Ernest K. Dishner
University of Northern Iowa
Thomas W. Bean
California State University, Fullerton
John E. Readence
Louisiana State University

D1535984

READING IN THE CONTENT AREAS:
IMPROVING CLASSROOM INSTRUCTION

**KENDALL/HUNT
PUBLISHING COMPANY**
Dubuque, Iowa

THE KENDALL/HUNT
LEARNING THROUGH READING SERIES
Lyndon W. Searfoss, *Consulting Editor*

C   402409   02

In memory of Cynthia Lorentz Cook

Contents

Part D: Putting It All Together

List of Contributors

Reprints

Richard L. Allington, State University of New York–Albany
Ernest K. Dishner, University of Northern Iowa
Richard A. Earle, McGill University
Paula J. Gaus, University of Arizona
W. John Harker, University of Victoria
Harold L. Herber, Syracuse University
Terry C. Ley, Auburn University
Anthony V. Manzo, University of Missouri–Kansas City
Joan B. Nelson, State University of New York–Binghamton
Vincent P. Orlando, Metropolitan State College
Charles W. Peters, Oakland (Michigan) Public Schools
John E. Readence, University of Georgia
Peter L. Sanders, Wayne State University
Lyndon W. Searfoss, Arizona State University
Robert E. Shafer, Arizona State University
Frank Smith, Ontario Institute for Studies in Education
Michael Strange, University of Texas
JoEllyn Taylor, Far West Laboratory
Keith J. Thomas, Arizona State University
Daniel J. Tutolo, Bowling Green State University
Richard T. Vacca, Kent State University
Joseph L. Vaughan, Jr., East Texas State University

Original Manuscripts

Ira E. Aaron, University of Georgia
Donna E. Alvermann, University of Northern Iowa
Sharon V. Arthur, Eastern Connecticut State College
R. Scott Baldwin, University of Miami
Thomas W. Bean, California State University–Fullerton

Jay S. Blanchard, Murray State University
Margaret Corboy, University of South Carolina
James W. Cunningham, University of North Carolina–Chapel Hill
Patricia M. Cunningham, Wake Forest University
Ernest K. Dishner, University of Northern Iowa
Linda A. Gambrell, University of Maryland
Lance M. Gentile, North Texas State University
David A. Hayes, University of Georgia
Eleanor J. Maddox, Phoenix (Arizona) Elementary Schools
John N. Mangieri, University of South Carolina
George E. Mason, University of Georgia
Lana McWilliams, Memphis State University
David M. Memory, Indiana State University
David W. Moore, University of Connecticut
P. David Pearson, University of Illinois
Thomas A. Rakes, Memphis State University
Ned Ratekin, University of Northern Iowa
John E. Readence, University of Georgia
Randall J. Ryder, University of Wisconsin–Milwaukee
Lyndon W. Searfoss, Arizona State University
Cyrus F. Smith, Jr., University of Wisconsin–Milwaukee
Susan J. Smith, South Carolina Department of Education
Robert J. Tierney, University of Illinois

Preface

Reading in the Content Areas: Improving Classroom Instruction presents preservice and inservice teachers with a foundation for content reading instruction. In completing this project, we have attempted to provide readers with a variety of viewpoints on the "state of the art" in content reading. As such, we have endeavored to acquire an authorship that represents various aspects of content reading instruction yet still believes that helping students to deal with the difficulties of content materials is equivalent to good teaching practices. This text also is a result of a recognized need for a source that presents not only a practical guide, but also a theoretical base for these instructional suggestions. At the same time, the editors recognize the fact that there are no simple solutions to the dilemma faced by intermediate and secondary teachers as they attempt to communicate content to their students.

The ideas presented here are by no means the answer to all the specifics of content reading instruction. The editors do believe that this text will provide college instructors with a means of presenting a comprehensive view of content reading. A positive feature of a book of readings is the opportunity for a methods instructor to use the book to augment a required course text which may contain gaps in knowledge. Although intended to stand alone, this book of readings may also be used in conjunction with *Content Area Reading: An Integrated Approach* (Readence, Bean, & Baldwin, 1981. Kendall/Hunt Publishing Company). As such, it is hoped that this text, whether used alone or in conjunction with another text, will make subject matter specialists *better* teachers of their content.

Part A of this book includes three chapters that introduce content area reading. Specifically, chapter one provides a justification and description of the philosophy behind content area reading. Chapter two examines the reading process and provides a framework for the strategies advocated in this text. Finally, chapter three defines the essential processes involved in content area reading.

Part B consists of two chapters designed to promote the instructional match between readers and text. Chapter four describes ways of selecting the content textbooks in specific classrooms, while chapter five provides diagnostic strategies to assess students' reading needs in the content classroom.

Part C provides four chapters of strategies for teaching in the content areas. Chapters six, seven, and eight discuss vocabulary development, comprehension instruction, and study strategies. Chapter nine offers suggestions for accommodating individual differences in the content classroom.

Finally, Part D provides the framework for the reader to integrate the ideas presented in previous chapters. Chapter ten describes the role of program design, program leadership, and teacher and student rights as content area reading programs are planned and implemented.

Obviously, such a large undertaking requires the help of many people. We are first indebted to those individuals who consented to write original manuscripts for this text. We also appreciate the willingness of those authors of reprinted articles who gave us permission to use the articles here.

Gratitude is extended to Alan C. Vincent for his faith in this project and to Lyndon W. Searfoss who served as consultant to this project.

Finally, we would like to thank those individuals who will read this text and are stimulated enough to implement what is being advocated here.

E. K. D.
T. W. B.
J. E. R.

Introduction

1

Content Area Reading: Justification and Description

There is an assumption by many middle and secondary grade teachers that, upon leaving the elementary grades, students should have mastered the skills necessary for efficient reading in content area subjects. Thus, these teachers may perceive their role as that of an information dispenser. This is unfortunate since the demands placed on students in coping with subject matter material differ greatly from those placed on students as they learn to read from narrative material in the early grades. For instance, concept load, technical vocabulary, and lack of experiential background can present numerous problems as these older students read content material. In addition there are students who have not successfully learned to read. Thus, there is a need for instruction that casts subject-matter teachers not as reading teachers, but as facilitators of learning who enhance their students' ability to learn from text.

In this chapter Dishner and Readence discuss the growing emphasis on content reading and assess the "state of the art." Additionally, they argue for a broader perspective incorporating listening, speaking, and writing as well as reading in helping students learn.

Allington and Strange point out the need for purposeful teaching and clearly formulated goals in helping students learn in the content areas. Furthermore, they state that such teaching is necessary if students are to be expected to develop an understanding of concepts presented in text.

Gentile describes reasons for students' inability to use the subject-matter texts effectively. Suggestions are offered to deal with these problems so that teachers may help students learn more efficiently.

Finally, Ley defines the challenge that faces all educators in middle and secondary schools—that of dealing with a myriad of reading problems presented by students. He elaborates on the notion that systematic reading instruction must be provided for students beyond the early grades.

Content Reading: Past. Present! Future?

Ernest K. Dishner
University of Northern Iowa

John E. Readence
University of Georgia

With the impetus gathered by such ideas as presented by Flesch (1955) in *"Why Johnny Can't Read"* and, certainly, by Allen's (1969) proclamation that every child should have the "right to read," a large portion of current educational writing has concerned the area of reading and reading education. Within reading education one particular facet of instruction, content area reading, has blossomed within the last few years. Articles, books, and conference sessions have been devoted to this very specific area of reading education (Herber, 1972; Laffey, 1972; Robinson, 1975).

What is the reason for this growing emphasis from reading educators? Previously, reading instruction was conceived from a basic skills approach which took place in the reading class—and only the reading class. If children had difficulty reading their textbooks, the approach was to reinforce those important skills considered necessary for successful reading. Many times the skills taught were isolated from the actual act of reading, and no differentiation was made in teaching reading to children using a basal reader or a content text.

The realization that "reading instruction in reading class only" was inadequate has finally surfaced. While the "closet clinician" has been busy remediating reading deficiencies, the remedial readers have been struggling with printed materials in their science, social studies, math, and English classes. That situation alone has caused reading educators to examine more closely the important area of content reading.

However, another stimulus, perhaps a more effective one, has been presented to reading educators from outside their profession. The emphasis on accountability in their instruction has prompted state departments of education and/or state school boards to become concerned over the reading achievement levels of their students graduating from their high schools. A dramatic trend had arisen over the past few years in the certification requirements for secondary education majors. In effect, states are beginning to mandate competence in reading.

Studies conducted by Estes and Piercey (1973) and Bader (1975) have pointed out this phenomena. In summary, they indicated that there was a 100% increase in the number of states requiring secondary reading preparation for certification in the two years between the studies. Furthermore, Bader pointed out that 55% of the states either had, or were considering, a reading requirement for secondary teachers.

"Used by permission from *Reading Horizons*, 1978, *19*, 78–81."

Together, the internal realization of the needs of content area reading and the trend toward reading requirements for secondary majors have brought content area reading to the forefront. However, with it have come a number of concerns. First of all, it is hoped that those individuals responsible for designing and implementing new preservice courses as a result of this impetus are emphasizing the important aspects of content area reading, rather than approaching the subject from the traditional basic skills point of view.

Second, there does appear to be a lack of understanding by many inservice reading specialists of the exact nature of content area reading. It is truly a sad situation when a reading specialist is approached by a content teacher with concerns about the reading difficulties of students in that particular content area, and can offer little or no specific assistance other than from a basic reading skills orientation. In many cases the misunderstanding by reading specialists concerning content area reading is due to the fact that they received little or no instruction in content reading themselves in their graduate reading preparation. As such, there is a general need to provide inservice for these individuals.

Third, complicating this growing awareness of content area reading are the objections raised by content specialists themselves. When presented with the need for such training, a typical response is—

> "But I was hired to teach history, not reading. I like history! I have an undergraduate degree in history because that is what I want to teach. If I wanted to teach reading, I would get a degree in reading!"

Such a response may indicate the possibility that the term "content reading" is too restrictive. Is it any wonder that the physical education, music, and art teachers are turned off by reading people? They are instructors of activity-oriented courses. Reading, they say, has little or nothing to do with their students' success in their activity-oriented courses! Yet, it can be argued that the technical vocabulary and concept load of music, art, and physical education is as extensive as that of English, social studies, or a host of other "core" subject areas.

Instead of pushing a philosophy which some content specialists find objectionable, perhaps a broader perspective of secondary reading is in order. This broader perspective not only can be a present aid in dealing with such objections by subject-matter teachers, but also has implications for future trends in content area reading. At the elementary level a growing emphasis in reading instruction is that of a total language arts approach (Moffett, 1973; Ruddell, 1974; Wilson and Hall, 1972). In such an approach reading is viewed as one of four communication processes, the others being listening, speaking, and writing. Since all four processes are interrelated and dependent in both process and function (Goodman, 1970), it can be argued that instruction in one communication process is reinforcing for another; i.e., instruction in listening, speaking, or writing is helpful for success in reading.

Can we, at the secondary level, separate these elements of language? Should we not take such a broader view at the secondary level? Since language is the mediational process for thinking (Ruddell, 1974), and since all content area courses require thinking skills, should we not provide students with experiences in all language or communication processes? If we conceive of the job of secondary education as the creation of a functioning member of society who is able to think and make rational decisions, then we should acquaint students in all subject areas with the power of language as a means to aid one in dealing effectively with the environment!

The need to furnish experiences in all language processes has been pointed out by Peck and Brinkley (1970) and Moore (1970). They indicated that students leaving the public schools and entering the junior college lack the language skills necessary to insure their probability of success in college level work.

Additionally, it can be legitimately argued that in all content courses, including those activity-oriented courses previously mentioned, students are required to use one, if not all, of the language processes in trying to deal with the content of the course. Listening, speaking, and writing, as well as reading, are required in all courses to deal with the language of that course!

Thus, the adoption of this broader perspective of content area reading deals with the current objections of content specialists and puts reading into its proper perspective—as one tool available for students to use in thinking, making better decisions, and dealing with their environment.

The intent of this article has been to assess the "state of the art" of content reading. Significant strides have been made in dealing with the needs of content area reading, yet significant advances still need to be made. It is hoped that content area reading can be examined from a broader perspective, i.e., perhaps educators should emphasize "content communication" in lieu of the narrower focus of content reading.

References

Allen, J. E. "Target for the 70's: The Right to Read." *American Education,* vol. 5, no. 10 (December, 1969), pp. 2–4.

Bader, L. A. "Certification Requirements in Reading: A Trend." *Journal of Reading,* vol. 19, no. 3 (December, 1975), pp. 237–40.

Estes, T. H. and Piercey, D. "Secondary Reading Requirements: Report on the States." *Journal of Reading,* vol. 17, no. 1 (October, 1973), pp. 20–24.

Flesch, R. *Why Johnny Can't Read and What You Can Do About It.* New York: Harper and Row, Inc., 1955.

Goodman, K. S. "Behind the Eye: What Happens in Reading." *Reading: Process and Program,* K. S. Goodman and O. S. Niles, Eds. Urbana, Ill.: National Council of Teachers of English, 1970, pp. 1–38.

Herber, H. L. *Teaching Reading in Content Areas.* Englewood Cliffs, N.J.: Prentice-Hall, Inc., 1970.

Laffey, J. L., Ed. *Reading in the Content Areas.* Newark, Dela.: International Reading Association, 1972.

Moffett, J. *A Student-Centered Language Arts Curriculum.* Boston: Houghton Mifflin, Co., 1973.

Moore, W. *Against the Odds.* San Francisco: Jossey-Bass, 1970.

Peck, R. E., and Brinkley, R. "College Reading Services for the Marginal Entrant." *Journal of Reading,* vol. 14, no. 1 (October, 1970), p. 19.

Robinson, H. A. *Teaching Reading and Study Strategies: The Content Areas.* Boston: Allyn and Bacon, Inc., 1975.

Ruddell, R. B. *Reading-Language Instruction: Innovative Practices.* Englewood Cliffs, N.J.: Prentice-Hall, Inc., 1974.

Wilson, R. M. and Hall, M. *Reading and the Elementary School Child: Theory and Practice for Teachers.* New York: D. Van Nostrand Co., 1972.

Remembering Is Not Necessarily Understanding in Content Areas

Richard L. Allington
State University of New York-Albany

Michael Strange
University of Texas

Improving comprehension in middle-grade content areas would be an easier topic to address if we had available validated theoretical models, and hence an understanding, of 1) how one learns from text, and 2) how intellectual operations develop in adolescence. Our current state of ignorance in these areas has been aptly summarized by Miller (1976) and Neimark (1975) respectively. We are then, like everyone else who would discuss improving comprehension of text, reduced to drawing upon the available body of literature and from this attempting to produce a framework from which useful strategies can be developed.

Goals and Instruction

Content area teaching is typically purposeful as opposed to incidental. For this purposeful teaching to occur, however, there must be goals for teaching; goals which go beyond the vague generalities and professional sounding platitudes too often associated with the various disciplines. We will not go as far as some and advocate goals which meet strict behavioral criteria, but for a variety of reasons the content area teacher must know what is to be taught and what is to be learned.

These goals have to reflect the dual role of the middle-grade content area teacher. In the middle grades the content area teacher has the distinctive and unique responsibility of developing effective application, utilization, and extension of reading abilities in content area texts (Allington, 1975). That is, the middle-grade teacher's role is one of producing students who know how to learn from printed material, thus attempting to ensure mastery of some of the most important prerequisite abilities for later learning, while simultaneously providing knowledge prerequisite to further learning in a particular discipline. The content specific knowledge must, of course, be identified but additionally the necessary learning strategies must also be identified. The middle-grade content area lesson then must not only produce content relevant learning but also provide the learner with skills and strategies for learning from text.

Instructional goals should be precise enough to allow the teacher to justify each assignment in relation to them. For instance, we should ask, "Why am I having students read page 33?" Is there information on that page that has been identified as important? Can a particular strategy for learning from text be employed? Or is it assigned because it follows page 32 and precedes page 34? Many pages in content area texts have nothing worth

"Used by permission from *Reading Horizons*, 1979, *20*, 60–64."

remembering, nor are any important concepts, functions, or relationships presented. We should argue that assigning these pages because they fall between more relevant material is justifiable, but only as long as the teacher is aware that the purpose is to maintain textual continuity. This rationale then cues the teacher that no test item should be drawn from that page. Students should not be tested on material simply because it is there. Test items must be related to the instructional goals set by the teacher.

This may seem blatantly obvious but we still visit content area classrooms which are totally text dominated. The teacher seems to have no goals except to get through the text. Now simply getting through a text may indeed be justifiable economically, and even politically, but it cannot be supported educationally. The teacher who adopts this position assumes no real responsibility for teaching, seldom setting any educational goals. Every page is page 33 and assessments are constructed with randomly selected statements from the text. Any statement, regardless of significance, may be turned into a test item (What was the tune the British band played when Cornwallis surrendered to Washington at Yorktown?).

Without clearly formulated goals the content area teacher has little guidance for developing either instruction or the assessment. Formulation of goals must precede instruction even in the most eclectic teaching environment. Both types of goals, content specific and generalize learning strategies, should be presented on the assessment. The type and level of assessment employed is a powerful shaping factor for student learning. If assessments do not relate to the goals then the students, particularly the brighter ones, adopt strategies which relate to success on the assessment. Assessments which require only remembering of minute details, for instance, focus student attention on these rather than on acquiring an understanding of the concepts, functions, processes, and relationships presented.

This leads us to another facet of goals, instruction, and assessment in content areas; remembering does not equal understanding. This is noted because goals sometimes become lists of data to be memorized, at least until the test (consider for a moment all of the facts we have forgotten from classes in which grades of A were earned). We are at this point quite sure that remembering what one reads is not itself a valid indicator of understanding, or comprehension. A rather simple demonstration of the validity of this contention will be found by reading the paragraph entitled "The CRT" and then completing the test items.

THE CRT

A CRT is a handy device. Of course, it cannot function without a central processing unit. The portable models need only a telephone pick-up to work. However, the most common access device is similar to an electric typewriter. With this combination a person can examine stored information prior to requesting hardcopy. It also allows a user to confirm input.

There are many uses for a CRT. Some models key mechanical responses such as opening valves, locks, etc. Of course direct mechanical manipulation requires a light sensitive model. These models are also useful in schools. The most common function is to present drill and practice exercises. However, due to the expense only about 1 percent of all classrooms have a CRT. Most experts predict that the CRT will become more common in schools. Some say it will replace the workbooks of today.

Answer True or False:

1. A CRT is a handy machine._____
2. A CRT needs a central processing unit. _____
3. There are probable CRT models. _____
4. A CRT allows a user to confirm input. _____
5. A CRT has a single use. _____
6. Most classrooms have at least one CRT. _____

Select the best answer:

7. The most common access device for a CRT is . . .
    a. a John Deere tractor   b. a CRT   c. an electric typewriter   d. none
8. CRT's are found in what percentage of classrooms?
    a. 1 percent   b. 1 percent   c. 10 percent   d. 100 percent
9. The CRT allows a user to examine information prior to . . .
    a. hand copy   b. impress   c. input   d. hardcopy
10. Most experts predict that the CRT . . .
    a.   will become common in schools.
    b.   fad will die out.
    c.   producers will market a color model.
    d.   will eliminate human teachers.

Write a short answer to the following question:

Describe in some detail how a CRT would be useful in your classroom.

Few teachers have difficulty correctly answering 70% of the items, even when the passage is removed after reading. Few, however, can describe a CRT (though most have had a direct experience with one). Simple questions on size, material, color, etc., cannot be answered. Likewise virtually none can answer the final question beyond simply regurgitating the statements from the passage. Thus while most readers are able to recognize all of the words and even remember much of the information, few ever comprehend what they have read, or understand the function of a CRT. This brings us to a crucial issue yet to be resolved. If comprehension is to be defined as an increase in information (Bormuth, 1969), then the performance on the CRT test is a demonstration of comprehension. However, it should be fairly obvious that little understanding has been generated. Remembering is not necessarily either comprehending or understanding. Only if the new information can be organized or associated with the previously known will understanding, or comprehension, take place.

How much learning in the content areas is of this type? Simple remembering of factual information but no assimilation, or cognitive reorganization. Do we really have as goals remembering whether Ben Franklin signed the Declaration of Independence, or how many miles Lee advanced into Pennsylvania, or the capitol of Oregon, or the major river in Brazil? Each of the above were drawn from social studies tests and by turning the items around we get what seem to be quite arbitrary and menial goals for learning. Similar examples abound in other content areas as well and these seem to suggest either goals that reflect rather low level expectations or test items discrepant from the original instructional goals.

Thus far remembering as an instructional goal has been criticized in relation to the content area skills role of the middle-grade teacher. However, similar criticism can be leveled in relation to the other role, that of developing learning skills. Factual recall is a necessary learning skill to be sure, but it is far from the most important or most powerful, particularly if recall goes no further than that found in the CRT task. Middle-grade students need to learn a variety of text processing skills particularly; assessing the value of information, identifying relationships, rapid identification of information relevant to a specific purpose, etc. A continual emphasis on recall of information leads to rote learning in content areas, students who can list exports without understanding the importance of exporting to an economy, students who can solve x but do not understand the underlying mathematical relationships, students who can list the genus and species of an organism without discovering the interrelationships of living things.

Goals are necessary for teaching. They do not have to be narrow or even measurable in the behavioral sense, but they do need to guide the teacher in planning instruction. They are even more useful for deciding whether one has reached the planned destination. However, goals for teaching are not enough, one must attempt to meet the goals with effective instruction and that is another point at which content area instruction at times breaks down.

From our standpoint what is called teaching in some content area classrooms is too often only testing or telling. To support this contention let us present two brief scenarios which can be observed in virtually any school on any day. In the first, the teacher simply assigns pages to be read with no further guidance and follows this with a test covering the material assigned. Or the teacher may simply use class time to question students on the assigned material. In the second scenario the teacher tells students a number of pieces of information and then also follows with a formal test or perhaps with the in-class questions. Both of these scenarios recur endlessly in the schooling process, and seem plausible methods for ensuring students have read assignments or attended to the lecture, but we need to examine whether either is truly teaching.

If the teacher simply writes "Read pg. 108–123" on the chalkboard and then later assesses student knowledge of this material, it would seem that instruction has not occurred. Even though pages have been assigned to be read, the teacher has not specified what is to be learned (unless one assumes everything on pages 108–123). Now suppose the student fails the test. Has the teaching failed? Perhaps it failed by omission but in the strictest sense teaching cannot be evaluated. How then should the failure be construed? If no teaching has occurred, what type of inadequacy is indicated?

It could be that the student has not read the assigned material, or perhaps could not read the material. It is also possible the student completed the assignment but did not have adequate experiences, or previous knowledge, to fully assimilate all the concepts presented. Then again the student may have completed the assignment and understood the material but failed to retain the specific information required for the test. The point is, the student failed the test but without a teaching component it is difficult to assess the relevance of this failure.

The student has failed to demonstrate the necessary independent learning skills and strategies, but we have identified the development of these as one of the two primary goals of the middle-grades content area teacher. The student has also seemingly failed to acquire the knowledge base one would consider prerequisite for further learning in the discipline, the other primary goal of middle-grade content area instruction.

Rather than continuing to beat this dead horse, let us summarize here by noting that in neither of the previous scenarios did the teacher develop either of the primary prerequisites; strategies or knowledge. These examples point out a major deficiency in content area instruction; too often aptitude and achievement is assessed without an instructional component. The learner has instruction in neither the development or refinement of processing skills and strategies nor in the development of an understanding of the concepts, processes, functions, or relationships presented in the text. At this point the teacher is only maintaining the status quo; those students who have the abilities or knowledge achieve, the others do not.

References

Allington, Richard L. "Improving Instruction in the Middle School Content Areas," *Journal of Reading,* 1975, vol. 18, pp. 455–461.

Bormuth, John R. "An Operational Definition of Comprehension Instruction." in K. S. Goodman and J. T. Fleming (Eds.), *Psycholinguistics and Reading,* Newark, Delaware: International Reading Association, 1969.

Miller, George A. "Text Comprehension Skills and Process Models of Text Comprehension," in H. Singer and R. Ruddell (Eds.), *Theoretical Models and Processes of Reading,* Newark, Delaware: International Reading Association, 1976.

Neimark, Edith D. "Intellectual Development During Adolescence," in F. D. Horowitz (Ed.), *Review of Child Development Research,* Volume 4, Chicago: University of Chicago Press, 1975.

Subject-based Reading Skills in Middle and Secondary Schools: Some Issues and Answers*

Lance M. Gentile
North Texas State University

Today there is a great deal of concern regarding many students' inability to use their subject-based textbooks effectively. Educators, parents, and school administrators frequently complain that students cannot or do not read widely and, moreover, do not appear to learn much from their reading.

Copperman (1979) reported evidence to demonstrate that reading achievement increases measurably in primary grades; reading achievement declines sharply in the middle and secondary years. Britton and Lumpkin (1978) concluded that imprecise readability labeling resulted in placing over seventy percent of the stories in middle grade readers above the designated level. They reasoned that this error may cause the abrupt drop in students' reading performance in these pivotal years.

*Written especially for inclusion in this text.

However, this problem is not restricted to reading texts in the middle schools. Numerous studies consistently report that textbooks for most subject areas in the middle and secondary grades tend to have inflated readability levels in relation to the reading skills of students having to use them (Calhoun & Horner, 1975; Daugs & Daugs, 1974; Hafner, 1977).

Nonetheless, the inappropriate assignment of readability levels to textbooks may account for only a portion of the difficulties encountered by pupils making the adjustment from reading in the initial school years to reading in the upper grades. Three signal factors that have received much less attention but share equal responsibility for this "middle and secondary slump" are:

1. The nature of reading tasks at lower and higher levels;
2. The lack of consistent and direct reading instruction provided middle and secondary school students to afford them successful passage from elementary school reading experiences, i.e., moving from story-based readers to subject-based texts;
3. The failure among many middle and secondary subject-area teachers to "personalize" their content for students and stimulate positive attitudes and real interest in these areas.

Reading Tasks at Lower Levels

During the first three years in school, most of what children are expected to read consists of simple narrative and dialogue. At this level emphasis is placed on "learning to read." Usually a single basal reader, comprised of stories and accompanied by a supplementary workbook containing practice lessons in word recognition and vocabulary development, forms the primary vehicle for teaching reading. Youngsters are taught the words, characters, plot, and setting that go along with these stories.

Readability levels may vary in these readers, but new terms are systematically repeated throughout each story's content. Ideas and events reflect many children's experiences, and most learn to read and understand these stories with a minimum of difficulty. In general, they are not hard-put to answer a teacher's disproportionate number of literal questions. Typically, the majority of questions asked in the elementary grades are of the literal, factual type, e.g., who, what, when, and where. Even when a teacher takes direction from questions provided in the basal reader's teacher's guide, literal questions still constitute fifty percent of those asked.

In this context reading is an "entertaining" experience. It is an attention-centered activity designed to appeal to children's interests. The teacher's message is, "Class, let's have fun as we read a story and answer some questions."

To insure that youngsters develop specific skills when reading these stories, most elementary teachers make good use of the Directed Reading Activity (DRA). The DRA leads children through the following step-by-step procedures and provides them ample opportunities to practice the basic mechanics of learning to read.

Readiness for reading (motivation and building background)
>   Interest readiness
>   Vocabulary and concept readiness
>   Intellectual and emotional readiness

Guided reading of the story
>   Silent
>   Oral

Rereading
>   Skill development activities
>>   Vocabulary study
>>   Word attack
>>   Comprehension

Follow-up activities
>   Extended reading

Whenever children have difficulty in mastering the concepts and skills required to succeed with these reading experiences, the elementary school frequently gets supplementary assistance from peer tutors, adult volunteers, teachers' aides, or other similar personnel.

Reading Tasks at Higher Levels

Circumstances change dramatically when youngsters enter fourth grade. At this point content subjects begin in earnest. Reading at this level and beyond means processing information for academic purposes, i.e., answering test questions or making written and oral reports employing higher level interpretations. For the remainder of their formal education, youngsters must deal with a wide range of technical or specific concepts and in many instances a host of unfamiliar vocabulary. Coupled with these circumstances, many teachers in the middle and secondary grades wrongfully assume that students have acquired the reading skills necessary to succeed in their subject areas.

To make matters worse, at the middle and secondary levels reading assignments are not necessarily attention- or interest-centered. For the most part they are not recreational or diversionary but obligatory, purposeful, language-centered tasks to which success and achievement in school are closely linked. The teacher's message is transformed from "Let's have fun . . ." to "Class, take out your math, language, science, foreign language, health, or social studies text, and *let's get to work!*"

The Lack of Consistent and Direct Reading Instruction

Contrary to what is done in the early elementary grades, i.e., using the DRA to help youngsters "learn to read," many teachers at middle and secondary levels devote little time to actual subject-based reading instruction (Durkin, 1979). As a result students have few opportunities to practice and apply the specific skills that will aid them in "reading to learn" using expository texts.

For students at middle and secondary levels most subject-based reading assignments contain several inherently difficult features. Teachers in these grades must devote ample time to helping students read for understanding by preparing them to cope with the following:

1. an absence of background experience related to the topic;
2. differentiated vocabulary;
3. main ideas and supporting details;
4. a possible lack of interest in the topic; and
5. graphics.

An absence of background experience related to the topic

A good portion of what many students are assigned to read in school may be unrelated to their prior experiences. Teachers should not assume that *comprehension* results merely because a youngster can "read" the words in a selection. Without building some background for the topic or ideas expressed in the reading material, teachers have little hope that youngsters will make appropriate responses to related questions. A host of background experiences can be developed by presenting films or film strips that pertain to the subject matter at hand, asking students to watch a particular television program treating the issues to be studied, reading to youngsters from associated materials and holding classroom discussions based on these readings, or listening to recorded speeches or messages that highlight key ideas from the text.

Differentiated vocabulary

Basically there are two levels of vocabulary that all students bring to the classroom, although there is a vast difference in the level to which these are developed. All students have acquired some degree of *receptive* and *expressive* speech. Receptive vocabulary refers to terms that students *recognize* in spoken or written form. Expressive vocabulary includes those words students can *employ* accurately when speaking or writing. Whereas most students' receptive vocabularies are much larger than their expressive ones, when reading textual materials there is a wide range of vocabulary items that are "unreceptive" to them. Teachers must teach the terms that appear throughout written material for which their students have little or no understanding if they expect them to read fluently.

The differentiated vocabulary that is most likely to cause problems for students falls into the following four classifications:

(a) **Multiple-meaning words**
   The *cell* is divided into four parts.
   The battery *cell* was deadened by a loss of water.
   A *cell* was mistakenly left open.
(b) **Technical or subject-specific words**
   The aphorism "*Divide* and conquer" may explain the Indians' defeat.
   Divide that answer by four.
   The Great *Divide* is one geographical factor to consider.

(c) **Colloquialisms or figurative expressions**

A *storm of controversy* arose over the issues.

Hitler's *storm* troopers held high status in Nazi Germany.

A *storm of protest* was levied against the speaker.

He *stormed out* of the discussions.

(d) **Abbreviations or acronyms**

The entire company, *etc.,* was left abandoned.

The prime minster lived in *Bldg.* 443 on 10th *Ave.*

An *R.N.* worked in the *Med. Lab.*

The *radar* (radio detecting and ranging) unit worked well.

The *scuba* (self-contained underwater breathing apparatus) gear was packed and ready to use.

Main ideas and supporting details

Subject-based reading assignments require students to locate main ideas and identify significant details if they are to carry on a reasonable discussion of the material. This is also extremely important if teachers expect students to perform well on tests or develop clear oral and written reports.

Generally, authors of texts posit the main idea of a paragraph in the first or second sentence, with supporting details subsumed in several successive sentences. At times a recapitulation of the main idea may appear in the penultimate or final sentence. Students should be given practice and direction in picking out main ideas and supporting details and in distinguishing among them. Without a thorough grasp of an author's hierarchical arrangement of thoughts, students are left groping for meaning and thereby waste a great deal of time and effort "reading" in haphazard or slipshod fashion. As a result, for many students, reading textual materials is seldom a coherent, logical experience, becoming instead a relatively "aimless voyage" through seas of print.

A lack of interest in the topic

Teachers must make every effort to create interest and generate enthusiasm among students for reading a particular part of a text. In an age when youngsters are bombarded by entertaining media, this is not easy. The use of films, humorous skits, role-playing activities, and oral readings or presentations from interested students, community members, or other "celebrities" may not only add zest to a reading assignment, but may also lend an air of authenticity to the material itself.

Graphics

Textbooks frequently contain graphs, diagrams, charts, maps, and other illustrations that help depict significant statistics or events but that are difficult for many young people to interpret. Teachers should take the time to instruct their students in the proper use of pictorial information and show them how to derive meaning from it.

The Failure of Many Middle and Secondary Subject Area
Teachers to "Personalize" Their Content for Students

In conjunction with the differences already mentioned, story and subject-based reading contrast in another important way. As stated earlier, middle and secondary teachers teach various academic subjects: math, English, science, foreign language, and others. Generally, a single assigned text serves as the primary vehicle of instruction in these classrooms. Each student must use these books to acquire the vital information and understanding necessary to pass tests, make reports, and participate in group discussions and activities. Thus, in the middle and upper grades, teachers are frequently denied the luxury and freedom to direct "the right material to the right child at the right time." *All* students are compelled to succeed with these texts, whether or not the texts:

are written on a level that corresponds to the reading abilities of students having to use them;

are attractively constructed and printed;

present information and material in interesting ways, concisely and accurately;

contain engaging illustrations or photographs;

treat topics that arouse students' attention or are of intrinsic concern to them; and

are preferred by particular teachers or are compatible with their views.

While many school districts mandate teachers to teach their courses using prescribed texts, this approach, if applied inflexibly, is doomed to fail. Today's youth have grown up in an intensely animated and entertainment-centered atmosphere; they are raised with television, motion pictures, records, radio, and toys of every description. As students, many not only expect to be entertained, but more often than not they demand it! Teachers in the middle and secondary schools cannot hope to "go it alone" with only the required text and a reading assignment of a certain number of pages to act as motivational underpinnings to their teaching; nor can subject material be taught in isolation of students' "real" world with only the written page used as a basis for learning.

For these reasons teachers must turn to supplementary resources and experiences as a means of embellishing or illuminating textual material. They must seek out those materials and persons that are capable of presenting ideas and issues in "personalized" or meaningful ways to students. This does not necessitate foresaking the class text, but under these circumstances, the text, though closely tied to the content, is not the singular focus of instruction. Through carefully planned and coordinated efforts, teachers can amass supplementary materials and organize auxiliary class activities in conjunction with the textbook to reaffirm or amplify students' knowledge of the world, interests, and life experiences.

Furthermore, the instructional material and methods (whether textually related or supplementary) should be viewed as a means to an end rather than as the goal of teaching content itself. Wendell Johnson (1946) said, "The value of a book is not in the book, it is in the subsequent behavior of its readers." The teacher's principal concern must be to develop able, interested, and enthusiastic learners in a particular subject field. This can only occur where teachers mold the following kinds of curricular adjustments and personal behaviors.

From a curricular standpoint, the following alternative instructional processes will aid teachers in expanding a textual-based curriculum into a successful subject-based "personalized" program:

Teachers can provide a wide selection of reading materials related to their subject matter. The textbook is only one resource. Readings of high interest and importance are readily available in library books, magazines, newspapers, and paperbacks. Nothing does more to bolster a subject area course of study than a variety of literature written at several levels of difficulty.

Teachers can make use of "interviews" or personal conferences with students to help determine the type of reading material most suitable to their interests and needs. These readings can serve as reinforcers to the textual assignments.

Teachers can allow students opportunities to discuss with them, a classmate, or the group some associated reading experiences. Most young people enjoy talking about their "personal" readings. Many are surprised at what they can and cannot recall during attempts to retell events or describe scenes and characters from the material. They frequently encounter confusion in these situations and find it necessary to refer back to the material or text to elucidate their ideas. This is common to adults as well as students, and students soon recognize how crucial it is for recall and clear comprehension.

Teachers can take advantage of every opportunity to combine textbook and supplementary reading experiences with other forms of media. They might incorporate into their daily lesson plans television programs, popular music, motion pictures, or cassette recordings dealing with issues presented in the class text or affiliated literature. This approach can assist teachers in developing broad communications activities that require students to listen, speak, read, and write. Introducing different topics linked to subject field through multi-media helps excite interest and encourage voluntary reading.

Teachers can make allowances and offer extra help for remedial students by developing listening tapes of various difficult sections of the text or by rewriting essential parts in language that is easier for these youngsters to read.

Teachers can let students interpret subject-based reading experiences through creative forms of expression: drama, painting, drawing, sculpture, dance, news reporting, and role-playing activities.

Teachers can make up subject-based reading lists for their individual fields and post these in the classroom, e.g., annotated bibliographies and reference indexes.

Teachers can group students according to their personal interests in a given subject area (for example, in history several youngsters may be intrigued with World War I or II, the Civil War, Watergate, etc.) or permit friends to work together in constructing projects and reports for the group.

Teachers can invite parents or other community members to address their classes concerning personal hobbies or interests that relate to specific subject areas. Students in middle and secondary schools should hear other teachers or professors, older students, working persons, and professional men and women expound on their diverse avocations. These people can share a wealth of ideas and provide interesting, exciting, and challenging experiences while serving as exemplary models or demonstrators of ways in which subject curricula connect to real-life pursuits. These individuals should become just as attractive examples to youth as amateur or professional athletes, musicians, and other entertainers or celebrities.

Technically, all kinds of curricular adjustments can be made in teaching academic subjects, but a course may still lack the most valuable adhesive of all, i.e., an interested/ interesting teacher. Consequently, from a personal standpoint:

Teachers must be avid readers of their subject material. As models for the students, a teacher's personal commitment to read widely in the field is essential.

Teachers must become acquainted with a broad range of subject-based literature in order to lead students in various directions.

Teachers must be eager *participants* in life. Adult enthusiasm for learning is highly contagious and will infect a majority of students. Much of what these young people learn in school is "caught" (to borrow a phrase from Dolores Durkin), not taught.

Teachers must possess a good program for study skills instruction to properly manage and sequence students' training along these lines.

Teachers must constantly be aware of individual students' differences and take steps to teach to them. They should be capable of adjusting teacher strategies and materials to meet the needs and varied personal interests of all their students.

An ideal subject-area course of study would be taught by an enthusiastic, imaginative person who tries to provide students with as many of the aforementioned curricular experiences as possible. It would also include what is known about human learning and habit formation. A total effort in the middle and secondary classroom is needed to offer students academic learning experiences that fully engage their emotions as well as their intellects. Hard evidence must be presented to youth that subject-based reading is distinctively rewarding and not something only certain people can do or enjoy doing.

References

Britton, G., and Lumpkin, M. Readability labeling: An answer to the middle grade slump. *Reading Improvement,* 1978, *15,* 162–169.

Calhoun, C., and Horner, B. Readability of first-year bookkeeping texts compared with students' reading level. *Business Education Forum,* 1975, *30,* 20–21.

Copperman, P. *The literacy hoax.* New York: William Morrow, 1978.

Daugs, D., and Daugs, F. Readability of high school biology materials. *Science Education,* 1974, *58,* 471–482.

Durkin, D. What classroom observations reveal about reading comprehension instruction. *Reading Research Quarterly,* 1978–79, *14,* 503.

Hafner, L. *Development reading in middle and secondary schools.* New York: Macmillan Publishing Co., 1977.

Johnson, W. *People in quandries.* New York: Harper and Row, 1946.

The Reading Problem in the Secondary School

Terry C. Ley
Auburn University

Secondary schools must provide for the furtherance of student reading skill development, and the principal must provide the well-informed leadership for such programs. Some key concepts about reading instruction are outlined here, and an extensive resource list is provided.

Taxpayers and the media are deeply concerned these days by what they perceive as serious limitations in young people's abilities to read, use standard English, and compute. Those "basic skills," variously defined, are the topic of discussion and argument wherever people interested in education gather.

Volleys are fired at PTA meetings and bridge clubs and on the pages of learned journals and popular weeklies. Moved to action, some interested parties have taken their concern to state capitals, where they have sought and, in some states, achieved legislation they hope will ensure accountability in education and competence in young people.

Those responsible for the education of students in middle, junior high, and senior high schools often become perplexed, frustrated, and angry when they discover that they are to be held accountable for their students' mastery of certain reading, writing, and arithmetic skills. It has not been easy for these teachers and administrators to abandon a well-worn but now clearly outdated theory that teaching such skills is solely the responsibility of the elementary school.

Regardless of technological changes that have had various effects on schools in recent decades, students must still read a great deal—and read well—in order to succeed in most schools. There is actually some evidence that today's adolescents read better, on the average, than previous generations of adolescents did, primarily because larger portions of the school-aged population remain in school longer. However, other evidence clearly shows that a sizeable portion of our school population cannot read easily or well.

Large numbers of otherwise marginal students who remain in school now find the reading they must do in biology or history classes, for instance, to be at best challenging and at worst discouraging. Such students inhibit their teachers' sense of professional success, too, because they do not learn the concepts and skills the teachers expect the textbooks to communicate. The resulting frustration can be channeled to positive action if teachers and administrators are willing to see reading not as a separate discipline taught only by specialists, but as a series of related skills developed throughout a lifetime.

Reprinted from *NASSP Bulletin*, 1979, *63*, 49–56, with permission of Terry C. Ley and the National Association of Secondary School Principals.

A Secondary School Obligation

Every secondary school has the obligation to continue the development of reading skills initiated in elementary schools. Current attempts to legislate accountability for instruction in certain basic skills, including reading, have implications for many sectors of our society. The implications for secondary school educators—and for those who prepare them for their jobs—are especially notable because these teachers traditionally have not been prepared to cope with their students' reading problems. In several states recent changes in certification and recertification standards, usually requiring some preparation in reading for all secondary school teachers, reflect growing awareness that accountability for reading instruction begins in teacher preparation programs and requires continual support through productive inservice efforts by local school districts.

In seeking to fulfill their obligation to prepare mature readers, secondary school educators should be aware of at least 10 concepts about reading and reading instruction, and should strive to reflect that awareness in their behavior as they build curricula and teach young people. While there is much more to be said about reading instruction, these key concepts summarize recent textbooks in the field—particularly those which deal with reading in the content areas—and serve as focal points for recent research in reading.

Space limits the development of each concept here, but anyone wanting to explore a concept further can find help by consulting the list of resources which follows this article.

1. Reading requires a set of competencies that develop at varying rates in individuals.

Those competencies undergo change as long as people continue to read. Among the elements of reading which require continuous development are: readiness for the reading tasks at hand; word study skills; vocabulary development; comprehension skills; critical reading skills; study skills; reading rate; ability to adapt rate and technique to purpose; and reading interests.

2. Students in any class represent a wide range of reading abilities, and the higher the grade, the greater the range.

Before meeting a heterogeneous eighth-grade class, a teacher can reliably estimate that the range between the best and the poorest readers in the class will be eight reading grade levels. The poorest reader may read at the fourth-grade level; the best, at the twelfth-grade level. About a third of the class will score near grade level (8.0) on standardized reading tests; about a third will score a year or more above grade level; and about a third will score a year or more below grade level.

Depending upon the school's dropout rate, by tenth grade the range will be 10 years; by twelfth grade, 12 years. The rule of thumb: in order to estimate the range of reading ability in a heterogeneous class at a given grade level, find two-thirds of the typical age of students in that grade. (Tenth grade: $2/3 \times 15 = 10$-year range.) The accuracy of this estimate may or may not be confirmed by achievement test scores for students in the class, but it should signal the many problems ahead for the teacher who plans to rely heavily on the reading of one textbook throughout a course. While grouping students by achievement will narrow the range somewhat, it does not permit teachers to assume that members of so-called homogeneous groups have the same reading strengths and weaknesses.

3. Readers are disabled for a variety of personal and school-related reasons, some of which educators can control.

These factors, summarized from Forgan and Mangrum (1976), influence reading achievement:

- *physical*—problems with vision, hearing, or general health;
- *language development*—meager vocabularies, substandard language models;
- *environment*—few positive experiences with reading outside of school;
- *aptitude for reading*—poorly developed visual and auditory memories, inability to classify or make judgments, limited pool of experiences;
- *social-emotional*—unhappy relationships with peers and family and poor concept of one's abilities and worth; and
- *educational*—poor teaching, inappropriate materials, perhaps no opportunity for any instruction in reading beyond the fourth to sixth grade.

4. Intelligence apparently influences the potential that students have for becoming skillful readers.

Reading requires visual and auditory discrimination abilities and other cognitive powers often explored by mental aptitude tests. Such mental abilities affect how rapidly people can learn to read. When given a reading achievement test, a hard-working, highly motivated student with limited intelligence may show only five months' growth after nine months of excellent instruction. That rate of growth may represent outstanding performance for that student. Given the same test, a gifted classmate may show evidence of 12 months' growth after nine months of instruction. As the years pass, the cumulative difference in the growth rates of the two students becomes increasingly evident until, in the tenth grade, those two students may represent the bottom and the top of the 10-year achievement range mentioned earlier. While intelligence factors appear to affect reading maturity significantly, it is important to remember that the other factors referred to in concept number three may influence readers to fall short of or exceed expectations that are based upon mental aptitude test scores alone.

5. Too many of the students in our secondary schools are expected to be able to read materials that are too difficult for them.

Readability formulae are commonly used to describe the relative challenge of textbooks. Most formulae are based on the premise that the challenge of a piece of reading is related to the lengths of its sentences and the length of its words. Normally, a readability of 8.0, or eighth-grade level means that even a reader on an eighth-grade reading achievement level *must have some direction* in order to read the material with 80 percent comprehension. Therefore, even selected textbooks that are "on grade level" (8.0 for a class of eighth graders) will be constantly frustrating to the third of a typical heterogeneous eighth-grade class which is reading from one to four years below the eighth-grade reading level. An even larger portion of the class will have difficulty with a "grade level" textbook if their teacher expects them to read it independently, with little direction or assistance. Unfortunately, the readability of textbooks frequently exeeds the level of the grade for which they are purchased, creating an even greater problem for readers and teachers.

6. *Text materials reflect the uniqueness of the content areas for which they are written.*

Reading a science text presents challenges not present in a mathematics text; both of them present challenges not present in narrative literature that one expects to find in an English class. In a sense, textbooks in each content area speak a language all their own, differing from textbooks in other content areas in vocabulary, sentence structure, paragraph and chapter organization, and graphic aids. Typically, it is comprehension of a content area's language which stands between students and their success in that content area. Content area teachers, who are experts with the languages of their respective fields, are best suited for assisting that comprehension. The content area classroom is the best setting for learning those special languages, too, for it is there that utility guarantees the constant reinforcement necessary to vocabulary and concept development.

7. *Teacher-constructed informal reading inventories allow teachers to assess how well students are able to read specific materials.*

Such inventories require that students read selected passages from one or more textbooks which the teacher anticipates using with the class. After reading a passage, students answer a series of questions written by the teacher to probe their understanding of what they have read. Scores indicate the appropriateness of a textbook for individuals or classes. Informal analysis of responses yields diagnostic information which should suggest areas requiring instruction.

8. *By directing student reading activity teachers can facilitate student understanding of concepts crucial to the content areas and encourage development of reading skills at the same time.*

Such direction begins as teachers consider diagnostic information they have gathered and anticipate the problems their students may have as they read a particular assignment. That anticipation results in prereading activity which prepares students for their reading; such activity motivates, builds concepts and vocabulary vital to comprehension, and encourages students to preview the selection and to establish specific purposes to guide their reading. Post-reading activity clarifies, reinforces, and extends the reading and provides for necessary skill development. Teachers unaware of the benefits of such directed activity are likely to continue to be gravely disappointed with the results of hastily given assignments which assume that all students in a class are capable of reading textbook material independently.

9. *When assistance from teachers is not enough—when reading skills are poorly developed and a single textbook inappropriate—teachers must seek alternatives to reading as the primary means of communicating concepts and skills important to their content areas.*

Some teachers use several textbooks written at a variety of readability levels and encourage students to share what they have read with mixed-ability groups. Others find that students who cannot read well can gain concepts and skills by watching a filmstrip or the teacher's demonstration, by hearing a recording or another student's report. A generous selection of print and nonprint resources is essential to any program that hopes to meet the diverse reading needs of the students it serves.

10. *A comprehensive secondary reading program should emphasize reading skills development in content area classrooms because that facet can have a great impact upon the entire student body. However, such a program must also offer developmental or remedial reading assistance to those who need or desire it, usually administered by a reading specialist or otherwise qualified teacher.*

In such programs, reading teachers offer elective courses which appeal to secondary school students possessing a wide range of reading abilities; they set up and supervise reading laboratories; and they assist content area teachers who are determined to encourage reading growth in their classrooms.

Challenge for All Educators

No brief treatment of reading instruction can adequately define the challenge that confronts all educators. It can, however, confirm suspicions that, instead of a single reading problem, we have before us a complex system of problems that eventually is reflected in test scores by which the public judges the efforts of students and educators. And a complex system of problems requires an equally complex system of responses.

Effective responses to the reading problem require the leadership of well-informed administrators. Piecemeal efforts by a few individual teachers, though admirable, are insufficient. Administrators initiate their schools' responses when they attempt to learn as much as they can about reading skills, and communicate their concern to their faculties. Such leaders involve knowledgeable and interested faculty members in school reading committees responsible for planning and implementing long-range inservice programs for all certificated staff. These administrators seek to hire teachers with preparation or experience in reading. They encourage and support experiments by teachers who wish to break comfortable but unproductive patterns. And they insist that the standardized reading achievement test be only one of many measures used for evaluating growth in reading.

Secondary school administrators cannot afford to relinquish their leadership responsibilities where reading instruction is concerned. They can seek the advice of specialists and enlist the aid of deputies to carry out portions of their school's response, but they must play a large role in the development of that response, for ultimately they must bear much of the responsibility for its success or failure. Most administrators need to know more about reading before they can begin to develop their school's response. The list of resources which follows should be helpful to those administrators—and to those teachers whose administrators ensure that their schools' professional collections contain as many of them as possible.

References

*Aukerman, Robert C. *Reading in the Secondary School Classroom.* New York: McGraw-Hill, 1972.
Burmeister, Lou E. *Reading Strategies for Secondary School Teachers.* Reading, Mass.: Addison-Wesley, 1974.

*These books contain chapters or sections devoted to each of several secondary content areas.

Dechant, Emerald V. *Improving the Teaching of Reading.* Englewood Cliffs, N.J.: Prentice-Hall, 1970.

Dillner, Martha H. and Olson, Joanne P. *Personalizing Reading Instruction in Middle, Junior, and Senior High Schools: Utilizing a Competency-Based Instructional System.* New York: Macmillan, 1977. (Consists of 13 self-instruction modules.)

Duffy, Gerald G., ed. *Reading in the Middle School.* Newark, Del.: International Reading Association, 1974.

Earle, Richard A. *Teaching Reading and Mathematics.* Newark, Del.: International Reading Association, 1976.

Forgan, Harry W. and Mangrum, Charles T. *Teaching Content Area Reading Skills: A Modular Preservice and Inservice Program.* Columbus, Ohio: Charles E. Merrill, 1976. (Consists of 10 self-instruction modules.)

*Hafner, Lawrence E. *Developmental Reading in Middle and Secondary Schools: Foundations, Strategies, and Skills for Teaching.* New York: Macmillan, 1977.

Harker, W. John, ed. *Classroom Strategies for Secondary Reading.* Newark, Del.: International Reading Association, 1977.

Harris, Albert J. and Sipay, Edward R. *How to Increase Reading Ability,* Sixth Edition. New York: David McKay, 1975.

Herber, Harold L. *Teaching Reading in Content Areas.* Englewood Cliffs, N.J.: Prentice-Hall, 1970.

Karlin, Robert. *Teaching Reading in High School: Improving Reading in Content Areas,* Third Edition. Indianapolis: Bobbs-Merrill, 1977.

McIntyre, Virgie M. *Reading Strategies and Enrichment Activities for Grades 4–9.* Columbus, Ohio: Charles E. Merrill, 1977.

Miller, Wilma H. *Reading Correction Kit.* New York: Center for Applied Research in Education, 1975.

Miller, Wilma H. *Reading Diagnosis Kit.* New York: Center for Applied Research in Education, 1974.

*Miller, Wilma H. *Teaching Reading in the Secondary School.* Springfield, Ill.: Charles C. Thomas, 1974.

*Piercey, Dorothy. *Reading Activities in Content Areas: An Ideabook for Middle and Secondary Schools.* Boston: Allyn and Bacon, 1976.

Preston, Ralph C., Ed. *A New Look at Reading in the Social Studies.* Newark, Del.: International Reading Association, 1969.

*Robinson, H. Alan. *Teaching Reading and Study Strategies: The Content Areas.* Boston: Allyn and Bacon, 1975.

*Shepherd, David L. *Comprehensive High School Reading Methods.* New York: Charles E. Merrill, 1973.

Thelen, Judith. *Improving Reading in Science.* Newark, Del.: International Reading Association, 1976.

*Thomas, Ellen Lamar and Robinson, H. Alan. *Improving Reading in Every Class,* Abridged Second Ed. Boston: Allyn and Bacon, 1977.

West, Gail B. *Teaching Reading Skills in Content Areas.* Orlando, Fla.: Sandpiper Press, 1974.

*These books contain chapters or sections devoted to each of several secondary content areas.

The Process of Reading to Understand

Reading is indeed a complex process. It is not simply a matter of sounding out words or memorizing lists of words. Complex psychological and linguistic processes are involved in reading, and research by cognitive psychologists and linguists have provided clearer insights into the act of reading. More importantly, this knowledge can influence teaching and learning in content classrooms since effective instruction must integrate theory with practice. As such, psycholinguistic inquiry has emphasized the effects of prior knowledge, memory, language knowledge, and text structure on a reader's ability to learn from content materials. Therefore, it is essential that content teachers be cognizant of those factors which influence the reading process since they can serve as important guideposts in day-to-day teaching.

A variety of viewpoints or aspects of the reading process are presented in this chapter. Specifically, Taylor emphasizes that what is basic to reading is making sense of printed language. Suggestions are offered to focus students' attention on this basic skill as they interact with print.

Shafer poses a question concerning the impact of psycholinguistics on classroom instruction. Specifically, he traces the development of the skills model of reading instruction and then outlines a psycholinguistic model and its potential applications for instruction.

Smith states that reading is impossible without prediction. A rationale for prediction is provided, advantages are cited, and applications to the classroom provided.

Tierney and Pearson review recent advances in reading comprehension pedagogy and research. Implications of these advances are discussed with the intention of providing teachers with guidelines to develop their own teaching procedures.

Making Sense: The Basic Skill in Reading

JoEllyn Taylor
Far West Laboratory

Have you ever heard a student read this way?
"I went home with my fry-end."((friend)
OR "She stopped to pick a flowed." (flower)
OR simply stop reading altogether because she did not "know" the next word? These students belong to the large group of ineffective readers who do not know or have forgotten what is basic.

Constructing Meaning Is Basic

What *is* basic in reading and the other language arts? To the effective language user it seems obvious that the communication of thought is what is basic. Whether the communication takes place verbally or through writing the receiver is never passive. He unconsciously does what is necessary for him to understand the message of the speaker or author. Using the signals (oral/written) as triggers, he constructs his own meaning which reflects his own language and life experience. His focus while receiving these signals, is "what sense can *I* make out of this?"

Vision of Whole Is Necessary for Parts to Make Sense

While taken for granted by effective readers, this demand for meaning seems to be the basic ingredient absent from the ineffective readers approach to print. Well-intentioned traditional instruction, rather than emphasizing a commitment to understanding, has distracted the reader by paying undue attention to the mechanics of the process (decoding, pronunciation, intonation, etc.). The ineffective reader, as indicated above, has no focus or goal beyond attempting to figure out the parts. There is a lack of awareness that the parts add up to a whole with potential meaning.

This disproportionate attention to mechanics can be likened to driving instruction. If the instructor were to isolate the use of the brake and accelerator, emphasizing mastery of those aspects prior to the learner's focus on total road awareness, the student might conceivably direct all of his attention to the pedals instead of the road! Obviously this does not make for effective driving. If, however, the student is first helped to understand the relationship of his car to the road and other vehicles, the use of the pedals and other instruments comes more easily and makes sense in the context of the total driving experience.

Reference Note

The author wishes to acknowledge Carolyn Burke, Marilyn Hanf Buckley, Jane DeLawter, Kenneth Goodman, Yetta Goodman, Dave Nettell, and Barry Sherman for their contributions during the preparation of this manuscript.

Reprinted from *Language Arts,* 1977, *54,* 668–672, with permission of the National Council of Teachers of English.

Such is the case with the young reader. If she first comes to realize the relationship between oral and written language and is aware that language is used to convey ideas, feelings, etc., this gestalt will assist her in plugging in the other subservient pieces, as they are needed and useful. With such an orientation, the readers might have made *these* substitutions, instead of those cited initially:

I went home with my girlfriend. (friend)
She stopped to pick a daisy. (flower)

My own findings and those of persons conducting research on miscue analysis are that, by and large, American children have enough phonics skills to become competent readers, but that phonics is not enough. If the reader were to seek meaning at all times, the universe of options would be narrowed to those items that are potentially reasonable. In, *The girl climbed the   fence*   (if fence is the unknown) the options are immediately limited to nouns that are "climbable." The field is severely reduced again when the "climbable" noun must begin with the letter *f*. A student maintaining a focus on making sense will not even entertain notions about words beginning with *f, fe, fen* or whatever, if they do not denote climbable nouns. This synergistic sorting system (processing the options simultaneously through semantic, syntactic and symbolic "filters") is a natural process and much more efficient than the traditional single-focused "What does it start with?" (symbolic) approach.

Natural Process of Self-Taught Reader Is Synergistic

Young self-taught readers verify these notions for us. Not influenced by conventional instruction, some five-year-olds have revealed to us their intuitive strategies for becoming readers.

First of all, these children have heard stories and enjoyed books from an early age. The adults in their families are seen reading daily for their own interest, needs, and enjoyment, as well as sharing reading time with the children.

After hearing some of their favorite stories read repeatedly and watching the print, these children begin to recognize some portions, and after a period of apparent memorization, phase into actually discerning the words themselves, without reliance on picture clues. Patterns begin to emerge in this process. "That word starts like my name." "These two look alike." "These are the same at the start." When asked, "How do you figure out something you don't know?", they respond with such statements as "I think about what would go there." or "I just say what would sound right."

Obviously, context and the speaker's sense of the language, are the major sources of cues. When one five-year-old was reading Silverstein's "Recipe for a Hippopotamus Sandwich" (1974) she stopped unsure before the word *mayonnaise*. Her teacher asked, "What *kind* of word is it?" She replied, "Food." He then asked, "What do you think it might be?" "It starts with *m* (sound)," she said, "so it must be *mustard* or *mayonnaise,* but it's long, so it must be *mayonnaise*."

By anyone's common sense criterion, such children are reading. They thoroughly re-tell and discuss the material they read. At the same time, these self-taught readers neither know, nor have they found a need to know:

- alphabet letter names
- sight words in isolation
- letter sounds
- phonics rules

As Frank Smith (1973) points out, this knowledge, if important at all, develops when one needs to spell, to locate words in the dictionary, etc., but is not necessary to be able to read. In fact, it distracts from the *basics* of reading. Beginning reading experiences build the reservoir from which these other skills develop. Attempting to teach these skills as a pre-requisite to reading actually violates the natural sequence that these self-taught readers make evident.

"Gestalt" Instruction Based on Natural Sequence

Effective reading instruction is a matter of developing or reinstating the student's natural desire to make sense of his world, in this case the world of print. Ways of doing this can be tailored to fit the level of the reader.

The Young Beginner: In the young child this intuitive demand for sense can be further developed by:

- watching while familiar stories are being read
- seeing known songs and poetry in print
- seeing product labels, ads, commercials
- dictating own stories and seeing them emerge in print
- reading *along with* competent readers
- silently reading (or looking at) books of own choice on a regular basis
- beginning independent reading on familiar, interesting topics, expressed in language similar to one's own
- learning to constantly ask one's self, does this make sense?

Having internalized this fervent demand for meaning, the young reader develops more and more refined thinking skills to deal with the unknown, bringing more experience and language knowledge to each new story and poem. A large storehouse of integrated experiences and sophisticated knowledge of grammar and spelling patterns are subsequently brought to bear on reading and writing tasks in all content areas.

The Older Reader with Difficulties: For the student who did not build her skills of reading in this natural way and is now not processing print sufficiently well to be able to re-tell a story after reading, the habitual demand for meaning must be established. A procedure such as the following can be very helpful in this re-orientation:

Tape record the student's present unassisted oral reading performance and listen to it, asking yourself:

I.	*Is she trying to make sense of it at all?*		
	A.	If so, *to what degree?*	
		1. How many sentences still make sense in the total context the way she read them?	☐
		2. How many sentences still make sense just as a single sentence?	☐
		3. What percentage do these two figures represent of the total number of sentences in the story?	☐
			Total ☐
	B.	In what *ways* is she striving for meaning?	
		1. Self-correcting	☐
		2. Logical substituting	☐
		3. Using her own dialect	☐
		4. Indicating dissatisfaction with nonsense	☐
II.	*Is she appearing* to settle for nonsense?***		
	A.	If so, *to what degree?*	
		1. How many sentences (as she read them) do not make sense?	☐
		2. What percentage do they represent? (or simply subtract the combined figure in IA, 3 from 100 percent)	☐
	B.	In what *ways* is she arriving at nonsense?	
		1. Substituting words that don't make sense	☐
		2. Making critical omissions	☐
		3. Pausing so long that she forgets what she has already read	☐
		4. Other	

You now have a broader view of what strategies the reader presently uses to process printed language. How can you use this information?

If she has few or no positive strategies (Section I), you may find the most direct route to instill the habitual demand for sense to be through her own oral language. After she dictates stories, descriptions, anecdotes, memorized songs, rhymes, ads, or any other spontaneous language, you can use this printed copy to help establish the concept that reading is merely listening to a long-distance speaker or interacting with someone who cannot be here now. By re-reading her own words *TO* her and *WITH* her, you can build the bridge from demanding sense from a speaker who is present, to demanding sense from the print of the absent speaker (author). The search for meaning is developed through the constant reminder, "Does that make sense?" This will not and should not always result in so-called "accurate" reading of the actual printed words. If we were to monitor our own reading we would discover frequent miscues to make the most sense of what we see. Children, too, who are reading effectively "replace words or phrases of a text, because, as they see it, what they are reading is not as sensible, common, or familiar as it should be" (Bettelheim 1976, p. 13).

---

*Appearing is used advisedly since we are assessing *oral performance,* not necessarily the actual reading "in the head." The two may differ, but this is an issue too complex to treat lightly here.

**Nonsense = less than sense, in this context. This does not imply random word-calling because most such miscues *do* display graphic similarity to the word in the original text (*think* for *thick*). Nonsense denotes semantic unacceptability or inappropriateness.

Later, or with a More Advanced Student: For a reader who strives to construct *some* meaning from printed stimuli, progress can be achieved by building on the already positive strategies. In fact, with the tape recording of his reading and the story text to follow, he may now become his own best teacher and evaluator. With a focus on, "Listen to see if it makes sense," readers usually spot the majority of their former semantically inappropriate miscues, and change them or sense the need to do so. In this practice, the emphasis shifts from teaching to learning and is more apt to develop along the natural lines demonstrated by the self-taught readers. The teacher's role becomes one of assisting the student in locating vitally interesting reading matter, urging predictions prior to reading, and discussing story content following the student's independent reading and tape monitoring. This could be accomplished in a small-group format as well.

Reading is learned by reading. Increasing mileage through print, and constructing sense of print are efficient avenues to reading competence. This may appear on the surface to be overly simplistic, but reading need not be regarded as a mysterious process. The miracle, if there is one, is the development of oral language, and this, coupled with the student's recall of life experiences, comprise the ever-increasing bank account from which he draws the "stuff" to make sense of printed language. Thus, teachers can perform one vital function in a student's development of reading competence: to reinforce or reinstate the desire to make sense of the world. This is what is basic to reading, to all of language, and to life itself.

References

Allen, P. David, ed. *Findings of Research in Miscue Analysis: Classroom Implications.* Urbana, Illinois: ERIC Clearinghouse on Reading and Communication Skills and National Council of Teachers of English, 1976.

Bettelheim, B. "On Learning to Read." *The National Elementary Principal* 56 (September/October 1976):pp. 6–14.

Britton, James. *Language and Learning,* Baltimore, MD: Penguin Books, 1972.

Goodman, Kenneth S. and Fleming, James T., eds. *Psycholinguistics and the Teaching of Reading.* Newark, Delaware: International Reading Association, 1969.

Goodman, Yetta M. and Burke, Carolyn L. *Reading Miscue Inventory Manual, Procedure for Diagnosis and Evaluation.* New York: MacMillan Co., 1972.

Hodges, Richard E. and Rudorf, E. Hugh. *Language and Learning to Read.* Boston: Houghton Mifflin Co., 1972.

Hunt, Dr. Lyman C., Jr. "The Challenge of Individualized Reading Instruction." Mimeographed. University of Vermont Reading Center, n. d.

Page, William D., ed. *Help for The Reading Teacher, New Directions in Research.* Urbana, Illinois: National Conference on Research in English and ERIC Clearinghouse on Reading and Communication Skills, 1975.

Silverstein, Shel. *Where the Sidewalk Ends: Poems and Drawings.* New York: Harper and Row, Publications, 1974.

Smith, Frank. *Psycholinguistics and Reading.* New York: Holt, Rinehart and Winston, 1973.

Taylor, JoEllyn. "Language and Reading in the Responsive Education Program." *The Responsive Education Program: For Children and Adult Learners.* San Francisco: Far West Laboratory for Educational Research and Development, 1976.

Will Psycholinguistics Change Reading in Secondary Schools?

Robert E. Shafer
Arizona State University

In his 1960 essay "The Major Aspects of Reading" William S. Gray summarized and illustrated a model of reading that he had been working on for three decades. This model proposed that a reader first learns to match sounds and letters, then combines these skills with phonics and "other word attack skills" to develop word perception. Gray postulated such word skills as syllabication (the breaking of words into their syllables), structural analysis (breaking words into bound and free morphemes), and context clues (inferring the meaning of the word from its position in a sentence or phrase).

Gray's influence on the field of reading has been great and for the past several decades the "skills model" of reading has held sway at all levels of school reading in the United States. More recently other models of reading have begun to emerge as a result of scholarship in such fields as cognitive psychology, linguistics, and information theory. This article traces the development of the "skills model" in the reading programs of secondary schools and outlines the characteristics and rationale of the psycholinguistics model of reading, suggesting its potential for secondary school programs.

Gray went on to say that the reader would proceed from reading words independently to reading sequences of words, such as phrases or sentences, and from this would gain a "literal comprehension" of a passage; for example, the reader would get the main idea of a paragraph by reading the topic sentence. Moreover, comprehension occurred at two further levels—the critical or evaluative, and the assimilative, where the reader would make a judgment as to the significance of the meaning, and then, if s/he were appropriately concerned with the meaning of what was read, would assimilate these meanings into her/his own consciousness.

Gray proposed that there were specific skills or abilities associated with these various "aspects of reading," and that the primary job of the reading teacher was to teach the skills associated with these different levels.

Although this description represents a tremendous oversimplification of Gray's model, I believe it to be accurate. The model was a remarkable one for its time; its pervasiveness and persistence into the present stand as testimony to the creative insight of its originator. Almost all of the instructional materials in beginning reading, and certainly most of the training programs for reading teachers even today, exemplify this model. It has become

"Reprinted with permission of Robert E. Shafer and the International Reading Association," January 1978 *Journal of Reading, 21,* 305–316.

known as the *"skills model"* or the *"taxonomic model,"*since the abilities associated with the various phases of reading can be broken down into a taxonomy which consists of major skills and various sets of subskills (Clymer, 1968).

Secondary Schools

The teaching of reading in the American secondary school has developed largely since World War II. It was called for in *The Improvement of Reading* by Strang, Traxler, and McCullough (first edition, 1946). The authors proposed that programs in reading be developed at all levels of schooling. It was followed shortly by a publication of the National Society for the Study of Education, *Reading in High School and College* (Gray, 1948), where similar proposals were made.

Suffice it to say that as secondary programs were developing throughout the 40s, 50s, and 60s, the most pervasive model of reading was the "skills model," according to which it seemed logical to assume that those readers who had difficulty in junior and senior high school somehow must have passed through the elementary grades without sufficiently developing those skills.

In the early stages, secondary school reading programs were generally remedial. Teachers would diagnose which sets of skills and subskills readers had not developed and group these students in special reading classes for such instruction. These programs called for intensive training for reading specialists and specialized materials and facilities in secondary schools (Bamman, 1964).

If remedial programs were based on a skills model, developmental programs were no exception. There was much confusion about the term *"developmental reading."* Many teachers asked, "Does developmental reading include remedial reading?" or more likely, in the early days, "What do you mean—teach reading in high school?" This question was answered by reading specialists of the time who proposed an integration of the skills model and the kinds of skills thought necessary for reading in the various subject fields.

The following answer by Margaret J. Early (1964) set the stage for many secondary school reading programs:

> "What do you mean—teach reading in high school?" Sometimes the question is asked truculently, by teachers still convinced that reading is a subject fit only for the elementary grades. More often the question reflects the genuine concern of teachers who are subject-matter specialists unacquainted with the methods and vocabulary of the reading specialist. The quickest way I know to answer the question, and keep the lines of communication open, is to draw a cone-shaped spiral.
>
> "This," I say, "is the line of direct instruction in basic reading skills. Here at the base, in the elementary grades, the spiral is tight, to represent heavy emphasis. This program of direct instruction tapers off gradually, but it never disappears, as it spirals upward into senior high school and college. By direct instruction we mean teaching word recognition, basic comprehension skills, locational skills, and rate of reading.

"This line," I continue, "represents only part of the program, the part which becomes less important in the secondary school. The more important phase is the application of reading skills to the learning of content in literature, history, mathematics, science, and other subjects. To visualize the whole meaning of 'teaching reading in the secondary school,' we must overlay this spiral with another one that begins narrowly in the primary grades and becomes broader as it reaches the upper grades."

These overlapping spirals show that the direct teaching of reading skills must proceed in an unbroken line from first grade through twelfth, reinforced, and indeed superseded, by a program which insures the application of skills in every subject where reading is an important means of learning. High school teachers can draw these implications: (1) they have something to contribute to the whole reading program, but they need not become reading specialists themselves; (2) even though emphasis on direct instruction decreases, it does not disappear; (3) the responsibility for this direct instruction is not theirs but the reading teachers'. Making a dual program work in reality, not simply on paper, requires expert teachers of reading and subject-matter specialists who understand and respect each other's goals, and can agree upon the means of achieving them.

In his influential book *Teaching Reading in High School,* Karlin (1964, pp. 37–38) based many of his proposals for secondary reading on Gray. As in most skills models, comprehension is seen by Karlin as proceeding from letters to words, and from words to meaning. The assumption is made that 1) words can be decomposed to letters, and 2) since we have been teaching letter identification for so many years, what readers must do is put letters together into words in order to recognize them and then proceed to larger units and ultimately to meaning.

As secondary programs developed, the major task confronting reading teachers was to enlist the aid of content teachers in teaching the reading of their special subject. Once again the pervasiveness of the skills model is overpowering. In his *Teaching Reading in Content Areas,* Harold Herber (1970, pp. 10–11) defines the responsibilities of the reading teacher and those of the classroom teacher:

> . . . the reading teacher says: *I have to teach these skills. What materials can I use to give instruction and provide practice on these skills? I don't care what the subject matter is just as long as the students have to use these skills in order to understand what they read.*
>
> And so the reading teacher finds the material, teaches the skills, and has the students engage in reinforcing practice. He hopes, of course, that the students will transfer these skills to their subjects and that the instruction they receive in reading class will help with assigned readings in each of their courses.
>
> Meanwhile, the content teacher says: *I have these ideas to get across to my students and this text—or these texts—develop the ideas quite well. I'll assign this material for homework so students, through their reading, will develop some understanding of these ideas. Now, in order for them to develop and use those ideas, there is a specific skill that the students have to use. It isn't "main idea," because the mere apprehension of the central thought is not the key to understanding this concept; nor is it "inference," because the author is rather straightforward in his statements; nor is it "recognition of assumption," because the author has identified his premises and has not relied on assumptions. No, in this particular selection the students have to read to "evaluate argument," and so that's the skill I will discuss with them for a moment before they begin reading the selection. Some of them will need more assistance than others so I'll have to provide a bit more guidance for them, but all of the students will have to employ this skill.*

This is the difference between the reading teacher and the content teacher with respect to the teaching of reading. The cliché "Every teacher a teacher of reading" has been interpreted by content teachers in light of the reading teacher's role and responsibility for teaching reading. Content teachers have rejected that role, and rightly so. Moreover, there has been a concerted effort to force on all content teachers the direct reading instruction properly engaged in by the reading teacher. This is unfortunate. There is no place for reading instruction, as reading teachers generally employ it, in content areas. There is a need for a whole new strategy in teaching reading through content areas, a strategy that uses what we know about the direct teaching of reading but adapts that knowledge to fit the structure of and responsibilities for the total curriculum in each content area.

Hundreds of articles have been written on how to adapt the teaching of reading skills to various content areas. Indeed, many of the new certification requirements for content teachers and reading specialists explicitly require courses involving reading in the content fields. Many junior and senior high schools now offer elaborate remedial and developmental programs, including programs in reading in the content fields.

Accountability and the Skills Model

Accountability measures have readily interfaced with the skills model. Following increased requirements for state certification of teachers, courses on the development of skills in word recognition, literal comprehension, and the so-called higher levels of comprehension have multiplied in colleges and universities. Although standardized tests are often used to measure school achievement and to comply with accountability requirements, skills-based criterion referenced testing in reading has also expanded. For example, McDonald and Moorman (1974) applied criterion referenced testing to evaluate minimal reading proficiency in the Phoenix Union High School District in Arizona. They used Barrett's (1968) "Taxonomy of Reading Comprehension" to develop performance objectives, such as 1) a functional reader will correctly identify stated main ideas; 2) a functional reader will correctly identify inferred main ideas. Test questions were developed to measure each of twelve performance objectives in twelve specific skills areas. The skills model has thus proved itself adaptable to both standardized and criterion referenced tests.

Given the years we have had to develop secondary school reading programs, the amount of published materials, and research done, it is interesting to note the concerned comments of specialists who have assessed school programs in secondary reading. Freed (1973), after surveying 485 school systems and the fifty U.S. state departments of education as to the nature and extent of secondary school reading programs, and the certification standards for teachers and specialists, concluded that:

> . . . secondary schools are still a long way from providing what William S. Gray suggested in 1948, "a program designed to promote maximum reading growth among all high school students in keeping with their individual capacities and needs." (Green, 1967)
>
> The lack of state mandates for both secondary reading instruction and for stringent teacher certification requirements is evident in viewing responses to the state department survey. . . . The survey of selected school districts reveals:
>
> —of the school districts that responded there may be as many as 34 percent of the junior high schools and 45 percent of the senior high schools that offer no reading courses

—in only 28 percent of the junior high schools and 5 percent of the senior high schools are all students required to take a reading course

—of the responding school districts, no more than half the reading teachers and almost none of the English teachers who teach reading are certified; but, in 21 percent of the schools, reading is taught by English teachers and in 37 percent by reading and English teachers. . . .

School districts go beyond state department requirements in providing reading instruction for their junior and senior high school students; however, the districts suffer from the lack of established certification standards. . . .

The most encouraging aspect of the findings is the acknowledged need for change. . . . Eighty-eight percent of the departments and 94 percent of the school districts believe that reading programs must be improved

In a survey of secondary reading activity in western New York state, Hill (1975) found that 77 percent of 172 responding schools reported some type of organized reading instruction in one or more of grades seven through twelve. He noted that more organized reading instruction occurred in grades seven and eight; local decisions in funding were key influences; organized reading instruction in middle schools (starting with grade five or six) is not necessarily carried through grades seven and eight; and there is a minimal involvement of content area teachers even in content related reading activities. All of this suggested to him that there is a need for some "hard, objective review" of content area reading instruction.

Hill also found that secondary reading programs continue to increase in number and, once established, in scope. He concluded that:

Nevertheless, the results are disquieting. There is little evidence of a vigorous, comprehensive thrust toward reading development in these schools. Much remains to be done in the reading preparation of both the classroom teacher and the secondary reading specialist. The data support balanced professional preparation (developmental, corrective-remedial, and content area strategies) rather than stress upon isolated approaches or singular methodologies.

In another recent look at secondary school reading, Early (1973) concludes:

In the past thirty years, the status of reading instruction in the secondary school has changed very little. In 1972 as in 1942, we are still debating the merits of special reading services and urging the whole school faculty to teach reading in the content fields. . . . It is the exceptional school system that offers courses in reading and study skills beyond eighth grade. Only in rare instances do I find high school departments other than English departments demanding teachers who are skilled in teaching reading.

In spite of three decades of development, including revision of certification requirements, extensive preparation of teachers in colleges and inservice programs, and a plethora of instructional materials on the market, these programs do not seem to be fulfilling their mission. Could it be that the skills model, the foundation for the programs themselves, has feet of clay?

A Psycholinguistic Model

It was Noam Chomsky in his books *Syntactic Structures* (1963) and *Language and Mind* (1972) who first focused attention on the ways in which human beings unconsciously acquire the rules of language. He proposed that these rules, which are acquired early in life, govern language behavior and that most of language learning is implicit knowledge. His work brought forth a plethora of studies of child language acquisition, much of which is still being pursued by such persons as Roger Brown (1973) and others.

It remained for scolars interested in the parallels between reading acquisition and language acquisition to develop a psycholinguistic model of reading. Most notable is Frank Smith, whose *Understanding Reading* (1971), *Psycholinguistics and Reading* (1973) and *Comprehension and Learning* (1975), combined information processing, cognitive psychology, and psycholinguistics in a psycholinguistic model of the reading process. Ken Goodman (1973) and Yetta Goodman and Carolyn Burke (1972) have also developed a psycholinguistic model and a program of research in miscue analysis to show how the model works and how one can apply psycholinguistics to improve the reading of young people.

Stated simply, in the psycholinguistic model, the reader is a continual seeker after meaning. The brain is constantly going through a decision-making process to decide what's out there in terms of incoming information and prior expectations, constantly attempting to reduce uncertainty by applying what is already known from previous experience to each incoming message.

According to the psycholinguistic model, within the brain there is a cognitive structure built up much the way Piaget has proposed in his theories of assimilation and accommodation (Ginsburg and Opper, 1969). As a human being learns to adapt to sets of new circumstances, cognitive categories are established in the brain, and *"feature lists"* for these categories are established for all that we know.

In order to identify an object as a word or a letter, something that is distinctive about it must be isolated. We then use these distinctive features to reduce the number of alternatives to what we are perceiving, and we ultimately reduce all uncertainty and achieve comprehension. Essentially, when we perceive, we 1) distinguish among objects, 2) put these objects into categories, and 3) assimilate or interrelate these objects with those we already know.

When the reader seeks meaning by using her/his cognitive structure, s/he is using *"implicit knowledge,"* a knowledge which s/he is not aware s/he possesses. S/he achieves comprehension or meaning when all cognitive questions are answered and there is an absence of uncertainty (Smith, 1975, p. 34).

In reading for meaning, the fluent reader is like the skilled radar operator who uses signal detection theory to identify hostile or friendly aircraft on a radar screen. As far as the radar operator is concerned, there are only two possibilities: a blip on the screen is either an aircraft or it is a cloud. In either case, the operator can make a correct identification, a *"hit."* However, there are two possible errors. The first occurs when no aircraft is present but the radar operator decides that one is—this is a "false alarm." The other occurs when there is an aircraft present but the operator mistakenly decides that the blip on the screen is a thundercloud—this is a *"miss."*

The radar operator would like to have a maximum number of hits and a minimum of false alarms and misses. But he cannot change the number of one without changing the total number of the others. He always has to decide where he will set his criterion for distinguishing planes from thunderclouds. He can set his criterion high: the higher the criterion, the more information required before making a decision. There will be fewer false alarms, but also fewer hits. There will be more hits if the criterion is set lower, but there will also be more false alarms.

What makes the radar operator decide to set his criterion high or low? He decides on the basis of the relative rewards or punishments for hits, misses, and false alarms. If he is heavily penalized for false alarms, he will set his criterion high, risking an occasional missed identification. If, on the other hand, he is willing to shoot down both friendly and enemy planes, and shoot at thunderclouds as well, and no one particularly cares, he will set his criterion low.

As readers, we go through processes of this sort each time we take a chance on a meaning. As Smith (1971, p. 25) has put it:

> The skilled reader cannot afford to set his criterion too high for deciding on word or meaning identification; we shall see that if he demands too much visual information, he will often be unable to get it fast enough to overcome memory limitations and read for sense. This readiness to take chances is a critical matter for beginning readers who may be forced to pay too high a price for making "errors." The child who stays silent (who "misses") rather than risk a "false alarm" by guessing at a letter or word before he is absolutely sure of it, may please his teacher but develop a habit of setting his criterion too high for efficient reading.

Perhaps we should ask ourselves if we are encouraging students to set their criteria low enough so that they are willing to be wrong in the process of risk taking in identifying words and meanings. To what extent do we encourage risk taking in classes at all? If, as Ken Goodman has proposed, reading can be defined as a *"psycholinguistic guessing game,"* then risk taking must be one of its most important aspects. What can we do to promote risk taking?

As readers sample the visual array which is print, using the cueing systems derived from their implicit knowledge of the way print is organized in English orthography (or in whatever language they are reading), some letters naturally follow certain others, and some almost never follow others. As fluent readers have continuing experiences with print, they become aware of the conventions of the printed page and build up within cognitive structure a storehouse of categories concerned with these conventions and consistencies. This knowledge of the conventions and consistencies of print is called *"redundancy."*

The same storehouse of knowledge is built up as implicit knowledge within cognitive structure concerning language itself. In learning language and using it constantly, we take over conventions and consistencies of which we are hardly aware. What appears to us to be a natural order of words is a highly developed aspect of human knowledge. It is an aspect which we were never taught but which we acquired with the other aspects of our language system, for example, our conventions of sound or phonology, and our storehouse of words. All of these conventions and consistencies of language are redundancies that we use to comprehend meaning. They represent a significant cueing system for us as we sample the printed page.

Another cueing system is derived from our previous experience, consisting of all of the meanings we've already stored away in cognitive structures. Linguists call this our semantic system. We use this cueing system every time we are called upon to sample the printed page and seek meanings there. This fund of knowledge is organized and stored in our long-term memory. In order to read fluently we must use our long-term memory.

Three Aspects of Memory

The psycholinguistic view of reading proposes that memory is essential in the reading process. One aspect of memory is known as the *"sensory store."* The sensory store (sometimes called the "visual image") contains perceptions we are making decisions about. Perhaps the second the brain decides that incoming information should be integrated with what is already known, information in the sensory store decays. This decay takes place very rapidly, probably in less than a second, unless the brain decides to put that information into short-term memory.

Short-term memory is the second aspect of memory, which holds raw information temporarily while the brain decides whether it should be put into long-term memory. An example would be the process of looking up a seven-digit telephone number and being interrupted while dialing the number on the telephone. We will probably forget the number if we are interrupted, since we would not have had opportunity to rehearse it and put it into long-term memory. We would probably have to look up the number again. Since we can hold only about four or five items in short-term memory, this is information that will be lost within a few seconds unless we renew it by some form of internal rehearsal. In a sense, short-term memory can be considered a bottleneck, since it can hold so little information.

The third aspect of memory is *long-term memory.* Only one item can get from short-term memory to long-term memory every five seconds. Whatever we get into long-term memory stays there for a long time. We may, in fact, have trouble getting things out of long-term memory, since we sometimes forget the ways we can get access to it.

In reading, all three aspects of memory are involved. As Smith (1971, pp. 78–79) has put it:

> In reading, as in any perceptual event, all three aspects of memory must be involved. Visual information is picked up from the printed page and held for less than a second in a sensory store. Much of the information in the sensory store must necessarily be lost, but some is transferred to short-term memory, where it can be held for a few seconds while further information from the sensory store is acquired. New visual information effectively wipes out the content of the sensory store immediately (which is supporting evidence for the view that most of the time we have our eyes open we are not taking in any information at all).
>
> How much information gets into short-term memory depends on its form. Short-term memory may contain only four or five elements at any one time, but each of these elements may be a single letter or a single word or possibly a meaning extracted from several words. Since sentence meaning cannot be determined on a sequential word-by-word basis, it is obvious that information from several printed words has to be held in short-term memory at any one time. The load on short-term memory can be reduced by "chunking" information in larger units (for example, by storing words rather than letters) but this involves making use of syntactic and semantic information that must already be stored in long-term memory. In fact, nothing could be identified—which means nothing could be perceived—if a contribution were not made by long-term memory, because it is there that is lodged the knowledge of the world to which all incoming information must be referred.
>
> The skilled reader usually keeps his eyes four or five words ahead of his voice while he is reading—a record of your eye movements if you were reading the present sentence aloud would have shown that your voice was only up to here/ when you eyes were here/. In other

words, a skilled reader probably keeps his short-term memory fully loaded while he is reading. The short-term memory bottleneck also suggests why even the slightest distraction is enough to make us lose the thread of what we are reading.

The reader must process whatever is being held in short-term memory—that is, lose it altogether or put it into long-term memory. Processing something into long-term memory can best be accomplished by *"chunking."* And the extent to which the reader is reading for meaning and for larger clusters of meaning will assist in chunking. In fact, the reader who is reading for letters or for words is under a tremendous handicap to chunk either letters or words. Even so, a good deal of information must be lost between short- and long-term memory, since a good deal is lost between sensory store and short-term memory.

Fluent readers must be parsimonious and insure that the information which is lost or discarded is least important. Fluent readers become aware of which information is the most meaningful in reading because they are using their semantic cueing system, that is, their knowledge of the world, in order to predict how relevant the incoming information will be. This process puts a premium on the use of redundancy in all of the cueing systems in reading.

Comparison with Skills Model

In many ways the psycholinguistic model proposes that reading takes place exactly the opposite from the way in which the skills model has taught us. Rather than going from sounds to letters to words to phrases to sentences to meaning, the fluent reader goes directly to meaning. To the extent that a beginning reader is becoming fluent, the beginning reader goes directly to meaning and through the totalities of meaning, establishes the meanings of smaller units—if indeed this takes place consciously at all. Readers are continually using the redundancies within their cueing systems to make predictions about meaning. They are continually reducing uncertainty and arriving at comprehension or meaning.

Most readers are unaware that the unconscious knowledge they have of the writing system of their language or of the world has anything to do with reading at all. It is essential that we as teachers make children aware of the importance their unconscious knowledge of writing and language has as they make predictions about meaning. Teachers will find that once they get past the term "psycholinguistics" and attend to what psycholinguists are actually saying about reading, they will find that much of their apprehension stemming from unfamiliar terminology will be overcome.

The following remarks from Smith's *Comprehension and Learning* (1975, pp. 184–85) may be taken as a guide for the development of future reading programs in the secondary school:

> . . . [R]eading cannot be considered a process of "decoding" written symbols into speech; it is neither necessary nor possible for writing to be comprehended in this way. Instead written language must be directly attacked for meaning—a process not usually "taught", at least not consciously to any significant extent—but learned by many children anyway. We will be better able to ask how children manage to learn to read, if we consider briefly what they must learn to do.
>
> It seems to me that fluent reading entails two basic skills, neither of which is unfamiliar to a child coming into the learning situation. The first skill is the prediction of meaning and the sampling of surface structure to eliminate uncertainty . . . a process that is fundamentally the

same for both reading and the comprehension of spoken language. The second skill is the ability to make the most economical use possible of visual information. Every child is also quite familiar with this need and skill because he has been making sense of other visual aspects of his world in this way since birth. . . . Neither of these skills, the prediction of meaning and the parsimonious use of visual information, is explicitly taught in school. But it is not necessary that these skills be taught. If he is put into an appropriate learning situation, a child will develop them—just as he has developed his skills for comprehending spoken language. And an appropriate learning situation is easily specified: A child can only learn to read by reading. Only by reading can a child test his hypotheses about the nature of the reading process, establish distinctive feature sets for words, learn to identify words and meanings with a minimum of visual information and discover how not to overload the brain's information-processing capacity and to avoid the bottlenecks of memory.

Applying Psycholinguistics

If the student is to read for meaning first, the meanings he or she already has will very much influence the assimilation and accommodation of everything read. Certainly long before the development of the psycholinguistic model of reading itself, many teachers have known this to be true. In the 1940s a young teacher in New York decided to try out some of the implications of Willard Olsen's research in child development by using self-selection and pacing in the development of what she called "individualized reading." Using children's picture books, she was able to demonstrate that children's development in reading is just as certain if good children's books are used rather than basal readers. Furthermore, more children retain a long-standing interest in reading as well (Veatch and others, 1973).

In the extension of her work in using key word vocabulary (as in the language experience approach), Veatch cooperated with Sylvia Ashton-Warner (1963) whose use of key words with the Maori children in New Zealand is another example of how a teacher's intuition has substantiated the newer psycholinguistic model.

Recently there are signs that the world of secondary reading instruction is becoming more than a plethora of kits, study guides, skill builders, and reading machines. Mavrogenes (1975) showed how the psycholinguistic knowledge within each reader can be used in a secondary school reading program. She concentrated on the ways in which redundancy, language experience, and literature can be intertwined.

Palmer (1974) applied psycholinguistic knowledge to the assessment of readability, and there are many implications in his writing for the measurement of reading achievement and assessment of reading ability generally, as well as for diagnosing the reading performance of an individual. Palmer is particularly interested in the ways in which short-based clause length, free modifiers, and a cumulative sentence influence "chunking." He urges further exploration of "significant factors of a rhetorical kind that influence the reader's cognitive ability to process information."

In 1965 Walker proposed individualized reading programs for secondary schools using what was then a developing literature for adolescents. Today, although such programs are by no means common, there are many more articles supporting and describing them as they exist in schools (for example, Ritt, 1976).

The continuing problem of reading in the content fields has been addressed by Sartain (1973), who proposed ways to interest students in reading for meaning in the various content fields by using the knowledge and interest they have in driver education. He branches from various aspects of driver education to a language experience approach to the area of content field reading. Language experience is a well-known method in the elementary school, yet few secondary teachers, insofar as a search of the literature reveals, have attempted this method in their reading programs, Sartain's article being a notable exception.

I propose that language experience and individualized reading have been validated by the psycholinguistic model of reading and are fertile areas which can be cultivated in the development of secondary school reading programs. These approaches may help us do what Frank Smith (1973) proposes in applying the psycholinguistic model to reading in general in his article *"Twelve Easy Ways to Make Learning to Read Difficult: And One Difficult Way to Make It Easy."* Smith urges teachers to use their basic intuitions about young people. His difficult rule to make reading easy is: *"The only way to make learning to read easy is to make reading easy."* He further states (p. 195):

> Learning to read is a complex and delicate task in which almost all the rules, all the cues, and all the feedback can be obtained only through the process of reading itself. Children learn to read only by reading. Therefore, the only way to facilitate their learning to read is to make reading easy for them. This means continuously making critical and insightful decisions—not forcing a child to read for words when he is, or should be, reading for meaning; not forcing him to slow down when he should speed up; not requiring caution when he should be taking chances; not worrying about speech when the topic is reading; not discouraging errors. . . .

The evaluations and assessments of reading in the secondary school show us what we already know—that there are still thousands of young people who not only find reading in the secondary school difficult but well nigh impossible. Is it not time that we begin a program to make learning to read easy in the secondary school?

References

Ashton-Warner, Sylvia. *Teacher.* New York, N.Y.: Simon and Schuster, 1963.

Bamman, Henry A. "Organizing the Remedial Program in the Secondary School." *Journal of Reading,* vol. 8, no. 2 (November 1964), pp. 103–08.

Barrett, Thomas C. "The Barrett Taxonomy of Cognitive and Affective Dimensions of Reading Comprehension." *Innovation and Change in Reading Instruction,* Helen M. Robinson, Ed., p. 19. Sixty-seventh Yearbook of the National Society for the Study of Education, Part II. Chicago, Ill.: University of Chicago Press, 1968.

Brown, Roger. *A First Language.* Cambridge, Mass.: Harvard University Press. 1973.

Chomsky, Noam. *Language and Mind.* New York, N.Y.: Harcourt Brace Jovanovich, Inc., 1972.

Chomsky, Noam. *Syntactic Structures.* The Hague, Netherlands: Mouton & Co., 1963.

Clymer, T. "What Is 'Reading'?: Some Current Concepts." *Innovation and Change in Reading Instruction,* Helen M. Robinson, Ed., pp. 7–29. Sixty-seventh Yearbook of the National Society for the Study of Education, Part II. Chicago, Ill.: University of Chicago Press, 1968.

Early, Margaret J. "The Meaning of Reading Instruction in Secondary Schools." *Journal of Reading,* vol. 8, no. 1 (October 1964), pp. 25–29.

Early, Margaret J. "Taking Stock: Secondary School Reading in the 70's." *Journal of Reading,* vol. 16, no. 5 (February 1973), pp. 364–73.

Freed, Barbara R. "Secondary Reading—State of the Art." *Journal of Reading,* vol. 17, no. 3 (December 1973), pp. 195–201.

Ginsburg, Herbert and Sylvia Opper. *Piaget's Theory of Intellectual Development.* Englewood Cliffs, N.J.: Prentice-Hall, Inc., 1969.

Goodman, Kenneth S., Ed. *Miscue Analysis: Applications to Reading Instruction.* Urbana, Ill.: National Council of Teachers of English, 1973.

Goodman, Yetta and Carolyn Burke. *Reading Miscue Inventory.* New York, N.Y.: Macmillan, Inc., 1972.

Gray, William S. "The Major Aspects of Reading." *The Sequential Development of Reading Abilities,* Helen M. Robinson, Ed., pp. 10–24. Supplementary Educational Monographs, No. 90. Chicago, Ill.: University of Chicago Press, 1960.

Gray, William S., Ed. *Reading in High School and College.* Forty-seventh Yearbook of the National Society for the Study of Education, Part II. Chicago, Ill.: University of Chicago Press, 1948.

Herber, Harold. *Teaching Reading in Content Areas.* Englewood Cliffs, N.J.: Prentice-Hall, Inc., 1970.

Hill, Walter, "Secondary Reading Activity in Western New York: A Survey." *Journal of Reading,* vol. 19, no. 1 (October 1975), pp. 13–19.

Karlin, Robert. *Teaching Reading in High School,* 1st ed. Indianapolis, Ind.: The Bobbs-Merrill Company, Inc., 1964.

Mavrogenes, Nancy A. "Using Psycholinguistic Knowledge to Improve Secondary Reading." *Journal of Reading,* vol. 18, no. 4 (January 1975), pp. 280–86.

McDonald, Thomas F. and Gary B. Moorman. "Criterion Referenced Testing for Functional Literacy." *Journal of Reading,* vol. 17, no. 5 (February 1974), pp. 363–66.

Palmer, William S. "Readability, Rhetoric, and the Reduction of Uncertainty." *Journal of Reading,* vol. 17, no. 7 (April 1974), pp. 552–58.

Ritt, Sharon Isaacson. "Journeys: Another Look at the Junior Novel." *Journal of Reading,* vol. 19, no. 8 (May 1976), pp. 627–34.

Sartain, Harry W. "Content Reading—They'll Like It." *Journal of Reading,* vol. 17, no. 1 (October 1973), pp. 47–51.

Smith, Frank. *Comprehension and Learning.* New York, N.Y.: Holt, Rinehart & Winston, Inc., 1975.

Smith, Frank. "Twelve Easy Ways to Make Learning to Read Difficult: And One Difficult Way to Make it Easy." *Psycholinguistics and Reading,* Frank Smith, Ed. New York, N.Y.: Holt, Rinehart & Winston, Inc., 1973.

Smith, Frank. *Understanding Reading.* New York, N.Y.: Holt, Rinehart & Winston, Inc., 1971.

Strang, Ruth, Arthur E. Traxler and Constance M. McCullough. *The Improvement of Reading.* New York, N.Y.: McGraw-Hill, 1961.

Veatch, Jeannette and others. *Key Words to Reading: The Language Experience Approach Begins.* Columbus, Ohio: Charles E. Merrill Publishing Co., 1973.

Walker, Jerry L. "Conducting an Individualized Reading Program in High School." *Journal of Reading,* vol. 8, no. 5 (April 1965), pp. 291–95.

The Role of Prediction in Reading

Frank Smith
Ontario Institute for Studies in Education

A growing number of analyses of reading are playing particular attention to the use that a reader must make of prior knowledge relevant to the material he/she is endeavoring to read (e.g. Goodman, 1968, 1970; Hochberg, 1970; Kolers, 1970; Smith, 1971, 1973). In formal psychological jargon this use of prior knowledge is frequently referred to as *hypothesis testing;* teachers know it more familiarly as *guessing;* and I shall refer to it as *prediction.* I believe that reading is impossible without prediction, and since it is only through reading that children learn to read, it follows that the opportunity to develop and employ skills of prediction must be a critical part of learning to read.

It is not necessary, however, that prediction be taught, for prediction is as much a part of spoken language comprehension as it is of reading. Children with sufficient verbal ability to understand written material that is read to them have both the competence and the experience to direct their ability in prediction to reading. My aim is to demonstrate that prediction is essential for reading, that everyone who can comprehend spoken language is capable of prediction, and that prediction is routinely practiced in reading by beginners as well as fluent readers.

Four Reasons for Prediction

1. Individual words have too many meanings. Words in our language tend to be multiply ambiguous, and the most common words have the most meanings (Fries, 1940). Everyday words like *come, go, have, take, table, chair* not only have a multiplicity of different meanings, they are often also ambiguous as to their grammatical function. How is the word *house* pronounced? The word cannot even be articulated until the reader knows whether it is a noun or a verb. The most common words in any language, the prepositions, have so many different meanings they take up more space in dictionaries than words in any other class. It should be noted, however, that speakers and writers are almost never aware of this potential ambiguity, and that listeners and readers are rarely aware of the multiplicity of possible meanings either.

2. The spellings of words do not indicate how they should be pronounced. There are over 300 "spelling-to-sound correspondence rules" of English (Venezky, 1967), and there is no rule that will specify when any of these particular rules must apply, or when the spelling to be "sounded out" is an exception. The rules of phonics are highly complex. To take a very simple example, how should a word beginning with *HO . . .* be pronounced?

Reprinted from *Elementary English,* 1975, *52,* 305–311, with permission of the National Council of Teachers of English.

The answer depends on whether the *ho* is followed by . . *t,* . . *ot,* . . *ok,* . . *rizon,* . . *use,* . . *rse,* . . *pe,* . . *ney,* . . *ist,* . . *ur,* . . *nest,* eleven different possibilities (all depending on what follows the initial letters, indicating that phonics must be applied from right to left).

3. There is a limit to how much of the "visual information" of print the brain can process during reading. Flash a line of about thirty random letters on a screen for about a tenth of a second and the most an experienced reader will be able to recognize is four or five letters. This four-letter or five letter limit in fact represents an entire second that it takes the brain to decide what these five letters are, it is not possible for anything else to be seen; a condition that can be characterized as "tunnel vision." In other words, for as long as one is trying to identify letters one after the other, reading is an impossibly slow and restricted process (Smith and Holmes, 1971).

4. The capacity of short-term memory (or "working memory") is limited (Atkinson and Shiffrin, 1970; Simon, 1974). Not more than six or seven unrelated items—say an unfamiliar telephone number—can be held in short-term memory at any one time. Try to overload an already filled short-term memory and other information will be lost. As a consequence, it is virtually impossible to read a word more than four or five letters long a letter at a time. By the time the end is reached, the beginning will be forgotten. It is similarly impossible to store the first words of a sentence while waiting to get to its end before making a decision about meaning. By the time the end of the sentence is reached, the beginning will have been forgotten.

Defining Prediction

There is a common feature underlying the four "reasons for prediction" that have just been listed. In each case the brain is confronted by too many possibilities; it must decide among more alternatives than it can handle. Decision-making takes time, and there is a fundamental rule that applies to every aspect of decision-making, whether it involves the identification of a single letter or word in line of type, or the comprehension of a sentence or an entire book. The fundamental rule is this: the greater the number of alternatives, the more time is required for a decision (Garner, 1962). Recognition is never instantaneous. We may be able to identify a letter or a word if it comes from a small set of known alternatives—when we know in advance that it is a vowel, or the name of a flower—but the same letter or word will be quite unrecognizable if it comes from a larger set of alternatives. The reason for this bottleneck is simple: the greater the number of possible alternatives, the more information the brain has to process in order to reach a decision. The art of fluent reading lies in the skilled reduction of the amount of visual information the brain has to process. If you know a letter will be either *A* or *B*, you need only a glimpse of that letter to decide which it is. But if the letter could be any one of the 26 letters of the alphabet, much more visual information will have to be taken into account.

My general definition of prediction is *the prior elimination of unlikely alternatives.* In the jargon of Information Theory, prediction is the reduction of uncertainty. The qualification "unlikely" in the preceding definition must be emphasized. "Prediction" in the sense in which I am using the word does not mean wild guessing, nor does it mean staking everything on a simple outcome. Rather prediction means the elimination from contention of those possibilities that are highly unlikely, and the examination first of those possibilities that are most likely. Such a procedure is highly efficient for making decisions involving language.

Prediction in Operation

Imagine that I have written 26 letters of the alphabet on 26 index cards, one letter to each card and that I shuffle the pack of cards, select one at random, and ask you to guess what that card is. You could very rightly object that since every letter is equally probable, nothing you know could in any way increase your chances of making a correct guess. Whatever letter you might choose to guess, the probability that you will be correct is exactly the same, namely, one in 26. On the average you would expect to make 13 guesses before you are likely to be right.

However, letters do not occur randomly in the English language. Some have a much higher probability of occurrence than others, for example the most common letter E is forty times more likely than the least common letter Z. If I asked you to guess the 17th letter of the 5th line of the 23rd page of a random sample of 1,000 books in any library, you would be correct forty times more often if you guessed E every time than if you consistently guessed Z. So when a letter is selected at random from English text, your prior knowledge of the language can obviously make a difference to your chances of making a correct guess.

It is easy to demonstrate that people can and do use their knowledge of the relative probabilities of English letters in this way, knowledge that often they are not aware they have. For example, one can ask an audience of several hundred people to write down their guess of what the first letter of a pre-selected six-letter word might be. In an example I demonstrated at the Reading '74 Conference at York University the pre-selected word was *STREAM*. The majority of people will write E, T, A, I, O, N, S, H, R, D, L or U, which happens to be the 12 most frequent English letters in order of frequency. Scarcely anyone will predict Z, Y, or J. Usually S happens to be the most common guess for the initial letter of six-letter words, by about one person in eight (as opposed to the one in 26 that would be expected if guesses were made at random). Tell an audience that the first letter is indeed S, and fully half of them will correctly guess the second letter T first time, and fully half again will guess that the third letter is R. Most people will then correctly guess that the fourth letter is E, and go on to be incorrect with their guess that the following letter is another E, although they will be correct on their second attempt with A. These days, K is usually the guess for the final letter, with M the successful second guess. In other words, by using their prior knowledge of the relative frequency of letters and groups of letters in English, people rarely have to labor through a dozen or more unsuccessful guesses before they can decide what the next letter of an unknown word might be. The average number of guesses is about three. (The statistically computed average number of alternatives that successive letters of English words might be is seven or eight, Shannon, 1951). The effect of such prior knowledge is considerable. Most English words remain recognizable if every other letter is obliterated, demonstrating that we scarcely have to look at most letters to identify them in words. A more graphic illustration of the saving that the prior elimination of unlikely alternatives can accomplish is that a single glance at a sequence of random *words* on a screen is usually sufficient to permit the recognition of two or three words, or twice as many letters than could be recognized if the *letters* flashed on the screen had been randomly selected.

But readers know far more about language than the relative likelihood of particular letters in isolated words. We can make excellent guesses about words in sentences. Take any book that happens to be handy, read the 1st couple of lines of a right hand page, and then guess what the next word will be when you turn the page,. You will not be right every time of course, but you will almost always guess a word that is possible. Remember, what is important is not to be absolutely correct, but to eliminate unlikely alternatives. Once again, statistical analyses of English texts have shown that although in theory an author might draw from a pool of fifty thousand words or more for the words to be used in a book, there are on the average no more than 250 alternatives available when he or she writes any particular word in that book (Shannon, 1951). The readers do not need to predict the exact word that will confront them. Nor need they predict more than a few words ahead. But if they can reduce the number of immediate alternatives from many thousands to a couple of hundred, they are taking a considerable burden from the limited information-processing capacity of the brain. Once again our illustrative experiment will demonstrate this saving: If the sequence of 30 letters flashed briefly on a screen comprises a single coherent sentence or meaningful phrase, then the viewer can usually see it all at one glance.

There have been hundreds of experiments showing that sequences of letters and words are identified faster, more accurately, and with less visual information, the more they correspond to possible sequences in the English language (a classic example is Tulving and Gold, 1963). The experiments demonstrate not only that individuals, including children, have a considerable prior knowledge of language that enables them to eliminate many unlikely alternatives in advance, but that this knowledge is exercised automatically, without the individual's awareness and without specific instructions to do so. But the prior rejection of unlikely alternatives is a characteristic of the way the human brain works. The reason we are rarely surprised by anything we see, even when we visit an unfamiliar setting, is that we always have a set of prior expectations about what we will in fact see. We do not predict everything, we would be surprised to see a camel in the harbor or a submarine in the zoo, but not *vice versa*. Nor are our predictions over-specific, we rarely predict *exactly* what we shall see next. Instead, we quite automatically and subconsciously eliminate unlikely possibilities from consideration.

The Advantage of Prediction

Prediction in reading, I have argued, involves the prior reduction of uncertainty by the elimination of unlikely alternatives. We never make our decisions as if we had no prior expectations; recognition and comprehension in such circumstances would always be disruptively time-consuming and tedious. Instead we seek just enough information to decide among the alternatives that are most likely. As a result, the four limitations on reading that I have discussed as reasons for prediction are very easily overcome, and there are other advantages as well.

Most words have many meanings, but if we are predicting, then we are usually looking for only one meaning of any particular word. You may not be able to guess if the next word is going to be *table* or *chair, sideboard,* or *coat-rack,* but if you know that it will refer to a piece of furniture, you will not even consider that *table* might be a set of numbers, or *chair* a verb. The reason neither speakers and writers are aware of the potential ambiguity of what they say is that they already know the meaning they are trying to express and do not consider alternative possibilities; they are embarrassed if a double-meaning is pointed out to them. Similarly listeners and readers expect a certain meaning if they are following (or rather predicting) the sense of what they are trying to comprehend; hence puns are so excruciating when eventually we manage to see them. Words may have a multiplicity and grammatical function taken one at a time, but in meaningful sentences they are rarely ambiguous.

The pronunciation of words may not be predictable from their spellings, but if you know what a word is likely to be, it is not difficult to use "phonics" to confirm or reject a particular expectation. As all reading teachers know implicitly, phonics is easy if you already have a good idea what the word is in the first place. If a child can predict that the next word is likely to be either *cow, horse,* or *sheep,* he or she will not need much knowledge of spelling-to-sound correspondences to decide which it is. It is in fact through such prediction that a mastery of *useful* phonic skills is acquired.

Obviously, prediction will speed up reading, and therefore help to overcome the limitation imposed by the brain's rather sluggish rate of information processing. The fewer alternatives you consider, the faster you can read, and the more efficient will be the reading that you accomplish. Reading with prediction means that the brain does not have to waste time analyzing possibilities that could not possibly occur.

The limited capacity of short-term memory is overcome by filling it always with units as large and as meaningful as possible. Instead of being crammed uselessly with half-a-dozen unrelated letters, short-term memory can contain the same number of words, or better still, the meaning of one or more sentences. In fact prediction works better at these broader levels; it is easier to predict meanings rather than specific words or letters, and very few letters or words need to be identified to test prediction about meanings.

The first of the bonus advantages of prediction in reading is that the reader is working already at the level of meaning. Reading is meaningful before the reader even begins. Instead of trying to slog through thickets of meaningless letters and words in the fond hope that eventually some nugget of comprehension will arise, the reader is looking for meaning all the time. If any possibility of meaning is to be found in a text, the predicting reader is the one who will find it.

The final advantage is of particular practical importance in many classrooms, namely that with prediction it does not matter if the reader's language does not exactly match that of the writer. Everyone can understand language that he or she could not possibly produce; that is why parents quickly learn to conduct their more intimate conversations out of the hearing of their pre-school children. Yet the language ability of children in schools is all too often evaluated by the speech that they *produce.* Few readers, even adults, can succeed in threshing out the sound of a sentence, word for word, unless they have a good prior idea of what the sentence as a whole means. There is no way a child can be expected to identify words as a *preliminary* to getting the meaning if the words are in fact not among those he or she would choose to express such a meaning. But with prediction, a "one-to-one match" is not required. It will not matter if a child *thinks* the author has written "John ain't got no candy", rather than "John has no candy", provided the meaning is understood and provided the teacher is not demanding literal word-for-word accuracy.

Prediction in the Classroom

Two basic conditions must be met if a child is to be able to predict in the manner that is essential for learning to read. The first condition is that the material from which children are expected to learn to read must be potentially meaningful to them, or otherwise there is no way they will be able to predict. The opposite of meaningfulness is nonsense, and anything that is nonsensical is unpredictable. Any material or activity that does not make sense to a child will make it more difficult to read.

But meaningfulness of materials and activities is not enough; children must also feel confident that they are at liberty to predict, to make use of what they already know. With prediction there is a constant possibility of error, but then readers who read without ever making errors are not reading efficiently; they are processing far more information than is usually necessary. The child who will become a halting, inefficient reader is one who is afraid to make a mistake. The worst strategy for any reader who is having difficulty understanding text is to slow down and make sure that every word is identified correctly.

The notion that prediction should be encouraged worries many teachers; it may sound as if a virtue is being made out of error. But one should distinguish prediction from reckless guessing. The guesser is usually the child trying to achieve what the teacher is demanding by getting every word right, no matter how little relation it bears to sense. A striking characteristic of older children with low reading ability is that they read as if they have no expectation or interest that the material might make sense, but are determined to get the words right at all costs.

Also, accuracy is overrated. There are only two possibilities for a mistake made during reading, either the mistake will make a difference to the meaning, or it will not. If the mistake will make no difference, if the child reads "house" instead of "apartment", then it will make no difference. There is no need to worry. But if the mistake does make a difference, if the child reads "house" instead of "horse", then the reader who is predicting will subsequently notice the anomaly, simply because he or she is following the meaning. The child who overlooks obvious errors of sense is not the child who rushes through to understand the gist of a passage but the one who tackles the passage one word at a time.

How then can prediction be taught? There are some obvious methods, such as encouraging a child to guess what a difficult word might be, and playing reading games where the teacher stops suddenly, or leaves an occasional word out, or makes an occasional deliberate mistake. But more important I think is that prediction should not be discouraged. Prediction is a natural aspect of language. The preferred strategies for a child who meets an unfamiliar word in an interesting story he or she is reading are the same as those for fluent readers: first skip, and second, guess. Sooner or later the child will have to predict if he or she is to become a fluent reader. Feedback is an essential part of all learning activities, but it can come too soon, or too often. A child who pauses before identifying a word may not want the teacher to help "sound it out", nor the rest of the class to tell what it is, he or she may in fact know what the word is and simply be wondering what it has to do with the rest of the sentence. A child who "makes a mistake" need not be "corrected" by having the teacher, or the rest of the class, say the right word immediately. If left alone he or she might self-correct in the following sentence, a far more valuable skill in reading than the blind ability to word-call. One of the beautiful advantages of reading *sense* is that it provides its own feedback; errors become self-evident.

One of the most formidable impediments to prediction, at all levels of reading, is anxiety. A child who is afraid to make a mistake is by definition anxious, and therefore unwilling to take the necessary risks of prediction. Individuals of any age labelled as reading problems will show anxiety, especially in situations where they feel they are being evaluated; their reluctance to predict will lead to laborious nonsensical reading, and their "difficulty" will become a self-fulfilling prophecy.

Prediction is not everything in reading. Other important considerations include the efficient use of short-term memory, the minimal use of visual cues, and the selection of an appropriate rate of speed for particular reading tasks, together with the acquisition of effective strategies for the identification of unfamiliar words from context. But these are all skills that come primarily through the practice of reading; they are fostered rather than taught (in fact many teachers are not aware of the extent to which these skills are involved in reading). The advantage of prediction is that it facilitates precisely the kind of confident, successful, and meaningful reading experience through which all of the critical skills of reading are acquired.

References

Atkinson, R. C. and R. M. Shiffrin, "The Control of Short-term Memory." *Scientific American,* August, 1970, 82–90.

Fries, C. C., *American English Grammar.* Appleton-Century, 1940.

Garner, W. R., *Uncertainty and Structure as Psychological Concepts.* Wiley, 1962.

Goodman, K. S., "The Psycholinguistic Nature of the Reading Process." In K. S. Goodman (editor), *The Psycholinguistic Nature of the Reading Process.* Wayne State University Press, 1968.

Goodman, K. S. "Reading: A Psycholinguistic Guessing Game." In H. Singer and R. B. Ruddell (editors), *Theoretical Models and Processes of Reading.* International Reading Association, 1970.

Hochberg, J. "Components of Literacy: Speculations and Exploratory Research." In H. Levin and J. P. Williams (editors), *Basic Studies on Reading.* Basic Books, 1970.

Kolers, P. "Three Stages of Reading." In H. Levin and J. P. Williams (editors), *Basic Studies on Reading,* Basic Books, 1970.

Shannon, C. E. "Prediction and Entropy of Printed English." *Bell Systems Technical Journal,* 1951, *30,* 50–64.

Simon, H. A., "How Big Is a Chunk?" *Science,* 1974, *183,* 482–488.

Smith, F. *Understanding Reading.* Holt, 1971.

Smith, F. *Psycholinguistics and Reading.* Holt, 1973.

Smith, F. and D. L. Holmes, "Letter, Word, and Meaning Identification in Reading." *Reading Research Quarterly,* 1971, *6,* 3, 394–415.

Tulving, E. and Gold, C. "Stimulus Information and Contextual Information as Determinants of Tachistoscopic Recognition of Words." *Journal of Experimental Psychology,* 1963, *66,* 4, 319–327.

Venezky, R. L. "English Orthography: Its Graphical Structures and Its Relation to Sound." *Reading Research Quarterly,* 1967, 2, 75–106.

Learning to Learn from Text: A Framework for Improving Classroom Practice*

Robert J. Tierney
P. David Pearson

We believe that if teachers understand the nature of reading comprehension and learning from text, they will have the basis for evaluating and improving learning environments. In this regard, we find many advances in the psychology and pedagogy of reading comprehension that provide exciting possibilities for changing our approaches to helping students learn how to learn from text. For example, in terms of texts, we present evidence that suggests that less reliance should be placed upon traditional readability procedures involved in text selection and use and that more credence should be given to teachers' impressionistic examinations of the extent to which a text fits with and might be used by selected students.

With respect to readers, teachers should recognize that a reader has a right to an interpretation and that reading comprehension is an interactive process involving more than a regurgitation of an author's explicit ideas. Readers should be encouraged to actively engage their background knowledge prior to, during, and after reading. They should be given opportunities to appreciate and evaluate the adequacy of their own perspective and other interpretations, to monitor their own progress through a text, and to discriminate new learnings from old knowledge.

Curriculum objectives might address: the importance, nature, and influence of a reader's background knowledge; the need for a variable balance between reader-based and text-based processing; and the importance of selected monitoring strategies as well as transfer skills. Widely practiced notions that compartmentalize comprehension into simple question types on a continuum from literal to inferred to evaluative should be rethought. Teaching prescriptions for how to process a text that disregard the everchanging interplay of text, purpose, and reader should be discarded. In their stead we advocate the adoption of teaching procedures that encourage students to monitor their own processing strategies—how they allocate attention to text versus prior knowledge, how they can tell *what* and *that* they know, and how to apply fix-up strategies when comprehension is difficult.

*Written especially for inclusion in this text.

In this paper, we will amplify each of the preceding notions about reading comprehension and classroom practice. First, we present some basic notions about reading comprehension. Thereupon, we discuss the implications of these notions for teaching. You should note that the suggestions for teaching are not intended to be exhaustive, exemplary, or very specific; instead, they are intended to provide teachers with guidelines and cursory examples of ways in which they might proceed to develop their own teaching procedures. We hope that the suggestions will be sufficiently explicit to guide adaptation and development.

Some Basic Notions about Reading Comprehension and Learning

Consider for a moment what is involved in comprehending the following passage:

THE DUST BOWL

During World War I, prices had tempted farmers to grow wheat and cotton in the former grazing lands of the Plains region. Plows and harrows broke up the deep, tough sod that had previously prevented erosion and conserved moisture in this semiarid region. When the years 1933–1935 proved unusually dry, there was danger that the region would become a desert. Terrible dust storms carried away topsoil in such quantities that even on the Atlantic seaboard the sun was obscured by a yellow haze. The water table of parts of the Plains region sank so low that wells ran dry. Between 1934 and 1939 an estimated 350,000 farmers emigrated from the "dust bowl." To take care of immediate distress, Congress provided funds so that dust bowl farmers could get new seed and livestock. On a long-term basis, the Department of Agriculture dealt with the dust bowl by helping farmers to plant 190 million trees in shelter beds, which cut wind velocity and retained moisture. Farmers were also encouraged to restore the Plains to what they had been in the days of the cattle kingdom and earlier—a grazing region.

Readers familiar with farming and the Plains area of the United States will likely recognize how the drought, forces of supply and demand, and soil changes interacted to contribute to the deteriorating conditions of the Dust Bowl era. They might be able to visualize the changing conditions of the topography and sense the frustration and anguish experienced by the farmers. Readers unfamiliar with farming but possessing first-hand experience with economic hardships might focus on the personal hardships and family upheaval associated with periods of depression. Readers who have experienced both farm life and economic hardship might even be able to go beyond visualizing the drought conditions to experiencing "a dryness of mouth" and "lump in their throats" as their interpretation of text triggers recall of specific experiences from the past.

The point of the example is that comprehension never occurs in a vacuum; it cannot proceed independently of a reader's fund of related experiences of background knowledge (or schemata [schema: singular], to use the recently rediscovered terminology of cognitive scientists). Comprehension is doomed to be at least somewhat idiosyncractic or at least conditioned by individual or group differences in background knowledge. And, in fact, there have been literally dozens of experimental demonstrations of the role that differences in background knowledge play in determining how students understand and retrieve information encountered in texts. Whereas this point may seem to belabor the obvious, current teaching and assessment procedures, with their emphasis on correct answers and preferred interpretations, seem to operate on the assumption that comprehension occurs independent of individual differences in background knowledge (a point to which we will return later in more detail).

How does comprehension proceed?

If comprehension is not simply a matter of mapping the author's message into a reader's memory, how then does it occur? Let us begin with an example, taken from Collins, Brown, and Larkin (1977):

WINDOW TEXT

He plunked down $5.00 at the window. She tried to give him $2.50, but he refused to take it. So when they got inside, she bought him a large bag of popcorn.[p. 3.]

With the initial statement, "He plunked down $5.00 at the window," the readers begin a search to build a model of the meaning of the text. One reader may invoke a racetrack scenario as a model; a second, a bank; a third, a movie theater. Each of these scenarios or models may be thought of as different schemata that different readers would invoke because of different levels of experience they have had with such scenarios in the past. Once invoked, each schema provides a framework for continuing the search to build a model for what the text means. For example, the racetrack schema creates expectations that bets, odds, horses, and jockeys will be mentioned soon, whereas the movie theater schema creates expectations for film title, certain types of food like popcorn, and a stage with a screen.

Cognitive scientists like David Rumelhart (1977; in press) say that schemata have certain *slots* that must be filled and that comprehension consists of recognizing specific items in a text that fill those slots. For example, "He" in the first sentence is a candidate for the "bettor" slot in a racetrack schema, the "depositor" slot in a bank schema, or the "movie-goer" slot in the movie theater scenario. As depicted in Figure 1, they may have constructed an initial model of the text involving, for example, a bank window with some bound slots (concepts enclosed by boxes) and some slots awaiting binding (concepts enclosed by circles). As readers proceed, they progressively refine their models: "She" is usually defined as the recipient of the money; "$2.50" is usually identified as change. Then with the statement, "So when they got inside . . . popcorn," readers usually recognize a conflict. They realize their models no longer match the text and are implausible, disconnected, and incomplete. To restructure their model, they might question previous interpretations (for example, that the female was a bank clerk or a bet taker) and shift to a different schema—from a bank or racetrack to a theater. Eventually it is likely that a model will evolve for readers that involves the purchase of two tickets and an attempt by a date to share the expenses. At this point, readers will sense that they have accounted for the text and that their interpretations are plausible, connected and complete—that is, their interpretations make sense, are coherent, and account for the text as well as their purposes for reading.

These same notions of reading comprehension can be applied to the passage "The Dust Bowl." With the initial statement, "During World War I, prices had tempted farmers to grow wheat and cotton in the former grazing lands of the Plains region," readers will likely

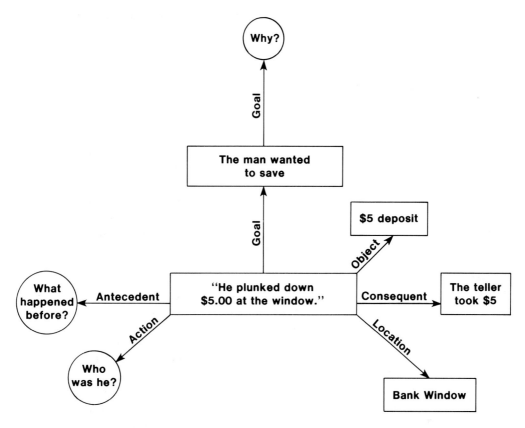

Figure 1. An initial stage in the construction of a model or scenario for the "Window Text."

activate their knowledge of farming and constrain these ideas in terms of the time period (World War I) and the type of farming to which the author alluded (wheat and cotton). As readers proceed, they are expected to relate these changes in farming—now focused on wheat and cotton—to plowing and the effects of plowing upon the conservation of moisture and potential for soil erosion. Across the next several sentences, "When the years . . . terrible dust storms . . . well run dry," readers need to activate other background knowledge, maintain their focus and progressively refine a model for the text. Assuming a singular purpose and adequate background knowledge, it is likely that readers will eventually develop a model for the text that involves an appreciation of the events causing the Dust Bowl crisis and what Congress did to alleviate the problem. Readers will then either tacitly or consciously consider the adequacy of their interpretation—in particular, the extent to which: (a) their purposes for reading the text have been met and accounted for in relation to the text; as well as sometimes (b) the relevance or transfer value of their acquired understanding.

A key point of schema theory, then, is that reading comprehension is akin to the progressive refinement of a scenario or model that a reader develops for a text. That is, reading comprehension proceeds and inferencing occurs via the refinement of the reader's model. As Collins, Brown, and Larkin (1977) described the refinement of the reader's model:

> The initial model is a partial model, constructed from schemas triggered by the beginning elements of the text. The models are progressively refined by trying to fill the unspecified slots in each model as it is constructed . . . and the search for relevant information is constrained more and more. [pp. 4–5.]

Within this framework, reader's schemata drive text processing toward the refinement of a model or scenario that "matches" the text against the reader's world and that is complete, interconnected, and plausible. That is, the reader's schemata will be involved in construction of a scenario to account for the elements and relationships within the text and the world as the reader sees it. If the reader's model seems tenable, then those schemata that comprise the model will be involved in the further text processing. If the reader's model seems untenable, then schemata will drive the reexamination, reconstruction, or restructuring of elements in the text to build a new model.

To summarize, the following statements can be made about reading comprehension: (a) a reader's background knowledge, including purposes, has an overriding influence upon the reader's development of meaning, and (b) reading comprehension involves the activation, focusing, maintaining, and refining of ideas toward developing interpretations (models) that are plausible, interconnected, and complete. In addition, there is a sense in which the reader's comprehension involves two other facets: the reader's *knowing* (either tacitly or consciously) that their interpretations for a text are plausible, interconnected, and complete ("make sense"), and, ideally, the reader's evaluation of the transfer value of any acquired understandings.

Pedagogical Implications

Recent examinations of instructional practices suggest that there is not much in the way of worthwhile practices for developing or improving comprehension in schools (Durkin, 1978–79; Tierney, LaZansky, & Schallert, 1981). Instead, there is and has been a lot of comprehension testing and practice (students working by themselves on worksheets or answering questions) and a great deal of informal assessment (teachers quizzing students about text selections). In most lessons, students are given passages to read. During or after reading the passages, teachers ask questions (either orally or via a worksheet). The responses, if discussed at all, focus on finding a right answer. In terms of skill acquisition, a high premium has been placed upon separated objectives that are unrelated to any comprehensive model of reading comprehension or learning and that are clustered around curriculum objectives or arbitrarily defined skill categories (e.g., literal, inferential, and evaluative comprehension) that give little attention to the role of a reader's background knowledge and the importance of improving a reader's abilities to learn how to learn (see note on p. 65). Reading comprehension is an area of the curriculum for which there has been little in the way of progress. Moreover, the changes that have occurred have not been tied to a careful analysis of the nature of reading comprehension and learning. We suggest that *if* teachers understand the nature of reading comprehension and learning, *then* they have the basis for determining what might facilitate and what might impede the development of comprehension and learning. We believe that a schema-theoretic perspective offers such a basis. Accordingly we suggest the following guidelines for implementing curriculum improvements. Our guidelines are tied to three traditional and interrelated segments in typical lessons for reading selections: preparing for reading, guiding reader-text interaction, and postreading comprehension and learning.

Prerequisite for reading: does the reader have schemata relevant for understanding a text?

Our first guideline addresses the empirically validated conclusion that a reader's prior knowledge has a pervasive influence upon understanding. Specifically, it is concerned with whether a match or mismatch exists between the purposes and prior knowledge of readers *and* the intentions and expectations of authors. That is, does the reader have the relevant schemata for a text?

Consider first the issue of match between an *author's intentions and a reader's purposes*. In our reviews of textbook materials we have encountered numerous examples where text intended for one purpose is forced to fit other purposes. With little regard for the integrity of a selection, some publishers seem to presume that text well-written for one purpose will be appropriate and well-written for other purposes. For example, in a certain biology textbook, the publisher uses a text describing the changing color of leaves to try to explain the physical process of these changes. The questions that are asked following the selection assume that the readers have been given many more details than the text provides; further, they totally disregard the descriptive-aesthetic functions that the text appears to serve. In the elementary classroom, simple narratives usually intended to be read for enjoyment are often sabotaged by an excessive use of poorly fitting questions (e.g., detail questions dealing with trivial information) under the guise of skill objectives.

What can teachers do? Prior to using text for pedagogical purposes, they can and should consider the functions that texts are intended to serve against the purposes for which a teacher intends and students will likely initiate. For example, text might be examined by first isolating the essential understandings that students are expected to derive from a text and then examining the extent and nature of support (usually in the form of concrete examples and analogies that can bind new learnings to old) for these understandings provided within the text. If the reader's purposes are quite unlike those intended by the author, and if the text cannot be augmented *even with teacher support* (i.e., the teacher provides the analogues and examples), then it should not be read to elicit those assumed understandings. Compare the obvious differences between the understandings that readers might be expected to glean from Stephen Crane's *The Red Badge of Courage* (1966), which uses the U.S. Civil War as background, and from a chapter on *The Civil War* in a history textbook. In the former, it is the themes of death, fear, and cowardice evoked by the experiences of a young man participating in war that are likely to capture the reader. In the latter, it is the facts and concepts that describe and define the Civil War that will be paramount. For Crane's treatment, it might be reasonable to expect a reader to glean an appreciation of the mood of the experience of war; for the textbook chapter, it might be reasonable to expect the reader to develop an appreciation of the causes, progress, and consequences of the Civil War. Even with a great deal of teacher support (including additional information, clarification, and other material), neither text could serve the purposes for which the other text seems intended.

Consider second the issues of mismatch between an author's expectations regarding audience and a reader's prior background of experience. There are many times when a text written for an audience with certain background knowledge is given to an audience with different or limited knowledge of this same topic. For example, note the difficulties an American reader will incur when trying to understand the following passage, even if it were revised to a lower readability level.

TODAY'S CRICKET

The batsmen were merciless against the bowlers. The bowlers placed their men in slips and covers. But to no avail. The batsmen hit one four after another along with an occasional six. Not once did a ball look like it would hit their stumps or be caught.

REVISED VERSION

The men were at bat against the bowlers. They did not show any pity. The bowlers placed their men in slips. They placed their men in covers. It did not help. The batsmen hit a lot of fours. They hit some sixes. No ball hit the stumps. No ball was caught.

Or consider the following segment taken from a biology text (Gallant, 1975):

"THE GARBAGE COLLECTORS OF THE SEA"

The garbage collectors of the sea are the decomposers. Day and night, ocean plants and animals that die, and the body wastes of living animals, slowly drift down to the sea floor. There is a steady rain of such material that builds upon the sea bottom. This is expecially true on the continental shelves, where life is rich. It is less true in the desert regions of the deep ocean.

As on the land, different kinds of bacteria also live in the sea. They attack the remains of dead plant and animal tissue and break it down into nutrients. These nutrients are then taken up by plant and animal plankton alike. Among such nutrients are nitrate, phosphate, manganese, silica, and calcium. . . .

It does not take too much effort to identify the readers for whom these texts, even if adapted for readability, might be inappropriate or incomprehensible. The first passage is written for an audience knowledgeable about cricket; the second passage is intended for an American high school student with an understanding of decomposition, continental shelves, body wastes, and bacteria. Without these understandings, we would predict that readers will have a great deal of difficulty reading the text and will likely develop incomplete or inappropriate interpretations for the text.

How can teachers assess whether a mismatch is likely to occur? It is our argument that traditional readability procedures (the use of formulas based upon word difficulty, word length, and sentence length, the use of the cloze procedure requiring the replacement of deleted words) will not suffice. Instead teachers should judge the adequacy of text for themselves. They should pursue an impressionistic evaluation of the demands of the text together with an assesssment of readers' prior knowledge. For purposes of illustration, an analysis of the "Garbage Collectors of the Sea" could involve an examination of the support given the concept of decomposition and an informal assessment of what students know. For example, *day and night* and *steady rain* provide ample support for the notion that *decomposition* is a never-ending process; considered as vague might be the locational reference to *continental shelf*—a term likely to be unfamiliar to most readers—and those aspects of the text specifying what decomposers are. To verify the possibility of a mismatch, teachers might informally assess the students' background knowledge by discussing with students what they know about these key concepts prior to reading.

If mismatches are inevitable, teachers have the following choices: dismiss the passage as inadequate or provide the students with the background experiences appropriate to the text. In terms of the latter, teachers might provide adjuncts or supplemental experiences prior to having students read the text. For example, teachers might support the use of textbooks with other reading material, media, activities, and experiences to supplement what students already know. As Rumelhart and Ortony (1977) have emphasized, "In all cases existing knowledge is utilized and required for the acquisition of new knowledge" (P. 117), or as Pearson and Spiro (in press) suggest: "Instead of asking the question 'what *does* the student *not know* that I have to help him or her learn?', educators should be asking 'what is it that the student *does know* that I can use as an anchor point—a bridge—to help develop the concepts that he or she needs?' " This implies that in those situations for which the reader lacks the background knowledge, teachers need to build bridges from what they already know or provide experiences or analogies (for example, a discussion of baseball as a means of understanding cricket) by which the reader can build such bridges for themselves.

Apart from specific action, teachers might offer a general program of schema development. Such a program might include field trips as well as films in conjunction with topics being read or discussed. It might involve students in activities that encourage their pursuit of or immersion in a topic through a variety of resources, for example, library materials and discussions with knowledgeable persons.

Guiding Reader—text interactions: do readers engage their schemata?

Our second guideline moves our discussion of pedagogy from prerequisites for dealing with text to the issue of student engagement with text. In particular, our second guideline assumes that readers already have adequate prior knowledge for dealing with text and asks whether they engage it. Many theorists and practitioners advocate strategies that are derived either directly or indirectly from these notions. For example, most basal reading lessons and several reading educators advise teachers to begin with either selected questions or a discussion of a story topic designed to activate background knowledge prior to reading. During reading, they often insert questions as a means of guiding or shaping a reader's understanding. Stauffer's (1969) Directed Reading-Thinking Activity (DR-TA) is one such procedure where setting purposes together with guided reading are integral. As Stauffer has stated:

> . . . either the reader declares his own purposes or if he adopts the purposes of others, he makes certain how and why he is doing so. He also speculates about the nature and complexity of the answers he is seeking by using to the fullest his experience and knowledge relevant to the circumstances. Then he reads to test his purposes and his assumptions. As a result, he may: one, find the answer he is seeking literally and completely stated; two, find only partial answers or implied answers and face the need to either restate his purposes in light of the new information gained or to suspend judgment until more reading has been done; three, need to declare completely new purpose. [Stauffer 1969, p. 40.]

There are numerous other strategies and practices ranging from advance organizers to study guides to prefatory statements to questioning strategies directed to these same ends.

In general terms, schema engagement relates to: (a) the reader's initial contact with a text, (b) the student's ability to relate his or her own background of experience to the information represented within the text, and (c) the student's ability to focus and refine his or her understanding of the text material. In particular, the notion of schema engagement addresses the issues represented by the following questions:

> Was the reader's schema engaged prior to reading, during reading, and after reading?
>
> To what extent did learning occur? Was the reader's relevant background of experience focused and structured during reading?

For teachers, schema engagement can be a serious problem among some of their students. A teacher may assume correctly that students have appropriate schemata for reading a text, only to discover in a postreading discussion that they did not engage those schemata while reading. Sometimes this problem manifests itself as a general lack of interest for reading a text or as an unwillingness to consider a topic or purposes prior to reading. In this regard, sometimes a schema engagement problem may be passage-specific—that is, it may arise for certain texts and not others. Sometimes schema engagement problems occur because readers fail to maintain schemata while reading. This may occur for a number of different reasons. First, readers may be predisposed to plod laboriously through any and every text they read. For example, readers may be devoting all their attention and capacity to decoding, leaving no room for comprehension. Second, poorly written text may make schema maintenance difficult if not impossible: for example, sudden shifts in topics, inadequate transitions, or poorly developed ideas may make the reader's task unduly difficult. Third, readers may be inattentive or distracted by too many or ill-considered adjuncts; that is, sometimes study questions and activities interrupt reading and cause a disruption of schema engagement.

What can teachers do? First and foremost, teachers should remain alert to whether students are engaging their schemata prior to, during, and after reading. Typically, a few well-placed and open-ended questions will generate a response from students that can or will suffice for such an assessment. If schema engagement problems are apparent, then teachers can adopt and adapt teaching procedures to meet the specific needs of readers. Since it is unlikely that a single procedure will be appropriate for all students in all situations and it is possible that teacher adjuncts may "do more harm than good," the following broad suggestions are presented only for purposes of exemplification.

Source of Problem	*Some Possible Solutions*
General reader inertia lack of interest	Use highly motivational material and functional reading material that necessitates a student reponse (e.g., following directions).
	Use adjuncts (inserted questions and study guide-type activities) that relate what the student is reading to what they know and might do.
Passage-specific problems	Alert students to what readers do. Encourage the application of strategies across variant text situations (e.g., have students relate what they do in successful situations with what they do in nonsuccessful situations).
Lack of focus and an inability to structure information	Have students develop "maps" or diagrammatic representations of the text.
	Provide adjuncts that encourage readers to focus and structure their ideas.
	Encourage students to use heursitics (who, what, when, where, why).
	Encourage notetaking and outlining.
Lack of focus due to laborious processing tendencies	Use texts that require or encourage greater student response.
	Encourage multiple passes through a text (skimming for the gist, rereading more carefully to check the relationship between key points, etc.)
	Highlight "reading for meaning."
Text-based problems (discontinuity, poorly developed ideas, etc.)	Prepare adjuncts to circumvent the difficulties (e.g., include statements that clarify the ideas represented within the text or encourage their omission)
	Encourage students to be the critics of poorly written text (e.g., have students evaluate poorly developed text and discuss how an author or reader might address these problems).
Overdependency upon teacher support	Avoid the use of any adjuncts that will displace the text.
	Use adjuncts sparingly and in conjunction with encouraging the reader to be self-initiating.
	Having students replace teacher adjuncts with their own probes.
	Discuss the purpose and role of any adjuncts.

Guiding reader-text interactions: does the reader exhibit flexible processing across different text read for different purposes?

Our third guideline is tied directly to our second guideline, but unlike our second it addresses the issue of monitoring reader-text interactions. As suggested earlier, with reference to figure 1, when readers interact with text they will and should acquire some information that was represented in the text and integrate it with information from their background knowledge. Certainly, there are situations for which it may be reasonable to expect a reader's understanding to remain close to the text; for example, when following a set of directions; alternatively, there are other situations for which it may be appropriate to expect a more reader-based interpretation. With this in mind, consider those situations when readers' interactive processing reflects a tendency to be either "too text-based" or "too reader-based." For example, consider the situation where a reader's interpretation is too reader-based, producing understandings that are "too loose" for the text and its intended purpose. What might be the ramifications if a science student read the following text too loosely?

The experiment that you are about to do deals with a property of light. For this experiment you'll need a penny, a cup, transparent tape, and a pitcher of water.

To perform the experiment, tape the penny to the bottom of the cup. Move your head to a point just beyond where you can see the penny.

Hold your head still, then slowly pour water into the cup. Be sure not to move your head.

Stop pouring if the penny comes into view.

Here, to explain or perform the experiment adequately, the science student cannot take liberties lest he or she err in the performance of explanation of the experiment. Unfortunately, readers with tendencies toward being too reader-based do not know *that* or *what* they do not know. They presume they know the material better than they actually do or need to. Particularly when the text deals with a familiar topic, readers assume that they know what is written. As a result, they often fail to recognize what might be subtle but important text signals. They fail to monitor their interactions with a text. In the context of many classrooms, these students escape identification, for they might be successful readers in most situations and, furthermore, can "bluff their way through" most teacher's questions.

What can a teacher do to help such students? First and foremost, teachers should alert students to the need to monitor their reading of texts differently for different texts. In text situations where a more text-based understanding is required, teachers might: alert the students to the need to read the material carefully; provide adjuncts (inserted questions or activities) that encourage students to monitor their developing interpretation; provide students with strategies such as outlining and notetaking for carefully reading the text; encourage students to consciously consider their purposes, their level of understanding, and ways to monitor that understanding; and have the students read the material in conjunction with carrying out some relevant activity (for example, an experiment in which successful performance is contingent upon a careful reading). Such students can be encouraged to consider the text more carefully by giving them questions that have two or three correct distractor choices, some of which come from the text and some of which do not. Students then can be asked to discriminate between correct text-based and correct knowledge-based answers.

Alternatively, consider the situation when a reader's understanding is too "text-based" for the text and purposes for reading. As Spiro (1977) has suggested, certain conditions of schooling may predispose a reader to ascribe to text an autonomy (and authority) that sponsors the separation of textual information from related prior knowledge. For example, a reader may minimize the interaction of his or her background of experience with a text to cope with the demands of answering a series of questions or the obvious demands of certain texts. Some may perceive the task of reading to be detached from self and tied to a text. In particular, they may perceive the task of reading to be detached from their own experiences. For example, in oral reading situations, in completing cloze activities (especially cloze activities demanding an exact-word replacement), and in response to a teacher's demand for a "more literal" interpretation, we would expect that students may misconstrue what reading comprehension is. They may decide, erroneously, that reading means a word-perfect rendition of a text.

What can teachers do in these situations? First, they should encourage readers to relate their background of experience to what they read and alert them to the importance of their own ideas, perspective, and purpose in any communication. Minimally, the reader should be asked to discuss his or her knowledge including a perspective about a topic in conjunction with a discussion of the author's perspective and what the author assumed the reader knew and might learn. Otherwise, the facilitation might be accomplished either through adjunct questions, activities, or appropriate variations. For example, sets of questions might be developed that encourage the reader to engage his or her own background of experience prior to, during, and after reading. Questions might encourage the reader to discuss his or her perceptions of what might happen and, at points during reading, what has occurred and any implications thereof.

To illustrate more specifically how this might proceed, here is a technique we have found useful. Begin by asking students what they think of when they hear the word X (where X is the topic that they are going to read about later). As they offer their associations, jot them down into categories (as yet unlabelled categories). For example, for *tree* the implicit categories might include parts of trees, kinds of trees, processes, products, and other tree-associated topics. Then go back and help the students to label the categories. Then ask them to read the chapter to learn more about X. After reading, return to the set of categories related to X and ask students to add new terms that they have acquired from reading. What one ends up with is a vivid demonstration of the student's preexisting schema, new learnings from the text, and the relationship between new and old information. The technique also maximizes the likelihood of schema engagement during reading.

Postreading comprehension and learning: is the reader's understanding adequate? Are new learnings transferable?

Our fourth guideline moves us from guidance and monitoring of text interactions to addressing the adequacy of readers' understandings. Central to our discussion are two notions: first, the realization that what is considered accuracy of understanding should be regarded as relative; second, the issue of transfer of new learnings.

Consider the notion that accuracy of a reader's understanding should be regarded as relative. The key point here is that what is considered an appropriate understanding is likely to vary from reader to reader and from context to context. That is, accuracy of understanding is relative and should be considered a function of individual reader and individual text characteristics, as well as a function of purposes for reading. In constructing an interpretation, a reader selects, inserts, substitutes, deletes, and connects ideas in conjunction with what he or she perceives as "making sense." And what "makes sense" depends upon the text as well as the reader's purposes and background knowledge. There are two postulates taken from Tierney and Spiro (1977) that are relevant to this notion:

1. A reader's selections, insertions, substitutions, omissions, and binding of ideas are *not* necessarily a sign of reader error.
2. It should not be assumed that each text has a single interpretation.

What implications does this notion hold for teachers? It would seem that teachers need to respect both authorship and readership. Indeed, accuracy of understanding is misleading unless defined in terms of the author's intentions and the readers' purposes. This means that teachers must recognize the readers' right to interpret a text at the same time that they instill in students a responsibility to address the author's intentions in writing the text. Integral to curriculum objectives that capitalize upon this perspective is the inclusion of goals similar to the following: the student is able to make judgments about his or her own understanding, the author's intentions, task demands, and strategy utilization. This will include objectives directed to having the student recognize alternative perspectives, the engagement of their own background knowledge, the plausibility of alternative interpretations, the viability of strategies for learning from various texts for alternative purposes, the nature of task demands (including author's intention and plan of organization), as well as nature and applications of new learnings. Integral to classroom practices, we suggest that teachers should assess the quality of a reader's interpretation in accordance with the following:

> To what extent was the reader's understanding adequate for the text and purposes for reading?
>
> When a reader's understanding diverges from some consensual author's intention, can the reader's interpretation be justified?

Current practices with their emphases upon correct answers and a single appropriate interpretation violate these principles. In their stead, we suggest that teachers need to move away from assessment procedures that sponsor a "single-correct-answer mentality" and generate devices that are open-ended and that allow for divergent responses. For example, after reading a selection, teachers might allow students to relate their own interpretations prior to prodding them with an array of questions. To move students away from "the right answer" orientation, students might be asked to rate or rank the plausibility of each response to a multiple choice question. In follow-up discussions different students can compare the rationales behind their various rankings or ratings. The acid test for student response quality should be "can it be justified?" rather than "is it right?". This criterion places the emphasis precisely where it should be placed: on the quality of students' reasoning abilities. Such a stance will also increase the likelihood that important rather than trivial aspects of text will receive emphasis.

Consider next the notion of transfer. The notion of transfer relates to whether a reader can apply what he or she has read or learned to other situations. At issue in any teaching reading comprehension situation should be two key considerations.

Is the reader able to recognize new learnings and potential application?

Is the reader able to apply skills acquired during instruction to other text situations without the support of such instruction?

These two questions can be translated into simple tests of comprehension: (a) can readers use the new knowledge they have acquired? and (b) can readers use the new strategies they have acquired when they encounter new texts on their own?

The issue of applying or using new knowledge places reading in a real-world context. The criterion assumes that students understand, remember, and evaluate new information more readily when they know its relevance to other experiences. That is, students should be asked to consider "the point" of what they have read, whether that point be for enjoyment, information gain, or to solve problems.

The second issue—applying learned strategies—gets at the heart of instruction. Presumably we teach so that students will become independent learners, no longer needing our intervention and support. Independence is the essence of transfer. Unfortunately, very few studies have addressed the transfer of strategy issue. From those few studies that have been reported, we are impressed that students rarely develop an ability to transfer or apply knowledge, skills, or strategies spontaneously—that is, when they are left to their own resources. Instead, they need to be guided toward transfer. This would include being alerted to when and how to use what strategies. By implication if teachers are to help students develop independent reading and learning skills, they should not assume that it will just happen. Situations and activities need to be implemented wherein students can try, discuss, and evaluate their strategy, skill, and knowledge utilization across a variety of reading situations. In this regard, teachers need to move beyond merely mentioning reading comprehension skills and begin helping students learn how to learn. There appear to be some general guidelines emerging from recent research on teaching reading comprehension that are relevant to this goal. One rather consistent finding is that students rarely acquire transferable abilities without being provided ample opportunities to develop and practice those abilities in a variety of relevant contexts. A key word here is *relevant*. Relevance pertains to the notion that students need to understand the purpose and function of reading strategies, comprehension, or learning as well as be given appropriate situations within which to explore their nature. If a reader is being asked to apply a strategy determining the main idea, the reader should do so within a variety of situations for which it is reasonable to find the main idea. Furthermore, readers appear to profit most from such learning experiences when they are given an explicit understanding of when, why, how, and what to do.

Concluding Remarks

It has been the purpose of this paper to draw upon recent developments in the study of reading comprehension as a means of examining issues or relevance to improving reading comprehension and learning from text. We have suggested that if teachers are to develop a reader's understanding, they should address the adequacy of their pedagogy against some basic notions about reading and learning. The notions that we have suggested are driven by a schema-theoretic perspective—a view that prompted the following questions as guidelines to instructional decision making.

- Does the reader have the relevant schemata for a text?
- Was the reader's schema activated (purpose, background knowledge, attention, focus, interest) prior to, during, and after reading? Was the reader's relevant background of experience activated during reading?
- Across reading material for different purposes, did the reader exhibit flexible processes in terms of activating, focusing, maintaining, and refining an interpretation? Was the reader aware of the strategies one could use to cope with different texts and purposes for reading?
- To what extent was the reader's understanding adequate for the text and purposes for reading? When a reader's understanding diverges from some consensual author's intention, did the reader justify his or her idiosyncratic interpretation? Did the reader recognize his or her perspective and the perspective of others?
- Was the reader aware of his or her level of understanding of a text read for different purposes?
- Did the reader recognize new learnings and their potential applications?

References

Collins, A., Brown, J. S., and Larkin, K. M. *Inference in text understanding* (Tech. Rep. No. 40). Urbana: University of Illinois, Center for the Study of Reading, 1977.

Crane, S. *The red badge of courage.* New York: Dell, 1966.

Durkin, D. What classroom observations reveal about reading comprehension instruction. *Reading Research Quarterly,* 1978–79, *14*, 481–533.

Gallant, R. A. The garbage collectors of the sea. In I. Asimov and R. A. Gallant, *Ginn Science Program* (Intermediate Level C). Lexington, Mass.: Ginn, 1975.

Pearson, P. D., and Spiro, R. J. Toward a theory of reading comprehension instruction. *Topics in language disorders,* in press.

Rumelhart, D. E. Schemata: The building blocks of cognition. In R. J. Spiro, B. C. Bruce, and W. F. Brewer (Eds.), *Theoretical issues in reading comprehension.* Hillsdale, N.J.: Erlbaum, in press.

Rumelhart, D. E. Toward an interactive model of reading. In S. Dornic (Ed.), *Attention and performance* (Vol. VI). Hillsdale, N.J.: Erlbaum, 1977.

Rumelhart, D. E., and Ortony, A. The representation of knowledge in memory. In R. C. Anderson, R. J. Spiro, and W. E. Montague (Eds.), *Schooling and the acquisition of knowledge.* Hillsdale, N.J.: Erlbaum, 1977.

Stauffer, R. G. *Directing reading maturity as a cognitive process.* New York: Harper and Row, 1969.

Tierney, R. J., LaZansky, J., and Schallert, D. *Secondary social studies and biology students use of textbooks.* Champaign: University of Illinois, 1981.

Tierney, R. J., and Spiro, R. J. Some basic postulates about comprehension: Implications for instruction. In J. Harste and R. Carey (Eds.), *New Perspectives in comprehension.* Bloomington: Indiana University, School of Education, 1979.

Note

Implicit within our discussion of the nature of comprehension has been the suggestion that inference and interpretation are as essential to acquiring an understanding as they may be to extending understanding after reading. This idea suggests that the widely espoused notion of a continuum from literal to inferred to evaluative has questionable validity. Not only does it lack validity as a statement about reading comprehension, it may have questionable utility as a curriculum guideline. There are many ways to acquire an understanding and at times different permissible understandings, regardless of whether these understandings be literal, inferential, or evaluative. Our point is that unless a great deal of thought goes into operationalizing curriculum procedures based upon these categories, teachers may find that they are forcing a student to deal with the literal when it would be more appropriate to address the inferred or evaluative. We believe that every act of reading necessitates inferential and interpretative understandings. In fact, students may need to deal with the inferential and evaluative prior to addressing the "literal."

3

Essential Processes of Content Reading

Decoding and comprehension—basic processes emphasized in helping children learn to read—are also essential processes involved in obtaining information from content materials. Open to question, however, is the extent to which content teachers should be involved in teaching these processes, particularly in the area of decoding. Decoding, unfortunately, is linked frequently—and sometimes exclusively—with phonics in the minds of many educators. Yet, it is only one aspect of decoding. Extensive use of phonics in content classrooms is questionable. With regard to comprehension, it must be remembered that reading words and remembering facts are not equivalent to the in-depth understanding of concepts needed to cope effectively with content materials. Additionally, there is a question as to what should be taught in the name of comprehension and how it should be taught.

Ryder specifically addresses the role of phonics in middle and secondary school subjects. He suggests that alternative forms of word analysis be pursued by teachers with students having difficulty with word pronunciation.

Cunningham discusses the processes involved in decoding unfamiliar words. She advocates instruction through the use of content to aide the reader in obtaining the meaning of unknown words and suggests the compare-contrast strategy to aid in pronouncing these unknown words.

Herber and Nelson suggest that teacher questioning may not always be the answer in directing students' reading of text material. Instead, they offer simulation strategies as the means to move students along a continuum toward independent learning.

Ratekin describes concepts about comprehension that content teachers need to understand. Processes that readers employ to enhance their own comprehension are also delineated.

Phonics in Middle/Secondary School Subjects

Randall J. Ryder
University of Wisconsin
Milwaukee

The ability to obtain meaning from text is, in part, dependent upon the efficient and rapid translation of alphabetic symbols into their spoken counterparts. Commonly, this letter-to-sound relationship has been referred to as word analysis and has constituted one of the most salient components of beginning reading instruction and secondary remedial reading instruction. Traditionally, word analysis has been taught by four strategies: phonics, structural analysis, syllabication, and context clues. Whereas each of these strategies, when effectively applied by the reader to written text, can assist in the pronunciation of words, it is phonics instruction that has received the greatest attention of educators and the general public.

As early as the mid-1800s, American reading educators have advocated phonics instruction as the single best approach to the teaching of reading. The basic principle of phonics instruction is that certain rules can be created that account for the pronunciation of letters (*a, b, f, g,* etc.) or letter clusters (*th, sh, sp,* etc.) in a consistent and accurate manner. By teaching the reader a group of rules that describes the pronunciation of letters and letter clusters, it is presumed that these rules will then be applied in a conscious and deliberate fashion to words that are not readily pronounceable but are present in the readers' listening vocabulary. Some of these rules are stated in terms of letter-sound correspondences that describe the sound(s) exemplified by a particular letter or cluster (*ck*→/*k*/, *kick*). Other rules are stated in terms of generalizations that describe the sound(s) exemplified by a group of letters or clusters (when two vowels occur together in an accented syllable, the first vowel usually has a long sound and the second vowel is usually silent). Thus, a beginning reader encountering the word *smoke,* for example, could apply the following generalizations and letter-sound correspondences:

1. *sm* is given the sound of /sm/ as in *sm*all
2. a vowel followed by a consonant then a final-*e* usually has a long vowel sound, thus *o* is given the long vowel sound
3. *k* is given the sound of /*k*/ as in *k*ite
4. final-*e* preceded by a consonant is not pronounced

Ultimately, the reader would combine the following sounds: /*sm*/ + /*o*/ + /*k*/ to arrive at a final pronunciation of the word (/*smok*/). Once pronounced, it is anticipated that the reader will then readily recall the word's meaning.

Written especially for inclusion in this text.

Phonics Rules and Regularities

Phonics is a system of rules that attempts to describe predictable letter-to-sound relationships existing in the English language. On the surface, it would seem plausible to assume that since there are twenty-six letters in the alphabet, there are most likely only twenty-six or so sounds produced by these letters. Unfortunately, this is not the case from the standpoint of the number of spelling units or sounds that exist in English. English spelling patterns have been found to consist of fifty-two major units; twenty for vowels and thirty-two for consonants (Venezky, 1967; 1970). The twenty-six letters of the alphabet are indeed functional units, yet so are certain combinations of these letters (i.e., *au, sp, ie, oa*). In fact, some of these combinations of letters, such as *th, ch, oo,* appear in words more frequently than some of the single letters. Thus the reader must not only recognize the variety of sounds that individual letters produce but also the sounds that letter combinations produce. Given that there are some forty distinct sounds in English and fifty-two major spelling units that represent these sounds, any attempt to create a set of rules that purports to capitalize on the apparent regularities of the letter-to-sound system will immediately encounter several shortcomings. First, there are many letters or clusters that consistently exhibit more than one sound. The letter *a,* for example, has seven different sounds (n*a*me, s*a*t, *a*bove, c*a*rt, v*a*ry, b*a*ll, w*a*r). Second, other letters and clusters may have different spellings yet share a common sound. Although represented by distinct spelling units, the underlined letters in the following words all have the same sound:b*a*by, st*ai*n, d*ay*, r*eig*n, th*ey*. Finally, certain letters or clusters under certain conditions produce no sound at all (yo*l*k, *k*now, hi*gh*, *h*our, com*b*, nat*u*ral, g*u*est).

While English does not display a one-letter, one-sound system, a description of the pronunciation of words in terms of specific letter-sound correspondences results in a rather predictable set of rules. In an extensive and systematic tabulation of letter-sound correspondences exemplified in the 6,000 one- and two-syllable words found to be in the comprehension vocabularies of six- through nine-year-olds, a total of 211 rules resulted (Cronnell, 1971). While many of these rules were written to account for exceptions inherent in other rules, the pronunciations of relatively few letters or clusters could not be described by this existing set of rules. Even though the set of rules produced by Cronnell contains descriptions of the letter-sound relationships inherent in the words examined, their usefulness for teaching purposes may be rather limited. The magnitude of an instructional program attempting to teach 211 rules to beginning readers would be a tremendous burden on the learner. Consequently, most phonic programs deal with generalizations rather than with letter-sound correspondences in an attempt to limit the number of rules provided to the learner. Unfortunately, as rules become more general their number of exceptions increase dramatically.

Several attempts have been made to determine the number of exceptions to commonly taught phonic rules (Clymer, 1963; Emans, 1967; Burmeister, 1968; Fry, 1964). In one such investigation (Clymer, 1963), forty-five phonic rules commonly taught in major reading programs were tested against the pronunciations of all words contained in those programs displaying a given letter or cluster described in the rule. Of the rules examined, only eighteen were found to predict the pronunciation of the letter or cluster with at least 75 percent degree of accuracy. Even among the rules that were found to be relatively useful, a few describe letter-to-sound relationships in such a vague manner as to be of questionable value to the reader. One of these rules, for example, states that when *c* and *h* are next to each other, they make only one sound. According to Clymer, this rule applied to every word appearing in elementary reading programs containing *ch*. While it is evident that *ch* produces a single sound, there are three distinct sounds of *ch* (*ch*ord, *ch*urch, *ch*alet) that are to some degree predictable from the following letter-sound correspondences:

1. *ch* followed by *r* or *l* has a *k* sound as in *Christ, chlorine.*
2. *ch* preceded by initial *s* has a *k* sound as in *school.*
3. *ch*, if not followed by *r* or *l* or preceded by *s*, is pronounced as in *cheap, church.*

Although the above letter-sound correspondences can account for the various pronunciations of *ch* with greater specificity than the *ch* generalization commonly found in elementary reading programs, noticeable exceptions still exist (ma*ch*ine, *ch*alet). Because most phonic instruction contains generalizations and letter-sound correspondences that have exceptions, certain reading authorities suggest that English does not, in general, display a predictable set of letter-to-sound relationships. Many of the rules examined by Clymer (1963) and others would support such a claim. However, more thorough examinations of English have shown that factors other than those described in phonic rules allow a much greater degree of predictability than was previously acknowledged (Venezky, 1967). One factor not acknowledged in phonic rules, which affects the pronunciation of certain clusters, is morpheme (unit of meaning) boundaries. The word *topheavy,* for example, contains two morphemes: *top* and *heavy*. The word *sphere* contains one morpheme. In the first circumstance, *ph* falls between two morpheme boundaries; consequently, it is pronounced as two distinct sounds (/*p*/ as in *pin,* and /*h*/ as in *held*). In the word *sphere, ph* does not fall on a morpheme boundary and, therefore, is pronounced /*f*/ as in *fish.* Admittedly, the effect of morpheme boundaries on students' ability to pronounce words is relatively small, yet it demonstrates the breadth of factors that allow the English spelling-to-sound system to be predictable.

Other factors found to influence the sound produced from a letter or cluster include the substitution of one sound for another (such as *i* and *y* as in *fight* and *bye*), the position of a letter or cluster in a word (initial *gh* as in *ghost*), and the accent (accent on vowel following *h* in *prohibit* gives *h* sound, whereas no accent on vowel following *h* in *prohibition* gives no *h* sound).

Despite the idiosyncracies inherent in the letter-to-sound system, there is general agreement among reading researchers and educators that phonic instruction combined with other word analysis skills is an important instructional tool for beginning readers. By drawing students' attention to certain letter-sound relationships through the teaching of phonics rules, it is anticipated that, despite the number of exceptions to rules, the student will approximate the pronunciation to such an extent that meaning-bearing clues and language-bearing clues will eventually allow the correct pronunciation of an unknown word. Many adults, if presented the word *victual* in isolation, would pronounce it as /*vic choo l*/ or /*vic tǝl*/. Placing the same word in the sentence, "The Beverly Hillbillies consistently referred to the food they ate as victuals" would allow most individuals to modify their original pronunciation to /*vi tǝls*/. Moreover, by drawing students' attention to certain letter-sound relationships, it is anticipated that more subtle regularities of the letter-to-sound system will be internalized. Through the continuous exposure of certain vowel digraphs (e.g., /ou/) initially learned by phonic rules, for example, most adults have internalized the effect that final consonants have on preceding digraphs (Ryder and Graves, 1980). Thus the pronunciation of *ou* as /au/ before *n, t,* and *d,* (*ground, trout, loud*) and as /u/ before *p, b,* or *ch* (*couple, trouble, touch*) is internalized, even though it is seldom directly taught.

Phonics in Content Areas

Inherent in the preceding discussion of phonic rules and the regularity of letter-to-sound relationships are several conclusions of the usefulness of phonics and implications regarding the importance (or lack thereof) of phonics instruction for middle/secondary students by content area teachers.

Many of the phonic rules currently used in today's reading programs are limited in their ability to accurately and consistently describe the pronunciation of letters or clusters. To impart rules upon middle/secondary students that are either so vaguely written as to be relatively useless or that exemplify large numbers of exceptions can only add to the persistent frustration that secondary remedial readers encounter. Tangential to this observation is the view held by most secondary reading teachers that the failure to acquire phonic rules upon entrance to secondary grades should not be dealt with by "more of the same" but rather by an attempt to use alternate word analysis strategies. The persistent use of phonics instruction for secondary students who have difficulty with word analysis largely ignores some of the basic assumptions that have made phonics useful for elementary students. When phonic rules are presented to elementary students, they are applied to material displaying a very limited and precisely controlled vocabulary. Most of the words encountered in elementary reading programs are already part of the readers' listening or speaking vocabularies. Once words are pronounced, they are immediately known. Such is not the case in middle/secondary content matter texts, which lack the controlled vocabulary evident in elementary reading materials. Consequently, even though these students may be able to apply their knowledge of letter-to-sound relationships to unfamiliar words, pronunciation by itself does not insure word meaning. Most middle/secondary students can readily pronounce *farrago* or *lagan,* yet without a rich contextual setting or the aid of a dictionary, few would recognize the meanings of these words. The major concern of content area teachers is teaching concepts through a structured instructional sequence of direct or vicarious experience. A concerted effort to teach phonic rules to these students in the confines of subject matter classrooms can only detract from these curricular objectives—a view supported by several reading authorities (Herber, 1978; Estes and Vaughan, 1978).

The appropriateness of phonic instruction for beginning readers, as previously mentioned, has been generally perceived as a useful instructional tool. Yet the practicality of phonics for older students is limited by a lack of evidence demonstrating its usefulness for older-aged students. In fact, recent findings demonstrate that low ability readers in the seventh grade have acquired a much greater knowledge of letter-to-sound relationships than was previously assumed. And by the time low ability readers reach the upper secondary grades, there is little difference between their ability to identify these relationships and the ability demonstrated by above-average readers (Ryder and Graves, 1980). Consequently, it is quite possible that phonic instruction in the confines of secondary reading programs themselves may be of limited value.

Alternative Strategies

Several alternatives to phonics are available to content area teachers concerned with developing their students' word analysis skills. One strategy is structural analysis, which not only provides the student with clues to the pronunciation of words but also clues to the word's meaning. While detailed and sequential instructional programs for teaching roots and affixes are not evident in most schools, the power of this strategy cannot be overlooked. Of the 20,000 most frequent English words, for example, 24 percent contain prefixes alone (Stauffer, 1942).

Providing the student with instruction in a relatively small number of roots, prefixes, or suffixes can unlock the pronunciation and meaning of many words. Once a root or affix has been learned, it can readily be applied to large numbers of words. Consider the total number of words that can be produced by various combinations of the following prefixes, roots, and suffixes:

Prefix	Root	Suffix
micro	toxin	s
anti	matter	
macro	biotic	
	body	

A second useful analysis strategy is that of pronouncing words to students prior to reading. As with most word analysis techniques, this method is useful for those words that are already part of the students' speaking or listening vocabularies but not part of their reading vocabularies. One technique would be the writing of, say, ten to fifteen words on a chalkboard. The teacher would then pronounce each word in the list to the students who would then repeat this pronunciation. The teacher could then write alongside the word two or three "known" words that would provide students with a clue as to their pronunciation. For example, if one of the difficult words on the board was *metamorphic,* the following words could be written alongside: *met a more tick.* This list could then remain on the board or be copied by the students to be used as a pronunciation key as the material was read silently.

Finally, one strategy seldom used in content area classrooms is the usage of word pronunciations provided in dictionaries. If content teachers could make provision for dictionaries to be available for students and provide instruction to facilitate understanding of pronunciation keys, then little if any teacher preparation or class time would need to be devoted to the pronunciation of words. Moreover, it would not be necessary to confront all students with instruction on words that may already be pronounceable. Dictionaries also provide a convenient source for students to independently acquire meanings as well as word pronunciation. Unfortunately, most students, as well as adults, will not refer to a dictionary while they are engaged in reading. Accordingly, their use should be limited to word analysis and word meaning activities prior to reading.

Conclusion

The teaching of phonic rules to beginning readers has been shown to be a useful technique to facilitate the pronunciation of words that are part of the students' listening or speaking vocabularies. And whereas there are many exceptions to a majority of phonic rules, it is apparent that there exist a variety of factors in English letter-to-sound relationships that allow them to be more predictable than is generally assumed. Secondary students have been confronted visually with large numbers of words during their education. Consequently, these students seem to have internalized letter-sound correspondences exemplified in these words with a relatively high degree of accuracy. This finding, in combination with the contemporary views of most secondary reading educators regarding the usefulness of phonics, strongly suggests that content area teachers consider alternate forms of word analysis instruction for the limited number of students who consistently have difficulty with pronouncing words.

References

Burmeister, L. E. Usefulness of phonic generalizations. *The Reading Teacher*, 1968, *21*, 349–56.

Clymer, T. The utility of phonic generalizations in the primary grades. *The Reading Teacher*, 1963, *16*, 252–58.

Cronnell, B. *Annotated spelling-to-sound correspondence rules*. (Technical Report No. 32), Inglewood, CA.: Southwest Regional Laboratory, 1971.

Emans, R. The usefulness of phonic generalizations above the primary grades. *The Reading Teacher*, 1967, *20*, 419–25.

Estes, T. H. and Vaughan, J. L. *Reading and Learning in the Content Classroom*. Boston: Allyn & Bacon, 1978.

Fry, E. A frequency approach to phonics. *Elementary English*, 1964, *41*, 759–65.

Herber, H. L. *Teaching reading in content areas* (2nd ed.). Englewood Cliffs: Prentice-Hall, 1978.

Ryder, R. J. and Graves, M. F. Secondary students' internalization of letter-sound correspondences. *Journal of Educational Research*, 1980, *73*, 172–78.

Stauffer, R. A study of prefixes in the Thorndike List to establish a list of prefixes that should be taught in elementary school. *Journal of Educational Research*, 1942, *35*, 453–58.

Venezky, R. L. English orthography: Its graphical structure and its relation to sound. *Reading Research Quarterly*, 1967, *2*, 75–106.

Venezky, R. L. *The structure of English orthography*. The Hague: Moulton and Company, 1970.

Decoding Demystified

Patricia M. Cunningham
Wake Forest University

Stop the average person in the street and ask him or her what reading is. You will probably get some blank stares and then some responses such as, "Reading is saying words." "Reading is figuring out the words." "Reading is getting meaning from something written." "Reading is thinking." All of these typical responses are correct. None, however, tells the whole story. In its simplest sense, reading can be conceived of as an act that requires figuring out what the words are and understanding what the words mean. The figuring out what the words are component is commonly called decoding. Decoding is the primary stumbling block to reading for most beginning readers. If Johnny knew that the squiggles, *I rode on a red train,* stood for the spoken version, he would have no trouble understanding or comprehending the meaning of this simple, familiar sentence. The older Johnny, on the other hand, may be able to read the words, *The light that is not absorbed by an opaque object is reflected by it,* without comprehending their meaning. Because most middle and secondary students have achieved the remarkable feat of being able to recognize immediately or figure out the correct pronunciation for almost any word, most attempts at helping older students become better readers are focused on the comprehension component of reading. This is as it should be. All readers have comprehension difficulties when faced with complex, unfamiliar material, and the ability to comprehend is never as good as it can be. Decoding, on the other hand, is a closed system that most middle and secondary students have mastered. Most—but not all. Some older students still experience a great deal of difficulty in figuring out what the squiggles on the page stand for. It is in an attempt to help this small but ever-present minority that this article is written.

Some of the readers who began reading this article have already stopped reading, and some of you who are still reading are doing so reluctantly. When most people think of decoding, they think of short and long vowels, diphthongs and digraphs and—worst of all— schwas! No self-respecting middle or secondary school content area teacher is going to take time away from his or her content to teach that stuff! I couldn't agree more. Not only do you not intend to teach that stuff, you shouldn't.

Older students who are still experiencing decoding difficulties have, in all probability, been taught and retaught the jargon and rules. They were and remain mystified by it all. There is, however, another approach. In the remainder of this article, I shall outline an approach to decoding, compatible with the older reader and with the aims of content area instruction. I shall attempt to demystify decoding for you so that you can demystify it for your students.

Consider what you do to identify words as you are reading. For the average adult reader, almost all words encountered in reading are recognized immediately. You don't know how you recognize them and can't explain the process any better than you can explain how you recognize and associate names with most of the people you know. When you first met most of the people you now know well, you were probably introduced to them and told their names. If you have the poor memory for names that I do, you probably didn't immediately identify the person's name the second time you met him or her and had to be told the name again or had to think for several seconds about where you met the person and then, from remembering the particular experience, you dredged up the name from the deep, dark recesses of your memory store. After several such encounters, however, you do learn the person's name well enough so that when you meet, you can identify that person effortlessly. You don't have to be told the name again and again, nor do you have to go through any intervening process to figure out the name—you just know it! So it is with words.

For our very first encounter with words, we are usually either introduced to the word and told its name, or we figure out that word using context or sound/letter clues (discussed in more detail later). After several encounters with that word, during which we might have to be told the word again or use some other device to remember it, the word becomes like a good friend—we just know it. In reading, a word that is recognized immediately and effortlessly in all contexts is called a sight word. For fluent readers, almost all words encountered are sight words. The words that are not sight words are those that we seldom or never encounter in our reading. This brings us back to you, the content area teacher. There are in every content area technical terms not usually encountered in the everyday reading done by students. If your students are to read your textbooks fluently, they must be introduced to the technical words and have enough encounters with those words so that the words become sight words—words immediately and effortlessly identified. This is not hard for the teacher to accomplish once the teacher realizes the importance of identifying the technical words, introducing them to the students, and providing enough repetitions.

Imagine, for example, that your science unit on light demands that your students be able to effortlessly and immediately identify the words *opaque, transparent, translucent, reflection, refraction, concave,* and *convex.* In relationship to each of these technical terms, your students probably fall into the following categories: (1) students who know the pronunciation and the meaning of the word; (2) students who know the pronunciation but not the meaning of the word; (3) students who know the meaning but do not recognize that the printed word stands for the spoken word they know; and (4) students who know neither the pronunciation nor the meaning for the word. Students who fall into the first category (few in number in most classrooms!) do not require meaning-oriented or decoding-oriented instruction in order to read and comprehend material containing these words. Students who fall into the second category need meaning-oriented instruction but not decoding-oriented instruction. Students in the third category need decoding-oriented but not meaning-oriented instruction; and students in the fourth category need both meaning- and decoding-oriented instruction. Most students would be in different categories for different words. Johnny, for example, may know the meaning and pronunciation for *transparent,* the pronunciation but not the meaning for *translucent,* the meaning but not the pronunciation for *reflection,* and neither for *opaque.* Rather than throw up their hands in despair at the task of discerning which students need what kind of instruction for which words, savvy teachers provide instruction that emphasizes meaning and pronunciation for all crucial technical terms.

This instruction takes many forms but usually begins with the teacher introducing the key terms, providing examples and definitions of each, and drawing from the students their accumulated knowledge about each. Recognizing, however, that repetition in various ways is essential for students to learn both the meaning and pronunciation of a new word, wise teachers provide a variety of experiences with the essential words. These experiences may include: displaying the words on cards on a bulletin board and beginning each lesson with a "practice quiz" in which the teacher supplies a definition or example of each word, the students write the appropriate word, and then self-check their word; fill-in-the-blank practice exercises in which the key words are each used several times; scrambled words and word-find activities in which words are matched to definitions and crossword puzzles. In constructing and carrying out these varied activities, the teacher plans the instruction so that students will all learn the meaning and pronunciation of the crucial words regardless of which category they were in prior to instruction. When the students are presented with the reading material containing these key words, they can both associate meanings with the words and effortlessly and immediately identify the printed words. The teacher who carries out this kind of prereading instruction is teaching decoding by assuring that crucial words are sight words for all readers.

Not all words that students need to identify can be taught in this direct fashion. Because of time limitations, the teaching of the pronunciation and meaning of words will necessarily be limited to those designated by the teacher as crucial and not apt to be known by most members of the class. Content area teachers can, as they carry out their content area instruction, help students figure out the identification of unknown words. This process is generally accomplished by the use of context or sound/symbol relationship clues. Since if a word is not immediately recognizable, the next quickest way to recognize it is to use the context of the surrounding words, that strategy, hereinafter referred to as the "blank" technique, should be directly taught to all students.

What do you do when, as you are reading, you come to a word that you do not immediately recognize or for which you do not have an appropriate meaning? If you are a good reader, you probably skip that word and continue reading until you finish that sentence and perhaps a few more sentences. The clues contained in the words preceding and following the unknown words often allow you to identify the unfamiliar-in-print word or fill in the meaning for an unknown word. While the identification of meaning for an unfamiliar word is not the focus of this article, an example should help to clarify how the context—surrounding words—often provides meaning for an unfamiliar word. A student who did not have a clear meaning for *translucent* could probably figure out a meaning when reading, *"The new frosted window pane was translucent. Light could pass through but you couldn't see through it."* The ability to use context clues to figure out meanings for unfamiliar words is crucial to reading comprehension, and a strategy for teaching this skill is described in Cunningham (1978).

Context can also be used to identify a word that you would recognize in its spoken form but are unable to decode in its written form. In this sentence, several _____ have been left _____ , but most readers will have _____ difficulty in filling in these words because the _____ words provide clues to the identification _____ the missing words. The previous sentence may be completed in several ways. Add the clue of word length (in this sentence, several _____ have been left _____ , but most readers will have _____ difficulty in filling in these words because the _____ words provide clues to the identification __ the missing words, and the missing words become more predictable. Add first-letter clues to word length (in this sentence, several w---- have been left o--, but most readers will have l----- difficulty in filling in these words because the r-------- words provide clues to the identification o- the missing words), and most readers would be able to read without difficulty the sentence: *In this sentence, several words have been left out, but most readers will have little difficulty in filling in these words because the remaining words provide clues to the identification of the missing words.* Because of the redundancy involved in any language, it is not necessary to be able to identify all words immediately and effortlessly in order to read with comprehension. It *is* necessary that the reader know that some words can be skipped and then figured out by reading on and thinking about what words would logically fit in those sentences. The additional clues of word length and beginning letter further narrow the possibilities. All good readers and few poor readers use context to identify unfamiliar in-print words.

Poor readers can be taught to use this valuable decoding strategy if teachers will provide them with materials in which many of the words are blanked out. The initial letter or letters (*sh, ch, th, ph, wh*) can be left visible, since most poor readers know initial letter sounds and can use them to narrow their choices. These materials, of course, would be informational material about the subject being studied. Students would be given a few minutes to silently read the entire passage saying "blank" when they got to each blanked-out word. The passage would then be read aloud, and students would volunteer their guesses for the blanked-out words. The use of an overhead projector and transparencies made from printed materials in which the missing letters have been taped over or blacked out with a watercolor marker allows the students to see the correctness of their guesses when the tape is removed or marking erased.

There are, however, some words that are not sight words and which cannot be identified by saying, "blank" and continuing on. When this happens, the good reader, as an avenue of last resort, applied his or her knowledge of sounds and letters to "sound out the word." This effort is a slow and laborious one and is often one at which poor readers cannot succeed.

The traditional approach for teaching students to sound out words is to teach them rules for dividing words into syllables and then more rules for figuring out the sound/symbol relationships for each syllable. There is, however, another avenue that leads to the goal of successful decoding.

Imagine that in your reading you encountered this sentence: *The man was bundiferous.* The made-up word, *bundiferous,* is not a sight word for you, and you cannot figure out its pronunciation from the context. Most of you have, however, assigned a pronunciation for this nonsense word. You probably pronounced the first part as *bun* and the last part to sound like *splendiferous.* How did you accomplish this remarkable feat? Perhaps you very rapidly divided the word into syllables and then equally rapidly applied rules to the individual syllables. It is also possible that you used a process that is called compare/contrast. Perhaps when you saw *bundiferous* you thought of the similar words, *bun* and *splendiferous.* Another possible route was to see the *bun* and then *ferous* as similar to the end of *coniferous*. The *di* part might have conjured up images of *ridiculous* or *indifferent*. Simply stated, I believe and have some research evidence to suggest (Cunningham, 1975–1976; 1979; 1980) that figuring out the sounds appropriate to combinations of letters may be accomplished by thinking of known words that have the same combinations of letters in the same place. If this is the case, a strategy that teaches students to compare and contrast unknown words to already known words will improve their ability to decode words. This compare/contrast idea has been operationalized as a teaching strategy with a game called *Mystery Word Match*.

To play this game, the teacher divides the students into two teams. Each team takes a turn asking a question about the mystery word, an important-to-content-learning word. Guessing the word after the first question is worth ten points. With each "no" answer, a point is subtracted, and the play moves to the other team. As long as a team receives a "yes" answer to its questions, it may continue to question until the identity of the mystery word is guessed. The team that guesses the word is awarded the number of points it is worth at that point. To begin the game, the teacher draws lines to represent the number of letters in the mystery word. Clue words are then written underneath and the students pronounce the clue words several times after the teacher. (Meanings for clue words should be quickly provided as this is felt necessary.) The play is carried out by the students trying to figure out which parts of the clue words are used in the mystery word. They ask, "Does the mystery word begin like _____ ?"; does the mystery word end like _____ ?"; does the mystery word have a middle like _____ ?" Here is an example for you to figure out.

Teacher: "The mystery word has eleven letters, -----------"
  (Draws eleven lines on board.)
  "Here are the clue words: illuminate
                                    transparent
                                    iridescent"
  (Teacher writes each clue word on board. Pronounces each. Students pronounce, define, and use in a sentence.)
  "Bill's team won the toss. They can go first. The mystery word is worth ten points."

Bill's Team Member. "Does the word begin like *iridescent?*"

Teacher: "No, it does not begin like *iridescent*. Cathy's team. Nine Points."

Cathy's Team Member: "Does the word end like *iridescent?*"

Teacher. "Yes it does." (Writes *cent* on last four lines: -------cent) "You may go again."

Cathy's Team Member: "Does the word begin like *illuminate?*"

Teacher: "No, I am sorry it does not. Back to Bill's team for eight points."

Bill's Team Member: "Does the word have a middle like *illuminate?*"

Teacher: "Good for you." (Writes *lu* on appropriate lines: ------*lucent).* "Your team may continue."

Bill's Team Member: "Does the word have a beginning like *transparent?"*

Teacher. "Yes, it does." (Writes trans: *translucent)* "The team may confer and name the word." (Team confers and triumphantly pronounces *translucent.* Teacher records eight points for Bill's team and discusses meaning of *translucent.* Game continues with next mystery and clue words.)

Mystery Word Match is fun and accomplishes two major purposes. The students learn some polysyllabic words that they can use as known words for comparison to unknown words which they encounter in their reading; and the students develop a mind set that encourages them, when faced with an unknown word, to try to think of words with similar parts for comparison and contrast of the unknown word. Of course, the mystery word should always be a word identified as a key word for the content being taught. If possible, the clue words should also come from the content area, since this increases the number of content area words students can immediately recognize. Mystery word and clue word matches are easy to construct. Make sure that the clue words have the same parts in the same place and that the spelling and sound of the similar parts are identical to those parts in the mystery word. Do not hesitate to use only two clue words for any mystery word, since the students should learn not to be limited to the syllable but to use the largest chunk of the word that they can pronounce by comparing it to a large chunk of a known word. (When two clue words are used, one begins like the mystery word; the other ends like the mystery word. The question about the middle is thus eliminated. Students love two-clue word mystery words since, if their first guess is right, they are almost assured of winning the points; and if the first guess of the opposing team is wrong, the other team will almost surely win!)

Here are some examples to get you started. (More examples can be found in Cunningham, Cunningham, and Arthur, 1981.)

democratic	*tricentennial*	*flourescence*
autocratic	tripod	incandescence
democracy	bicentennial	flouride
federalist	*convention*	*dissonance*
federation	controversial	resonance
imperialist	invention	disappointed
gyroscope	*inversion*	*controversy*
gyration	insurance	introvert
telescope	collusion	contemporary
hieroglyphics	reversal	glossy

In this article, decoding has been described as a simple and natural process that can be easily incorporated into any content area instruction. By emphasizing meaning and decoding as new words are introduced, teachers can help students to achieve more fluent reading. By teaching students to immediately and effortlessly incorporate technical terms into their store of sight words, to use context as a first attempt to decode unfamiliar words, and to compare and contrast those not decipherable using context to already known words, teachers can improve students' reading of content area materials and at the same time demystify decoding for these students.

References

Cunningham, P. M. Applying a compare/contrast process to identifying polysyllabic words. *Journal of Reading Behavior,* 1980, in press.

Cunningham, P. M. A compare/contrast theory of mediated word identification. *The Reading Teacher,* 1979, *32,* 774–778.

Cunningham, P. M. Investigating a synthesized theory of mediated word identification. *Reading Research Quarterly,* 1975–1976, *11,* 127–143.

Cunningham, P. M. Teaching vocabulary in the content areas. *NASSP Bulletin,* 1978, *63,* 112–116.

Cunningham, J. W., Cunningham, P. M., and Arthur, V. *Middle and secondary school reading.* New York: Longman, 1981.

Questioning Is Not the Answer*

Harold L. Herber
Syracuse University

Joan B. Nelson
State University of New York, Binghamton

The interrogatives "who, what, where, when, why, and how" are standard tools for the inquiring reader. A reader who can apply these interrogatives independently has the necessary skills for selecting pertinent information, for developing concepts by perceiving relationships within and across that information, and for synthesizing those concepts with others drawn from previous experience.

These interrogatives are also basic to *questioning,* a teacher's most frequently used instructional tool. Most teachers regularly use questions to guide students' reading of text materials, believing this to be an effective way to help students acquire the information and ideas in the text. Some teachers are also aware that reading skills are implicit in the application of questions to text materials. These teachers have two objectives in their use of questions: 1) to teach the content in the text, 2) to teach the reading skills necessary for answering the questions being asked.

The validity of these two objectives seems obvious. However, a careful reflection on what these objectives assume, particularly the second one, raises serious questions about that validity. When one directs students' reading with questions, there is an implicit assumption that students already have the reading skills necessary for a successful response to those questions. If the students do indeed possess those skills, then such questioning is

*Reprinted with permission of Harold L. Herber and the International Reading Association, *Journal of Reading,* 1975, *18,* 512–517.

perfectly valid. But if students in fact do not already have those skills, then directing their reading with questions that assume they do is misdirected teaching.

Is it valid to use a teaching procedure which, on the one hand, is designed to teach a skill but, on the other hand, assumes prior possession of that skill in order to perform the required task? This is what happens when a teacher attempts to teach interpretation, for example, by asking interpretive questions of students who need help in learning how to interpret. If students can answer the interpretive questions, do they not already possess the interpretive skills? If they do not possess the skills, does asking questions that require the use of the skills really teach them the skills?

It seems very probable that for instruction in how to read with good comprehension, questioning is not the answer.

Consider what is assumed for students by the science teacher in the following lesson on pollution. The reading selection in the science text focuses on carbon monoxide as a major air pollutant. The authors have organized their information and ideas using the cause-effect pattern of organization. Some of the cause-effect relationships are explicit; others are implicit. To acquire the information and to perceive the concepts imbedded in the material, students need to be able to read for cause-effect, an important part of the comprehension process.

Prior to giving the reading assignment, the teacher and students engaged in appropriate activities to prepare for the reading. Assume, then, the teacher knew that his students needed help in learning *how* to read for cause-effect. His instructional purposes were 1) to develop students' skill in reading for cause and effect and 2) to guide their learning of the content of the reading selection. To aid in accomplishing those purposes, he gave them the following questions:

1. What percentage of all air pollution is caused by carbon monoxide?
2. Why is carbon monoxide a major pollutant?
3. How does CO poisoning effect a person's body?
4. Where does much of our CO poisoning come from, other than automobile engines?
5. What is the most obvious way to reduce air pollution?
6. How do society's priorities relate to air pollution?
7. What have you observed concerning pollution that suggests people would rather not face reality?

Some of these questions are at the literal level. Others are at the interpretive, requiring students to perceive cause-effect relationships across information from several places in the text. Still others are at the applied level of comprehension, requiring students to synthesize ideas from the reading selection with ideas from other sources or experiences.

Are these good questions? Surely they are. Are they appropriate questions? No, they are not, *if* the intended objectives are to be believed. The questions may be appropriate for students who already know how to read for cause-effect relationships, but they are premature for those who lack the experience and skill. For students who have not learned how to manipulate information and ideas in this fashion, questions that in reality assume possession of that skill do little to develop it. Using questioning to direct students' search for information or ideas assumes at least some competency and independence in the process essential for the search.

Questions Are Valuable

None of this is to suggest that questioning is poor teaching procedure in the absolute sense. Speeches have been given, conferences organized, papers, articles, and books written on questioning as an instructional device. Anyone conversant with education cannot doubt the appropriateness of questioning.

The art and science of questioning is fundamental to good teaching. Well-formed questions can stimulate both critical and creative response from students as they interact with one another or the text material. Questions can be adjusted to the needs of students and their ability to respond, ranging from simple to profound, concrete to abstract. Good questions can reinforce the reading skills that students already have by providing practice on the application of those skills. Many teachers use study guide questions for that purpose. Good questions, accompanied by reinforcing feedback on the nature and quality of the responses, can raise the students' levels of sophistication in their use of the reading skills implicit in those questions. Many teachers provide students with study guide questions to serve as the basis for small group discussions to accomplish that purpose.

But what happens when students do not possess the skills to practice or reinforce? What does one do when questions do not seem appropriate or do the job? It is very likely that there needs to be a procedure that is preliminary to the application of good questioning strategies. This could well be the application of good *simulation strategies.*

Consider a different approach to the same lesson on carbon monoxide. The teacher guides students through the same appropriate activity to prepare them for reading the text. The purposes for reading are the same. But the manner in which the teacher guides the students is different. The following materials are given to the students and the teacher goes over the directions orally to make certain they understand how to perform the task.

Carbon Monoxide

Part I. Directions: Here are twelve sets of words or phrases and numbers. The words or phrases in each set are separated by a line. You are to decide if the first word or phrase in a set stands for a possible cause of what the second word or phrase stands for. The numbers at the end of each set tell you the page, paragraph, and lines where you can find the information to help you decide. Work together to make your decisions. Be ready to show the information in the text that supports your decisions.

_____ 1. Carbon monoxide/more than 51 percent air pollution (113,1,1–3)
_____ 2. Automobile engines/80 percent carbon monoxide emissions (113,1,6–7)
_____ 3. Incomplete combustion/significant percent of CO emissions (113,1,4–7)
_____ 4. Carbon monoxide/danger, illness, death (113,2,1–3)
_____ 5. One gallon gasoline/three pounds CO (113,2,6)
_____ 6. Mild CO poisoning/highway accidents (114,1,1–2)
_____ 7. Faulty exhaust systems/poisoned people (114,1,9–11)
_____ 8. CO poisoning/oxygen starvation (114,2,1–2)
_____ 9. Hemoglobin and CO/strong chemical bond (114,2)
_____10. Heavy smoking/permanent combination of hemoglobin and CO (115,0,4–6)
_____11. Inhaling CO/trouble with hearing (115,1,9–11)
_____12. Reduction in traffic/obvious remedy (115,1,1)

After part one is completed by students and discussed, they do part two. Again, the teacher goes over the directions to insure understanding of the task.

> *Part II.* Directions. Read each of the following statements. Check those you believe to be reasonable. Think about the work you did in Part I of this guide as well as other ideas you have about pollution.
>
> _____ 1. People will risk their lives to have what they want.
> _____ 2. What a person wants is not always what he needs.
> _____ 3. Good replaces bad more easily than bad replaces good.
> _____ 4. What you can't see won't hurt you.
> _____ 5. A surplus can cause a shortage.

Now, what is the difference between the two lessons and the procedures they represent? The obvious difference is that one is based on a set of questions while the other is based on a set of words and phrases and a set of statements. But within that obvious difference is an important distinction and the potential for *simulation.*

You will note that the materials for the second procedure really present possible answers to the questions posed in the first procedure. But the *teacher* asked those questions *of himself* rather than of his students. As a skilled reader of science material, he was able to discern the cause-effect relationships and to express them by a series of related words or phrases as well as by a set of sentences. He then took these, his own answers to his own questions, and presented them to his students as a series of alternatives for them to consider. Their task was to take those "answers" and determine if the information in the text or ideas from their store of knowledge and experience either supported or denied their validity or reasonableness. Students discussed the alternatives among themselves in small groups and later with the teacher. In those discussions the question that was constantly raised in reference to decisions about the validity of alternatives was "What's your evidence?" Students responded to that question by identifying information from the text or ideas from their experience to justify their decisions. Thus, they went through a simulation of the process the teacher went through when he created those alternatives in the first place.

As a skilled reader, the teacher could perceive relationships within the information and could state those relationships. On the other hand, when students are not skilled readers, they may experience great difficulty doing what the teacher can do well. But when asked to find support for statements that do express possible relationships across information in the text, they can locate that information. In finding support for the statements, the students deal with the text in almost the same way the teacher did in creating the statements. They develop a feeling for the skill the teacher had to apply when creating the statements.

Simulation can be defined as an artificial representation of a real experience; a contrived series of activities which, when taken together, approximate the experience or the process that ultimately is to be applied independently. As it pertains to the process of comprehension in reading, simulation would be to contrive a set of activities which approximate what one does when one comprehends independently. In our example, the activity approximates reading for cause and effect, providing a representation of that experience. Repeated over time, experiences of this type give students a feeling for processes which are part of reading comprehension.

Independent Questioning

With that feeling as the base and the reference point, and with the confidence that comes from success, students then can respond more readily to questions that require the application of the skill in order to produce their own answers. The teacher can explain that the process is almost the same: they still look for relationships and they still think about what ideas those relationships represent; but now they develop their own expressions of those relationships. With the previous simulated experience providing a pattern to follow, they are in a much better position to produce such answers than if they had not had that experience.

The principle operating here is that it is easier to recognize information and ideas than it is to produce them. Using that principle as applied to the difference between responses to statements and responses to questions, one can establish an instructional sequence that moves students along a continuum of independence.

1. The teacher prepares statements for students' reactions. References are added to indicate where students might look in the text to determine if there is information to support the statements (page, column, paragraph, if necessary).
2. The teacher prepares statements for students' reactions. No references are given.
3. The teacher prepares questions for students to answer. References are added to indicate where students might look in the text to find information which, when combined, might answer the question.
4. The teacher prepares questions for students to answer. No references are given.
5. Students survey the material, raise their own questions and answer them.
6. Students produce statements of meanings, concepts, and ideas as they read.

Within each of these steps in the sequence one can accommodate a range of ability and achievement by the sophistication of the statement or question. Steps 1 through 4 are teacher-directed; steps 5 and 6 are student-directed.

Earlier it was stated that using questions to guide students' reading in order to develop reading skills is really based on the assumption that students already have the skill; otherwise they would not be able to answer the question. To be sure, the simulation as represented in steps 1 and 2 in the above sequence also makes some assumptions, but not nearly so many. Students identify, they do not produce, the valid responses. The assumption is that when they encounter the information in the text they will see the connection between that information and the statements. If they do not, it may be because the statement is too abstract. So you make it more concrete, adjusting statements just as you would adjust questions.

The next time you guide students' reading, ask yourself the questions you would normally ask them—questions that deal both with the content of the selection and the comprehension process essential to understanding that content. Then give the students your answers as a series of alternative statements to respond to. Depending on your students' achievement levels, you may want to provide references for them as suggested above. Make certain the statements aren't too sophisticated for them. However, do not be afraid to have the students think beyond the literal level of comprehension. Then be ready for responses and for justifications you may not have thought of yourself. These will come if, after students have responded to the statements and are discussing them with you, you keep asking the all-important question, "What's your evidence?"

And *where* does all of this happen? Right in the regular content area classroom, of course. And *who* does it? The regular classroom teacher. *How?* As indicated above. *When?* As often as it seems profitable; as consistently as time and logic will allow. *Why?* Because students need the help; they need to be shown how to do what their teachers require them to do. *What?* We said, "Because. . . ."

Concepts in Comprehension for Content Area Teachers*

Ned Ratekin
University of Northern Iowa

For some time content area reading "experts" have been rapping on classroom doors and gesturing through windows with the hope of being invited to enter just long enough to share their vital information on how students learn from course materials. The number of teachers opening their classrooms to this information is encouraging. But many others, after a glance toward the commotion, hesitate to become involved with outside ideas from content reading literature or from inservice resources based on its concepts.

The reasons for this hesitancy are not difficult to understand. Much content reading literature emphasizes the responsibility of content specialists to teach students how to learn from course texts—that is, how to read the textbook. This appeal often leads teachers to negative interpretations, such as: (1) content teachers are expected to make up for poor instruction in reading by their students' previous teachers; (2) they must add the burden of teaching reading to their duties; (3) priorities for content learning and the prestige of a discipline must give way to development of prerequisite abilities; (4) students are held back by reduced course content; and (5) content teachers are expected to prepare themselves in a new field.

The fact is that the fast growing literature on content area reading is most impressive in demonstrating its value as an aid rather than as an addition to content area teaching. Herber (1978), for example, has made a significant contribution through integrating concepts from past research and shaping the direction of experimentation and practice in content area reading.

Despite this effort, the thrust of information on content area reading is blunted by misconceptions and apprehensions held by teachers. To a science teacher, teaching science and teaching reading in science are not the same thing.

An approach is needed that removes the perceptions of content reading as an added and foreign duty, one that presents it as facilitating the purposes of the content area teacher. The concept of interface—the integration of information from separate disciplines—is a popular and productive notion. It implies a contribution that meets objectives of each discipline.

*Written especially for inclusion in this text.

Recent studies concerning comprehension of discourse contain many implications for content area learning that may be interfaced with the content teacher's knowledge of concepts and objectives in a discipline. This paper summarizes several of these concepts. This review reveals that guiding learning from text, or reading, is an instance of guiding students' comprehension of concepts through any media; as such, guiding students' reading is not an extra burden unjustly left for the content teacher, but rather a direct opportunity for content teachers to perform in their role of helping students develop course concepts.

The Nature of Concept Development

A brief comment on the nature of concept development seems necessary as a background for this review of information on comprehension and text reading. The goal of a content teacher is to provide the environment and experiences that will lead students to new concepts. Any teacher will testify that placing students in the presence of information and events does not automatically generate concepts. Since a concept is an internalized construction that represents reality, and not the reality itself, concept development requires an active interaction between the learner and events or objects in the environment that allow the learner to "invent" the new concept. A successful interaction leads to ownership of the concept by a learner; that is, a concept label such as "erosion" or "detente" or "plot conflict" will each trigger an expected set of elements. The interaction typically requires a readiness on the part of the learner in terms of previously learned concepts, ability to carry out pertinent mental processes, language that allows access to ideas, and a reason for the effort. Whether a student is listening, viewing, reading, or manipulating, the problem of the teacher is in many ways the same: how well does the activity allow a learner to interact so that a reconstruction of concepts (comprehension) results from the experience? The teaching task is to create a "fit" between the learner and new information that will allow the interactions necessary for concepts to develop.

Factors That Determine a Comprehension Fit

Comprehension of text is achieved to the degree that a reader is able to interact with a text in relation to three variables: the concept background or context in which information is presented, the language in which information is presented, and the cognitive activity the reader engages to follow an author's thought or to reconstruct the author's meaning. The remainder of this paper summarizes information related to these three variables and briefly suggests implications from this information that may be of value to the content area teacher.

1. *The concepts, real world experiences, or assimilated knowledge held by the learners as they approach the learning experience will determine their understanding.* This is a well-recognized truth with a long history of documentation. Although basic it is not trite; many of the problems in school learning emanate from lack of provision for this factor. Both Bruner and Piaget have demonstrated that new concepts, or new world knowledge, grow from previously held concepts. Bruner, in fact, implies that new concepts are old concepts refined by the addition of new attributes, leading to expanded categories of knowing, or by

discrimination of conditions in which previous concepts do not apply. Piagetian theory indicates that intellectual growth from perceptual to cognitive knowledge is a product of continuous restructuring to conform to new cognitive or perceptual evidence.

Recent work by several scholars in comprehension have approached this precondition for learning through a field of study termed *"schema theory"* (Anderson, 1977). This theory retains the views of previous cognitive theorists but provides a practical format for understanding the impact of former experiences on understanding a current communication. In schema theory, past experiences of a person are viewed as organized according to events that tend to recur. Driving a vehicle, attending a football game, being a father, sitting alone in the woods each form a schema. The more repeated the experience, the firmer the schema; and the more various the experiences within an event, the richer the schema. Attending football games at an elementary school, at a large university, within a prison, and in Canada would create a more diverse schema for "football game" than just viewing professional football on TV. Also, schemata (the plural form of schema) are hierarchical and interacting. The schema "football game" would include a subschema "cheerleaders", which may include additional subschemata for "jumping" and "hollering." All of these would fit into a larger macroschema of "athletic event."

The useful idea in this is that a term or incident that identifies an event (such as football game) immediately unlocks a flood of interlocking elements, or framework, known to be related in that event. In any specific event the particular items will not be known, but the slots in the framework form a readiness for information to be completed. Searching for elements to fit slots in the hypothesized framework forms the necessary interaction for comprehension.

It should be noted that schemata can confuse as well as facilitate comprehension, as any person who has tried to watch a rugby contest with a schema for a football game can verify. Comprehension depends, in part, not only on the existence of concepts and schemata but also on the particular schema that is dominant at a particular time in relation to the information being presented.

2. *Comprehension is determined by the fit between the language of an author and a learner.* Although language is not the only vehicle to learning, presenting information through language—spoken or written—is a basic approach in education. The elements of vocabulary and sentence form are crucial in the fit between information and learner.

There are two routes by which the words used in a communication will assist the learner in comprehending the ideas presented. Either the words will immediately trigger concepts that can be brought to the understanding, or the learner must use problem-solving strategies to hypothesize a possible concept for a term not immediately recognized. Problems in immediate identification of word meaning result when either the learner lacks the concept represented (the word is not recognized, even if pronounced), or the term is not recognized as representing a concept that is actually known by the learner. That is, a student may have the concepts represented by *obese, turgid,* or *transient,* but does not recognize the vocabulary used for these concepts. Discrimination of these two quite different sources of "vocabulary" problems is important for analyzing a comprehension fit. The first implies a comprehension problem due to concept development, whereas the second implies a problem due to word knowledge.

In either case, when a word does not excite a concept, the learner must use cues from within the word and within the language context to estimate a meaning. Word analysis, or the use of meaning-bearing parts of a word, and use of context clues are the strategies more frequently employed to aid comprehension at this point. The surrounding information may provide an explanation of an unrecognized term; the most obvious example is a direct definition, or examples, illustrations, and graphics that supply attributes of the concept represented by the unfamiliar term.

Comprehension of vocabulary, therefore, is dependent on concept background, word knowledge, ability to use strategies to take advantage of word and text clues, and the fit between these abilities in the learner and how well the text itself provides for analysis.

In addition to vocabulary, sentence form or structure can be a major factor in comprehension. As words merely awaken concepts, so sentences represent associations among ideas. The written or spoken sentences are not the ideas. Any idea (deep structure) or meaning of an author can be represented in a variety of written or spoken forms. This surface structure varies not only in vocabulary but also in syntax. A learner may present an idea using vocabulary and a sentence quite different from the vocabulary and sentence used by a text presenting the same idea. The structure normally used by a learner (sentence schema) is the best basis for predicting the structure of information being received. In other words, comprehension of information will be determined in part by the ability of a learner to predict the language elements being received. The expectation of a certain language pattern may be viewed as a type of schema, with blank slots predicted and ready to be filled with specific information. If the schema projected does not fit the information, then there is a lack of readiness, and thus, comprehension suffers.

Comprehension of text by a reader, therefore, is dependent on the fit between language patterns of the learner and the language patterns used by an author.

3. *Comprehension by the learner is also determined by the cognitive processing employed to complete and transform schemata on the basis of the new information being received.* The fact that there is no meaning in surface communication, only in the receiver, and that information is meaningful only when concepts are already known may lead to the bizarre conclusion that a person can only understand what he or she already knows. How, then, can a person learn new concepts and gain new information? It is obvious that the crucial component of comprehension is the thinking, or cognitive activity, carried out by a learner who is presented with information. It is the thinking process, the search for meaning, that determines completion of schema slots or the reorganization of schemata. Just as world knowledge and language elements form a readiness through schema predictions, pertinent directions of thought also form a schema of readiness to receive information.

Cognitive psychologists have labored long to lay bare the intricacies and complexities of mental processing, attempting to identify repeated patterns of relations that characterize the flow of thought. A host of models, hierarchies, and taxonomies have been devised from this work by practitioners as a guide to identifying the desirable fit between a learner's thinking pattern and the thinking demands presented by a communication.

Patterns of logical organization included in such taxonomies as a guide to instruction in comprehension usually include, but are not limited to, the following: cause-effect; comparison and contrast; order in time and sequence; and inductive listing (Niles, 1965). Other models incorporate mental operations such as relating, classifying or categorizing, ordering, making deductions, making inductions, and combinations of these operations that result in transposing, projecting, and inferring (Barrett, 1970).

Establishing a fit in such thought processes between a learner and the communication requires not only that the learner can carry out the thinking demanded by the information, but also that the learner can predict the thinking pattern or schema being used by the writer or speaker. Teaching students to think in various logical patterns is important, but the additional ability to predict logical form is necessary for a reader to experience efficient comprehension. The more a reader has been sensitized to the logic of a selection, by personal skills or the guidance of a teacher, the more readily that reader will understand the author.

Considerable research has been generated recently in an attempt to identify patterns of discourse and the ability of readers to match the author's text structure. One area of this research is concerned with story grammar—the elements in a narrative such as conflict, plot structure, setting, and episodes (Mandler and Johnson, 1977). Another aspect of this research is concerned with expository structures such as problem-solution, comparison, antecedent/consequent, description, and collection (Meyer, Brandt, and Bluth, 1980). There is some evidence that as children learn to read they tend to assimilate the story grammar structure as a basis for comprehension; even content area materials for lower grade children often appear in this narrative form. Higher level content area texts are almost exclusively expository in structure. This conflict between narrative and expository schemata forms a major barrier for children in attempting to comprehend content area texts. In fact, Anderson (1979) has concluded that many learners will reorganize expository information so that it will fit a narrative schema in order to make sense from information being read.

Ability to predict and follow the logical flow of information obviously allows a learner to understand relationships among ideas. This understanding results in the identification of main ideas or conclusions derived from the underlying attributes or causes. Therefore, the skills of determining main ideas and recalling details are not isolated skills but simultaneous products of a successful fit in processing information.

In addition to logical organization as an element in cognitive processing, there is a factor commonly termed "levels of comprehension" that is used to describe the depth and amount of information from a learner's world knowledge schema that is necessary to understand and use a given communication.

The three levels most widely identified in taxonomies of comprehension are literal, interpretive, and applied. The applied level often includes aspects of critical thinking and appreciation (Herber, 1978).

It may be useful to return to the schema model to clarify the functions of these three levels in comprehension. As a learner hypothesizes a schema in which to receive information, a host of possible items and relations is generated. These items are placed in the schema readied for specific information. For example, if a reader is learning about the government in a democratic country, a schema would probably include an electorate, elected officials, and a head of government (as well as many other probable slots). As the reader gains information on the specific country under study, specific items are placed in these slots. It may be discovered in the text that the electorate is limited to landowners, that to be elected a person must be at least forty years old and is called an elder, and that the head of government is called a moderator. The original schema is intact, although the subschemas of qualification for office may need to be expanded to include more alternatives.

Comprehension occurs, then, when a reader shares a schema with a writer. The process of comprehension is the effort by a reader to reorganize his or her schema in order to maintain a shared schema with the writer. The content of the reorganization is based on the information and relations provided by the writer. The processes of reorganization are provided by the thinking skills of the reader.

Literal comprehension occurs when the reader identifies elements of the shared schema in direct statements by the writer. When a reader comprehends on the literal level, he or she does not refer to any aspects of the shared schema except the meanings represented in direct statements of the author. If a reader comprehends only on the literal level, there are two possible explanations: either the reader is heavily dependent on the author for all elements of the schema (that is, the reader has no personal knowledge or experience to assist the author in constructing the schema) or the reader is unsophisticated in the ability to integrate personal experiences into the author's schema.

On the interpretive level of comprehension, the reader must not only identify information to complete slots in the schema, but also the author expects the reader to apply additional information from the reader's world knowledge schema in order to complete the author's intended meaning. With few exceptions, text materials require the reader to use interpretive-level comprehension in order to grasp the author's intended meaning. The author-reader interaction is actually a dialogue in which the author excites aspects of the shared schema, expecting the reader to share in aspects of the content not specifically stated. This expectancy represents the author's respect for the reader and may even generate a sense of intimacy. Interpretive level comprehension, then, is discovering what the author means on the basis of both what is stated (literal level) and what is assumed to be known or can be concluded.

As Pearson (1979) has made clear, it is difficult to conceive of a truly literal level of comprehension; but it is important to note that, although inferences may enhance understanding, they do not necessarily lead to an interpretation of the author's intended meaning. Suppose the text on the mythical government states: "Moderators were elected for life; needless to say, the country has seen numerous assassinations." Inferences that could be drawn by the reader might include explanations for the assassinations of persons elected for life. Such explanations may include the possibility of despicable or senile rulers removed for the public good or an ambitious person's strong drive for the political power of the presidency leading to removal of the incumbent. These understandings would enhance the communication but may not in themselves be the major intended meaning. In this passage, the interpretation intended by the author may be that there are pitfalls inherent in that form or all forms of government or that some systems work better than others.

Problems on the interpretive level of comprehension may result from a reader's inability to draw inferences that enhance the author's meaning or from difficulty in synthesizing the literal and inferred understandings into the major intended meanings of the author.

The applied level of comprehension is really not direct interaction with text information at all, but rather the realization that information understood from text has implications for other events beyond the text ideas themselves. In schema theory terms, this means that ideas understood can be related to other schema through common larger, macroschema frameworks.

Assume that a student has read three stories in which these three different events occurred: a girl speaks to an "uncool" boy in front of her friends; a boy turns down a scholarship in order to keep a family together; a man substitutes himself for an innocent man condemned to execution. When the student, after reading the third story, claims that the three are all alike in that they represent acts of courage requiring sacrifice, that student is demonstrating an applied level of comprehension.

For another example, students may be asked to find a similarity in events from their reading related to the development of nuclear energy, increased land tillage, and replacement of refugees. The students who realize that solving some problems may result in other more serious problems will be using the applied level of comprehension.

The applied level of comprehension involves the analysis-synthesis or convergent-divergent sequence of search, which first requires identification of significant aspects of a specific text, followed by a creative searching for other personal knowledge and experience that shares these significant aspects. These applied level understandings are frequently the major objectives of instruction in content areas.

Another aspect of applied comprehension involves the value standards that a reader brings within a schema to a selection. These value standards, whether intrinsic or provided as part of the instruction, lead to evaluation and appreciation as forms of reaction to text material.

It is generally accepted that the act of comprehension is not a linear sequence, but rather an interaction of the cognitive processes previously summarized. It seems naive to view comprehension as a linear flow of activity beginning with word identification and moving through word meaning, sentence meaning, passage meaning, and finally integration with other knowledge. It is just as misleading to view comprehension as beginning with a purpose and full-blown schema at the top, followed by discovery of more and more specific information to complete a schema. It is more realistic to view comprehension as composed of constant interactions between and among the variables of organization and levels of processing, with top-level schemata tentatively directing the search for specific information and new information altering the schemata in which the search continues (Rumelhart, 1977). This interaction must include language and word and graphic variables as well as the affective elements of purpose and interest.

Content teachers certainly are not expected to build a separate curriculum for developing skill in comprehension or in the strategies of interaction. It is just as difficult to expect students to mature in comprehension of text materials through direct reading instruction that often has a vacuum of relevant content. It is more useful to view a knowledge of the comprehension process as a valuable tool to guide content teachers in determining practical teaching strategies in helping students build concepts.

Several resources now exist that provide practical suggestions for content area teachers to interface with their own knowledge of the concepts, language, and problem-solving strategies in specific content areas. The following summary of implications from text comprehension identifies aspects of instruction in which these strategies may be implemented:

1. Content teachers who analyze materials from which they expect students to learn concepts will discover such readiness factors as: demands for prerequisite concepts;

vocabulary, language structure and logical reasoning characteristics of the author; the degree to which interpretation or inference is required; provisions within the text for presenting concepts; and skills needed to use resources in the text to build concepts.

2.   Assessing the ability of students to read a text will provide insight into the degree of guidance in understanding the text needed by different students and will identify students with whom a specific text may not be usable.

3.   Comprehension is a product of a meaningful search for information. The motivation for reading is created by guaranteeing an intersection of the schemata in which students are living through their personal problems and pleasures and the schema of materials they are asked to read in order to build concepts. Creating this intersection requires some introductory activity.

4.   In addition to providing purposes for reading, activities that precede reading prove valuable for clarifying prerequisite concepts, anticipating probable vocabulary problems, and establishing the various schemata for events, language, and thinking processes demanded by the text for comprehension. The specific elements to be included in this prereading activity are, of course, determined after discovering the fit between the demands of the materials and the ability of students.

5.   Guidance in processing text information gives readers the opportunity to interact with information in order to build concepts. This guidance, often in the form of questions or statements for analysis, may take the form of actually leading a reader through the processes of comprehension on the literal, interpretive, and applied levels.

6.   Assimilation and extension activities will provide an opportunity for readers to gain a firm grasp of the concepts met during reading and allow them to integrate new concepts into their own schemata.

References

Anderson, R. C. Schema theory and reading: A progress report. Paper presented at the National Reading Conference, San Antonio, Texas, 1979.

Anderson, R. C., and Spiro, R. J. *Schooling and the acquisition of knowledge.* New York: John Wiley and Sons, 1977.

Barrett, T. C. A taxonomy for reading comprehension. Paper presented at the International Reading Association, Anaheim, California, 1970.

Herber, H. L. *Teaching reading in content areas.* Englewood Cliffs, N.J.: Prentice-Hall, 1978.

Mandler, J. M., and Johnson, N. S. Remembrance of things parsed: Story structure and recall. *Cognitive Psychology,* 1977, *9,* 111–151.

Meyer, B. J. F., Brandt, D. M., and Bluth, G. J. Use of top-level structure in text: Key for reading comprehension of ninth grade students. *Reading Research Quarterly,* 1980, *1,* 72–103.

Niles, O. S. Organization perceived. In H.L. Herber (Ed.), *Developing study skills in secondary schools.* Newark, Del.: International Reading Association, 1965.

Pearson, P. D. Recent views on the nature of reading comprehension; Teaching models. Paper presented at the Reading Comprehension Workshop, Cedar Falls, Iowa, 1979.

Rumelhart, D. E. *Toward an interactive model of reading.* University of California, San Diego: Center for Human Information Processing, 1976.

Promoting the Instructional Match: Reader and Text

4

Selecting and Introducing
the Textbook

It is imperative that content teachers know the approximate difficulty level of printed materials being used in their courses. In this way they can attempt to compensate for any mismatch between reader and text. Unfortunately, texts are frequently chosen according to teacher intuition and/or some type of readability estimate. Both of these approaches have limitations when considered in the light of our current understanding of those features that make textbooks more understandable and useful as learning tools. Additionally, there are certain practices that teachers can employ in making the best possible connection between students, materials, and the content to be learned.

Nelson cautions that readability formulas provide only estimates of reading difficulty and are not absolute measures. She presents other concerns about readability measures and then offers suggestions to content teachers for their use.

Harker presents five criteria for the selection of content materials. To demonstrate these criteria, they are applied to a representative text, and conclusions are made concerning their use.

Alvermann and Dishner point out that what must be considered in promoting student learning is the interaction between students, content, and materials.

Readability: Some Cautions for the Content Area Teacher

Joan Nelson
State University of New York at Binghamton

Professional textbooks that promote reading instruction in content areas typically recommend that classroom teachers use a readability formula to determine the appropriateness of subject area text materials for their students. Good advice? It depends.

Every teacher should be able to estimate the reading difficulty of materials that students are expected to read. Obviously, it is useful to have some objective means for making this estimate. The most widely used readability formulas (Dale-Chall, 1948; Flesch, 1951; Fry, 1968; McLaughlin, 1969) employ some measure of sentence length along with some measure of word difficulty to determine a grade level score for printed materials. The score is usually based on sample passages drawn from various parts of the text, and it represents an estimate of the average reading difficulty of the full text. Different formulas yield slightly different readability scores for a given selection, but teachers can use the score as one factor in evaluating reading material for student use.

Readability scores provide *estimates* of reading difficulty, not firm and absolute levels. Recommending the use of readability formulas is good advice if their limitations are communicated along with their recommendation. However, some suggestions of how to use the information derived from a formula call into question the appropriateness of recommending their use in the first place. Content area teachers are frequently advised to use readability scores to match the reading difficulty level of text materials to the reading achievement level of individual students. Occasionally, it is suggested that teachers should rewrite text materials to conform to readability criteria. Based on both practical and theoretical considerations, these recommendations are questionable at best and may be harmful in practice unless caution prevails.

While it may make very good sense for a reading teacher to choose or prepare materials for reading instruction that approximate the reading achievement level of the individual student, a variety of factors make it impractical and perhaps even inadvisable for content area teachers to do the same. The curriculum for the reading teacher is the reading process, most often defined as a set of reading skills. The reading teacher analyzes specific skill needs of individual students and selects or prepares material that lends itself to the sequential development of needed skills.

The curriculum of the content area teacher, on the other hand, is a set of ideas and generalizations related to the subject of study (Herber 1970). For the subject area teacher, the most important consideration in selecting text material is whether it communicates the essential facts, concepts, and values of the subject in a logical sequence, a sensible organi-

Reprinted with permission of Joan Nelson-Herber and the International Reading Association, *Journal of Reading,* 1978, *21,* 620–625.

zation, and an interesting and attractive format. Readability is an important factor, of course. It would be foolish to expect students to comprehend material written far above their reading level no matter how well it presented the essential information. However, given the wide range of reading achievement to be found in a typical class at the middle or secondary school level, it is unrealistic to expect subject area teachers to locate material containing the essentials of the subject for each level of reading achievement represented in the classroom.

According to Burmeister (1974) and others, the typical tenth grade classroom encompasses a range of eleven grades of reading achievement, from fourth grade to college level. Even if it were possible to approximate this range with several sets of material containing the essential information, it would be inappropriate to assume that students could comprehend any given text simply because readability scores matched reading achievement scores. Too many factors other than sentence length and word difficulty are involved in comprehending content area material to make any such assumption.

Readability formulas do not generally consider such variables as levels of abstraction, complexity of concepts, figurative and poetic language, multiple meanings, technical and scientific vocabulary, variations in format and organization, and a host of other factors related to the comprehensibility of subject area reading materials. [Some readability formulas do consider sentence complexity and, to some extent, concept load. They are, however, more complicated to calculate, and their use is generally confined to researchers. Klare (1974, 1975) provides an excellent summary of readability formulas for interested readers.] Neither do they take into account the variability of reading difficulty within text material except in the averaging process. More important, readability formulas do not measure the interest, the motivation, the language competence, or the experiential background of the reader in relation to the specific content of the text.

Take the following social studies sentences as an example: "The leader often becomes the symbol of the unity of the country. No one will run against him." These sentences are relatively short and they contain few multisyllabic words. According to readability criteria, the sentences would appear to be appropriate for junior high school text material. However, the difficulty an eighth grade reader might experience in comprehending these sentences has little to do with readability criteria. Consider the information that the student must integrate:

1. The special meaning of *leader* in the social studies context.
2. The word *often* used to mean "in many cases" rather than "repeatedly."
3. The sense of *becomes* as meaning "grows to be" rather than "is suitable to."
4. The abstract concept of *symbolism*.
5. The abstract concept of *unity*.
6. The word *country* as a political unit rather than as a rural area.
7. The idea of *run against* as in an election.
8. The implication of a cause and effect relationship between the ideas presented in the two sentences.

There is no question that the context of the full text would support the ideas being presented. Unfortunately the surrounding sentences are likely to contain other abstractions, multiple meaning words, and implied relationships that pose their own comprehension problems.

It is clear, then, that the danger is not in advising teachers to use readability formulas as an aid in evaluating student textbooks; the danger is in promoting the faulty assumption that matching the readability score of materials to the reading achievement scores of students will automatically yield comprehension. Far too many teachers make textbook reading assignments on the basis of that faulty assumption and then fail to comprehend why students fail to comprehend.

Rewriting Text Materials

Recommendations that teachers rewrite text materials to meet readability criteria are based on another faulty assumption—that shortening sentences and changing multisyllabic words automatically make a reading passage easier. According to Pearson (1974–75, p. 160), "Such recommendations reveal a common error in interpreting correlational data by assuming that correlation means causality."

Readability formulas are based on correlational data. Correlation is simply an index of relationship. Although sentence length correlates with passage reading difficulty, it is not necessarily the cause of the reading difficulty. It may be that concept complexity causes both longer sentences *and* reading difficulty. Clear communication of complex concepts may *require* longer sentences. Thus, the reading difficulty of a passage would be caused by complex concept load which results in a longer sentence, rather than by sentence length itself. Shortening the sentence without changing the concept load may not enhance comprehension. Indeed, there is a growing body of evidence and opinion (Pearson 1974–75, Dawkins 1975, Klare 1974–75) to suggest that arbitrarily shortening sentences may *increase* the difficulty of the reading task by rendering explicit relationships obscure.

Pearson uses the following example:

(a)   Because the chain broke, the machine stopped.
(b)   The chain broke. The machine stopped.

Though sentence (a) is longer, the causal relationship is made explicit by the subordinating conjunction. In (b) we have reduced the sentence length but have placed a new inferential burden on the reader. The causal relationship must be inferred 1) from the proximity of the ideas presented and 2) from the reader's background of experience with machines.

The increase in difficulty may not be apparent here, because most people have had some experience with machines; however, where subject area textbooks are presenting ideas that are *new* to the reader, that is, *beyond the reader's experience,* such causal relationships might be impossible to infer, as in the following sentences which might be found in an economics textbook: "Businessmen are forced to lower investment. They change their production and employment levels to return to equilibrium." Does a cause and effect relationship exist between the two sentences? If so, which is cause and which is effect? Unless the reader is familiar with the economic principles of income determination, it is impossible to be sure. Compare the longer sentence: *"Because* businessmen are forced to lower investment, they change their production and employment levels to return to equilibrium." The relationship is made explicit, leaving the reader free to ponder the meanings of the words themselves.

What about the words themselves? According to Klare (1974–75, p. 96), "the word or semantic variable is consistently more highly predictive than the sentence or syntactic variable when each is considered singly." It might seem to make sense, then, to change difficult or multisyllabic words to meet readability criteria. Unfortunately, the words that are most likely to cause a high readability score for a content area textbook are the technical vocabulary and the special meaning words of the subject area. For example: in mathematics—*multiplication, rectangular, hypotenuse, variables, adjacent, circumference, congruent;* in social studies—*peninsula, totalitarianism, historical, equilibrium, vegetation, distribution, discrimination, industrialization, reciprocity;* in science—*elements, chemicals, reaction, reagent, acceleration, condensation, chromosomes, photosynthesis, precipitation.*

These are only samples of the kinds of content words which are either multisyllabic or do not appear on lists of commonly used words such as the Dale-Chall list (1948). They are, nevertheless, essential to subject matter comprehension. It would be foolish to suggest that teachers rewrite materials to change or eliminate these words when they represent the very substance of the subject the teachers are trying to teach.

To return to our earlier economics example, the words *businessmen, investment, production, employment,* and *equilibrium* are those which most readability criteria would suggest changing for reading ease. However, these words represent the technical vocabulary of the subject. Without an understanding of these words, students would be crippled in their study of economics. These words should be taught, not changed or eliminated. Thus, instruction, not a readability formula, becomes the key to comprehension of subject area material.

A content area textbook is not really designed for independent reading. It is a teaching tool designed to present facts, concepts, and values that are beyond the current knowledge and experience of the reader. The textbook uses the technical vocabulary of the subject to convey that information. Imbedded within that text are abstractions, comparisons and contrasts, cause and effect relationships, and sequences of events related to the subject. The use of a formula based on word difficulty and sentence length to match the readability score of material to reading achievement score of the reader does not automatically yield reading comprehension. Comprehension of the text requires the integration of what is new to the reader with his or her own background of experience. The reader makes sense of what is unfamiliar by relating it with the familiar.

The essence of good teaching is showing the learner how to do what is required to be successful (Herber 1970). The teacher provides the link between the familiar and the unfamiliar through instruction. The more experience the reader has had with the vocabulary and concepts of the subject, the easier the textbook will be to read and comprehend. Instruction in content area reading includes:

1. Putting students in touch with their own experience that relates to the new ideas being studied.
2. Teaching vocabulary in a way that relates the new words to previous experience to give the learner a context for meaning.
3. Guiding reading to provide the support needed to understand new ideas by setting purposes for reading; calling attention to organization; preparing material to demon-

strate relationships such as cause-effect, comparison-contrast, and sequences; and preparing material to aid students in reading for information, interpretation, and application.

4. Providing post-reading activities to encourage rereading, discussion, and reinforcement of the new ideas in the context of the student's own world of experience.

Teaching strategies to accomplish such reading instruction in content areas have been amply described and demonstrated in Herber (1970, 1978), Robinson (1975), Shepherd (1973), Herber and Nelson (1977), and others.

Suggestions for Content Teachers

The preceding ideas can be summarized by some suggestions to content area teachers.

1. Learn to use a simple readability formula as an aid in evaluating text material for student use.
2. Wherever possible, provide text materials containing the essential facts, concepts, and values of the subject at varying levels of readability within the reading range of your students.
3. Don't assume that matching readability level of material to reading achievement level of students results in automatic comprehension. Remember that there are many other factors that affect reading difficulty besides those measured by readability formulas.
4. Don't assume that rewriting text materials according to readability criteria results in automatic reading ease. Leave rewriting of text material to the linguists, researchers, and editors who have time to analyze and validate their manipulations.
5. Recognize that using a readability formula is no substitute for instruction. Assigning is not teaching. Subject area textbooks are not designed for independent reading. The best way to enhance reading comprehension in your subject area is to provide the kind of instruction which prepares students for the reading assignment, guides them in their reading, and reinforces the new ideas through rereading and discussion.

References

Burmeister, L. *Reading Strategies for Secondary School Teachers.* Reading, Mass.: Addison-Wesley, 1974.

Dale, E. and J. Chall. "A Formula for Predicting Readability." *Educational Research Bulletin,* vol. 27 (1948), pp. 11–20, 37–54.

Dawkins, J. *Syntax and Readability.* Newark, Del.: International Reading Association, 1975.

Flesch, R. *How to Test Readability.* New York, N.Y.: Harper & Row, 1951.

Fry, E. "A Readability Formula That Saves Time." *Journal of Reading,* vol. 11, no. 7 (April 1968), pp. 513–16, 575–78.

Herber, H. *Teaching Reading in Content Areas.* Englewood Cliffs, N.J.: Prentice-Hall, 1970, 1978.

Herber, H. and J. Nelson. *Reading across the Curriculum: Staff Development Programs.* Homer, N.Y.: TRICA Consultants, 1977.

Klare, G. "Assessing Readability." *Reading Research Quarterly,* vol. 10, no. 1 (1974–1975), pp. 62–102.

Klare, G. "A Table for Rapid Determination of Dale-Chall Readability Scores." *Educational Research Bulletin,* vol. 31 (1952), pp. 43–47.

McLaughlin, G. "SMOG Grading—A New Readability Formula." *Journal of Reading,* vol. 12, no. 8 (May 1969), pp. 639–46.

Pearson, P.D. "The Effects of Grammatical Complexity on Children's Comprehension, Recall, and Conception of Certain Semantic Relations." *Reading Research Quarterly,* vol. 10, no. 2 (1974–1975), pp. 155–92.

Robinson, H.A. *Teaching Reading and Study Strategies.* Boston, Mass.: Allyn & Bacon, 1975.

Shepherd, D.L. *Comprehensive High School Reading Methods.* Columbus, Ohio: Charles E. Merrill, 1973.

Selecting Instructional Materials for Content Area Reading*

W. John Harker
University of Victoria

Content area instructional materials are learning devices, not just sources of content area information. When selecting instructional materials, it is necessary to ensure that they provide the information required for students to achieve content area learning objectives. But it is equally necessary to ensure that they do not frustrate students' learning by imposing barriers to reading and understanding.

This article presents five criteria for the selection of content area instructional materials that will support rather than frustrate student learning through reading. The five criteria are readability, concept load, background information, organization, and format and style. Each of these criteria will be considered in turn, and its application will be demonstrated through an analysis of *Man in the Tropics* (Carswell, Morrow and Honeybone, 1968), a textbook used in eighth grade social studies in British Columbia.

Readability

Readability as determined through readability formulas is often the first criterion used to select instructional materials. In 1963, Klare noted that over thirty different readability formulas existed. Since that time, a number of new formulas have been developed, including the relatively simple Fry (1968) and SMOG (McLaughlin, 1969) formulas. Most readability formulas use different combinations of sentence length and vocabulary difficulty to determine reading difficulty, while others include sentence complexity in their calculations.

But readability formulas can prove disillusioning. Often reading materials determined to be at the same level of reading difficulty cause students different degrees of reading difficulty in the classroom. Also, when different formulas are applied to the same material,

*Reprinted with permission of W. John Harker and the International Reading Association, *Journal of Reading,* 1977, *21,* 126–130.

they often yield different readability levels. Further confusion arises when students find materials with relatively low readability levels to be more difficult than expected, and the reverse.

The reasons for these anomalies lie in the nature of readability formulas themselves. Since methods for determining vocabulary difficulty and sentence length vary among formulas, as do the mathematical calculations used, the lack of consistency among the reading levels derived from different formulas is not surprising. And since formulas do not account for the complexity of ideas contained in reading materials, instances of "easy" materials proving difficult are understandable, since unfamiliar, complex concepts can be expressed using elementary vocabulary and short, simple sentences.

Readability formulas do provide a relatively quick guide to reading difficulty if their shortcomings are recognized and they are used together with other criteria. For example, *Man in the Tropics* checks out at a grade nine reading level using the Fry formula but at a grade twelve level using the SMOG formula. About the only conclusion the teacher can draw from this information is that this material may be too difficult for most eighth graders. (The teacher may also be quietly thankful he is not teaching grades nine, ten, eleven, or twelve, in which case he would not know which formula to believe, or whether to believe either of them!)

Concept Load

According to Piaget (1971), it is only as students enter the period of formal operations from about age eleven onward that their conceptual development has advanced to the stage where they can internally build and manipulate abstract ideas without reference to concrete examples. This suggests that secondary students have only recently acquired the ability to comprehend abstract concepts, and that the nature and number of concepts introduced in content materials must be recognized as a major determiner of reading difficulty.

Concept load can be estimated by establishing the number of concepts introduced and their degree of complexity and level of abstraction. An examination of *Man in the Tropics* reveals that this book is likely to prove conceptually difficult for most eighth graders. The content of the book is beyond most students' direct experience. Moreover, students encounter a virtual avalanche of abstract concepts relating to geology, vegetation, climate, population, and agriculture, each concept being described by new technical vocabulary. This evidence supports the conclusion drawn from readability formulas that this book is going to be heavy going for most students in grade eight social studies.

Background Information

Since background information contributes directly to concept development, students' background information is closely related to concept load in determining the reading difficulty of instructional materials.

The teacher's first task is to determine the author's assumptions about students' background information and their previous learning experiences. Are these assumptions consistent with the background that students can be expected to bring to the new learning tasks? If these assumptions are not consistent, students will lack a context for new learning and comprehension difficulties will result.

Searching for the authors' assumptions about students' background information pertaining to the content of *Man in the Tropics* proves to be a futile exercise. Aside from a passing reference in the preface to "the range of ability of the students who will use this book," the authors make no direct reference to the students for whom their text is intended. One can only infer from the heavy concept load imposed by the content of their text that the authors assume considerable background information on the part of the reader.

The extent to which students will in fact possess this information can best be determined by the teacher. The importance of the teacher's role in deciding the appropriateness of instructional materials is highlighted here. In the case of *Man in the Tropics*, the eighth grade social studies teacher who is familiar with the social studies curriculum will be in the best position to determine what background information she can legitimately expect students to bring to this text based on their previous school experience.

Organization

Assuming that instructional materials present concepts consistent with students' backgrounds, one must also consider whether these concepts are organized to guide learning.

The teacher should check whether the internal organization of instructional materials provides a smooth continuity of ideas. Are concepts developed sequentially? Does one idea lead logically to the next? The provision of valid content alone does not ensure that this content will be organized in a clear and logical manner which is apparent to the reader.

Turning to *Man in the Tropics*, one finds a poorly organized text. While rich in content area information, the organization of this information fails to guide the development of students' geographical concepts. Rather than organizing their text around geographical concepts and developing these sequentially in order of their complexity and difficulty, the authors have chosen to organize their text around the different geographical regions studied. The result is that the stage of conceptual development and the amount of background information assumed to be possessed by students reading the first chapter are essentially the same as what are assumed in the final chapter; no development in learning through reading is provided for.

Format and Style

The format and style of instructional materials are also key considerations in determining reading difficulty. Obviously, students will read attractively laid out, colorful, and well illustrated instructional material in a more purposive manner and with greater success than they will "textbookish" material which promises little more than boredom.

Equally important is the author's style. Is the material written in a ponderous, overly academic style, or does the author project an empathy for the reading and learning tasks confronting students by writing in a manner which engages their attention and guides their thinking? No dilution of content or conceptual rigor need result from instructional materials written in approachable and appealing styles.

A further consideration is the provision of special features to aid learning. Graphic aids, illustrations, maps, glossaries, and appendices all assist student learning when they are well integrated with the text of the material. The specific nature of these aids will vary widely from one content area to another. In assessing the effectiveness of these aids, the teacher should check that they are located where they are needed within the material, and not relegated to the back of the book or placed several pages away from their optimally useful location in the text.

The format and style of *Man in the Tropics* are adequate but not outstanding. There are ample illustrations, and the text is written directly to the student, thereby giving the student a sense of active involvement in the material. Special features abound in the text, but a careful examination of them reveals flaws in their placement and content.

For example, the first paragraph of the first chapter refers the student to a figure which does not appear until three pages later, and further on in the text the student is directed to compare the facial features of two racial groups in a series of photographs, only to find just one of the groups represented!

The five criteria for materials selection outlined here are suggestive, not prescriptive. Additional or different criteria may be indicated in specific learning situations and in particular content area. However, the application of these five criteria will give a general framework for selecting instructional materials which support student learning of content through reading.

Should the grade eight social studies teacher adopt *Man in the Tropics?* Ultimately, the decision must be based on knowledge of the students. But the evidence revealed by the analysis illustrated here strongly suggests that this text will make difficult reading for most eighth graders. Readability, concept load, assumed background information, organization, and certain aspects of format all contribute to a difficult text. Significantly, no one category of information is sufficient to classify accurately this text. But taken together, the information from the various categories presents a composite picture of a piece of instructional material which may be all too typical in its inadequate recognition of the learning needs of the students for whom it is intended.

References

Carswell, Gordon E., Robert Morrow and B.C. Honeybone. *Man in the Tropics.* Toronto, Ont.: Bellhaven House, 1968.

Fry, Edward. "A Readability Formula That Saves Time." *Journal of Reading,* vol. 11, no. 7 (April 1968), pp. 513–16.

Klare, George R. *The Measurement of Readability.* Ames, Iowa: Iowa State University Press, 1963.

McLaughlin, Harry G. "SMOG Grading—A New Readability Formula." *Journal of Reading,* vol. 12, no. 8 (May 1969), pp. 639–46.

Piaget, Jean. *Science of Education and the Psychology of the Child.* New York, N.Y.: Viking Press, 1971.

The Student Connection:
Content ⇢ Students ⇠ Materials

Donna E. Alvermann
University of Northern Iowa

Ernest K. Dishner
University of Northern Iowa

How often have you heard someone emphatically state, "I teach students—not skills and content!" While we would count ourselves among those who support such a humanistic perspective on teaching, we would also question the assumptions behind the statement. Is it possible, for instance, to teach secondary students without regard for major concepts in the content areas? We think not. Nor do we believe that students learn in a vacuum, devoid of materials that, when properly selected and used, can serve as vehicles for content and skills. Rather, we propose that teachers keep students clearly in the forefront of their thinking as they plan instructionally, making students the "connection", so to speak, between that which is to be learned (content) and the means by which it is to be learned (materials).

The task is not a simple one. There are no easy solutions. In fact it is important to realize that no formula, no set of guidelines currently in existence, nor any soon-to-be-discovered remedy will make the task any easier in the future. Reality, not pessimism, guides our reasoning in this matter. However, what the authors of this article *can* offer the reader is an overview of some established as well as new practices in reading that are thought to enable the teacher to facilitate the student connection.

What follows, then, is a discussion of the important match between the subject matter *content,* that which is to be learned; the *student* and what he or she brings to the learning task in the way of life experiences (knowledge and skills); and instructional *materials,* a primary source of knowledge. Finally, an attempt will be made to bring these factors together through a discussion of some possible implications for classroom instruction. The following diagram (fig. 1) represents the important relationship of students to content, content to materials, and materials to students. The interface that results from combining all three elements provides the framework in which to discuss instructional implications.

Content

Various guidelines/sources should be used to determine the specific content to be taught in a given classroom. State and local curriculum guides provide an initial source for course content. Local curriculum committees and departmental faculties help to further shape the specific course content. However, the ultimate decision as to what content will be taught, and importantly, what specifics will be emphasized, rests with the classroom teacher. Consideration of content must precede material selection. At the same time, content cannot be considered separate from the student population to be served.

Written especially for inclusion in this text.

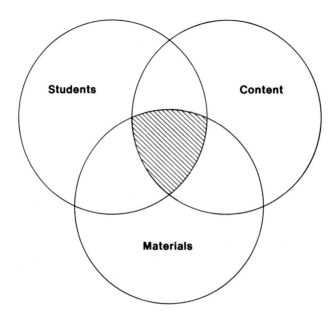

Figure 1. Comprehension: an interface of student knowledge factors.

Herber (1978) provided some important guidelines for decision-making relative to content instruction. It is important to note that the following discussion links content selection with a consideration of that student population.

Identification of concepts and process

Preliminary to all good instruction is the time teachers spend thinking about what it is they want their students to learn. Traditionally, middle and secondary teachers have considered this phase of the preparation period as tantamount to identifying the major concepts that must be taught in their subject area. However, preparation time includes an additional dimension when Herber's (1978) idea of functional reading instruction is considered. In his approach to teaching reading in the content areas, content determines process (reading skills). "That is, both the concepts which are developed and the manner in which the related information and ideas have been organized and presented in the information source will dictate the reading/reasoning process a reader must apply to that source in order to read it successfully" (p. 26). Preparation time viewed from this perspective, then, would include analyzing content to establish concepts as well as identifying reading processes required to learn these concepts.

Perhaps it is important here to make a brief comment to those preservice and inservice teachers who operate in predominantly "activity-based" subjects, e.g., music, art, and physical education, to name a few. The same process described above applies to those subject areas as well. That is, during the preparation of a unit, one must identify the major understandings that students should possess at the end of that unit; but, in addition, an activity-based instructor might also ask, "What major activities should my students be able to perform as a result of my teachings?" The logical question, then, to follow would be, "How will my students learn to perform these activities?" The answer to that question will result in the process, i.e., the instructional strategies that will be utilized to accomplish the objectives(s).

It is certainly not realistic to believe that all concepts are of equal importance. It is equally naive to believe that all vocabulary terms related to a single concept are of equal importance or that all terms will be mastered equally well by all students. A systematic approach to vocabulary selection is needed that results in the "realistic" teaching of content.

Selection of vocabulary terms

Once the concepts and reading processes required to understand these concepts have been identified, decisions must be made concerning the selection of vocabulary to teach. Since instructional time is limited, it is important for the teachers first to prioritize the identified concepts. One might categorize each concept into one of three groupings—(1) most important, (2) important, and (3) least important. Those concepts that are deemed "most important" are those that everyone in the class should master—they are essential to the subject as a whole and likely will serve as prerequisite knowledge for future learnings. Those concepts labeled "least important" are reserved for the best students. Often times these understandings can be taught to the high achievers through individual assignments or through small research group activities. Finally, the "important" concepts fall somewhere in between the other two categories.

Once the concepts have been prioritized, the teacher can utilize Herber's (1978) four criteria for separating those words that must be carefully taught from those that can be presented in other ways. He recommended that teachers first identify and list all vocabulary terms relating directly to the concepts to be taught. Stated another way, the classroom teacher should identify those terms essential to a description/explanation of each concept. Obviously, then, the very act of prioritizing concepts has resulted in a prioritizing of vocabulary terms.

Second, the list should be narrowed by applying the criterion of relevant value—in other words, select those key terms that contribute most to students' understanding of a concept.

Third, as a result of either formal or informal techniques for assessing students' background experiences, the teacher should be in a position to narrow the list even further so that only those terms for which the students have no prior understanding are included. The eliminated words can be used in reinforcement activities where they provide contextual clues for helping students unlock meanings to unknown words.

Finally, Herber recommended that the last criterion be applied in two steps. In the first step, words that appear both on the list of remaining terms and in the textbook reading assignment should be selected. The second step of the selection process enables teachers to facilitate students' independence in acquiring word meaning in the future. In this step, where emphasis is placed on skills instruction rather than content, teachers should select those words that lend themselves most readily to teaching through the use of context, structural analysis, and reference sources. The entire process is not as time consuming as it might first appear. Herber pointed out that most teachers, given practice, will soon be able to simultaneously apply the first three criteria and thus have adequate time left to devote to the final criterion.

Students

Since much of what secondary students are expected to learn must be read and extracted from textbooks, it is essential that their experiences be at least somewhat congruent with the author's experiences. Specifically, students must be able to bring some background knowledge to the content and, furthermore, be able to recognize different types of structural organization used by the author.

Content congruency

Whether students ultimately understand their text assignments will depend in part on whether they are able to predict the important elements within the content. According to Sorenson (1980), readers who have appropriate experiences will be able to make predictions on a global (meaning) level as well as on a lower order (vocabulary, syntax, orthography) level. In expanding McCabe's (1980) formula, Sorenson (1980, p. 62) viewed a reader's anticipatory behavior in the following manner:

$$Ra = (F) \, C \, E_u \text{ meaning } + \, C \, E_u \text{ vocabulary } + \, C \, E_u \text{ syntax } + \, C \, E_u \text{ graphic features}$$

That is, anticipatory reading (Ra) is a function (F) of the amount or units (u) of prior experience (E) that a reader has that are congruent (C) with the author's experiences on both the global and lower order levels. Psycholinguistically speaking, students who engage in the anticipatory reading process will need to use fewer visual cues as they sample the text in order to accept or reject their anticipations. This should result in greater fluency (hence, better comprehension) since readers will be concentrating on chunking meaning units rather than attending to individual words.

Teachers who understand what constitutes anticipatory reading place themselves in a better position to predict those features of a textbook assignment that will most likely interfere with students' comprehension. Once having identified potential incongruencies, teachers are then able to intervene with appropriate instructional strategies.

Structure congruency

Whether students make use of the author's organizational structure will also have an effect on what is ultimately comprehended and recalled. Meyer (1979), for example, described a number of studies involving ninth graders' recall of expository passages. Most of the students who were rated high in comprehension ability used the same top-level structure (e.g., descriptive, comparison/contrast, cause/effect) as the author when they recalled information from the passage. Furthermore, those same students remembered more of the main ideas and supporting details a week later than those students who did not use the author's top-level structure. In contrast to the high comprehenders, most ninth graders with poor comprehension skills approached the task without an effective organizing strategy. For those students, it appeared to be a matter of simply trying to remember everything, a formidable task for even the best of readers!

Materials

Although content area teachers have identified the major concepts and the reading processes required to help students learn those concepts, planning is not complete until the textbook has also been analyzed. Sometimes in making textbook assignments, subject area teachers attribute ideas to a textbook that are not actually there. Herber (1978) noted that this phenomenon is understandable in view of the fact that teachers, as experts in their subject areas, unconsciously supply the missing information. The problem arises when teachers *assume* that students will glean the same information from the assigned reading. To eliminate the resultant confusion and frustration, Herber suggested that teachers analyze the text by placing themselves in the position of their students. Reading the text as hypothetical students, teachers will then be able to identify the gaps that occur due to limited meaning vocabulary and lack of experience in the subject area. In this way, teacher expectations of what concepts the students should gain from their reading will be based on fact rather than on assumption.

Following are several suggestions for conducting a content analysis of the assigned textbook.

(1) Through a process identified by Gagné (1970) as "chaining", teachers can determine if sufficient *details* exist in the text for grouping into *concepts*. In turn, it is necessary to determine if the *concepts* are developed clearly enough for students to use in deriving *principles*. The validity of this entire process rests, quite naturally, on how well the text and curriculum objectives match.

(2) Tierney, Mosenthal, and Kantor (1980) proposed that teachers analyze the purposes for which a text is intended. This task enables teachers to determine whether their purpose for making an assignment can best be served by the text in question. For a complete explanation of this type of content analysis, the reader may want to refer to the Tierney and Pearson article in this book.

(3) Perhaps one of the most thorough content analyses can be made using Meyer's (1979) guidelines for textbook selection. First, content area texts should assist students in determining what is essential information versus nonessential information. Texts with clearly identifiable top-level structures provide the best source of this information. Second, textbooks should contain preview sections or introductions to alert the reader to the main ideas. Likewise, summary sections are needed to repeat those main ideas. Third, titles and subheadings should focus on the main ideas and explicitly signal the author's top-level structure. For example, a section comparing the French Revolution to the American Revolution should be titled "Revolutions in France and America: Did They Differ?" rather than "The French and American Revolutions." The first title draws the student's attention to the author's top-level structure, that of comparison/contrast. Fourth, content area textbooks used with average and below average readers should contain explicit signaling of relationships within

sentences. For instance, "Because steamboats were no longer able to compete with trains, the Erie Canal fell into disuse" is preferable to "Steamboats were no longer able to compete with trains. The Erie Canal fell into disuse." As Nelson (1978) pointed out, "shortening sentences may *increase* the difficulty of the reading task by rendering explicit relationships obscure" (p. 623). Fifth, if concepts considered important by the teacher are buried in details, it is imperative that additional material be used to emphasize the concepts. Finally, Meyer suggested that teachers should "avoid text where topics are discussed primarily by listing attributes with unspecified interrelationships" (p. 11). Ironically, whereas this type of top-level structure (descriptive) is the least facilitative for the reader (Brandt, 1978; Meyer & Freedle, 1979), it reportedly occurs most frequently in secondary textbooks (Bartlett, 1978; Niles, 1965). A study strategy found useful in compensating for text organized with a descriptive top-level structure will be discussed in the last section of this article.

Since the discussion thus far has focused on the textbook as an instructional resource, it seems appropriate to remind readers of the variety of other material available, such as magazines, films, videocassettes, transparencies, and simulation kits. In fact, with little or no modification, most of Harker's (1977) five criteria for selecting content area texts can be used in making decisions about these alternative resources as well.

Implications for Instruction

Up to this point we have conveniently separated the factors that influence how content area teachers teach students into three categories—content, students, and materials. Quite naturally, these categories are not mutually exclusive. For instance, we select certain content words for careful teaching based on our knowledge of students and whether or not the words appear in their textbooks. Likewise, we are apt to focus reading assignments on concepts that we deem important to teaching the curriculum—and (we hope) the students. The following examples are an attempt to illustrate how the three interacting factors can be translated into instructional practices by content area teachers interested in facilitating the student connection.

Example 1

As mentioned earlier, teachers frequently discover that there is not sufficient time to carefully teach all the vocabulary terms that they consider essential for students' understanding of textbook assignments. Consequently, many content area teachers have turned to the structured overview as a vehicle for helping students perceive relationships between familiar and unfamiliar words. Originally conceived as a means for helping students develop a sense of the structure of concepts within a curriculum area (Barron, 1969), the structured overview quite naturally facilitates students' knowledge of how textbooks are structured as well. Thus, the meaning of *mercantilism* can be developed at the same time that essential elements from a textbook chapter are highlighted in this abbreviated version of a structured overview (fig. 2). Since research indicates that students benefit from being able to predict, prior to reading, those elements in text that are important (Brown & Smiley, 1977; Collins et al., 1977), an overview such as that shown in figure 2 would seem to make good sense.

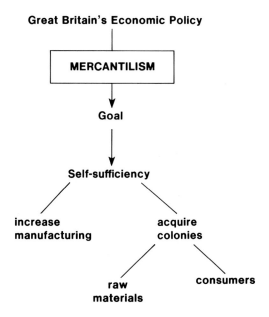

Figure 2. An abbreviated example of a structured overview.

There is even some evidence suggesting that poor readers may benefit from being told directly what is and is not essential in text (Pichert, 1979). Also, if an old adage is to be believed, "one picture is worth a thousand words!"

Example 2

An idea derived from working with a group of tenth graders (Alvermann, 1980) further illustrates the versatility of the structured overview. Briefly, these students were provided with a comparison/contrast structured overview to compensate for the effect of text that was organized with a descriptive top-level structure. A typical situation in which this strategy might prove effective can be illustrated using a secondary social studies text. In *A History of Our American Republic* (Laidlaw, 1979), the growth of sectionalism in the United States is described by first listing details concerning the industrial Northeast. Nine pages later, similar categories of information are related to the agricultural South. Finally, after seven more pages, the growing West is described, again with similar categories. By presenting a comparison/contrast overview (fig. 3) prior to making a reading assignment, teachers can increase the probability that students will anticipate essential text elements *and* perceive relationships among the separate sections of the textbook. Furthermore, if students are encouraged to contribute to the overview, teachers may find they have a custom-made diagnostic tool for determining whether the readers' experiences are congruent with the author's experiences.

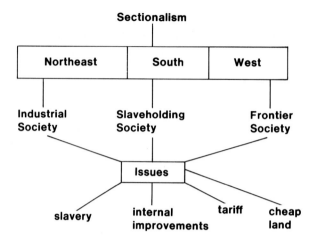

Figure 3. An example of a comparison/contrast overview.

Example 3

For textbooks to be effective instructional tools, both readers and writers must possess certain proficiencies. Teaching students to recognize that authors communicate for certain purposes to certain audiences is part of the implicit contractual agreement to which Tierney and LaZansky (1980) refer when they speak about the rights and responsibilities of readers and writers. What better way for students to learn to recognize this *implicit* agreement than for teachers to make it *explicit*. How teachers might go about helping students appreciate the reader-writer agreement may be best understood by way of example.

Consider the hypothetical situation in which a textbook author is faced with the choice of presenting an esoteric term or several commonplace substitutes (Adams & Bruce, 1980):

(a) The discovery of a number of fossilized porbeagles in Kansas is intriguing.
(b) The discovery of a number of fossilized mackerel sharks in Kansas is intriguing.
(c) The discovery in Kansas of the fossilized bones of a number of large, ocean-dwelling fish is intriguing.

As Adams and Bruce pointed out, the author was forced to relinquish the specific meaning of the intriguing discovery when simpler words were substituted for the precise term, porbeagle. If, perchance, sentence (a) rather than (b) or (c) were to appear in a high school biology text, teachers would need to discuss with students the purpose for the author's particular choice of words. Once students develop a sense of why an author writes in a particular way, they are less apt to complain about "the impossible text."

Summary

The three factors that influence how content area teachers teach students—content, materials, and students themselves—have provided the focus of this article. Although each is essential in its own right, together they contribute to the all-important interface that results due to the overlapping relationships among the three. This is as it should be. Moreover, teachers who view the interface as fertile ground for instructional planning can be assured that they are making headway in achieving the "student connection."

References

Adams, M., & Bruce, B. *Background knowledge and reading comprehension.* (Reading Educ. Rep. 13). Champaign, Ill.: University of Illinois, 1980.

Alvermann, D. E. *The effects of graphic organizers, textual organization, and reading comprehension level on recall of expository prose.* Unpublished doctoral dissertation, Syracuse University, 1980.

Barron, R. The use of vocabulary as an advance organizer. In H. L. Herber and P. L. Sanders (Eds.), *Research in reading in the content areas: First year report.* Syracuse, N.Y.: Reading and Language Art Center, 1969.

Bartlett, B. J. *Top-level structure as an organizational strategy for recall of classroom text.* Unpublished doctoral dissertation, Arizona State University, 1978.

Brandt, D. M. *Prior knowledge of the author's schema and the comprehension of prose.* Unpublished doctoral dissertation, Arizona State University, 1978.

Brown, A. L., & Smiley, S. S. Rating the importance of structural units of prose passages: A problem of metacognitive development. *Child Development,* 1977, *48,* 1–8.

Brown, A. L., & Smiley, S. S. The development of strategies for studying texts. *Child Development,* 1978, *49,* 1076–1088.

Collins, A., Brown, A. L., Morgan, J. L., and Brewer, W. F. *The analysis of reading tasks and texts.* (Tech. Rep. 43). Champaign, Ill.: University of Illinois, Center for the Study of Reading, 1977.

Gagné, R. M. *The conditions of knowledge.* New York: Harcourt, Brace, Jovanovich, 1966.

Harker, W. J. Selecting instructional materials for content area reading. *Journal of Reading,* 1977, *21,* 126–130.

Herber, H. L. *Teaching reading in content areas* (2nd ed.). Englewood Cliffs, N.J.: Prentice-Hall, Inc., 1978.

McCabe, P. P. Formula for compromise. *Journal of Reading,* 1980, *23,* 488–489.

Meyer, B. J. F. *Structure of prose: Implications for teachers of reading.* (Research Report 3). Tempe: Arizona State University, 1979.

Meyer, B. J. F., & Freedle, R. O. *Effects of discourse type on the recall of young and old adults.* Manuscript submitted for publication, 1979.

Nelson, J. Readability: Some cautions for the content area teacher. *Journal of Reading,* 1978, *21,* 620–625.

Niles, O. S. Organization perceived. In H. L. Herber (Ed.), *Developing study skills in secondary schools.* Newark, Del.: International Reading Association, 1965.

Pichert, J. W. *Sensitivity to what is important in prose.* (Tech. Rep. 149). Champaign, Ill.: University of Illinois, 1979.

Sorenson, N. L. Expanded formula for anticipatory reading. *Journal of Reading,* 1980, *24,* 62–63.

Tierney, R. J., & LaZansky, J. *The rights and responsibilities of readers and writers: A contractual agreement.* (Reading Educ. Rep. 15). Champaign, Ill.: University of Illinois, 1980.

Tierney, R. J., Mosenthal, J., & Kantor, R. N. *Some classroom applications of text analysis: Toward improving text selection and use.* (Reading Educ. Rep. 17). Champaign, Ill.: University of Illinois, 1980.

5

Assessing Reading Needs in the Content Classroom

For instruction to be maximally effective, teachers must be able to assess their students' knowledge and skills so that they can bridge the gap between what students bring to the learning task and what they will be learning. Such assessment will provide a foundation upon which teachers can build appropriate instruction. Without such assessment, teachers will be forced to make uninformed assumptions about what students do and do not know and what they can and cannot do. The effective means of obtaining the information necessary to make appropriate instructional decisions concerning students is informal assessment that is administered silently, rather than orally, to the total class simultaneously and is based upon representative text materials that students will be utilizing.

Rakes and McWilliams provide a rationale for informal diagnosis in the content areas. Specific techniques such as the group reading inventory and the cloze inventory are described.

Vaughan and Gaus pose an alternative to traditional informal testing techniques. Several suggestions are offered to teachers who seek to gather diagnostic information concerning their students.

Assessing Reading Skills in the Content Areas

Thomas A. Rakes
Memphis State University

Lana McWilliams
Memphis State University

The use of textbooks in most subject area classrooms is a generally accepted practice in schools across the country. Each fall teachers begin their classes using one or two textbooks for an enrollment of students whose reading achievement levels vary greatly. This paper deals directly with the issue of evaluating how well students can read textbook material. Three procedures are particularly appropriate for use during the first few class meetings and perhaps later, as a follow-up during the spring of the same school year.

A Need for Informal Diagnosis in the Content Areas

It would not be unusual to find a range of reading ability among students that may vary as many as six to eight grade levels in some classrooms. Such a range of achievement can present a difficult problem for teachers who use one basic textbook.

Textbook reading has presented difficulties even for good readers who are considered to be reading on or above grade level. Many textbooks currently in use are written on a vocabulary, concept, and readability level several years above the grade level in which they are being used. In addition to high readability levels, there is a problem created by the expository style of writing. This type of reading is not only more difficult for many students, but it is also less interesting to read than material written in a narrative style. Most youngsters learn to read using a narrative type reader, commonly referred to as basal readers. Beginning in the middle grades a transition from basal to content textbook reading is usually assumed.

In the past, upper grade teachers have been primarily trained to teach content and have not felt they had either time or knowledge to diagnose and teach the reading skills required by their subject area. Since the 1960s, reading authorities have been recommending informal assessment techniques with increasing popularity. However, these teacher-made tests have not been widely used by content area teachers. With the push in the late 1970s and early 80s for competency testing, informal classroom techniques may be dealt another setback. The new call for competency and achievement testing does not, however, contribute directly to classroom instructional practices. Formal tests, by their very nature, require the need for external scoring, delayed reporting of results and—for classroom impact—the need for curricular alterations to "match" the perceived weaknesses found by the tests. Many

Written especially for inclusion in this text.

formal testing programs are designed to provide a gross effectiveness index rather than specific information about student strengths and weaknesses. The formal tests that do offer individual profiles are not, in most cases, tied directly to the books or other instructional programs currently used in a given classroom. Informal test procedures such as those discussed in this paper are not intended to replace formal testing but, instead, to provide practical, immediate information not otherwise available.

The need for assessing reading performance in content areas can hardly be denied. Our primary concern is how to structure a group diagnostic test so that results will provide direction for further teaching considerations. The means of assessment must be content specific, easily constructed and scored, group administered, and representative of the type of reading skills that students would be expected to use in their science, history, or other subject area classes. For these purposes, a description of three types of instruments is provided for use in content area materials. Each of the three types of procedures may be adapted for use in middle through high school level classes.

Surveying Content Area Reading Interests

Reader interest is vital to maintain comprehension of nearly any written material. For interest surveys to be helpful, we must be able to assume that the information obtained is reasonably accurate. For this reason it is suggested that interest surveys be administered in an untimed and relatively brief format of no more than one or two pages in length. Teachers should keep in mind that the purpose of such surveys is to gain some indication of reader interest and/or knowledge about a particular subject area.

Content interest inventories are generally of three types: An open-ended projective type; a more structured, directed-response type; or an instrument using titles and annotations for a specific subject area. Projective instruments usually take less time to construct, but more time is required to score and interpret responses. Ten to fifteen statements may be used to elicit responses. The following examples could appear as a portion of a history interest inventory.

1. If I were to name three famous leaders from earlier days, they would be _____ _____ .

2. The time period that I know most about in our nation's history is _____ _____ .

3. In the past my history classes have been _____ _____ .

4. If I had the chance to study only one time period in history, it would be _____ _____ .

For those persons who are interested in a more content-directed survey, figure 1 presents a model for English teachers.

1. Listed below are several areas of study in English classes. Indicate your preferences for study in these areas by placing the number 1 by the topic you most prefer to study, 2 by the next most preferred topic, etc.

_____ drama

_____ poetry

_____ essay writing

_____ short stories

_____ parts of speech

_____ writing social and business letters

_____ creative writing

_____ history of the language

_____ novels

_____ punctuation

_____ biography

_____ vocabulary study

_____ sentence diagramming

2. List the subjects you are now taking in rank order from most interesting to least interesting.

3a. If you had a choice, would you choose to a take another course in English?

A. Yes

B. No

C. Undecided

b. Write a short paragraph about your answer to 3a.

4. Listed below are several pairs of activities. Look at the pairs, one at a time, and draw a circle around the activity you would find most interesting of the two.

1. solving an algebra problem

diagramming a sentence

2. reading about Lee's surrender at Appomattox

writing about the character of Huckleberry Finn

3. acting out a part in a play

carrying out a laboratory experiment in conduction of electricity

4. writing an original short story

learning to use a slide rule

5. seeing a filmstrip about the structure of the atom

reading a novel about World War II

6. measuring distance in metrics

tracing route of Cherokee Indians during early days of America

7. seeing a film about the customs of the Japanese

attending an exhibit of and lecture about birds

5. Put a check by those things you have done in the last two months because you chose to and not because you had to.

_____ wrote a personal letter

_____ attended a play

_____ wrote a creative story

_____ read a novel

_____ wrote a poem

_____ wrote a business letter

_____ attended a concert

_____ spent your own money on a magazine

_____ visited a museum

_____ drew or painted a picture

_____ listened to an informative lecture

_____ watched an educational TV program

Of the things you checked above, which did you enjoy doing the most?

Figure 1. Content interest inventory—English. (Reprinted with permission from Kendall/Hunt Publishing Company, *Content Inventories:* English, Social Studies and Science, 1979, 212–214.)

6. Indicate whether you have read any works of the authors listed below by placing a check mark beside the name. In the blank beside the author's name, write the title of the work you have read.

_____	1. Mark Twain	_____
_____	2. William Shakespeare	_____
_____	3. Edgar Allen Poe	_____
_____	4. Eugene O'Neill	_____
_____	5. Ernest Hemingway	_____
_____	6. John Steinbeck	_____
_____	7. Charles Dickens	_____
_____	8. Jack London	_____
_____	9. James Michener	_____
_____	10. Maureen Daly	_____
_____	11. Robert Frost	_____
_____	12. Alfred Lord Tennyson	_____
_____	13. Carl Sandburg	_____
_____	14. Robert Heinlein	_____

7. Indicate below which type of reading you prefer:

_____ 1. adventure

_____ 2. science fiction

_____ 3. mystery

_____ 4. factual accounts of historical events

_____ 5. biography

_____ 6. poetry

_____ 7. drama

_____ 8. animal stories

_____ 9. romance

_____ 10. "how-to" books

Figure 1. Continued.

A third type of interest survey involves having students rank their preferences for a listing of titles accompanied by brief descriptions about the work. The reader's responses should reflect the type of topics that interest each respondent. Vaughan and Gaus (1978) recommend a pupil interview as a follow-up to the ranking process.

Interest surveys may be constructed using the current textbook or a previous text for reference points. When used for early semester data gathering, teachers can sometimes recognize details about how students feel toward the subject area and, to some extent, how much they know about the subject. Information from interest inventories should be summarized on a whole-class basis as well as reviewed for individual student comments. Students are often very honest and, perhaps, painfully direct about their feelings toward certain academic subjects. Without a survey of some type, teachers will never know the extent of interest—or disinterest—that students have about their studies.

Using a Group Reading Inventory

Group reading inventories (GRI) are useful for obtaining information about how well students can read their textbooks and for isolating specific textbook handling and comprehension difficulties. Administered in two parts, a GRI is a group test constructed from textbook material that students have not previously read. Part one of the test is used to measure a reader's ability to use book parts, illustrative material, and reference skills (See figure 2).

Part two of a GRI is designed to measure a reader's ability to answer comprehension questions after reading a portion from a textbook.

Part One: Using Book Parts

Introduction: These questions are designed to help you understand the organization of your text and to enable you to use it more effectively. You may use your text in answering the questions.

1. Where would you look to locate a short story in the text if you could not recall the title or the author?
   a) Glossary
   b) Table of Contents
   c) Literary Terms and Techniques
   d) Index of Authors and Titles

2. If you came across the word "demagoguery" in your reading in the text, where would you look *first* for a definition?
   a) Table of Contents
   b) Literary Terms and Techniques
   c) Glossary
   d) The Composition and Language Program

3. The study and discussion questions for most of the literary works in the text are found:
   a) in the Table of Contents.
   b) after each selection.
   c) in the Index of Fine Art.
   d) immediately before each selection.

4. If you were asked to define "simile," where would you look *first*?
   a) Glossary
   b) Table of Contents
   c) Preface
   d) Literary Terms and Techniques

5. If you were asked to list some of the works of John Steinbeck, but you could not remember any of the titles, where would you look?
   a) Index of Fine Art
   b) Index of Authors and Titles
   c) Table of Contents
   d) Picture Acknowledgments

6. Where would you look to locate the page number of the special indexes?
   a) Glossary
   b) Table of Contents
   c) the last page of the text
   d) Preface

7. If you were told to read "A Narrow Fellow in the Grass" and you did not know its genre or author, where would you look?
   a) Exercises in the Text
   b) Glossary
   c) Table of Contents
   d) Index of Authors and Titles

Figure 2.

8. Where would you find reading and writing topics for poetry?
   a) in the Table of Contents under Poetry
   b) Literary Terms and Techniques
   c) Practice in Reading and Writing: The Novel
   d) Exercises in the Text

9. Where is "Practice in Reading and Writing" located in each chapter?
   a) at the beginning of each chapter
   b) after each literary work
   c) at the end of each chapter
   d) before each literary work

10. If you wished to find detailed information and background material on each genre, where would you look?
    a) in Literary Terms and Techniques
    b) in the Glossary
    c) at the end of each chapter dealing with that genre

11. If you wished to locate a picture of Vincent Van Gogh, where would you look in the text?
    a) Index of Authors and Titles
    b) Picture Acknowledgments
    c) Index of Fine Art
    d) Art Credits

12. If you were asked to find an *example* of "alliteration" in a literary work, where would you look *first?*
    a) Exercises in the Text
    b) The Composition and Language Program
    c) Literary Terms and Techniques
    d) Glossary

13. Look at your table of contents and give, in order, a brief description of its major divisions and subdivisions.

Part Two: Group Reading Inventory—English

Introduction: Read this selection to find out how the early novel developed and the various forms it took.

The Novel

One of the nicest pleasures in life for many people is to curl up in a comfortable place and read a good novel. Novels have been in existence for a relatively short time, compared to other forms of literature. For example, the drama has existed for centuries, whereas the novel came into being only about three hundred years ago. Basically, a novel can be defined as a long story, written in prose, and having many characters and more than one plot.   1

Prior to the development of the novel in its present form, stories were often written in verse. These verse stories were known as "romances" during the Middle Ages. Usually the stories revolved around characters such as kings, queens, knights-in-armor, and other heroes. Rarely were ordinary people and their problems ever subjects for romances—they were considered unfit subject matter for literature.   2

During the Renaissance, dating between the fourteenth and sixteenth centuries, people began to see that ordinary people and their lives could be interesting and meaningful subjects for stories. There were also many other economic and scientific changes occurring that convinced people to change their point of view about life and literature.   3

Figure 2. Continued.

Among these important changes were the geographical expansions of many countries, which led to increased trade in far-off places. Merchants were acquiring wealth and moving into larger cities. These were people who were practical and realistic, and they wanted to read about people like themselves rather than make-believe heroes and worlds of fantasy. Also, the newly invented and continuallly improved printing press was making it possible for large quantities of books to be printed and available at relatively low cost for everyone to read.   4

Early Novels

To please the new readers, storytellers began writing their tales in prose. They discovered that the adventures of ordinary people could be just as exciting as the tales of heroic deeds by extraordinary people. Often the characters in the new literature were former servants who wandered from place to place, becoming involved in some honest and some dishonest adventures while seeking their fortunes. The term "picaresque," from the Spanish word *picaro* meaning "rascal," came to be used to describe the humorous tales of these rogues' adventures.   5

An English author, Daniel Defoe, was among the first to write about an ordinary trader, shipwrecked on a desert island. This eighteenth century novel, *Robinson Crusoe,* describes all the human emotions and adventures Crusoe experiences while on the island. Another English author, later in the eighteenth century, also chose an ordinary person to center his story around. Henry Fielding wrote *Joseph Andrews,* in which he describes the adventures of a young servant as he wandered about meeting different people. Novels that are stories of heroes traveling about, having exciting adventures, are called "adventure" or "journey" novels. There are many of these types of novels in both English and American literature. Some examples include *David Copperfield, Oliver Twist, Huckleberry Finn,* and *Tom Sawyer.*   6

The "plot" novel was another type of novel developed in eighteenth century England. These novels, unlike the adventure novels, are usually set in only one place and have fewer characters. Their compelling stories are usually about love between men and women, fathers and sons, mothers and daughter, and between friends. These works help readers better understand how other people, like themselves, feel, think, and react to others and to their environments. The customs and problems of real people in real life have typically been reflected in novels through the period of time in which they have passed.   7

Comprehension Questions

The Novel

1. What is a novel?

2. What was the "picaresque" novel?

3. Approximately when did the novel come into being?

4. What is a "plot" novel?

5. How did the invention of the printing press affect literature?

6. What are "romances?"

7. How does the "plot" novel differ from the "adventure" novel?

Figure 2. Continued.

8. If our society were only composed of the very rich and the very poor, with no middle class, what type(s) of novel(s) might we have today?

9. How did exploration affect the merchants?

10. What type of modern literature do you think may have been an outgrowth of space exploration?

11. What are two examples of "adventure" or "journey" novels in English or American literature?

12. How might the mass media (television, newspapers, etc.) negatively affect the novel today?

13. Why did the novel develop the way it did?

14. What social topics might be found in modern novels today?

Figure 2. Continued.

Test construction—instructions for construction of a GRI follow:

Part one—using book parts

Using the adopted textbook for the class, construct eight to twelve questions that require a knowledge of book parts and reading the illustrative material that may appear in the specific text being used. Part one of figure two contains examples of questions for this section of a group reading inventory. While a multiple-choice format is used in the sample, questions such as these may be used by having students look up their answers in their textbooks. "On what page would you find information about our sixteenth president?" "What does the dotted line on the chart on page 00 represent?" "On what page does chapter six begin?"

Part two—silent reading

1. Choose a passage of approximately 500 words from the first fifty pages of the book that the class will be using. The passage should be material not previously read and should be complete in overall concept or story theme.

2. Count the total number of words in the passage and write that number down.

3. Develop from twelve to fifteen comprehension questions covering the material to be read in the book. Questions should be designed to require the reader to respond to main idea, factual, vocabulary, and inferential type questions. These questions may be either open-ended or multiple-choice format.

4. Prepare an answer sheet that includes all original questions and possible answers. A model key is shown in figure 3.

Skill	Question and Possible Answers	Paragraph
Main Idea	1. What is a novel? (long, prose story with many characters and more than one plot)	1
Context	2. What was the "picaresque" novel? (stories of adventures of rogues or rascals who traveled about the country; from the Spanish word *picaro* meaning rascal.)	5
Detail	3. Approximately when did the novel come into being? (during the Renaissance; between fourteenth and sixteenth centuries).	3
Context	4. What is a "plot" novel? (stories of love between people, set in only one place and having few characters)	7
Detail	5. How did invention of the printing press affect literature? (large quantities of books available at reasonable cost)	4
Context	6. What are "romances?" (stories written in verse usually about kings, queens, knights, or other heroes)	2
Detail	7. How does the "plot" novel differ from the "adventure" novel? ("plot" novels are usually set in one place and have fewer characters)	7
Inference	8. If our society were only composed of the very rich and the very poor, with no middle class, what type(s) of novel(s) might we have today? (answers will vary).	
Detail	9. How did exploration affect the merchants? (gave them more markets in which to sell products)	4
Inference	10. What type of modern literature do you think may have been an outgrowth of space exploration? (science fiction)	
Detail	11. What are two examples of "adventure" or "journey" novels in English or American literature? (*David Copperfield, Oliver Twist, Huckleberry Finn, Robinson Crusoe,* or *Joseph Andrews*).	6
Inference	12. How might the mass media (television, newspapers, etc.) negatively affect the novel today? (answers will vary)	
Main Idea	13. Why did the novel develop the way it did? (people were becoming more practical and realistic; discovered the "ordinary" could make good stories (answers will vary)	
Inference	14. What social topics might be found in modern novels today? (answers will vary)	

Performance Levels

IND	0–2 questions missed
INST	3–5 questions missed
FRUS	6 or more questions missed

Total Number of Words in Passage _____

Figure 3. Answer key: The Novel.

5. Label the type of skill each question is intended to measure and note page and paragraph references for later discussion with the class.

6. Develop a summary chart to record class performance. A sample chart is shown in figure 4.

Student Names	Group Reading Inventory							Study Skills Assessment				
	Cloze Level & %-age	GRI Level & %-age	Words per Minute	Main Ideas (Questions 1,13)	Context (Questions 2,4,6)	Details (Questions 3,5,7,9,11)	Inference (Questions 8,10,12,14)	Using Book Parts	Locational Skills	Organizing & Retaining Information	Reading & Interpreting Graphic Aids	Reading for Different Purposes
Sample: Doe, John	47	80	225	✔	0	0	✔	✔	✔	0	0	✔
1.												
2.												
3.												
4.												
5.												
6.												
7.												
8.												
9.												
10.												
11.												
12.												
13.												
14.												
15.												
16.												
17.												
18.												
19.												
20.												
21.												
22.												
23.												
24.												
25.												

Figure 4. Class Summary Chart. (Reprinted with permission from Kendall/Hunt Publishing Company, *Content Inventories:* English, Social Studies and Science, 1979, 230.)

Test administration and scoring—instructions for administering and scoring a GRI are as follows:

1. Explain the purpose of the inventory and inform the class members that they will be expected to answer questions without rereading the material.

2. For Part one of the test, ask students to use their texts to answer the questions. Observe the class and note those readers who exhibit difficulties locating the information.

3. For Part two of the test, ask students to open their texts to the designated reading selection and briefly introduce the material.

4. As an optional procedure, some teachers may wish to obtain some measure of reading rate. To do so a teacher should ask the students to read the material silently and, when they have finished, write down the time spent reading (in minutes and seconds). If a classroom clock is not available, a teacher may serve as timekeeper. After allowing two to three minutes to pass, a teacher may write the time every ten minutes on the chalkboard by erasing the previous time and entering the new time (e.g., 3:10, 3:20, 3:30). As students finish they simply look at the board and note their elapsed time. A words-per-minute rate can be computed by dividing the total words in the selection by the reading time (words ÷ time = w.p.m.).

5. After having read the material silently, students should record their time and raise their hand. The teacher then brings them the prepared questions, which they must answer without referring back to the reading selection. In some classes where a majority of the students may likely have difficulty, it may be necessary to allow students to keep their books open while answering the questions. Although this practice is not preferred, it does allow for some degree of evaluation and relieves frustration on the part of some readers. In such classes, scoring will need to be interpreted on a very strict basis with more complete answers expected due to students being allowed to reread the materials while answering the questions.

6. When scoring the test, teachers can apply the following criteria: 80 percent and above—reader should find the textbook easy to read; 65 percent to 79 percent—reader should need some instructional assistance to read and understand the book but can be expected to use the book. Below 65 percent—book is probably too difficult, and the reader will require much assistance and supplemental help to use the book. Practical information can be gained by recording the particular kinds of questions that each student misses. Instruction should then be initiated that would focus on teaching material in a manner that would enable students to use the skills they appear to have mastered and at the same time provide practice improving their ability to answer the types of questions they find most difficult.

Using a Cloze Inventory

For several years cloze tests have been considered to be an easy-to-use group placement technique. The test can be administered to an entire class in twenty to thirty minutes and, in most instances, will discriminate between those students who can and cannot read the book from which the test is taken. When used for screening content area reading ability, a cloze test appears as a reading selection with words omitted at regular intervals. The following procedure should be followed when constructing a cloze test using information from a subject area textbook.

1. Select a passage of approximately 400 words from the first fifty pages of the adopted textbook.
2. Leaving the first and last sentences unchanged, retype the selection inserting a blank in place of every seventh word. A minimum of fifty blanks is suggested. The finished test should be similar in format to figure 5. Number each blank.

Earthquakes

An earthquake Is a sudden shaking of the earth. When a part of the earth

_____ suddenly, it causes a pattern of _____ to travel in all directions and _____ some
1   2   3

distance. These waves are the _____ felt as a result of the _____ earth.
4   5

There are several types of _____ . One type is caused when large _____ of rock
6   7

under the earth change _____ . Volcanic eruptions can cause quakes and _____ explosions
8   9

can also create tremors.

The _____ dangerous type of quake is usually _____ by the sudden shifting of huge
10   11

_____ of rock under the earth. The. _____ movement and change of the earth
12   13

_____ pressure upon these rocks until the _____ becomes so great that the rocks
14   15

_____ displaced. The place where the shifting _____ is usually along a line or _____ in
16   17   18

the earth called a ''fault.'' _____ cities can be destroyed or a major _____ created by this
19   20

type of quake. _____ point of greatest destruction in an _____ is usually directly above
21   22

where the _____ has taken place. This is called _____ epicenter. At least once a year
23   24

_____ great quake of this nature occurs _____ in the world.
25   26

The waves of _____ caused when a quake occurs spread _____ all directions from
27   28

the center. The _____ used to measure the intensity of _____ movement is called a seis-
29   30

mograph. In _____ to study the effects of earthquakes, _____ have set up seismology cen-
31   32

ters all _____ the world. At times the movements _____ quakes are so slight that only
33   34

_____ with the use of the seismograph _____ detect them. At other times, the _____ are
35   36   37

so great that people as _____ away from the center as a _____ miles can feel them.
38   39

Figure 5. Science: Cloze placement inventory.

Several side _____ can occur after an earthquake that _____ as much damage as
                     40   41
the quake _____ . One of these is the "sea _____ " that happens near coastal cities. These
           42   43
_____ waves are often called tidal waves; _____ they have nothing to do with
 44   45
_____ movements of the ocean. These sea _____ result from quakes under the ocean
 46   47
_____ under the land near the coast _____ from submarine landslides caused by the
 48   49
_____ of the sea floor.
 50
Although scientists know a great deal about where earthquakes are most likely to occur,

they still can not predict when they will happen; perhaps someday this will be possible.

Figure 5. Continued.

3. Prepare a "sample" cloze test containing six to ten blanks. The sample may be duplicated, shown on an overhead transparency, or printed on the chalkboard. This sample should be used prior to administering the complete cloze inventory.
4. Prepare an answer sheet showing the exact word that originally appeared in the book for each blank on the cloze test.

The following directions are suggested for administering and scoring a cloze test:

1. Each class member should participate in a cloze practice session immediately prior to completing the actual cloze inventory. Ask the students to complete the sample. Discuss the correct choices and stress the ideas that only exact word replacements will be counted as correct responses. Students should also be informed that a score of around forty percent correct is acceptable and that guessing is acceptable.
2. Hand out copies of the test and allow twenty to thirty minutes of silent reading time for completion of the test.
3. Each paper must be scored individually. A quick method of scoring can be developed by using an exact copy of the cloze test and cutting out ¼" rectangular notches for each blank. Above each blank write in the correct word. To score, simply place the key over a student's paper and compare answers. Misspelled words may be counted as correct if they appear to represent the original word. Percent correct scores may be interpreted as follows:

58 percent and above—reader should find the text book easy to read.

37–57 percent—reader should need some instructional assistance to read and understand the book but can be expected to use the book.

Below 37 percent—book is probably too difficult and the reader will require much assistance and supplemental help to use the book.

A table is provided in figure 6 to aid in rapid conversion of number of correct answers to percent and to determine reading placement levels. For those whose scores fall below 37 percent, a group reading inventory or perhaps an individual reading test should be admin-

Directions: First locate the number of correct responses in the far left column. Next, move across to the right stopping under the number representing the total deletions in the selection. Where the two intersect will be the reader's percent correct.

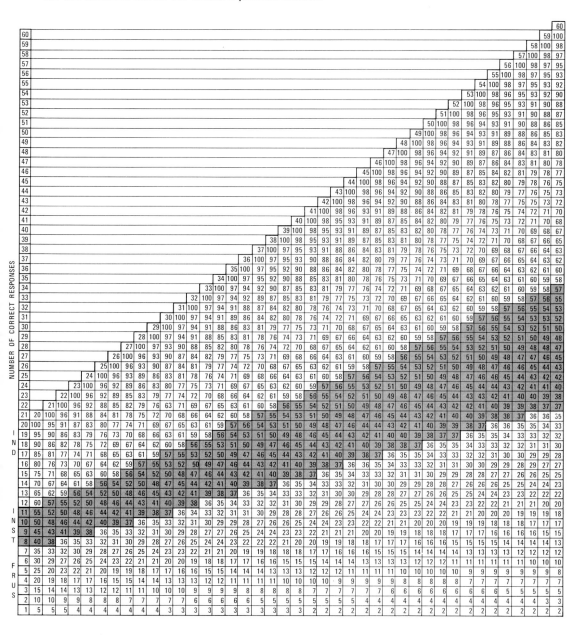

Figure 6. Cloze placement table. (Reprinted with permission from Kendall/Hunt Publishing Company, *Content Inventories:* English, Social Studies and Science, 1979, xii.)

istered. Some users may also wish to analyze cloze test errors on the basis of "type of substitution." Some readers may tend to miss specific kinds of words or words appearing in a particular part of sentences. If these patterns exist, it would be appropriate for a content teacher to initiate corrective measures to remediate the observed problem and in turn, to improve overall reading competency.

Three separate types of informal assessment have been suggested for measuring content reading skills. Each procedure provides a direct means of providing valuable information for either improving reading in the subject area or as a placement aid. For placement purposes, the cloze inventory is recommended. If both placement and diagnostic information are needed, use of a group reading inventory would be suggested. In most classes some type of content interest inventory would be helpful. Without the type of information provided by informal content-related tests, subject area instruction can, at best, be based upon intuition and/or a preconceived combination of ideas and instructional activities for a total class. In such classes, individual—or even intraclass—reading differences are usually all but ignored.

References

Dishner, E. K., and Readence, J. E. Getting started: Using the textbook diagnostically. *Reading World,* 1977, *17,* 36–43, 46–49.

McWilliams, L. J., and Rakes, T. A. Assessing reading skills in science. *Science and Children,* 1980, in press.

McWilliams, L. J., and Rakes, T. A. *Content inventories: English, social studies, and science.* Dubuque, Iowa: Kendall/Hunt, 1979.

Rakes, T. A. A group instructional inventory. *Journal of Reading,* 1975, *18,* 595–598.

Rakes, T. A., and McWilliams, L. J. Bridging the gap: Alternatives to standardized testing. *English Journal,* 1978, *67,* 193–198.

Vaughan, J. L., and Gaus, P. J. Secondary reading inventory: A modest proposal. *Journal of Reading,* 1978, *21,* 716–720.

Secondary Reading Inventory: A Modest Proposal*

Joseph L. Vaughan, Jr.
East Texas State University

Paula J. Gaus
University of Arizona

Rummaging through the daily mailbox accumulation, Mickey, the reading specialist at Salmugundi High School, comes upon the inevitable memos:

From Betsy T. (a biology teacher): "Can you retest Rodney? His standardized test score says he can read on grade level, but he doesn't understand our text and refuses to participate in class."

*Reprinted with permission of Dr. Joseph L. Vaughan, Jr. and Paula J. Gaus and the International Reading Association, from the *Journal of Reading,* 1978, *21,* 716–720.

From Mark Haskings (a new English teacher): "Would it be possible for you to test Brenda J. for reading ability? She seems to be out of it, but she says she reads the stories."

From Jan and Fred (team teachers in U.S. history): "Mickey, can Rocko read? He claims he can't and he is driving us both *crazy!*"

Mickey, knowing exactly what to do, mentally crosses lunch off the list of activities for the day, hastily scribbles responses to each of the teachers, and heads for the dog-eared file marked Informal Reading Inventory (IRI). Aptly trained in its use as a diagnostic instrument, Mickey prepares to bridge the gap between formal diagnosis and those instructional practices appropriate for use in a classroom.

The preceding scenario accurately depicts moments in the real-life experiences of many secondary level reading specialists. Although such scenes are true to life, we feel compelled to point to a basic inconsistency. The use of an IRI, in its traditional format, *with adolescent readers,* often does not provide the in-depth, pertinent information necessary to bridge the gap between formal diagnosis and instructional practices appropriate for use in a classroom.

The predominant values of an IRI, as it is traditionally used, are 1) to identify a student's independent, instructional, and frustration reading levels, and 2) to determine the appropriate level of a specific basal series in which a student should be placed for instruction. While the identification of reading levels and the placement in appropriate basal readers are meaningful for elementary specialists and teachers, of what value can such information be in a diagnosis of secondary level readers?

Consider these specifics. First, secondary level students are not taught from basal readers. Second, interest is a major factor in adolescents' reading performance, yet interest as a factor is rarely considered in an IRI. Third, adolescents are expected to read many different types of material, but this variety is rarely accounted for in an IRI. Fourth, oral reading is often *not* representative of adolescents' reading habits. Fifth, oral production of words from graded word lists does not adequately indicate a student's knowledge of what those words mean.

Our purpose here is to propose a workable alternative to the traditional IRI that can provide pertinent, in-depth information about adolescent readers. Such suggestions have been made before, most notably by Johnson and Kress (1965) in their practical, even authoritative, handbook *Informal Reading Inventories.* In fact, our proposal has evolved largely due to an absence of modified formats based on ideas suggested by Johnson and Kress. We have been further motivated by Froese's (1974, p. 120) finding that although "numerous reading authorities advocate the use of informal reading inventories at the secondary level," in terms of their development and research, "there are few studies related to the secondary level."

For a diagnostic instrument of reading ability to be of maximal value, it must afford opportunities to examine as many aspects of a reader's behavior as possible. Such an instrument designed for adolescent readers should, therefore, include an assessment of 1) comprehension of varying types of material; 2) knowledge of vocabulary; 3) awareness of key content area concepts; 4) ability to vary approach according to type of reading assignments; 5) skill in critically analyzing various types of content area material; 6) ability to cope with unfamiliar vocabulary; and 7) the effect of instruction on the various aspects of reading, especially comprehension and the preteaching of key vocabulary terms.

General Framework

The framework of a secondary reading inventory (SRI) should consist of several reading selections on each of four reading levels. Four reading levels are considered sufficient for diagnosing adolescent readers because, as Dale and Chall (1948) noted, reading levels, especially beyond the fourth grade, are only approximately related to grade levels and often overlap. The four reading level ranges we propose to include in an SRI are upper elementary, intermediate, secondary, and advanced secondary. The corresponding grade levels associated with those reading levels are fifth-sixth, seventh-eighth, ninth-tenth, and eleventh-twelfth.

Within each of these four levels of an SRI would be five selections based on a variety of material from which adolescents are most often required to learn. These categories of material include 1) fiction, 2) factual narration (e.g., biography, or historic description), 3) social studies exposition, 4) scientific description and exposition, and 5) problematic or directional exposition (e.g., math word problems or vocational "how to" material). Additionally, in order to provide a diagnostician with an opportunity to assess the difference between a student's comprehension when aided by some intervening instructional assistance, each selection might be divided into two parts. In effect, the framework of the proposed SRI would consist of 20 passages, with five selections on each of four levels.

Interest Inventory

How does the specialist begin to place students within this general framework? An important factor in reading comprehension is students' interest. Pikulski (1974, p. 145) states, "there would be almost universal agreement that readers who are highly motivated to read something can enjoy that material, even if word recognition and comprehension challenges are very significant." Understanding the degree of interest a student has in various selections becomes, therefore, important diagnostic information. If a student's interest in a selection is at least moderately high, his or her comprehension of the material is likely to be proportionately increased. The opposing condition may similarly and inaccurately deflate comprehension scores.

An interest inventory, then, composed of titles and brief descriptions of the five selections on each level of the SRI, could be incorporated into what is usually termed a "pupil interview." The inventory can be designed so that the annotations of the selections from each level are all on a single page. The annotations, usually several sentences, should provide the student with a brief idea of the selections. The student can rank on the page itself the selections for each level in the order in which he or she would prefer to read them.

A brief discussion with the student after he or she has completed the ranking process for all four levels may provide additional insights into the student's interests and attitudes. For example, if the student consistently ranks fiction high and science low, this reflects an attitude toward those types of classes, an attitude which can dramatically affect performance. Thus, a science teacher, in this case, would have to realize that efforts must be made to improve the student's attitude toward science as an important first step toward helping the student learn science. Let us caution you, however, that a student's interest based on annotations may not accurately reflect his or her interest *after* the selection has been read. A student may *become* interested (or disinterested) in a selection as he or she is reading (Olshavsky 1977), so it may be valuable to discuss the degree of interest after a student reads a selection as well as before.

Traditionally, the entry level for an IRI is based on performance on an informal word recognition inventory. This activity seems to have little value in a diagnosis of an adolescent, since the emphasis is on oral production of words rather than on identification of the meanings of those words. We suggest, therefore, that the first testing activity, per se, be a vocabulary check based on sources such as the graded word lists provided by Taylor and Frackenpohl (1960). This type of vocabulary assessment will require research substantiation, especially to identify predictive levels for comprehension, but it can provide insights into the overall vocabulary proficiency of an adolescent reader in the absence of research that clearly identifies functional criteria.

Comprehension

As for determining where to begin the actual reading component in a diagnosis of an adolescent, we suggest beginning with a silent reading selection on the upper elementary (UE) level, one that the student indicates is in the middle of his or her interest inventory for that level. Until more substantive research can be conducted to reconfirm or to suggest otherwise, we propose that the traditional criteria of 70 to 90% comprehension be considered indicative of adequate comprehension for instructional purposes. (This is, however, one of the more important areas for immediate concern by researchers.)

If a student's comprehension is adequate on the selection from the upper elementary level, the diagnosis should proceed to several higher levels until comprehension falls below an acceptable range. As with the initial selection on the upper elementary level, the selections on the higher levels should represent the midpoint of the student's interest as determined by the responses to the interest inventory. The purpose of this level-by-level progression is to identify the highest level at which the student can comprehend material on an "instructional level."

Since an SRI consists of five selections on each level, it affords an opportunity to assess a student's ability to comprehend a variety of material on what initially seems to be the maximal "instructional level." Having determined that "maximal instructional level," a diagnostician can proceed to determine the degree of variance in comprehension based on selections from areas of interest other than the midpoint area. This will provide information especially pertinent to the content area teachers who will be teaching the student and can provide in-depth information for a tutor or specialist who may eventually be working with the student.

Another aspect of comprehension which one may want to assess is the effect of instruction. Since the SRI as proposed, and the traditional IRI for that matter, involve having a student read a selection without instructional guidance, this factor is often important to examine. Recall that we have proposed that each selection of each level be divided into two parts. The second part can be used to examine oral reading proficiency or the effect of instruction on comprehension. The effect of instruction may be most pertinent with those selections that students indicate they have not adequately comprehended on their own, but that certainly would not be the only time that assessing the effect of instruction might provide additional information.

Directly related to examining the instructional effect on a student's comprehension is the degree to which a student might increase comprehension when directed to read for one or more specific purposes. Adolescents who have reading difficulties often read to remember everything as if they were reading a story where the object is to discover what happens in a plot. When reading exposition, however, this strategy of reading to remember everything often creates problems because there is so much to remember. With a second part of each selection available, a diagnostician can use strategies such as a directed reading activity or a directed reading-thinking activity to determine whether a student's comprehension is likely to improve with instructional guidance.

The relationship between vocabulary and comprehension is one of the few clearly established factors in reading ability. Therefore, an assessment of a student's comprehension of key vocabulary terms should be considered following the reading of each selection. It is not unusual that a student's comprehension be flawed because of a failure to understand certain key terms, especially in content area material. A brief discussion of the key concept words following a comprehension check can often identify the source of a difficulty. For some students, any instruction must be preceded by a discussion of the key concept terms. Thus, as a final component of an SRI, we suggest that the diagnostician have a list of the key terms within each selection so that when a student has indicated some difficulty in comprehension, the ideas directly related to those terms can be more thoroughly examined.

The SRI we propose as an alternative to the traditional IRI can guide the construction of alternative forms of diagnosis which can subsequently be put to the test of substantive research. We hope that others will join us in the production of specific tests or subtests based on this model and in research efforts to verify or disconfirm the utility of these tests as valid indices of adolescents' reading ability.

References

Dale, E. and J. Chall. "A Formula for Predicting Readability." *Educational Research Bulletin*, vol. 27 (January 21 and February 17, 1948), pp. 11–20, 37–54.

Froese, V. "IRIs at the Secondary Level Re-examined." *Interaction: Research and Practice in College-Adult Reading*, P.L. Nacke, Ed., pp. 120–24. Twenty-third Yearbook of the National Reading Conference. Clemson, S.C.: National Reading Conference, 1974.

Johnson, M. S. and R. A. Kress, *Informal Reading Inventories*. Newark, Del.: International Reading Association, 1965.

Olshavsky, Jill Edwards. "Reading as Problem Solving: An Investigation of Strategies." *Reading Research Quarterly*, vol. 12, no. 4 (1976–1977), pp. 654–74.

Pikulski, J. "A Critical Review: Informal Reading Inventories." *The Reading Teacher*, vol. 28, no. 2 (November 1974), pp. 141–51.

Taylor, S. and H. Frackenpohl. *EDL Core Vocabulary. Research and Information Bulletin No. 5* Huntington, N.Y.: Educational Developmental Laboratories, Inc., 1960.

Strategies for Teaching in Content Areas

6

Content Area Vocabulary Development

The importance of systematic vocabulary development in content areas should not be underestimated. Consider the fact that each content area presents students with a new, different, and extensive set of terminology. Without teacher attention and instruction to this novel terminology, students' comprehension will necessarily suffer. For this reason, considerable attention to vocabulary development is basic to effective instruction in the content areas. Therefore, teachers need to be aware of a variety of strategies they may employ to enhance vocabulary development.

Moore and Arthur describe a strategy that not only enhances vocabulary development, but also involves the use of production to enhance comprehension of text passages. An example is provided, and cautions concerning its use are discussed.

Smith discusses the use of graphic organizers as a means of enhancing vocabulary and comprehension in pre- and postreading situations. A rationale for its use and examples of both pre- and postgraphic organizers are provided.

Readence and Searfoss discuss the positive aspects of utilizing categorization as a means of enhancing vocabulary development. Three specific strategies are described with examples provided.

Mangieri and Corboy describe various reinforcement activities that teachers might construct to extend vocabulary development in a postreading situation. Categories for such activities are delineated, and accompanying examples are given.

Possible Sentences

David W. Moore
University of Connecticut

Sharon V. Arthur
Eastern Connecticut State College

Students encounter unfamiliar vocabulary during subject matter reading assignments on a regular basis. Indeed, the general purpose of most reading assignments in subject matter classrooms is to introduce students to new concepts and vocabulary. The problem is that students generally need help acquiring such information. Direct instruction is needed to help students understand the meanings of new terms and the relationships among those terms. Possible Sentences is a technique that teachers can use to provide this instruction.

Rationale

The main purpose of Possible Sentences is to enable readers to independently determine meanings and relationships of unfamiliar words in content reading assignments. The capacity of context to provide a meaning for words is clearly demonstrated by this technique. Moreover, students' meaning vocabularies for a particular topic being studied in class are emphasized. This emphasis occurs because Possible Sentences concentrates on specific words that are taken from a passage to be read.

Several activities occur during a Possible Sentences lesson. First of all, students predict relationships between the unfamiliar terms that are to be encountered in an upcoming passage. Because of this activity, motivation to read is aroused, and appropriate mental sets are created. The tendency of prediction activities to motivate and focus readers has been discussed extensively (Stauffer, 1969). Additionally, prediction activities allow teachers to evaluate students' familiarity with concepts prior to formal instruction. Such activities provide a good indication of students' entry level into a learning task.

Locating evidence to justify statements also occurs during Possible Sentences. This higher-order reading activity occurs because the relationships that are predicted during the prereading phase of this lesson are presented again for evaluation during the postreading phase. Consequently, students need to cite specific parts of their reading assignment that either support or refute the predicted relationships.

Finally, Possible Sentences is a technique that structures both reading and writing activities. Students not only recognize contextual setting of words, but they produce original contextual settings. That is, students note an author's context, which is provided for target words, and then the students create their own context for the identical target words. Vocabulary instruction that includes reading as well as writing activities is generally recommended by educators and is supported by research (Gipe, 1978–1979).

Written especially for inclusion in this text.

Procedure

There are four steps in a Possible Sentences lesson. In the first step, the teacher lists key terms of a passage that are defined adequately by their context. These target words are presented to the class, and each word is pronounced several times. In step two, a student pairs any two words on the list and dictates a sentence using them. The teacher writes the sentence on a chalkboard or on an overhead transparency and underlines both words from the list. The sentence is written exactly as the student dictates, even if the information it contains is not accurate. This exact transcription is necessary for the evaluation phase that occurs later. Another student then pairs any two words on the list and uses them in a sentence. Students may use words already placed in previous sentences if they wish, but eventually they should include each word on the list in at least one sentence. The teacher continues recording sentences until a specified time period elapses, until a specified number of sentences have been created, or until students can produce no more.

In step three, students read the passage for the purpose of checking the accuracy of their classmates' statements. Then, with the passage available for reference during step four, the sentences generated prior to reading are evaluated: which ones are accurate? which ones need further elaboration? which ones cannot be validated because the passage did not deal specifically with them? This evaluation calls for careful reading and directed discussion. The original sentences that prove to be inaccurate should be rectified or else omitted in accordance with the information clarified during this step.

Finally, after evaluating and modifying the original sentences, the teacher may call for new ones. As these new sentences are dictated, other students may challenge them as inaccurate, unknowable, or incomplete and then quickly check the text for confirmation. The final, acceptable statements then should be copied into the students' notebooks or folders.

Example

The above section provides a general description of Possible Sentences; what follows are sample components of a Possible Sentences lesson that was based on a passage about the movement of valley glaciers. The sample components of this lesson are sequenced below as they would occur in an actual situation. First, the target words are presented; second, students produce "possible sentences;" third, the assigned passage is read; and fourth, final modified sentences are created.

Target Words

iceberg	terminal moraine
Jean Louis Agassiz	valley glacier
Muir Glacier	

Possible Sentences

Jean Louis Agassiz discovered *Muir Glacier.*

There are many *icebergs* in the *Muir Glacier.*

An *iceberg* floats in the ocean, and a *terminal moraine* is on the ground.

Icebergs come from *terminal moraines.*

Muir Glacier was formed by a *terminal moraine.*

Assigned Passage

Movement of Glaciers

The movement of apparently solid ice down valleys is somewhat like the flow of rivers. The process has been studied by many scientists. Jean Louis Agassiz, the great Swiss-American naturalist who first proposed the idea of the great Ice Age, drilled holes in a row across a glacier and erected flags in them. His survey of the positions of the flags showed not only that the glacier moved forward, but also that the center moved faster than the sides.

Ground-up materials are carried in the glacial ice and dropped at or near the edge of the glacier where melting occurs. These materials make up the terminal moraine—a ridge at the ice margin—and other glacial deposits.

Where valley glaciers move into the sea, they break off in great blocks or icebergs. The great Muir Glacier of Alaska fills a basin of about 350 square miles. It moves out into the sea along a two-mile front, with an ice cliff from 250 to 300 feet high. The glacier extends hundreds of feet below sea level and may yield icebergs 1,000 feet thick. (J. V. Dodge and W. R. Dell, Eds. *Britannica Junior Encyclopaedia,* vol. 6. Chicago: Encyclopaedia Britannica, 1964, p. 355)

Final Modified Sentences

Jean Louis Agassiz studied *valley glaciers* and learned that their centers moved faster than their sides.

Some *icebergs* that break off *Muir Glacier* are 1,000 feet thick.

An *iceberg* floats in the ocean, and a *terminal moraine* is on the ground.

Valley glaciers form ridges of land that are called *terminal moraines.*

Several points should be considered while inspecting the preceding Possible Sentences sample. An important point is that the original reading passage on glaciers was included here in order to demonstrate how the five target words were chosen. The criterion for target words is that they comprise "key vocabulary with clear defining context." As can be seen by referring to the original passage, the five terms selected for this sample lesson are key, or essential, to understanding the major points of the passage. Additionally, the meanings of these terms are explicitly stated or else directly implied by the defining context. In other words, the five terms were chosen because they were important to the passage and because students could be expected to figure out their meanings through the use of context.

It should be noted also that the dictated sentences reveal some pertinent information about the participants in this activity. Specifically, most of the original sentences contained inaccurate information, but all of them were credible. This credibility suggests that the students' conceptual backgrounds were appropriate for this passage and that the students were prepared to accommodate the new information. In addition, the accuracy of the students' final sentences provides evidence that the meaning and the relationships of the five terms were identified correctly. The ability to paraphrase a passage is a good indication of reading comprehension (Anderson, 1971).

Finally, the greater complexity and the richness of the final sentences indicate how this activity expands students' linguistic performance. Students typically produce more elaborate syntax as they modify their original sentences. This increased production is especially evident when students retain original word pairs when stating a corrected relationship between the words.

Comments

There are some pitfalls in directing students' attention to context that teachers should realize before planning Possible Sentences lessons. First, teachers should take great care to choose key terms that have meanings that can be readily grasped from the context. Although context can provide substantial information to readers about the meaning of unknown words, it does not provide such information invariably. Deighton (1959) best summarized this condition with his statement ". . . while context always *determines* the meaning of a word, it does not necessarily *reveal* that meaning" (pg. 2). For example, the three sentences displayed below contain an uncommon technical word, *felodese,* along with an identical number of surrounding words, ten, to make up the immediate context. However, these sentences clearly vary according to the amount of direct defining context that they provide:

1. His felodese totally shocked some people and merely surprised others.
2. Some people resort to felodese to escape from their problems.
3. Felodese, or suicide, is the ultimate form of deliberate self-destruction.

As can be seen, sentence 3 is devoted entirely to explaining the uncommon term that it contains. There is practically no ambiguity about the meaning of *felodese.* By the same token, sentence 2 substantially constrains possible meanings of the new term, but it does not give away the meaning of the word. As mature readers know, people can resort to a variety of licit and illicit activities to escape from their problems. *Sports, television,* and *daydreaming, drugs, gambling,* and *fighting* are all possible synonyms for *felodese* within the context of sentence 2. And finally, sentence 1 provides practically no direct clues about the meaning of the uncommon word. Readers would be able to "use context" to determine the meaning of *felodese* only if there were additional defining clues available in other sentences.

Several sources provide an introduction to or a review of the various types of context clues that directly reveal the meaning of words. Deighton (1959), Ames (1966), Dale, O'Rourke, and Bamman (1971), Johnson and Pearson (1978), and others have defined such types of direct clues as "formal definition," "example," "summary statement," "apposition," and "reflection of tone or mood." However, nearly all those who have defined types of context clues caution teachers that instruction should center on actually using such clues and not on labelling the various types.

To repeat, context always determines the meaning of words, but it does not always reveal their meaning. Thus, teachers should select only unfamiliar words that are embedded in relatively clear defining contexts when contextual activities such as Possible Sentences are carried out. The five terms selected from the sample passage on glaciers clearly meet this criterion.

A final caution about directing students' attention to context clues to build meaning vocabulary deals with levels of understanding. When context explicitly states or directly implies a word's meaning, it does so at a symbolic level (Cunningham, Cunningham, and Arthur, 1981). That is, words are defined by their relation to other words. Although this level of understanding is important and often is the only way a term can be understood, other activities should be provided whenever possible to help students understand new terms at more personal, concrete levels. This means that follow-up instruction should be provided after meanings for technical terms are apprehended through Possible Sentences. This instruction should be designed to clarify and elaborate new word meanings through direct experience or by directly associating the new terms with students' previous experiences and concepts. For example, the meanings of the scientific names for the parts of a flower (e.g., *stamen, pistil, anther, filament, petal*) may be grasped at a symbolic level by learning their definitions. Knowing that *stamen* is a "spore-bearing leaf that produces a male gamete" is a form of symbolic knowledge. However, flower parts can be elaborated by having students dissect and label them, by showing pictures of flower parts, and by discussing students' observations of various plants.

Of course, the phenomenon underlying many terms cannot be directly experienced in regular classrooms. Students will never meet Abraham Lincoln, a terminal moraine cannot be brought in for inspection, nor can the abstract phenomenon that is represented by the term *fidelity* be dissected on a table like the concrete item that is behind the term *flower*. Nevertheless, elaboration activities such as films, pictures, simulations, and discussion can be provided that allow students to indirectly experience the majority of concepts that are introduced in text. By providing meaningful associations and by making the terms more vivid, teachers can help students better understand and retain the new vocabulary that they acquire from the context of a reading passage.

The teaching technique described here, Possible Sentences, is intended to help readers independently determine meanings and relationships of unfamiliar terms in content passages. It is a structured language activity that is designed to motivate students, set purposes for reading, and review learnings following the reading. The primary steps in this teaching technique call for students to dictate "possible sentences" that contain at least two target words, read the passage from which the words were selected, and then evaluate and modify the original sentences. Before conducting a Possible Sentences lesson, teachers should be certain that the target words are clearly defined by their context. In addition, follow-up instruction should be provided for students after they apprehend word meanings from context so that those meanings are related to students' experiences and understandings.

References

Ames, W. S. The development of a classification scheme of contextual aids. *Reading Research Quarterly,* 1966, *2,* 57–82.

Anderson, R. C. How to construct achievement test items. *Review of Educational Research,* 1974, *42,* 145–170.

Cunningham, J. W., Cunningham, P. M., and Arthur, S. V. *Middle and secondary school reading.* New York: Longman, 1981.

Dale, E., O'Rourke, J., and Bamman, H. A. *Techniques of teaching vocabulary*. Palo Alto, Calif.: Field Educational Publications, 1971.

Deighton, L. C. *Vocabulary development in the classroom*. New York: Columbia University Press, 1959.

Gipe, T. P. Investigating techniques for teaching word meanings. *Reading Research Quarterly,* 1978–1979, *14,* 624–644.

Johnson, D. D., and Pearson, P. D. *Teaching reading vocabulary*. New York: Holt, Rinehart and Winston, 1978.

Stauffer, R. G. *Directing reading maturity as a cognitive process*. New York: Harper and Row, 1969.

Instructional Applications of Graphic Organizers*

Cyrus F. Smith, Jr.
University of Wisconsin-Milwaukee

Since Ausubel (1960, 1963, 1968) first introduced the advance organizer, educators and learning theorists have confronted an interesting dilemma. Specifically, research indicated that the advance organizer facilitated learning, but practice showed it to be difficult to construct and use in an instructional context. Barron (1969) helped to alleviate this problem when he suggested a change in the format of the advance organizer. Prior to 1969, advance organizers had been presented as prose passages. Barron changed them to tree diagrams that utilized the vocabulary of the concept to be learned, thereby depicting the interrelationships between key words and terms. Barron called his modification the structured overview.

Structured overviews have gained considerable attention in recent years as useful teaching tools. Teachers have found that structured overviews assist them as they plan their classes and that they have multiple applications for in-class use. The structured overview, like its predecessor the advance organizer, was originally intended as a readiness activity. The thinking was that if the learner was presented with a familiar structure or experience prior to the introduction of new information, then the familiar structure or experience would serve as a cognitive foundation to which the new information could be attached. Classroom practice, however, has shown that structured overviews are equally useful as assimilation or follow-up activities. This expansion of the structured overview's ability has led to a more inclusive nomenclature. Thus, to answer the need for precision among educators, structured overviews are now being referred to as graphic organizers. This paper will discuss the graphic organizer in two major ways. First, it will be discussed as a planning tool that helps teachers clarify their instructional objectives. Then it will be discussed as either a readiness or an assimilation or a follow-up instructional strategy.

---

*Written especially for inclusion in this text.

Consider the following graphic organizer:

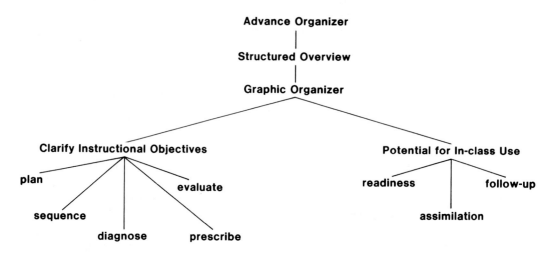

It describes the evolution of the graphic organizer. It has been inserted here to show how the development of a graphic organizer aids a teacher in clarifying instructional objectives. Please note that the discussion to follow has been sequenced along two continuums. That is, no branching occurs until after the inclusion of the term "graphic organizer." The two less inclusive terms, "clarify instructional objectives" and "potential for in-class use," indicate two major uses of the graphic organizer. These uses are further defined by the inclusion of even more specific modifiers, which are placed beneath them. This constant diagramatic progress from general term to less inclusive term to specific term has application across all subject areas. Teachers can plan their lessons more effectively, decide the most appropriate ways to sequence instruction, and evaluate both their teaching and the learning of their students. This last component is important for two reasons. One, the graphic organizer allows the teacher to determine how a lesson is developing (diagnosis); and two, it then guides or directs students as they strive to attain the lesson goals (prescription).

When developing a graphic organizer as a planning, readiness, or assimilation activity, the following sequence of steps is suggested (Earle & Barron, 1973; Herber, 1978; Smith, 1979; Smith & Kepner, 1980).

1. Analyze the vocabulary of the learning task, listing all words and terms that you feel are representative of the major concepts that you want the students to understand.
2. Arrange the list of words diagramatically to depict logical relationships.
3. Evaluate your arrangement. Can words be added or deleted to more clearly depict the relationships essential to the concept under discussion?
4. Before introducing the graphic organizer to students, decide which of the words and terms they should be able to add through reading or listening and delete them for the time being. However, keep a master copy for your reference.

5. When the concept to be learned is introduced, use the chalkboard to display the graphic organizer (step 4) to the students. Encourage them to apply knowledge previously learned by adding any words to the diagram that more fully complete it. Tell them that the diagram will serve as a study aid in that they will be expected to add additional words and terms to it as they partake in the lesson. Further, ask students specific questions that will direct them in this task.

6. During the course of the lesson, have students add to the diagram appropriate words and terms that they uncover, thereby relating new information to that previously learned. As this process develops, insist that students sufficiently explain their additions either as individuals or in small or large group discussions.

Instructional applications of these six steps fulfill an earlier assertion regarding the planning, readiness, and assimilation uses of the graphic organizer. Smith (1979, pp. 4–9) and Smith and Kepner (1980, pp. 11–24) have presented more detailed examples of this process in the contexts of English and mathematics lessons, respectively. The reader is directed to these references, since they are useful, practical classroom applications of graphic organizer development.

The graphic organizer can also be used as an in-class follow-up small group activity (Barron, 1978; Herber, 1978; Smith, 1979; Smith and Kepner, 1980). When used in this fashion, students apply subject matter concepts or understandings by exploring and analyzing the relationships that exist between and among words, terms, or symbols. In order to illustrate this usage as a postgraphic organizer, the reader is urged to do the following activity.

Directions: *Cut along the lines to separate the words and terms listed below. Choose the most general term. Then, arrange the remaining words and terms beneath it in such a way that logical relationships are depicted. Some terms may be used more than once. Terms may be added by using the blank slips. Not all of the terms need to be used. Be prepared to explain or justify your arrangement.

Literal	Interpretation
Analysis of Relationships	Valuing
Application	Cause/Effect
Comprehension	Sequence
Comparison/Contrast	

One *possible* depiction of the organization of these terms may be found at the end of this article.

Teaching applications of the postgraphic organizer are several. For instance, the use of small groups reduces the teacher/student ratio of one to twenty-five to one to three, and groups can be structured by skill, ability, or interest to reflect the academic range within a class. As groups proceed with the task, the teacher is free to circulate, observing and/or

*If you wish not to cut this page of the book, use small slips of paper and write one term on each slip. Then follow the directions as described.

providing assistance to students as needed. If the teacher notices that most groups are having difficulty understanding the key relationships of the idea or concept being taught, then wholesale reteaching would be appropriate. If difficulty is limited to a few groups, then immediate small group instruction is provided for some while other groups proceed independently. Regardless of which situation occurs, the teacher should challenge groups to explain and justify the graphic organizers that they have developed.

Please note that several different graphic organizers can be developed from the same list of words and terms. This is significant in at least two respects. Runyon (1978) found that the use of postgraphic organizers not only allowed him to view students' perceptions and understandings of abstract concepts in a chemistry curriculum, but he also found that some students developed graphic organizers that gave him new perspectives on familiar ideas. Secondly, a whole class discussion that focuses on several student-developed graphic organizers provides an effective review and summary in which the interrelationships of words and terms are compared and contrasted. In this type of discussion, students are able to share the perceptions and understandings that they discovered in small groups. In effect, students have the opportunity to examine an idea from several perspectives. This use of the graphic organizer lets students think at cognitive levels above primary meaning and allows the teacher to guide and direct their thinking about ideas or concepts.

To develop a postgraphic organizer, the teacher selects approximately twelve words or terms that evince general, less inclusive, and specific interrelationships. These are presented with the directions and in the format presented previously in this paper. Students should be familiar with the format of the graphic organizer before proceeding with the activity. At least fifteen minutes should be allocated for graphic organizer construction. Time allotted for discussion will vary from subject to subject and from class to class. Smith (1979) has provided sample postgraphic organizer formats for several content areas.

This paper has discussed instructional applications of the graphic organizer. Like its predecessor, the advance organizer, the graphic organizer meets the three conditions that Ausubel (1960, 1963, 1968) feels are necessary for learning abstract subject matter. These conditions are: (1) the material to be learned must be organized; (2) the learner must have a cognitive foundation to which new ideas can be anchored; and, (3) the learner needs a willingness and a strategy to learn new information. The graphic organizer fulfills these conditions in at least two ways. It helps teachers to plan their instruction and it is a useful readiness, assimilation, or follow-up activity. More specifically, the graphic organizer provides the teacher with an instructional framework for formulating, clarifying, and evaluating instructional objectives. It focuses students' attention as they read by actively involving them in the task at hand. It serves as a surrogate teacher in small group discussions by providing students with a means to analyze the relationships about a concept. And, finally, it assists the teacher in subsequent whole-class discussions by providing a concrete visual reference as students debate the merits of the concept being examined.

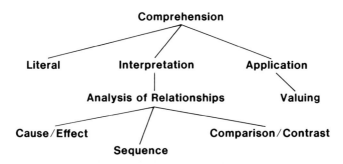

Example of possible graphic organizer—comprehension terms from activity on page 145.

References

Ausubel, D. P. The use of advance organizers in the learning and retention of meaningful verbal material. *Journal of Educational Psychology,* 1960, *51,* 267–74.

———. *The psychology of meaningful verbal learning.* New York: Grune and Stratton, 1963.

———. *Educational psychology: A cognitive view.* New York: Holt, Rinehart, and Winston, 1968.

Barron, R. F. The use of vocabulary as an advance organizer. In *Research in reading in the content areas: First year report.* H. L. Herber and P. L. Sanders, (Eds). Syracuse, N.Y.: Syracuse University Press, 1969, 29–39.

———. Research for classroom teachers: Recent developments on the use of the structured overview as an advance organizer. In *Research in reading in the content areas: Fourth report.* H. L. Herber and J. D. Riley, (Eds). Syracuse, N.Y.: Syracuse University Press, 1978, 171–176.

Earle, R. A. and Barron, R. F. An approach to teaching vocabulary in content subjects. In *Research in reading in the content areas: Second year report.* H. L. Herber and R. F. Barron, (Eds). Syracuse, N.Y.: Syracuse University Press, 1973, 84–99.

Herber, H. L. *Teaching reading in content areas* (2nd ed.). Englewood Cliffs, N.J.: Prentice-Hall, Inc., 1978.

Runyon, J. P. Instructional uses of structured overviews in the high school chemistry classroom. Unpublished Master's thesis, The University of Wisconsin-Milwaukee, 1978.

Smith, C. F. *The structured overview: Theory and practice.* Madison, Wis.: Wisconsin Department of Public Instruction, 1979.

Smith, C. F. and Kepner, H. S. *Reading in the mathematics classroom.* Washington, D.C.: National Education Association, 1980.

Teaching Strategies for Vocabulary Development

John E. Readence
University of Georgia

Lyndon W. Searfoss
Arizona State University

If young people are to read with understanding and enjoyment, they must develop their vocabularies. Obvious? Of course, but teachers can speed up vocabulary growth by involving students in discovering and comprehending words and the ideas they convey. One especially useful technique for doing that is categorization. This technique improves prediction and problem-solving skills, but more importantly, it helps students find some sense and order in their own experiences. Three aspects of categorization, *Word Fluency,* the *List-Group-Label Lesson,* and *Feature Analysis,* are useful from primary grades through graduate school. The greatest benefit will come from using them in the order presented below.

Word Fluency

Word Fluency is a vocabulary development technique in which one of two participants attempts to generate as many vocabulary words as possible in sixty seconds. All that is needed is a pencil, paper, and a watch or clock with a second hand. When *first* doing Word Fluency, you should demonstrate the technique with a student *before* the entire class begins to try it. Once the steps to Word Fluency are clear, pairs of students usually are able to work well independently.

In communicating the directions to students, say,

> I want to see how many words you can name in one minute. Any words will do, like *story, book,* or *friend.* When I say 'ready' you begin and say the words as rapidly as you can and I will count them. Using sentences or counting numbers are not allowed. You must use separate words. Go as rapidly as you can. Ready! Go!

Let the students go first and tally their words on a sheet of paper. If students hesitate for ten seconds, remind them that any words will do. Students experiencing difficulty in the beginning may be motivated if you say, "Look around the room. What do you see?" or "Think of something we did in today's class." Stop at the end of one minute.

Next, alternate roles. Students time and count while you name words. This is the key to Word Fluency, for you can *model* categories of words for the students. Instead of randomly naming words, as most students would do, you can give words in categories so they hear how you organize words (and how much more rapidly words can be given when they are categorized). Again, responses are tallied and the activity ended in sixty seconds.

Reprinted from *English Journal,* 1980, *69,* 43–46 with permission of the National Council of Teachers of English, John E. Readence and Lyndon W. Searfoss.

In scoring responses, words are counted, and all words are acceptable except (1) repetitions, (2) number words, and (3) sentences. Emphasis is placed on categorizing by awarding participants extra points for categories of at least four words. The score for the activity is the total number of words named in one minute plus the points awarded for categorizing. Graphs may be used so students can chart their progress. A line graph might be used to illustrate student advances, but visible, graphic signs of success should be reinforced by you. As students become accustomed to this technique, their scores will naturally rise with the graphs providing the incentive to continue the activity.

The follow-up is particularly important. When your portion of the activity is completed, you should ask the students, "How did the words I named go together (categories)?" Since extra points are given for such categories, the demonstration can give students incentive to do well with Word Fluency, and thus, develop their vocabulary.

When the students become familiar with this activity, you can vary the activity by limiting words named in one minute to a particular category, or set of categories, e.g., things associated with conflict, qualities of a character in a story, etc. Begin this use of Word Fluency by stating, "Today, when we say words, let's think about the short story we read yesterday and only say words you remember from that story." In this way students will name words associated with a particular lesson (category) and enhance their understanding of vocabulary related to the story. Word Fluency could be repeated frequently throughout the development of a unit of study or short stories to aid students in remembering and reinforcing new vocabulary related to the unit or stories under study.

List-Group-Label Lesson

The List-Group-Label lesson was originally conceived by Hilda Taba (*Teacher's Handbook for Elementary Social Studies.* Reading, Massachusetts: Addison-Wesley, 1967) to help students handle technical vocabulary in elementary level social studies and science classes; the concept of the lesson can be broadened to improve systematically the vocabulary and categorization skills of students in all grades.

To begin a List-Group-Label lesson, a blackboard, a large sheet of paper, or something comparable is needed to record responses. A one-word topic is selected as a stimulus and written at the top of the blackboard or paper. Topics may be drawn from a school event, a short story or poem being studied, or a current news item.

Students are asked to think of words or expressions related to the stimulus word. For instance, you might ask, "Think of any word you know that reminds you of the word *conflict.*" Responses are recorded and you should accept all words, making no judgments (including telltale facial expressions). The list of words given by the students should be kept manageable. Approximately twenty-five words is a good number of words, depending on the stimulus word and grade level of the students. After all the students have had an opportunity to offer words, stop the listing by saying, "I'll take two more words." Below are listed words students might generate using the stimulus word previously mentioned, *conflict.*

Conflict

death	murder	hate
lose	war	love
win	resolution	man
yell	dilemma	personal
scream	pain	hostage
fight	maturity	people
poison	guns	enemy
bombs	knives	friend

Next, reread the list orally, pointing to each word as it is pronounced. The students, individually or in small groups, are told to construct smaller lists containing at least three words that have something in common from the large list previously obtained. Words in the large list may be used in more than one category as long as the grouping is different. With small groups, a recorder should be selected by each group to record the group's categories and lists of words.

After they have completed grouping words by categories, record the list of words and categories on another part of the blackboard or another sheet of paper. The initial master list must be visible for easy reference. It is important that you ask the individual or group to explain or defend their thinking as the category is recorded. In this way all students will learn from seeing other categories and hearing why and how words are grouped. From the list of words generated by the stimulus word, *conflict,* the following are possible categories:

1)   hate, love, scream, yell, fight, pain = emotional reactions
2)   death, murder, lose, win, war, hate, maturity = results of conflict
3)   man, friend, enemy, personal, hostage = people in conflict
4)   guns, poison, knives, bombs, people = weapons of conflict

Since the grouping and labeling could present problems for some students, you might decide to take students through the List-Group-Label lesson by modeling their thinking for them. Another way of getting started is to construct a first category and title it until the students understand the procedure. You might list words and have students determine an appropriate label. Finally, if students or groups have words they cannot fit into a neat category, tell them to start a "misfit" list. As categories are compared, students will learn one list of misfits is rarely like another student's or group's list.

Feature Analysis

Feature Analysis derived from the theoretical construct of cognitive structure described by Frank Smith (*Comprehension and Learning.* New York: Holt, 1975) is the way in which human beings organize knowledge. D. D. Johnson and P. D. Pearson (*Teaching and Reading Vocabulary.* New York: Holt, 1978) refer to a version of this technique as semantic feature analysis. Smith stated that as a human being processed new information (1) categories were established in one's mind store and (2) rules (feature analysis) were formulated to place objects (words, ideas) into these categories. Finally, category interrelationships were established in the mind store so one could determine how objects could be related, yet be unique.

In practice, Feature Analysis enables students to see how words are related and, at the same time, see how they remain unique. It should begin with categories already known to students and is particularly appropriate as a post-reading activity to refine and extend students' understanding of ideas. The key to Feature Analysis is *starting slowly* so students build upon an understandable structure. We have found that if you use Word Fluency and List-Group-Label until both you and your students are familiar with them, Feature Analysis is much easier to use. There are six steps in Feature Analysis.

Category selection

Select a category name to begin the lesson. The category should be familiar to students. To illustrate we will continue with *conflict*.

List words in category

Once the category is selected, the teacher, or preferably the students, supplies words which name objects or ideas related to the category. In the case of the category of "conflict," we can begin with a limited number of words dealing with media events or literature. For purposes of illustration, we will use the words, "Walter Mitty, Mr. Spock, and Iran."

List features

You must now decide which features, or traits, are to be explored in the category. Start with only a few features; students will later build onto these. For our example, features to be explored are whether conflict (a) is personal, (b) deals with hate, (c) deals with fantasy, and (d) deals with reality.

After the first three steps of Feature Analysis have been completed, we have a matrix which looks like this:

	Conflict			
	personal	hate	fantasy	reality
Walter Mitty				
Mr. Spock				
Iran				

Indicate feature possession

Students are guided through the matrix to learn whether, in this case, conflict possesses a particular feature. Again, ask students to defend their thinking. A simple + or − system can be used to indicate feature possession. Students who become accustomed to Feature Analysis may use a more sophisticated system to indicate feature possession, such as a form of the Lichert scale (*always, most of the time, sometimes, a few times, never*). Our matrix for the category of "conflict" could look as follows using a + or − system:

	Conflict			
	personal	hate	fantasy	reality
Walter Mitty	+	−	+	−
Mr. Spock	+	−	−	+
Iran	+	+	−	+

Add words/features

At this point students have indicated feature possession, and they should be asked first to generate new words to be added to the matrix, followed by new features to be analyzed. You may wish to set a limit on either the number of words and/or features to be added to the matrix; however, fewer words and features are usually generated as categories become more abstract in nature or become further removed from students' backgrounds.

In our example, words such as "Richard Cory" and "M.A.S.H." may be added. Other features might include "war," "death," and "resolution." When students generate additions to the matrix, they are expanding their vocabularies and developing ideas through categorization.

Complete and explore matrix

Students complete the matrix by using the same feature possession system as before with the new words and features. Our final matrix might look like that shown below.

	Conflict						
	personal	hate	fantasy	reality	war	death	resolution
Walter Mitty	+	−	+	−	−	−	−
Mr. Spock	+	−	−	+	−	−	+
Iran	+	+	−	+	+	+	−
Richard Cory	+	−	−	+	−	+	+
M.A.S.H.	+	+	−	+	+	+	+

Exploration, the final part of this step, completes Feature Analysis. Students analyze the matrix to see how words relate within a category yet remain unique. For instance, they may see that patterns of conflict can be entirely different from one another—their *uniqueness*. Specifically, they may see that even though all characters or people in the media may be in conflict, only certain ones deal with reality or war or are resolved. On the other hand, they might note that a category (conflict) does have certain common elements. Mr. Spock and Richard Cory, both characters in conflict, have much but not everything in common. Likewise, the characters of M.A.S.H. and the people in Iran share some common traits.

Exploring the matrix is best accomplished when students examine and discuss rather than follow your leads. If students wish, they may further expand the matrix on their own, and you may extend discussion by exploring various parts of the matrix in greater depth. You may decide, for example, to explore further how conflict is resolved in each case.

In summary, teachers can foster and speed up vocabulary growth by involving students. These categorization techniques incorporate active student learning. Additionally, they require little teacher preparation to be successful. By proceeding from one simple technique, Word Fluency, to a more difficult technique, List-Group-Label, and from these to something even more complex, Feature Analysis, all of us can help our students read with more understanding and enjoyment.

Reinforcing Vocabulary in the Content Classroom: The Why and the How

John N. Mangieri
University of South Carolina

Margaret Corboy
University of South Carolina

The teaching of reading in content subjects is multifaceted. Its key ingredients include—but are not limited to—the following: the reading abilities of the students, the curriculum, the instructional techniques employed, and the content materials themselves. Since each of these components is a subject for intense study of and in itself, we have chosen to select and focus upon only one—vocabulary development.

In this article we seek to accomplish two goals. First, we will describe the role that vocabulary plays in a content area. Second, strategies for acquiring and reinforcing content area vocabulary will be presented. Thus, this article will deal with both the *why* and the *how* of vocabulary as it relates to the content classroom.

Vocabulary in the Content Classroom: The Why

The importance of vocabulary in understanding content materials is obvious. Books and other instructional devices are comprised of words. If students are to derive meaning from these materials, they must possess an understanding of a significant portion of the words contained in them.

At the present time, much is known about vocabulary acquisition and reinforcement. Cunningham, Cunningham, and Arthur (1981) offer

> ". . . some important principles to keep in mind about what words are and how they are learned:
> 1. Understanding and applying appropriate meanings is essential to reading comprehension.
> 2. Meaning vocabulary includes not only words but also phrases, symbols, abbreviations, initials, and acronyms.
> 3. It is impossible to make definite statements about the size of a person's meaning vocabulary because words do not have "a meaning."
> 4. Most people's *receptive* vocabulary (words they understand while listening or reading) is larger than their *expressive* vocabulary (words they use in speaking or writing).
> 5. Many words have several different but related meanings, usually listed under a single dictionary entry.
> 6. Some words have several unrelated meanings, which are usually listed as separate entries in the dictionary.
> 7. As people read and listen, they particularize their general meanings for words—a process termed *instantiation.*

Written especially for inclusion in this text.

8. *Denotations* are factual, literal meanings of words.
9. *Connotations* are interpretations or value judgments attached to words.
10. Most words are learned through many different encounters in different contexts over a period of time.
11. Words are learned through direct experience, indirect experience, and symbolically.
12. The words that ought to be taught are those which students need to learn in order to understand the content they will be listening to or reading. In a content analysis, the teacher lists important concepts and then determines which words must be known in order to master or grasp these concepts." '[pp. 23–24.]

Given the complexity of most content area materials and the reading ability of the students utilizing them, in all likelihood a pupil typically will be required to read selections containing numerous unknown words. Much of this unfamiliar vocabulary will be *technical words,* "those which deal mainly with a specific field of knowledge or experience" (Robinson, 1975, p. 57).

Estes and Vaughan (1978) point out one of the problems regarding vocabulary in a content classroom. They state: "One's understanding depends on the appropriateness of the vocabulary with which an idea is expressed. That is, if a reader is to comprehend, the vocabulary of what is being read must be appropriately suited to the level, or stage, of conceptual development" (p. 98). Aukerman (1972) discusses another facet of the problem of technical vocabulary in content materials. He says: "It is not so much the use of specific, scientific, and technical words that increases difficulty, but how words are introduced and defined" (p. 23).

By aiding in the introduction, learner acquisition, and reinforcement of technical words, the teacher paves the way for optimum comprehension of subject matter. Thus, time and effort spent on the part—vocabulary development—helps to insure mastery of the whole— understanding of content.

It is hoped that the issue of *why* content teachers have a responsibility for insuring that students understand their specific subject's technical vocabulary is apparent. After all, they are the specialists in a given academic area. It is they who know the relative importance (or nonimportance) of a particular word in a given area of study. Content teachers are in a prime position to determine whether an author has adequately defined a technical item in a material and can readily call these important specialized words to the attention of their students. In addition to the aforementioned, content teachers, through their daily interactions with students and subject matter, are able to assess the degree to which students have *acquired* and *retained* key technical vocabulary.

It should be noted that if students are to genuinely understand vocabulary, they must be given more than a mere exposure to technical words. Such words must not only be identified, but the teacher must also provide the students with opportunities to acquire and retain them. Acquisition and retention will occur only if a teacher consciously seeks to make it happen. In fact, the learning of technical words can be an exciting effort, limited only by the creativity and diligence of a teacher.

Vocabulary in the Content Classroom: The How

Since the importance of vocabulary instruction in the content areas has been discussed, it is time to focus on *how* such instruction can be implemented. The specific exercises included in this article are those that teachers have found to be successful in introducing and reinforcing vocabulary. These exercises have been organized according to the following classification system: (1) recognition level; (2) meaning level; and, (3) relationship level. These exercises illustrate that vocabulary instruction need not be dull, and they are offered as interesting alternatives to the use of routine vocabulary notebooks and dictionary drills that are commonly found in content classrooms.

The first step in teaching vocabulary in the content areas occurs when the teacher identifies the key terms and plans strategies for introducing and reinforcing them. A teacher has the option of incorporating these exercises at a number of points in direct instruction. Prior to the reading of the selection by the students, exercises may be used to introduce terms and provide motivation for reading. Presented after the reading of the passage, these exercises provide an opportunity for discussion and reinforcement of the terms with respect to the concepts developed. In addition, these exercises provide a rather novel alternative to vocabulary evaluation.

Although a sample exercise may illustrate the vocabulary of a particular content area, the use of that exercise is in no way limited to that specific subject. For example, the central word puzzle is based on vocabulary selected from a chapter in a chemistry textbook. This same exercise could be adapted to any one of the other content areas. As you examine these exercises, keep in mind their adaption to your specific content area.

Also, one's concept of vocabulary in the content classroom should not be confined to these exercises per se. The following activities at each of the three levels—recognition, meaning, relationship—are representative of the type of activities that a teacher might use with individuals or an entire class. It should be remembered that the primary purpose of these exercises is to aid students in the mastery of technical vocabulary in a content area.

I. Recognition level

Recognition of the words presented on the printed page is the first step in the reading process, since it is essential that students be able to recognize words that they encounter in a given passage. Therefore, recognition exercises such as the following are best used by teachers *prior* to the reading of the passage in order to insure that students will readily recognize these terms when they subsequently appear in print. It is suggested that recognition-level exercises be introduced orally by the teacher so that the students will have the benefit of hearing the pronunciation of each term while concurrently looking at its visual form.

A. Word Search*

Directions: The names of nine explorers are listed at the left. Locate each one in the puzzle and draw a line around it.

Explorers of the New World

Verrazano
Magellan
LaSalle
Cartier
De Soto
Brulé
Joliet
Marguette
Nicolet

```
S O J P R N C A R T I E R
M N B O C H I X C H G A N
A B S H L I N C K E L D A
R A L V N I N T O M K E W
Q U A P E L E B U L A S N
U M B T A R S T U C E O A
E C P V E E R P S H M T U
T U R O C H P A L L A O M
T R U R H W E X Z U X E B
E S T M A G E L L A N C R
T E F I M O M L I M N E U
R A H T P O U G A U P O L
X N I C L R A P T S O C E
U P R L A S A L L E A R M
A D O V I V N T A G E L S
S O W T N O T F I G H O T
```

B. Word Scramble

Directions: As your teacher calls out each word, rearrange the letters to write it correctly.

1. EINIFNIT   _ _ _ _ _ _ _ _
2. NIBYRA   _ _ _ _ _ _ _
3. NEVN   _ _ _ _
4. TIANQUOE   _ _ _ _ _ _ _ _
5. CEMLADI   _ _ _ _ _ _ _ _

*Exercise based upon usage of *The Free and the Brave* by H. Graff.

The words to be called orally by the teacher and presented visually to the students after they have written their responses are:

INFINITE

BINARY

VENN

EQUATION

DECIMAL

C. The Right Word*

Directions: Look at the first word in each row. If the word is repeated on that line, circle it. If the word is not repeated, do not mark anything.

1. *millimeter*	millimicro	milliner	millimeter	millipede
2. *kilometer*	kiloliter	kilometer	kilovolt	kilohertz
3. *centimeter*	centiliter	centime	centimo	centipede
4. *meter*	metric	metier	metis	miter
5. *volume*	voluble	volutin	volume	voltine
6. *kilogram*	kiloparsec	kiloton	kiloliter	kilogram
7. *meniscus*	meninx	meniscus	menace	memsahib
8. *kinetic*	kinesis	kinetin	kinesics	kinema
9. *cylinder*	cynical	cymatium	cyclone	cylinder
10. *megahertz*	megalith	megaton	megabar	megaspore

II. Meaning level

As was previously discussed, recognition of words is the first step in the reading process. The next level consists of a student's determining the meaning of a word in terms of the context of the material.

The exercises shown in this section are aimed at the development of meaning vocabulary. A caution should be noted: administration of these exercises in isolation from the textbook or other references constitutes *testing* rather than teaching. Since the intent at this level is to *teach* rather than to test, students should be directed to consult their textbooks when completing these exercises.

Meaning level exercises may be used effectively at two different points in time. *Prior to the actual reading of a passage,* a student may be directed to scan the material in order to determine the meaning of the given terms and then complete the respective exercise. In this capacity, a foundation of word meaning is developed prior to the student's encountering the terms in print. *After reading the passage,* the student may be directed to consult the text in completing the exercise, thus clarifying and reinforcing the meanings of the terms presented in it.

*Exercise based upon usage of *Physical Science* by C. Barman, M. Schneiderwert, J. Rusch, and W. Hindin.

A. Central Word Puzzle*

Directions: Dmitri Mendeleyev developed the original periodic table of elements. Show your knowledge of the currently used periodic table by examining the descriptions below and writing the correct terms next to the corresponding numbers.

```
 1.                                    R   A   D   I   U   M
 2.                         — — — — — M
 3.                             — — — — I — —
 4.                         — — — — T — — — —
 5.                             — — R — — — —
 6.                             — — I — — — —
 7.                             — — M — — — —
 8.                             — E — — — — —
 9.                             N — — — — — — — —
10.                             — — D — — — —
11.                         — — — — — E —
12.                             — — — L — — — —
13.                         — — — — E —
14.                             — — Y — — —
15.                             — — — E —
16.                             V — — — —
```

1. most chemically active member of the calcium family
2. Group I family on periodic table
3. Group II family on periodic table
4. parts of atoms in the outer shell
5. horizontal row on the periodic table
6. number appearing above an element's symbol
7. vertical column on periodic table
8. element with atomic number 2
9. Group V family on periodic table
10. first element on the periodic table
11. Group VII family on the periodic table
12. Group VIII family on the periodic table
13. appears below an element's chemical symbol
14. element with atomic weight of 15.9994
15. number of electrons in outer shell of Group III family
16. within a given group, the number of outer-shell electrons does not _____ .

*Exercise based upon usage of *Modern Chemistry* by H. Metcalfe, J. Williams and J. Castka.

B. Malapropisms*

Directions: Underline the words that are misused in the following sentences and substitute the correct terms. This first item has been completed for you.

habitat

1. The place in which an organism lives is its <u>inhalant.</u>
2. During cold weather, many plants enter a dorsal period.
3. An organism's occupation is its nix.
4. Navel plants and animals live only in salt water.
5. Land plants are celestial and are totally dependent upon presidio for water.
6. Flesh-eating animals are called carnivals.
7. Symposium is a relationship that means "living together."
8. The tapeworm is considered a parasol because it harms its hostel in deriving nourishment from it.
9. In mutilation, two organisms benefit from living with each other.
10. Insteps are animal behaviors that are not taught but come naturally.

C. Sentence Selection**

Directions: Place a check in front of those phrases that combine with the underlined word to make a true statement. The first item has been completed for you.

1. A <u>kilometer</u>
   - ✓ measures length.
   - _____ is equal to two miles.
   - ✓ is equal to 1000 meters.
   - _____ is abbreviated by the symbol k.

2. A <u>metric ton</u>
   - _____ is equal to 2000 pounds.
   - _____ is abbreviated by the symbol mt.
   - _____ is equal to 1000 kilograms.
   - _____ measures mass.

3. A <u>meter</u>
   - _____ is equal to 100 centimeters.
   - _____ is equal to 1000 millimeters.
   - _____ is equal to 1000 milliliters
   - _____ measures volume.

4. A <u>gram</u>
   - _____ is abbreviated by the symbol g.
   - _____ is equal to 1000 milligrams
   - _____ can be measured with a metric ruler.
   - _____ has the mass of a paper clip.

*Exercise based upon usage of *Modern Biology* by J. Otto and A. Towle.
**Exercise based upon usage of *Physical Science* by C. Barman, M. Schneideruert, J. Rusch, and W. Hindin.

5. A <u>liter</u>

_____ is equal to a gallon.

_____ is used to measure liquid volume.

_____ is equal to 1000 milliliters.

_____ is equal to 100 centimeters.

D. Crossword Puzzle*

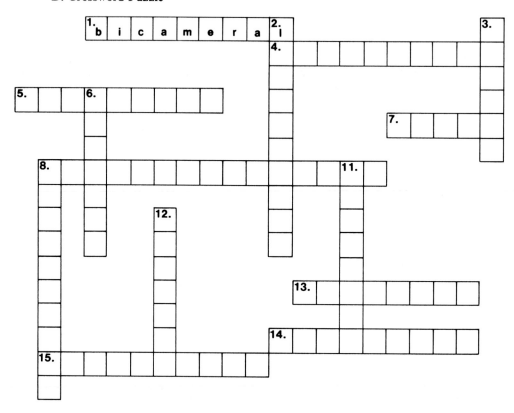

ACROSS

1. two-house legislature
4. process by which law is passed by the people
5. _____ pro tempore serves in absence of the lieutenant governor
7. committee composed of members of both houses
8. the redrawing of district boundaries
13. name of lower house in Calif., Nev., N.J., N.Y., and Wis.
14. name of lower house in Md., Va., and W. Va.
15. one-house legislature

*Exercise based upon usage of *Our American Government and Political System* by D. Wit and A. Dionisopoulos.

DOWN

2. in thirty states, _____ governor serves as president of the senate
3. upper house
6. presiding officer in lower house
8. process by which law is repealed by the people
11. only state with unicameral legislature
12. type of committee that works when legislature is not in session

E. Synonym Selection*

Directions: Place a check next to each word that is a synonym for the preceding underlined word. There is at least *one* synonym listed in each item. The first item has been completed as an example.

1. redress
   - ✓ correction
   - _____ destruction
   - _____ application
   - ✓ reparation

2. usurpation
   - _____ explanation
   - _____ seizure
   - _____ humiliation
   - _____ estimation

3. abolish
   - _____ extinguish
   - _____ establish
   - _____ annul
   - _____ eliminate

4. impel
   - _____ force
   - _____ join
   - _____ urge
   - _____ question

5. perfidy
   - _____ faithfulness
   - _____ treachery
   - _____ loyalty
   - _____ allegiance

6. abdicated
   - _____ synthesized
   - _____ relinquished
   - _____ renounced
   - _____ announced

7. acquiesce
   - _____ accept
   - _____ object
   - _____ reject
   - _____ comply

8. magnanimity
   - _____ honor
   - _____ revenge
   - _____ worthlessness
   - _____ tyranny

III. Relationship Level

After the words are recognized and appropriate meanings are attached to them, the student is "ready" to deal with vocabulary at the relationship level. It is at this level that relationships between and among words are discovered. Through this analysis and a student's

*Exercise based upon usage of "The Declaration of Independence," July 4, 1776.

"linkage" of words, concept formulation is initiated. Since the recognition of the word and understanding of meaning are prerequisite to the relationship level, these exercises are best used after students have had sufficient opportunity (i.e., at the end of a chapter) to acquire and use the designated technical vocabulary.

A. Analogy

Analogy exercises require students to examine words in relationship to one another. Oral introduction is required by the teacher to illustrate the relationship exhibited and to acquaint the students with the punctuation used in abbreviating the items. For example:

toes : feet   ::   fingers : hands

is read as:

toes are to feet as fingers are to hands.

Some of the relationships that can be exhibited through the use of analogy are listed below.

Directions: Read each analogy, then select and circle the word that belongs in the blank.

Part to whole
skin : man   ::   feathers: _____
fish   bird   turtle   lion

Place
Washington, D.C.: Potomac   ::   New York: _____
Mississippi   Missouri   Hudson   Snake

Classification
Reptilia : snake   ::   Amphibia: _____
fox   frog   cow   starfish

Person and place
Armstrong : moon   ::   Columbus: _____
America   India   China   Spain

Person and role
Carter : President   ::   Mondale: _____
Secretary of State   Vice-president   Speaker   Chief Justice

Place and object
Detroit : car   ::   Chicago: _____
cotton   clothing   meat   paper

Paired associate

    Starsky : Hutch   ::   Marquette: _____

    Joliet   Livingstone   Stanley   Cartier

Object and function

    olfactory nerve : smell   ::   optic nerve: _____

    taste   see   hear   touch

Number

    3 : 9   ::   7: _____

    49   28   56   14

Cause and effect

    food : obesity   ::   smoking: _____

    diabetes   arthritis   psoriasis   cancer

Antonym

    enlarge : decrease   ::   attract: _____

    repeal   repel   draw   entice

Synonym

    exterminate : annihilate   ::   perplex: _____

    evict   explain   bewilder   annoy

B. Classification*

Directions: Governments can be classified according to the following three categories. Under each of the three categories, select and write the term that appropriately describes the government of the corresponding country. Be prepared to justify your choices.

	geographical distribution of political power UNITARY CONFEDERATE FEDERAL	relationship of executive with legislature PRESIDENTIAL PARLIMENTARY DICTATORIAL	relationship between those governing and those being governed DEMOCRATIC AUTHORITARIAN
UNITED STATES	federal	presidential	democratic
GREAT BRITAIN			
FRANCE			
SOVIET UNION			
CANADA			
JAPAN			
CUBA			
YUGOSLAVIA			

*Exercise based upon usage of *Our American Government and Political System* by D. Wit and A. Dionisopoulos.

C. Checklist*

Directions: Review the tactics listed below. If labor utilizes a specific tactic, put a check under the column labeled "labor."

If management utilizes a tactic, put a check under that column.

If a tactic is used by labor as well as management, put a check under the column labeled "both."

	Labor	Management	Both
1. picketing			
2. slowdowns			
3. injunctions			
4. strikes			
5. featherbedding			
6. strike breaker			
7. propaganda			
8. boycott			
9. restrictions of output			
10. lockouts			
11. political pressure			

D. Identifying Relationships**

Directions: Circle the three words in each line that have something in common. On the line below, briefly describe the relationship of the words you have circled.

1. (incisors)   pharynx   (canine)   (molars)   adenoid

    types of teeth
_____

2. appendix   mouth   esophagus   adenoids   stomach
_____

3. tongue   liver   colon   taste buds   salivary glands
_____

4. cementum   erepsin   enamel   pepsin   dentine
_____

5. duodenum   jejunum   ileum   lacteal   caecum
_____

*Exercise based upon usage of *Consumer Economic Problems* by R. Warmke and E. Wyllie.

**Exercise based upon usage of *Modern Biology,* by J. Otto and A. Towle.

6. trypsin	ptyalin	lactase	lipase	amylase

7. glycerin	erepsin	lacteals	lactase	matlase

8. larynx	mucus	saliva	pancreas	hydrochloric acid

Concluding Comments

Effective teachers know that they must aid students in understanding the words unique to their content fields. Lamberg and Lamb (1980) suggest: "Because many teachers regard vocabulary as an important component of content area learning, they provide regular, systematic instruction in selected terms and symbols, which designate key concepts in their content area. . . . Many other teachers, however, provide only sporadic attention to vocabulary; they assume, incorrectly, that all students should be able to learn the new words and concepts without assistance" (p. 31).

In conclusion, Herber (1978) states: "If independent activity is expected and students have not been *shown how* to perform that activity, the teaching is assumptive. It neglects the critical factor in good instruction: that is, that students must be *shown how* to do whatever it is they are *expected* to do independently" (pp. 215–216).

References

Aukerman, C. *Reading in the secondary school classroom.* New York: McGraw-Hill, 1972, p. 23.

Barman, C., Schneiderwent, M., Rusch, J., and Hindin, W. *Physical science* (2nd ed.). Morristown, N.J.: Silver Burdett, 1979, section entitled "Excursions"; ninth-grade level.

Cunningham, J. W., Cunningham, P. M., and Arthur, S. V. *Middle and secondary school reading.* New York: Longman, 1981, pp. 23–24.

"The Declaration of Independence", Philadelphia: 1776.

Estes, T. H., and Vaughan, J. L., Jr. *Reading and learning in the content classroom.* Boston: Allyn and Bacon, 1978, p. 98.

Graff, H. *The free and the brave.* Chicago: Rand McNally, 1980, Chapter 3, "The French Experiment"; eighth-grade level.

Herber, H. L. *Teaching reading in content areas.* Englewood Cliffs, N.J.: Prentice-Hall, 1978, pp. 215–216.

Lamberg, W. J., and Lamb, C. E. *Reading instruction in the content areas.* Rand McNally, 1980, p. 31.

Metcalfe, H., Williams, J., and Castka, J. *Modern chemistry.* New York: Holt, Rinehart, and Winston, 1978, Chapter 5, "The Periodic Law"; 11th grade level.

Otto, J., and Towle, A. *Modern biology.* New York: Holt, Rinehart, and Winston, 1977, Chapter 35, "The Amphibians"; Chapter 41, "Nutrition"; Chapter 49, "The Habitat"; high school level.

Robinson, H. A. *Teaching reading and study strategies: The content areas.* Boston: Allyn and Bacon, 1975, p. 57.

Warmke, R., and Wyllie, E. *Consumer economic problems.* Cincinnati, Oh.: South-Western Publishing Co., 1977, Chapter 5, "Production in the American Economy"; Chapter 7, "Labor-Management Relations"; tenth-grade level.

Wit, D., and Dionisopoulos, A. *Our American government and political system* (2nd ed.). River Forest, Ill.: Laidlaw Brothers, 1977, Chapter 2, "Types of Modern Government"; Chapter 25, "The State Legislatures"; eleventh- and twelfth-grade level.

7

Comprehension Strategies in Content Areas

Without a doubt, the essence of content area instruction is comprehension instruction. Unfortunately, recent studies have pointed out that comprehension instruction in classroom situations appears to consist mainly of information dispensing, interrogation, and assessment. This is obviously the antithesis of what should be going on in the name of comprehension instruction. Teachers need to have access to a variety of strategies that (a) capitalize on students' prior knowledge, (b) guide their reading of text material, and (c) reinforce their learning after reading. Thus, teachers must be knowledgeable about strategies designed to enhance comprehension in prereading, reading, and postreading situations.

Manzo describes three instructional methods to enlarge comprehension in content area reading. Specifically, all three activities incorporate oral languaging as part of the total lesson structure.

Vacca emphasizes the importance of readying students to read their class assignments. He explicates the various components of the prereading stage of an instructional lesson.

Tutolo focuses his discussion on the study guide, a means to direct students' reading of a text assignment. Specifically, he describes two types of guides and discusses their value in content area instruction.

Thomas also advocates the use of guide material in instruction. Additionally, he suggests the use of modified cloze techniques in guide material and illustrates three types of such guides.

Bean recommends the use of content redefinition as a means of introducing vocabulary in a prereading situation. Furthermore, he suggests coupling that with the use of two comprehension strategies to enhance long-term retention of key vocabulary and concepts in reading and postreading situations.

Thomas describes a strategy that requires students to preview material to predict responses to six key questions. With the predictions serving as purposes for reading, discussion of the various conjectures ensues in the postreading phase.

Cunningham discusses the use of questions in prereading, reading, and postreading situations. Specifically, he focuses his discussion on questions that: (1) diagnose what students already know; (2) guide students' learning; (3) stimulate students' thinking beyond the text; and, (4) focus on specific learnings.

Finally, Arthur focuses on writing as a means of enhancing students' learning. A writing strategy for all classrooms is described, followed by specific suggestions for writing in various content areas.

Three "Universal" Strategies in Content Area* Reading and Languaging

Anthony V. Manzo
University of Missouri–Kansas City

The term "reading in the content areas" is a code name for means and methods by which to improve reading, language, and thinking in every classroom.

The basis for the content area reading movement is twofold: there is the belief (1) that developmental skills—such as reading, language, and thinking—need to be nurtured continuously and rather explicitly throughout the school years, even in college, and (2) that the content area teacher is in the best position, in terms of daily contact with students, to promote these skills concurrently with the skills and objectives of each content class.

To this basic objective and rationale, three elaborations can be added as guidelines for developing actual instructional practices in the content areas. The first is that the content teacher probably teaches best when s/he serves as a model of effective reading behavior (Manzo, 1969). The second says that the notion of concurrent methods should not be limited to content and reading skills, but can be extended to thinking skills (Herber, 1970) and selected language skills and attitudes about learning (Manzo and Casale, 1980). The third idea, which further elaborates the first two, says that the teacher can best model and impart these skills, abilities, and attitudes when interacting with students in "oral languaging" (Manzo and Sherk, 1978).

"Oral languaging," as used here, means a discussion structured to promote a reciprocal ("give and take") exchange between the teacher and students, so that they may influence one another's thinking and language behaviors.

The stress on language needs some definition and explanation. Language, here, means the words one knows and tends to speak. These words, theorists such as Sapir tell us, have a greater influence on the person speaking than on the one listening (Mandelbaum, 1958). Put another way, to be taught new ways of speaking is tantamount to being taught new ways of understanding, thinking, and acting.

*Reprinted with permission of Dr. Anthony V. Manzo and the International Reading Association, *Journal of Reading,* 1980, *24,* 146–149.

Thus, when a student is taught to read and to "language" better, the likelihood is that s/he is being taught how to think and feel differently as well. From this we can infer that the value of altering a student's way of "languaging" (Postman and Weingartner, 1969), or speaking and thinking, can have a profound influence on the student's affect, to the extent of heightening the individual's willingness and determination to read and to study in a given discipline.

I have fashioned three relatively simple instructional methods of almost universal applicability from these guiding ideas. One, called the Oral Reading Strategy, is *"text specific,"* i.e., it is designed to be employed with a specific piece of text and to help the student to read it with greater fluency and comprehension. The other two, the C/T/Q and Question-Only strategies are understood better as *"non-textual"* or bracing methods, i.e., intended to help a student to build a richer foundation in the language, thought and attitude of a discipline, and therefrom to grow in reading and content knowledge.

Oral reading strategy

The Oral Reading Strategy has the teacher periodically (once per week) read aloud a brief selection (approximately two pages) of a text while students follow along in their textbooks. The teacher then asks students to "translate" or put things into their own words as s/he stops at logical points. In content-rich material, this might mean pausing after each paragraph, with the likelihood that students reread individual sentences and even phrases. Since this strategy is primarily a readiness activity designed to motivate students and develop their concept background, when accomplished, they should read silently thereafter.

The confusions revealed, questions raised and informal (incidental) help rendered with vocabulary, author style, basic concepts, and key questions make this a solid content area reading and languaging lesson.

C/T/Q strategy

C, T and Q is a simple reminder to the teacher (1) to isolate key Concepts, key Terminology and key Questions around which a unit of study is built, and (2) to teach these in advance of reading, much as in the DRTA (Stauffer, 1969), but then again as a follow-up activity after silent reading.

It is valuable to have students record C/T/Q points in their notebooks. In this way, the information is available as a map or continuous reference to guide them through subsequent lessons and home/school reading assignments.

The special value of C/T/Q is that it causes the teacher to think through and share with students the most essential and uncluttered elements of language and thought germane to a unit of study.

This method is especially valuable when combined with the next, the Question-Only Strategy (Manzo and Legenza, 1975), which helps students learn how to arrive at the central concepts, language and thoughts of a unit by their own wit and analysis.

The question-only strategy: a stepwise method

Step 1: The teacher announces a topic to the class and explains the rules of the interaction. Students are told that they must learn all that they can about the topic solely by their questions, after which they will be given a test on the topic. The test, they are told, will cover *all* the information which you, the teacher, consider to be important, whether or not the students extract the information from you with their questions.

Step 2: The class questions and the teacher answers fully but without undue elaboration.

Step 3: The test is given. A class discussion follows in which note is made of the questions raised and those which should have been.

Step 4: Students are directed to read their texts carefully or to listen to a short lecture in order to discover what they failed to learn through their initial questions.

(Optional) Step 5: A follow-up test is given. The combined scores from the first and second tests are a good index of a student's growth in grasp of key ideas and facts.

Instructions for installation

The value and creditability of new methods are always reduced, at the beginning, by certain predictable inhibitions on the teacher's performance. The reflections which follow are added in the hope of reducing some of these inhibitions to the successful adoption of the methods described in this article.

One of the darkest and best kept secrets of teacher education is that teaching effectiveness, contrary to the beliefs of naive researchers, actually is diminished when new methods are first being learned and employed. The reasons are simple.

First, the teacher's "cognitive dissonance" level (Festinger, 1957) is raised in the new situation. Cognitive dissonance occurs any time an individual is faced with reconciling opposing drives. (My use of the term is broader than the usual, though within Festinger's conceptualization.) In the case of teaching, the teacher has not always freely chosen the new method. Pressure is put upon teachers to try new approaches, by professors and administrators and indirectly by students. This causes dissonance, or ambivalent feelings.

After the teacher "elects" to try the new method, there is additional dissonance associated with the method itself. The teacher may think: "If it does work, shouldn't I have thought of it earlier? What if it is a better way to go, but *I* can't make it work? Maybe it would be best if it didn't prove workable; then I wouldn't have to face the likelihood that there are other books, ideas, and courses of study out there which need to be sought out and tried." In other words, the teacher experiences cognitive dissonance about both the new method and the need to try it out.

Also, early attempts to use anything new are fraught with miscalculations. Recognizing this, the teacher is bound to experience insecurity and "performance anxiety." Together, these have the effect of narrowing the teacher's attention, to the detriment of students and their individual needs.

This scenario is not so discouraging as it may appear. Consideration of an analogous situation, learning to drive a car, suggests that the problems can be overcome in a relatively easy fashion.

When first we learn to drive, we dare not play the radio, carry on a conversation, or take in the scenery. As our driving becomes more and more habitual, we can do all of these things and more. So it is with new methods. It is important to continue to use them until dissonance is reduced, comfort is increased, and we can once again become sensitive and aware of student needs.

A conservative estimate, based upon personal teaching and teacher training experiences, suggests that a new methodology needs to be employed not more than two to four times for the benefits to outweigh the initial drawbacks. Unfortunately, there is a strong tendency to abandon new ideas and methods before the completion of even a single full trial.

In short, to install and embed these methods to full benefit, employ each, completely, at least three times. To add luster to performance, compare notes with enthusiastic and experienced colleagues, and adapt the methods to personal style and the unique situations in which they are to be employed.

References

Festinger, Leon. *A Theory of Cognitive Dissonance*. Evanston, Ill.: Row, Peterson, 1957.

Herber, Harold. *Teaching Reading in the Content Areas*. New York, N.Y.: Prentice-Hall, 1970.

Mandelbaum, Donald G., ed. *Selected Writings of Edward Sapier in Language, Culture, and Personality*. Berkeley, Calif.: University of California Press, 1958.

Manzo, Anthony V. "ReQuest: A Method for Improving Reading Comprehension through Reciprocal Questioning." *Journal of Reading*, vol. 12 (November 1969), pp. 123–26, 163.

Manzo, Anthony V., and Ula Casale. "PASS: A Problem Solving Approach to Study Skills." *Reading Horizons*, vol. 20 (Summer 1980).

Manzo, Anthony V., and Alice Legenza. "Inquiry Training for Kindergarten Children." *Journal of Educational Leadership*, vol. 32 (April 1975), pp. 479–83.

Manzo, Anthony V., and John K. Sherak, "Languaging in the Content Areas: The LICA Design." . *Journal of the New England Reading Association*, vol. 13 (Winter 1978), pp. 28–32.

Postman, Neal, and Charles Weingartner. *Teaching as a Subversive Activity*. New York, N.Y.: Delta Books, 1969.

Stauffer, Russell G. *Teaching Reading as a Thinking Process* . New York, N.Y.: Harper and Row, 1969.

Readiness to Read Content Area Assignments*

Richard T. Vacca
Kent State University

There's a consensus among reading people that readiness should be a practical part of reading instruction at every teaching level. Karlin (1964, p. 236), for example, agrees that while the readiness concept has been applied to primary reading, "its influences may be felt at each instructional level." The goal of readiness to read in content areas presumes that students will be mentally and psychologically prepared to begin a reading assignment—in a state of mind which will promote learning.

As a general principle, readiness refers to the ability of an individual at a given age to cope adequately with the demands of a cognitive task (Ausubel, 1963). Frederick's (1968,

*Reprinted with permission of Dr. Richard Vacca and the International Reading Association, *Journal of Reading*, 1977, *20*, 387–392.

p. 18) review of research on readiness activities generally indicates that, "Pre-learning experiences can be used to advantage in readiness if experiences: 1) lead to a concept, 2) are relevant to the concept, and 3) provide a direction in learning the concept." Ausubel (1963) argues that there is little disagreement that readiness always crucially affects the efficiency of the learning process. He indicates, however, that little if any significant research has been conducted in the classroom. As far as readiness for reading is concerned, Marksheffel (1966) reiterates that it is intrinsic to reading at every instructional level, but admits that it has received "insufficient attention and is little understood" by reading personnel.

Since the 1960s, however, readiness to learn through written discourse has been analyzed from many investigative perspectives. Insights have emerged; promising instructional procedures have been introduced into the literature.

In particular, a great deal of experimental activity has focused on Ausubel's (1963, 1968) theory of "meaningful reception learning." It's appropriate, therefore, to consider the developments arising from this theory and the implications they have for those content teachers who themselves are "ready" to expand their instructional repertoires.

First, however, consider the following review of where the reading field has been with readiness-to-read methodology. This will provide a framework in which to understand better the implications of meaningful reception learning for readiness to read in content areas.

Readiness to Read in Retrospect

Part of the readiness concept states that individuals must know certain things before they can learn specific, additional materials, or that they must develop certain skills before they can develop others. Because readiness is an inferred mental state, teachers unfortunately have little direct knowledge of an individual's state of readiness. Nevertheless, through detailed knowledge of a student's educational background and the use of diagnostic tools, fairly shrewd inferences can be made about readiness for a specific reading task.

Classroom teachers in elementary schools attempt to ensure children's readiness to read by giving them preparatory activities. These procedures have become traditional. In reading methods textbooks or basal teaching manuals, lesson formats typically espouse a "readiness stage" which emphasizes in one way or another: 1) setting purposes, 2) building background and experiences, and 3) teaching unfamiliar vocabulary. The same steps can be applied at all grade levels and in all content areas.

If taken at face value, these activities usually are beguiling to the unsuspecting teacher. Armed with an undergraduate or graduate course in reading (if any at all), he/she may begin classes with the idea that a dash of new vocabulary here and a sprinkling of questions there will suffice in preparing readers for the learning task ahead. Obviously this is an oversimplification of readiness methodology. Nevertheless, much more than the routine of a readiness stage is required to prepare students.

A structure is needed that will help learners link what they know with what they will study. Herber (1970), in discussing how a teacher can structure a lesson through which both content and reading can be taught, elaborates on the stage of preparing the student for the lesson. In Herber's instructional framework, preparation presumes the necessity of cognitive readiness and has several interdependent elements:

1) Motivation
2) Background information and review
3) Anticipation and purpose
4) Direction
5) Language development

1) *Content teachers use those motivational techniques which best fit their style and personality.* They determine which approach actually will arouse a particular group of students for a specific lesson. The witty start, the dramatic presentation, the novel prelearning experience are all useful in sparking excitement or curiosity about the material to be read.

2) *As students get set for the reading task, they need a frame of reference for the concepts they will encounter and acquire.* Background information helps build this framework, providing a context into which new information can be fitted. There is a need to review common experiences and relate them to the subject matter, to enlarge and strengthen the context of the topics which the students will be dealing with in the reading assignment.

With respect to this frame of reference, one of Stauffer's (1969, p. 53) criticisms of the readiness activities of basal readers should be heeded. He questions whether a brief, teacher-directed talk session ever "builds" experiences or leads to concept development: "Will talking about a hungry lion . . . or a circus or an Indian, build concepts?"

Similarly, a social studies teacher once spoke of her experience with an eighth grade class on the island of Guam. She was teaching about the coal resources of the U.S.A. During her readiness period, she wished to clear up possible confusion by telling students that *coke* was not to be mistaken for a popular soft drink. She then spent several weeks on the unit using pictures, projects, reports and the like. Finally, she gave a test in which one pupil, responding to a particular question, wrote, "I know coke is made from coal—but it still tastes good." Clearly, as Stauffer (1975, p. 9) suggests, "Concepts are not acquired by artificial explanations and compulsory memorization, but by giving students a chance to acquire them in, by, and through their functional contexts."

3) *During the preparation period, teachers try to help students anticipate what they'll be dealing with and set a purpose for their reading.* The essential question, however, is, "Set whose purpose?" Students'? Teacher's? How does a teacher reconcile his/her purpose(s) with those of students who may have no particular interest in the topic? According to Herber (1970, pp. 33–34) students establish reading purposes through the structure provided by the teacher:

> The structure provided by the teacher should reflect his own preparation for the lesson: he has determined the ideas he believes are important enough for students to acquire. He encourages pupils to be receptive to those ideas as they read. He also determines how the students must read the material in order to develop those ideas, and he gives students direction in the application of those ideas. Consequently, students read for the purpose of developing specific ideas, and they do so with a conscious application of specific, appropriate skills.

4) *Another part of ensuring readiness to read is that content teachers give students directions as to specific skills which they will need in order to handle the subject matter in their next unit.* Since these skills differ according to the subject, the teacher must analyze the reading material to determine which will be needed.

5) *Finally, teachers prepare readers for the technical vocabulary they will encounter.* Students should become familiar with key vocabulary and gain a degree of facility with it before they read.

In retrospect the preparatory aspects of readiness to read should help students to link the "given"—what they already know or the skills that they have—with the "new"—what they are about to learn. The bulk of effective "reading instruction" in the content areas may very well come before students read—during the preparation component of a teacher's lesson. Hansell (1976, p. 309) accurately states,

> . . . teachers may help students to read texts, articles, or books by helping them understand the content before they deal with it in print. . . . The problem of content teachers then becomes, in the words of an eighth grade teacher in Boston, one of "convincing the students that they know more than they think they do about my subject."

Since the 1960s research involving "meaningful reception learning" has introduced a number of developments affecting cognitive readiness. These developments do not require classroom teachers to alter drastically what they already know about preparing students to read. Rather, they can be adapted to the procedures described above. In this way content area teachers are in a position to increase their instructional repertoires and approach readiness from a wider intellectual perspective.

Basing their work on Ausubel's belief that an individual's wealth of knowledge is organized hierarchically in terms of highly generalized concepts, less inclusive concepts, and specific facts, experimenters have studied extensively the use of "advance organizers" as an aid to learning and retaining concepts. Advance organizers attempt to maximize the cognitive readiness of learners prior to a new task. Ausubel maintains that cognitive structure—"an individual's organization, stability and clarity of knowledge in a particular subject-matter field at any given time"—is a major factor in learning and retention. Learning is facilitated to the extent that previous knowledge is clear, stable, and organized.

Ausubel suggests that advance organizers, if constructed and used properly, would enhance learning and aid retention because they tend to clarify and organize an individual's cognitive structure prior to a learning task. Advance organizers presumably contain the necessary relevant "subsuming concepts" which enable learners to fit new meaning into previous frameworks.

An advance organizer, then, is defined by Ausubel (1968, p. 214) as preparatory paragraphs which provide:

> . . . relevant ideational scaffolding, enhance the discriminability of the new learning material from previously learned related ideas, and otherwise effect integrative reconciliation at a level of abstraction, generality, and inclusiveness which is much higher than the learning material itself. To be maximally effective they must be formulated in terms of language, concepts, propositions already familiar to the learner, and use appropriate illustrations and analogies.

Baker (1976) has reviewed fifty-two published research reports dealing with Ausubel's theory of meaningful reception learning. His exhaustive review establishes that the majority of studies conducted *since* Ausubel's investigations have been nonsupportive. More than two-thirds of the studies, though, are short-term, "one shot," experiments rather than prolonged investigations. Moreover, more than twenty different forms of advance organizers have been investigated.

One of the major limitations of advance organizer research has been the lack of a commonly accepted operational definition that allows for careful replication. Baker suggests future studies could profit from a detailed analysis of Ausubel's theoretical base, rather than on his specific treatment—the advance organizer.

A structured overview is a preparatory activity which has its roots in Ausubel's theoretical base of meaningful reception learning (Barron, 1969). More and more it is mentioned in the literature on reading instruction (Catterson, 1974; Manzo, 1975; Hansell, 1976). Thus far, the International Reading Association has published two monographs in its Reading Aids Series which serve as excellent content area reading resources for math and science teachers. Both monographs (Earle, 1976; Thelen, 1976) provide a description and numerous examples of the structured overview adapted as a readiness procedure in math and science classes.

Structured overviews are visual diagrams of the key vocabulary of a learning task "in relation to more inclusive or subsuming vocabulary concepts that have been previously learned by the student" (Estes and others, 1969, p. 41). Earle (1969) devised a set of directions to make the construction of overviews a non-time consuming and realistic task for teachers:

1. Select every word that you intend to use in a unit that you think is necessary to the students' understanding what you want them to understand.
2. Take the list of words and arrange them and rearrange them until you have a diagram which shows the relationships which exist among the ideas in the unit.
3. Use an overhead or write the diagram on the chalkboard the first day of the lesson (or use as a prelearning experience before students read). Explain why you arranged the words the way you did and have students contribute as much information as possible.

The Figure represents a structured overview that was constructed by Joseph Janoch, a ninth grade social studies teacher from Lyons Township High School, LaGrange, Illinois.

Structured Overview: Social Studies Unit

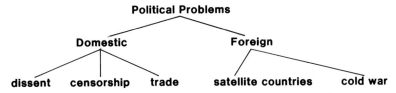

Purpose: This is used before the chapters on Foreign Affairs and Eastern Europe. The major concepts are shown in a comparison-contrast pattern. Either write this on the board or place it on an overhead projector. Describe the overview, supplying more in-depth answers as the questions warrant.

Note the hierarchy of major concepts, their connection to one another, in the reading selection. The social studies teacher has an opportunity to preteach key technical terms, draw upon students' understandings and experiences with the terms. Possibly the teacher will have students relate several of the terms to previous study or learnings within the course. Furthermore, notice the implicit comparison-contrast pattern expressed in the structured overview. What better way to provide directions for the needed reading skills that will be applied to this selection than to have students visualize it through the diagram! The structured overview provides a visual map, a network, that permits students to see the relatedness of the important concepts in an overall unit or specific reading assignment to be studied.

The structured overview thus can become an important preparatory tool in the perception of relationships and the acquisition of concepts. In addition, it may very well have an additional "side benefit." After continued use of the structured overview in research in a classroom setting, Earle (1969, p. 53) notes the reaction of one teacher: "Preparing and using the overview made my teaching easier, I knew exactly where I was going. . . ." The structured overview, then, is a way of helping classroom teachers to clarify their content objectives and to identify precisely the major ideas to be encountered and acquired by students.

References

Ausubel, D. P. *Educational Psychology—A Cognitive View.* New York, N.Y.: Holt, Rinehart and Winston, 1968.

Ausubel, D. P. *The Psychology of Meaningful Verbal Learning.* New York, N.Y.: Grune & Stratton, 1963.

Baker, R. L. "Meaningful Reception Learning." *Research in Reading in the Content Areas: Third Year Report,* H. L. Herber and R. T. Vacca, Eds. Syracuse, N.Y.: Syracuse University Reading and Language Arts Center. In Press.

Barron, R. F. "The Use of Vocabulary as an Advance Organizer."*Research in Reading in the Content Areas: First Year Report.* H. L. Herber and P. L. Sanders, Eds. Syracuse, N.Y.: Syracuse University Reading and Language Arts Center, 1969

Catterson, J. H. "Techniques for Improving Comprehension in Mathematics." *Reading in the Middle School,* G. G. Duffy, Ed., pp. 153–65. Newark, Del.: International Reading Association, 1974.

Earle, R.A. *Teaching Reading and Mathematics,* Newark, Del.: International Reading Association, 1976.

Earle, R. A. "Use of the Structured Overview in Mathematics Classes." *Research in Teaching Reading in the Content Areas: First Year Report,* H.L. Herber and P.L. Sanders, Eds. Syracuse, N.Y.: Syracuse University Reading and Language Arts Center, 1969.

Estes, T. H. and others. "Three Methods of Introducing Students to a Reading-Learning Task in Two Content Subjects." *Research in Reading in the Content Areas: First Year Report.* H. L. Herber and P. L. Sanders, Eds. Syracuse, N.Y.: Syracuse University Reading and Language Arts Center, 1969.

Frederick, E. C. A Study of the Effects of Readiness Activities on Concept Learning. Unpublished doctoral dissertation, Syracuse University, 1968.

Hansell, T. S. "Increasing Understanding in Content Reading." *Journal of Reading.* vol. 19, no. 4 (January 1976), pp. 307–11.

Herber, H. L. *Teaching Reading in Content Areas.* Englewood Cliffs, N.J.: Prentice-Hall, 1970.

Karlin, R. *Teaching Reading in High School.* 1st ed. Indianapolis, Ind.: Bobbs-Merrill, 1964.

Manzo, A. V. "Guided Reading Procedure." *Journal of Reading,* vol. 18, no. 4 (January 1975). pp. 287–91.

Marksheffel, N. A. *Better Reading in the Secondary School.* New York, N.Y.: Ronald Press Co., 1966.

Stauffer, R. G. The Dimensions of Sound Reading Instruction. Paper presented at the 25th Annual Reading Conference. University of Delaware, Newark, Delaware, 1975.

Stauffer, R. G. *Directing Reading Maturity as a Cognitive Process.* New York, N.Y.: Harper & Row, 1969.

Thelen, J. *Improving Reading in Science.* Newark, Del.: International Reading Association, 1976.

The Study Guide—Types, Purpose, and Value*

Daniel J. Tutolo
Bowling Green State University

Students' poor comprehension of expository texts is a problem that concerns most content teachers. A contributing factor is the extensive concept load found in most content area texts. The reader simply does not know what ideas are important and what topics deserve concentrated study.

The teacher can improve student learning by designing study guides which lead the learner to the important concepts explained in the textbook. This article will define the study guide and provide an example of both the interlocking and noninterlocking types. The purpose of study guides will be clarified, and, this author's opinion will be offered concerning the value of guides.

A study guide is a teaching aid written by the teacher to be used by the student to assist the student in developing reading skills for the purpose of enhancing comprehension of textual material. A guide is usually a typewritten copy keyed to the textbook that can be placed beside the text while the student is reading. The student refers to the guide, then the text, or vice versa. Or, the student may refer back and forth to guide and text while reading the associated text.

The guide represents a plan or strategy to be followed by the learner to enhance comprehension. The guide, as written by the teacher, identifies a reading task or objective and offers a plan or strategy for the reader. The assumption is that comprehension will be enhanced when directions which stipulate goals are in close proximity to the textual material containing the relevant information.

The guide is a simulator of the experience and understanding which the teacher wants the student to have. It assumes that many students have difficulty reading expository text and must be guided carefully so as to experience success at their level of competence.

*Reprinted with permission of Dr. Daniel Tutolo and the International Reading Association, *Journal of Reading,* 1977, *20,* 503–507.

Guides can be designed to lead students through levels of comprehension from literal to interpretive to applicative. Or, they can be designed to focus on internal patterns of paragraphs like comparison/contrast cause/effect and main idea/detail. Or, they can be designed to lead students through specific skill development like conclusions, arguments, relationships and generalizations.

Types of Study Guides

Interlocking study guide. In the case of the interlocking study guide, statements proceed from the literal level of meaning (Herber's model, 1970) to the interpretive level of meaning to the applicative level of meaning. The three levels of thinking required of the reader do not intermix. All literal questions are grouped together, all interpretive questions are grouped together, and so on. The sequence of thinking in the interlocking guide always moves from literal to interpretive to applicative.

By keying the statements in some way, the guide can serve as a valuable help in individualizing instruction. Suppose that all literal statements are marked with one star (*). Immature readers can be asked to respond to these statements, while average and brighter students can be expected to respond to two-star and three-star statements. Thus the class is divided into three ability groups all following the same guide yet responding to different parts of the guide.

Research is not yet clear whether concentrating on one kind of thinking is a better approach to learning. Certainly, however, this approach can insulate some students against failure. An immature reader who is guided to respond to literal statements and questions is far more likely to be successful, particularly if this student has a history of quitting or giving up when confronted with complex reading tasks.

Noninterlocking study guide. In the case of the noninterlocking study guide, no such hierarchical thinking is encouraged. The teacher is free to include in the guide any direction that will help the reader to process the information (Cunningham and Shablak, 1975). The thinking necessary for understanding might vary from literal to application and back to literal again as the reader moves through the connected discourse.

The purpose of the study guide is to prepare a plan for reading the text.

Interlocking Levels Guide

Read "Tragedy" on page _____ of your textbook. After you have completed the reading, respond to this study guide. Try to answer correctly without returning to the text material. However, if you are not sure of an answer feel free to reread the assignment and then mark your study guide. Notice that the guide has questions and statements separated into three categories. Section one—the one starred items—calls for your recall of facts as stated in the text. Section two—the two starred items—calls for a different kind of thinking called interpretation. Here you must decide what the author meant by what was said. Section three calls for a third kind of thinking called application. In this section you will be expected to use the facts and interpretations to solve a problem.

Remember, read the account carefully and try to respond without going back to the text. This guide will attempt to measure your recall of information. If, after you have carefully read the guide, there are answers you are not sure about, feel free to return to the text to reread.

Now: Read "Tragedy."

Tragedy

The townspeople regarded "Death Hill" as appropriately named. Over the years sixteen lives had been lost as a result of automobile accidents on the dangerous turns. Despite flasher lights warning of the peril, visitors to the area often miscalculated the turns, with the result of bent fenders and bruised egos. The fatality rate in the teens indicated the problem was far greater than property and ego damage alone.

It wasn't until the town lost two of its own on the second and most dangerous turn that talk began in earnest of building a bypass around "Death Hill." State engineers had been contacted and a preliminary study was now in progress. In projects of this type the state paid ninety percent and the local townspeople ten percent. Most local people considered the project cheap at any price for they had known Becky and Jerry all of their lives. Each time they met the family survivors here or there around town, it served as a silent reminder of the loss that could have been avoided.

Factual questions: Remember, a fact can be verified by going directly to the text for the answer.

Code: * literal **interpretation
    *** application

* According to townspeople "Death Hill" was

    A. a poor nickname
    B. appropriately named
    C. a passing fancy
    D. the greatest local problem

* The preliminary study was intended to determine the cost of

    A. a tunnel through the hill
    B. widening the highway
    C. a bypass
    D. extensive safety measures

Interpretation: Remember, you are to try to determine what the author meant by what was said.

** What is meant by "the town lost two of its own"? Write a one paragraph explanation: _____

** Select the answer that most nearly represents what the author meant when he said "most local people considered the project cheap at any price."

    A. Cost is no object where safety is involved.
    B. This was one death too many.
    C. The ninety percent-ten percent ratio was appealing.
    D. Local conscience was now involved.

Application: Considering the facts and ideas as expressed, can you solve these problems?

*** Assume you are the editor of the local newspaper. Six months has passed since City Council received the preliminary report and no action has yet been taken. Write an editorial encouraging positive action on the part of Council to approve a bypass road.

*** The City Council has approved the bypass and now must raise $100,000 as its portion of expenses to construct the bypass. Suggest ways the community can raise this amount.

Noninterlocking Levels Guide

Code: * literal
        ** interpretation
        *** application

  * Read paragraph one of "A New Way of Life for Americans." When energy was abundant and cheap we could produce goods more _____

*** Read paragraph two carefully. List several reasons why this adjustment would be difficult for Americans.

  ** In paragraph three what is meant by "increasing the quality of life"?

*** Reread paragraph three with this question in mind. Is it better to produce many different kinds of breakfast cereals to appeal to every taste or to limit production only to cereals that are tasty and high in nutritional value? Respond to the question in writing. Tell why you feel as you do.

A New Way of Life for Americans

The energy shortage can be expected to influence the cost of goods and services for years to come. When energy was abundant and cheap we could produce goods more economically and thus sell them at a lower per unit cost. Now that energy is expensive and the goods produced higher priced we must make more careful choices about the things we buy.

Perhaps we will have to give up the idea of an extensive wardrobe, two cars for every family, two or more weeks vacation every year, and other signs of our affluent society. One very visible sign of affluence which may be on the decided decline is the department store loaded with consumer goods to appeal to every taste. This adjustment will be difficult for a nation used to consuming so much.

But, when we look at the future it may be better to produce and sell products which increase the quality of life rather than simply appeal to insatiable wants. Appealing to our insatiable wants never made us very happy anyway. Perhaps if we direct our efforts as a nation toward producing and consuming goods that enhance the quality of life, we can look forward to a society which takes a more realistic view of wants and the satisfaction of these wants. With the energy shortage upon us this new way of thinkimg is worth a try.

One way to eliminate the need for study guides is to write expository texts that are easier for students to read. The problem is, as we know, at what level we write these texts when reading levels of students in a typical class are likely to vary considerably. The usual formula used to measure this variance, as suggested by curriculum experts, is two thirds of the median chronological age of the students. With fifteen year olds, this means a spread of reading achievement of ten years.

It perhaps makes more sense to adopt a book which most students in the class can read and then prepare study guides to enhance comprehension of the students. This is easier said than done. Certainly high school teachers are not going to spend countless hours generating study guides to assist all students. It often is easier to set the book aside and assume the responsibility for lecturing and providing the information in other ways.

Teachers, however, might be convinced to generate study guides on those parts of the textbook which contain essential ideas, concepts, and generalizations. Let us suppose that a teacher selects some key concepts that are taught in November of the school year. The teacher carefully prepares the study guide to aid in comprehension of these concepts. The teacher wants mastery of these concepts because instruction throughout the rest of the year will build on these basic ideas. An hour spent generating a guide is an investment that pays dividends many times throughout the year.

If we keep in mind that a study guide once generated can be used over again the next year, we truly have a good investment in teacher time and not an intrusion on important teacher time.

At any rate the use of the study guide makes textbook teaching easier. One can reason that the textbook is not that important and all would agree. Yet, 80 to 90 percent of teachers use a text adopted by their school district. Textbooks are likely to be around for a long time. The problem is not the textbook, in my view, but rather the inflexible use of the textbook. Study guides increase this textbook flexibility and make it possible for more students to be successful in their reading.

Extensive research has been conducted into the effect of questions and statements presented to students to enhance comprehension of textbook reading. Although the research does not mention study guides by name, it is the basis on which we can build our thinking.

Two of the people who have contributed immeasurably to research on questions are Lawrence Frase (1970) and Ernst Rothkopf (1970). Their work indicates that both questions and statements provided the reader while reading connected discourse do aid in retention of prose material.

Ronald Carver (1972) has written a scathing denunciation of this, claiming adequate controls were not utilized. Two of the variables not adequately controlled are reading time and plan or strategy used by the individual.

Carver pointed out that students will certainly learn more from exposition if they spend more time reading the text. A study guide encourages more reading time and it is the increased reading time that enhances comprehension, not any special qualities in the guide itself.

Carver continued by pointing out that the strategy used by the readers was never clarified in the research. A study guide provides the needed strategy.

In future, carefully replicated classroom research, such as is currently being conducted by Harold Herber, may provide us with more clues as to how to build better study guides.

References

Carver, Ronald P. "A Critical Review of Mathemagenic Behaviors and the Effect of Questions upon the Retention of Prose Materials" *Journal of Reading Behavior,* vol. 4, no. 2 (Spring 1972), pp. 93–118.

Cunningham, Dick and Scott L. Shablak. "Selective Reading Guide-O-Rama: The Content Teacher's Best Friend." *Journal of Reading,* vol. 19, no. 5 (February 1975), pp. 380–82.

Frase, Lawrence T. "Boundary Conditions for Mathemagenic Behaviors." *Review of Educational Research,* vol. 40 (1970), pp. 337–48.

Herber, Harold L. *Teaching Reading in Content Areas.* Englewood Cliffs, N.J.: Prentice-Hall, Inc., 1970.

Rothkopf, Ernst Z. "The Concept of Mathemagenic Activities." *Review of Educational Research,* vol. 40 (1970), pp. 325–36.

Modified CLOZE: The InTRAlocking Guide

Keith J. Thomas
Arizona State University

From time to time modified versions of the *CLOZE* procedure have been cited for their potential as instructional techniques appropriate to the teaching of reading (Jongsma, 1971; Thomas, 1978). When written closure format is applied selectively to subject matter materials the resulting products are unique forms of study guides heretofore overlooked in the professional writing on content reading methodology.

Recently, Tutolo (1977) helped clarify the essential constructs of study guides as proposed by Herber (1970) and Cunningham and Shablak (1975). An important differentiation was made between interlocking and noninterlocking guides. In the former, the sequence of thought processes required of the reader is always hierarchical; in the latter, hierarchical sequencing is merely incidental (Tutolo, p. 504). Irrespective of the sequencing involved, both types of guides have one characteristic in common: they consist of a series of questions or directives posed for the reader, statements which the student must refer, react, and/or respond to either before, during, or after reading the textual material.

The modified *CLOZE* applications described by this writer represent a different approach to the development and use of study guides. Structurally, the proposed guides are designated as in*tra*locking. This term was coined because in each guide illustrated the reading skills utilized, the content understandings enhanced, or the cognitive processes emphasized are all interwoven *within* the text itself. The intralocking guide is not an ancillary aid as is the case with the interlocking and noninterlocking types. It is not a series of questions or guiding statements accompanying the reading material. Because of its closure format, the intralocking guide is an *integral* part of the textual material. Consequently, use of this type of guide and the process of reading become a totally integrated learning experience.

Before illustrating various types of intralocking study guides, certain assumptions and propositions regarding their development and implementation need identification and elaboration.

1. Students are capable of functioning with their assigned content textbooks. Competency in basic word-identification skills and comprehending behaviors is assumed. Intralocking guides were not conceptualized for remedial instruction but rather for developmental, content-oriented reading experiences. However, they can be adapted for use with students of lower achievement levels provided appropriate textual material is available. Also, different types of intralocking guides may be created for different students depending on individual needs and teacher flexibility.

2.   Students are capable of reasoning in a manner consistent with the demands of content reading tasks. For example, students are witnesses of and participants in antecedent-consequent activity in their daily living; inferential and judgmental thinking are commonplace. They do not need to be taught *how* to think, but rather to experience the need for application of thinking skills during reading activities. What is necessary pedagogically is the shaping and structuring of the learning environment so that the desired reasoning will be applied. Consequently, processing behaviors or thinking skills do not need to be "simulated," but rather stimulated.

3.   Each guide is designed for a specific purpose. Learners know the purpose of the guide and the behaviors to be applied, but not the products of the guide. Products are learned inductively as the guide is completed.

4.   In some respects the intralocking study guide is more difficult to develop than interlocking and noninterlocking varieties. Consequently, it is not presumed that all content teachers will wish to take advantage of the special qualities inherent in the intralocking type. It is, however, an excellent tool for the reading specialist to develop as part of his/her instructional repertoire for use with students as a supplement to any specialized reading methodology already employed by content teachers.

5.   The intralocking study guide may not have universal application to all content reading materials or instructional settings. Modifications are certainly possible and new applications may be conceptualized periodically by creative content teachers.

6.   Because of the specificity of intralocking guides, they are especially suitable for short selections of textual material. Practically speaking, they are probably best developed from content selections that have been edited from textbook chapters. The typical content teacher's preparation time is at a premium; this may preclude the possibility of developing such additional instructional aids. Again, reading specialists can provide substantive help by assisting their "content colleagues" in constructing these guides.

As mentioned, the intralocking study guide involves application of *CLOZE* format. In each of the examples that follow, selective deletion patterns have been utilized. Terms chosen for deletion were identified in accordance with procedures established for preparing each type of guide. These procedures are in concert with the specific instructional objective for which each guide was developed. Selection of specific items for deletion are expected, however, to vary among teachers and differing subject materials. Three types of intralocking guides have been devised and field-tested; each is explained in detail and accompanied by a specific illustration.

The Content Guide

The first type of intralocking guide is designed to assist the reader in identifying the specific ideas and information deemed most important in the content selection, hence the term "content guide." The guide itself is merely a reproduced portion of the text in which key lexical items have been deleted and replaced with blanks of uniform length. Lexical items (the nouns, verbs, adjectives, and adverbs of traditional grammar) are often considered the "meaning-bearing" words of language; attending to these specific terms, therefore, is generally crucial to comprehending the basic information presented by the author.

In developing the guide, selection of terms to be deleted is best effected through a three-step process. First, as the teacher reads and studies the chapter content, key ideas should be noted. Second, the sentences or the sentence in which each key idea is stated should be identified. Third, within that sentence (or those sentences) terms which complete the key idea should be selected for deletion.

The closure format of the guide forces readers to specifically attend to the deletions, hence the information the teacher desires students to retain. Which specific terms are actually deleted is left solely to teacher judgment. However, there should be sufficient contextual support to at least suggest an appropriate response for each blank, provided the ability to logically follow the ideas presented has been maintained. As students read the selection, closure is reached, meaning is attained, and the guide is completed.

In the following selection, note the terms which were deleted. (For purposes of illustration the words are included in parentheses.) Analyzing the deletions reveals the ideas the teacher has deemed important for retention.

> During the Reconstruction Era, not everything went smoothly for the new governments of the South. Sometimes (money) was spent wastefully. Because of poor management and inexperience, the roads and bridges cost (more) than they should have. Also, many government officials, both (white) and black, took advantage of the unsettled times to put money into (their) own pockets. This was true in the (North) as well as the South. For example, if a road builder wanted a contract from the state government, he might have to give a handsome sum to the government (official) in charge. One (corrupt) governor of Louisiana is said to have made a million dollars in various deals when he was in office. Also, costly luxuries were purchased with public funds. For instance, in the South Carolina capitol building there was a refreshment room for state senators where whiskey, wine, and cigars were served at (public) expense.[1]

When the selection has been completed, discussion of student responses provides a logical culmination to the reading experience. Students may also be referred to the original text for confirmation of their choices. The desirability of exact-word replacements may be contingent upon the specific terms deleted; in some instances these are important, in others they may be inconsequential.

Teachers who have used this *CLOZE* application report that it is an effective "reading guide," since it highlights and directs attention to the most important ideas, much the same as a list of guiding questions. The advantage of this type of guide over the ancillary list of questions, however, is that it requires the student to reason with the author's input *during* reading without having to interrupt continuity in information processing by referring to a series of disconnected questions.

The Structure Guide

Writers of textbooks often develop ideas and present information according to various organizational patterns. Readers must perceive these thought patterns if they are to comprehend the relationships between and among the ideas developed by an author. Compre-

---

[1]From George Mannello, *Americans All,* pp. 125–126. Reprinted by permission from the publisher: Amsco School Publications, Inc.; copyright © 1973.

This summer I read about a teacher who claimed to have taught a thief, a schizophrenic, an evangelist and a murderer all in the same classroom.

The thief was a tall boy who hid in the shadows and whom the other children avoided. The schizophrenic rarely spoke but gazed at the teacher with tiny eyes filled with terror. The evangelist was class president and the most popular boy in school. The murderer sat and stared out the window, occasionally letting out a shriek that would shiver the glass.

Apparently, now the thief stands looking through the bars of his prison cell. In the state mental hospital the schizophrenic is restrained from beating his head on the floor. The evangelist sleeps in the church yard, victim of a disease contracted during his missionary work. The police no longer search for the murderer ever since he was, himself, killed in a bar-room brawl.

The teacher concludes that all of these students sat in his classroom and listened as he taught. He said he must have been a great help to them. "After all," he said, "I taught them the difference between a noun and a verb, and how to diagram a sentence."

As we begin this new year, whether we are students, parents, administrators or teachers, let us consider what it is that we really want to accomplish in the next nine months. Of course, as an educator, I would never say that knowing the difference between a noun and a verb is unimportant. Naturally, any skill we learn which helps us communicate with others enables us to feel better about ourselves and our place in the world. But what I am saying is that a new school year can give us the opportunity to set goals and "take stock" of ourselves to be certain that our daily priorities reflect our commitment to what is good and of enduring value.

Kenneth W. Smith, Chaplain

classroom and his co-curricular program.

His last five summers have been spent as a teacher at Pine Crest of an intensive enrichment program for minority students. In this program he has covered such classics as MacBeth, Death of a Salesman, The Crucible and The Brave New school forensics programs in the Eastern United States, is president of the Florida Catholic Forensics League, the largest league in the NCFL. Host director of the NCFL Grand National Tournament in May which involved over 1600 people, Lee has also hosted Florida's largest tournament for the last hension facilitated by recognition of these patterns enables readers to sort and store information in meaningful categories thereby enhancing retention and recall.

Reading authorities have pointed out the necessity of recognizing developmental patterns associated with various subject matter materials, especially the social sciences (Robinson, 1964; Aaron, 1963). Fortunately for the reader the type of organizational structure is often cued by key words or phrases. Applying the *CLOZE* format to paragraphs from textbooks by deleting key words that cue certain patterns can help facilitate the reader's discovery, awareness, and/or recognition of these important elements. Such an instructional aid makes a valuable intralocking study guide that focuses students' attention toward the specific ideational relationships the writer has established.

In the following example, the writers begin the paragraph with two statements regarding a particular orientation toward taxation policy. These statements are followed by a series of essentially "if . . . then" cause/effect statements which explain the reasoning behind the theoretical position. To understand the position, readers must understand the supporting cause/effect relationships.

> Many people are taking the position that present high tax rates on the higher income brackets is a handicap to the economy of the country. They urge that reduction in these rates should be given more serious consideration than an overall tax reduction in all income brackets. (If) , for example, a manufacturer has the major portion of his profits or other income taxed away, he will not have the funds necessary to enlarge his factory, or to put in labor-saving and cost-saving equipment which is essential for increasing the efficiency of his operations. (If) he cannot increase efficiency and (hence) reduce the costs of producing his product, the public will not get the advantages of possible improved technology and advancement of science. Such a situation, they say, will tend to hinder progress of the entire national economy. (If) carried far enough a tax policy of this kind could actually stifle economic growth.[2]

In this sample key words were deleted to emphasize the relationship of subsequent statements to the central idea in the paragraph.

Vacca (1973) has provided a helpful list of key words and phrases that cue patterns of simple listing, time order, cause/effect, and comparison/contrast. His list provides an appropriate corpus of terms for possible deletions in developing the intralocking structure guide.

Simple Listing: to begin with . . . ; first . . . ; secondly . . . ; next; then. . . ; finally
. . .

Time Order: on (date); not long after; now; as; before; after; when.

Cause-Effect: because; since; therefore; consequently; as a result; this led to; so that; nevertheless; accordingly; if . . . then.

Comparison-Contrast: however; but; as well as; on the other hand; not only . . . but also; either . . . or; while; although; unless; similarly; yet. (Vacca, p. 78).

Again, in preparing this type of guide, the teacher must be cognizant of organizational patterns which are especially critical to following the author's development of the topic.

[2]From Mortenson, Krider, and Sampson, *Understanding Our Economy,* pp. 377–378. Reprinted with permission from the publisher: Houghton-Mifflin Co.: Copyright © 1967, 1964.

Herber (1970, pp. 54–58) has outlined a procedure that should prove helpful in this matter. As with other intralocking guides, discussion of terms selected by students should follow completion of the activity.

The Concept Guide

The third type of intralocking guide is designed to help students with concept formation, refinement, and/or extension. In this guide, the *CLOZE* format is utilized in deleting technical or specialized vocabulary terms, the "labels" used by the author to present key concepts.

Depending on the nature of the textual material, the concept guide may be developed according to one of two patterns. In some textbooks, for example, the author may include paragraphs which are intended to define or explain the meaning of specialized or technical vocabulary pertinent to the topic under discussion. Since the language of the subject matter is central to thorough understanding of the material, readers need to pay special attention to author input whenever such paragraphs are included in a chapter.

In the following example, note how the authors have developed the idea of "society" by comparison and contrast with a previously defined term "culture." Notice also how *CLOZE* has been applied to delete some of the key words which develop the concept. In using this guide the student is required to manipulate mentally the basic ideas which the authors chose to help establish and fix a meaning for the label "society."

> Society, like culture, is a word that has common and scientific meanings. The society page of the newspaper illustrates the common meaning. (Scientifically) , a society is an organized group. You use the word in this way when you speak of a debating or dramatic (society) . Social, in the scientific sense, has to do with the ways in which people are (organized) . There are social forces at work in families, clubs, cities, states and countries.
>
> Our modes of (organization) are, of course, part of our way of life. The two words "culture" and "society" are intimately (related) . The distinction between the two is important, nevertheless. Canada, for example, has two languages—French and English. The French- and English-speaking Canadians are (organized) as one country. Two cultural groups in one political (society) make for complications in Canadian affairs, as you will read in Chapter Six. Can you think of similar examples?[3]

In some instances, especially when paragraphs of definition are not characteristic of the author's style, teachers may select a portion of the chapter in which, a technical or specialized term occurs with marked frequency. This situation accounts for the second possible pattern for the concept guide.

When a concept label appears repeatedly, it is usually framed in sentences which detail many of its attributes. By deleting the word each time it appears, the reader's attention is specifically focused on the attributes since the label has been removed. Even if the reader is unable to identify the missing word (if the word is not in his/her oral-aural vocabulary at all) "teaching" word meaning is greatly simplified because students have already manipulated the ideas represented by the label. As an example, in the following paragraphs the same word (in singular, plural, or adjectival form) has been deleted each time it occurred.

[3]From Jones and Murphy, *Geography and World Affairs,* p. 25. Reprinted by permission from the publishers: Rand McNally Co., copyright © 1971.

The Structure of _____

    In earlier chapters we have used the term _____ but so far we have made no attempt to give a mental picture of an _____ . What is an _____ and what does it look like? _____ are so tiny that they cannot be seen even through the most powerful microscope and, for this reason, scientists will never know what _____ look like. However, for more than 70 years scientists have been hard at work on many kinds of experiments, hoping to shed some light upon the problem of the structure of _____ . A good deal of information on _____ structure has been discovered and, as a result, models of _____ have been designed in accordance with these discoveries. Nor should it be surprising that, as new knowledge is acquired, drastic changes have had to be made in these working models. It is therefore reasonable to say the present-day model of an _____ may not account for the new discoveries of tomorrow. In such a case the present model would again have to be changed.

    The term _____ is one of the oldest of all scientific terms; indeed, it was used by the philosophers of ancient Greece more than 2000 years ago. The Greeks thought that matter was made up of tiny indivisible particles which they called _____ . They compared _____ with the building blocks of their temples and, to them, an _____ of copper, like a block of stone, could have all kinds of sizes and shapes. This was a very crude idea. Nonetheless, it persisted through the centuries. Not until the early part of the 19th century was the concept of an _____ drastically changed.[4]

When students work with this type of intralocking concept guide some will determine the deleted term on the bases of general knowledge and background information. If these factors are insufficient, often the teacher merely has to write and pronounce the word for the students: definitions will have already been formulated from the contextual information. Ames (1975) has described the effectiveness of this approach for teaching content terminology. (Incidentally, the deleted base term in the illustration was *atom*.)

    The intralocking study guides as previously described and illustrated are not intended to replace the interlocking and noninterlocking varieties. The modified *CLOZE* format of the former does represent an alternative to the typical organization of the latter; an alternative which, because of its unique structural features, enhances the fusion of reading/thinking skills with content acquisition. This type of fusion, after all, seems to be one of the primary purposes of stressing developmental reading in subject matter areas.

References

Aaron, Ira E. "Developing Reading Competencies Through Social Studies and Literature." *Reading As An Intellectual Activity,* I.R.A. Proceedings, No. 8, 1963, pp. 107–110.

Ames, Wilbur S. "Instructional Uses of the CLOZE." Speech presented at the Twentieth Annual Convention of the International Reading Association. New York, May, 1975.

Bickel, Charles L., Neal D. Eigenfeld, and John C. Hogg. *Physical Science: A Modern Approach,* Revised Edition. New York: American Book Company, 1970.

Cunningham, Dick and Scott L. Shablak, "Selective Reading Guide-O-Rama: The Content Teacher's Best Friend." *Journal of Reading,* Vol. 18, No. 5 (February, 1975), pp. 380–382.

Herber, Harold L. *Teaching Reading in Content Areas.* Englewood Cliffs, New Jersey: Prentice-Hall, Inc., 1970.

---

[4]From Bickel, Hogg, and Eigenfeld, *Physical Science: A Modern Approach,* p. 217. Reprinted by permission from the publisher: American Book Company; copyright © 1970.

Jones, Stephen B. and Marion Fisher Murphy, *Geography and World Affairs*. Chicago: Rand McNally and Company, 1971.

Jongsma, Eugene. *The Cloze Procedure As A Teaching Technique*. Newark, Delaware: International Reading Association, 1971.

Mannello, George. *Americans All,* Vol. I. New York: Amsco School Publications, Inc., 1973.

Mortenson, William P., Donald T. Krider, and Roy J. Sampson. *Understanding Our Economy*. Boston: Houghton Mifflin Co., 1967.

Robinson, H. A. "Teaching Reading in the Content Areas: Some Basic Principles of Instruction." *Improvement of Reading Through Classroom Practice*. Newark, Delaware: International Reading Association, 1964, pp. 35–36.

Thomas, Keith J. "Instructional Applications of the CLOZE Technique." *Reading World,* Oct. 1978.

Tutolo, Daniel J. "The Study Guide—Types, Purpose and Value." *Journal of Reading,* Vol. 20, No. 6 (March, 1977), pp. 503–507.

Vacca, Richard. "A Means of Building Comprehension of Social Studies Content." *Research in Reading in Content Areas: Second Year Report,* Harold L. Herber, editor. Syracuse: Syracuse University, 1973, pp. 75–82.

Comprehension Strategies: What Makes Them Tick?*

Thomas W. Bean
California State University, Fullerton

Today, more than ever before, it is possible for us to feel overwhelmed by the vast array of comprehension strategies promoted in the professional literature. The growing list of acronyms and abbreviations (e.g., CARWET, DLL, GRP, etc.) are enough to make us a little apprehensive about trying any of these exotic-sounding devices. Yet many of these comprehension strategies share some underlying psycholinguistic principles that may serve to demythologize their esoteric labels. In order to explore the existence of such an underlying psycholinguistic base, we need to first consider the origin of our most cherished comprehension strategies and their more recent "clones."

It may come as no surprise to you to learn that most comprehension strategies are basically "armchair" inventions intuitively derived from ingredients of learning theory and lesson structure. Relatively few classroom research studies exist to support or refute the use of our more popular teaching activities (e.g., the directed reading activity, study guides, etc.). Despite both the informal development of comprehension strategies and an absence of empirical evidence attesting to their effectiveness, they all share some common psycholinguistic features that make them "tick."

We can explore these underlying psycholinguistic features by examining three representative strategies that might be integrated in a traditional prereading-reading-postreading

---

*Written especially for inclusion in this text.

lesson format. The first strategy, context redefinition (Cunningham, Cunningham, and Arthur, 1981), illustrates two psycholinguistic principles inherent in a successful prereading strategy.

In context redefinition, key vocabulary terms are selected by the teacher and listed on the board. Students then brainstorm to predict possible definitions for each of the words. For example, see if you can write a definition or synonym for the two words that follow.

1. *eggrails:* _____

   _____

2. *mushburgers:* _____

   _____

Now read the following selection to see if you need to modify your initial hypotheses.

She preferred a surfboard with *eggrails* for slow, sloppy waves. A board with rounded edges was ideally suited to this afternoon's conditions. The wind was blowing straight onshore, creating bumpy *mushburgers*.

Experience with context redefinition confirms that it helps increase students' motivation to actively comprehend a reading assignment. But what are the two underlying psycholinguistic principles that seem to make it tick?

First, context redefinition acknowledges the role of the reader's prior knowledge in the comprehension process. Indeed, you probably guessed that "eggrails" and "mushburgers" referred to foods based on their graphophonic similarity to "eggrolls" and "hamburgers" in addition to your greater experience with eating as opposed to surfing. Secondly, the introduction of surrounding context provides a model of the process that a fluent reader employs to modify initial hypotheses. In short, context redefinition treats comprehension as an interactive process that is neither exclusively reader-based nor exclusively text-based.

Should you decide to give context redefinition a try, the essential steps are:

1. Select key vocabulary from a reading or listening selection that students are going to encounter.
2. Present the words in isolation and brainstorm to predict some possible definitions or synonyms.
3. Provide context by having students read or listen to key portions of the selection.
4. Redefine the words based on their contextual meaning.
5. Verify these definitions with a glossary or dictionary.

Although context redefinition highlights the psycholinguistic principles of prior knowledge and contextual analysis in comprehension, it does have one limitation. If context redefinition is used in isolation from a comprehensive lesson structure (i.e., prereading-reading-postreading), it is not likely to engender long-term retention of the key vocabulary and related concepts from the lesson. Long-term retention of information requires critical analysis (sometimes called "deep processing"), organization (sometimes called "chunking"), and systematic rehearsal (Bransford, 1979). By integrating context redefinition with two additional approaches—the Directed Listening Lesson (Cunningham et al., 1981) and the Guided Reading Procedure (Manzo, 1975)—these additional psycholinguistic factors come into play.

The Guided Reading Procedure (GRP) and Directed Listening Lesson (DLL) share the following parallel steps.

1. Set a purpose for reading (GRP) or listening (DLL) to a selection. For example, read to compare and contrast surfboard designs for differing wave conditions.
2. Have students read (GRP) or listen (DLL) to a key portion of the text. For example:

    She preferred a surfboard with eggrails for slow, sloppy waves. A slow board with rounded edges was ideally suited to this afternoon's conditions. The wind was blowing straight onshore, creating bumpy mushburgers. Luckily, she had decided to bring two boards to the beach today. Her fast pintail with its hard rails had been just right for the hollow and glassy early morning surf. After lunch she switched to her swallowtail for the sloppy, onshore conditions.

3. Have students brainstorm everything that they remember from the selection while you record this verbatim on the board.
4. A brief rereading of the selection may be needed to clarify inconsistencies or retrieve missing information.
5. Organize the information in categories or a skeletal outline. Below is an example of (a) how one might organize information into categories; and an example of (b) a skeletal outline.

(a) Categories

WAVE CONDITIONS	SURFBOARD DESIGN
hollow, glassy	pintail: fast, hard rails
sloppy, mushy	swallowtail: slow, soft rails

(b) Outline

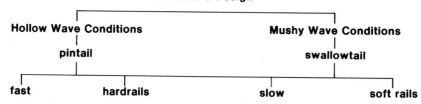

6. Provide follow-up activities that will reinforce the long-term retention of this information (e.g., a fake pop quiz in teams, vocabulary games, etc.).

The Directed Listening Lesson and Guided Reading Procedure extend students' prior knowledge of a topic that might be introduced using context redefinition. All three strategies increase active time on-task. This factor, coupled with the analytical discussion of textual information, contributes to the deep processing necessary for long-term retention (Bransford, 1979). Finally, the organization of concepts into categories or a hierarchical structure facilitates the retrieval of textual information.

In summary, comprehension strategies such as context redefinition, the Directed Listening Lesson, and the Guided Reading Procedure do indeed share some common characteristics that make them "tick." They all seem to embody psycholinguistic principles that are known to foster comprehension. The task that remains is for you to field-test, modify, and integrate the various strategies. In this way we can eventually verify what our pedagogical intuition and psycholinguistic understanding of the reading process currently hint at.

References

Bransford, J. D. *Human cognition: Learning, understanding, and remembering.* Belmont, Calif.: Wadsworth, 1979.

Cunningham, J. W., Cunningham, P. M., and Arthur, S. V. *Middle and secondary school reading.* New York: Longman, 1981.

Manzo, A. V. Guided reading procedure. *Journal of Reading,* 1975, *18,* 287–291.

The Directed Inquiry Activity: An Instructional Procedure for Content Reading*

Keith J. Thomas
Arizona State University

The Directed Inquiry Activity is a modification of the Directed-Reading-Thinking-Activity as originally developed by Dr. Russell Stauffer. The DIA includes various features of DRTA methodology, but is designed specifically to help "direct" students through reading assignments with content materials containing an abundance of factual information and details, much of which should be retained by the reader. The DIA utilizes a framework of conjecture regarding six points of inquiry: Who? What? When? Where? Why? How? Students preview the material and are then encouraged to predict responses to these six key questions as preparation for reading the selection. Predictions are treated as purposes for reading; the reading is followed by review and discussion of the various conjectures.

Reading specialists and content teachers may not completely agree with Sanders (1969), but his following comments about textbooks are reasonably accurate.

> . . . the textbook is weak in that it offers little opportunity for any mental activity except remembering. If there is an inference to be drawn, the author draws it, and if there is a significant relationship to be noted, the author points it out. There are no loose ends or incomplete analyses. (p. 158)

*Reprinted from *Reading Improvement,* 1978, *15,* 138–140, with permission of Keith J. Thomas and Project Innovation.

Although Sander's remarks are generally directed at assisting teachers in developing appropriate questions for post-reading experiences, his suggestions have important implications for prereading activities with subject matter materials as well. For example, in the middle and upper grades both students and teachers report the need for learners to assimilate as many facts and basic understandings as possible (Thomas, 1975). This need is readily understandable; most comprehension taxonomies are hierarchical and presume mastery of explicitly stated information before interpretive, critical, creative, or applicative thinking can be successfully employed (Smith, 1963; Barrett, 1968; Herber, 1970, pp. 62–63). These higher levels of cognitive operations, incidentally, represent the types of thinking most teachers apparently desire to stimulate during discussions that follow content reading experiences.

One problem for the content teacher and the content learner, therefore, seems rather obvious: what can be done to facilitate sorting, categorizing, and retrieving the myriad facts and details so frequently found in textbooks used during content lessons? Manzo's (1975) Guided Reading Procedure appears to be one technique which may be of assistance to both teachers and students. However, the GRP is essentially a "reflective thinking" strategy and does not necessarily help the reader organize his/her thoughts *before* encountering the material, unless the teacher includes some special previewing activity such as ReQuest (Manzo, 1969). And what precedes the reading may have at least as much influence, if not more, upon student success with the content lesson.

Acting on the expressed needs of middle- and upper-grade students and their teachers, this author developed a procedure which addresses itself to Sander's charge that "students deserve the right to participate in the thinking. They deserve the right to reason with raw, undigested ideas." (1966, p. 158) Based on the *Directed-Reading-Thinking-Activity* as developed by Stauffer (1969a; 1969b; 1970; 1975), extended and modified by Valmont (1972), and adapted by Hansell (1976), the procedure is specifically designed to help "direct" students through content materials containing an abundance of factual information, much of which *should* be retained by the reader. The *Directed Inquiry Activity* retains many features of DRTA methodology, but differs in one significant aspect. The DIA utilizes a framework of conjecture regarding six specific points of inquiry: Who? What? When? Where? Why? How?

The DIA begins with students surveying a portion of the material about to be read, perhaps just the title in short selections. With longer assignments, entire chapters for example, several beginning paragraphs may be read; illustrations and topical headings or subheadings may be studied as well. After surveying, students are encouraged to predict responses to the six key inquiry questions which have been listed on the chalkboard by the teacher. The teacher records predictions under appropriate categories, providing verbal feedback (elaboration upon student conjectures) and helping to elicit further points of information he/she desires the students to learn. Thus, although predictions originate with the students, the teacher helps shape thinking through skillful questioning. As predictions are listed under each point of inquiry, interrelationships among the ideas are traced across categories through further class discussion initiated by teacher feedback. The predicting and elaborating phase serves a two-fold function: (1) it establishes purposes for reading, and (2) it helps to fix an anticipatory mind-set toward the specific forthcoming reading experience.

When predicting terminates, students read the assigned material to verify and confirm (or reject) their hypothesized ideas and information. The actual reading is followed by a critical analysis of the predictions. Conjectures are reviewed and discussed; additions, deletions and/or modifications of the recorded material are made under appropriate inquiry categories.

The DIA can be used with students at any grade level and is easily adaptable to a variety of specific content areas. (Social Studies is particularly well-suited). However, since the teacher plays an active role as facilitator during the DIA, careful preparation is necessary and several considerations warrant particular attention. The teacher must be thoroughly familiar with the content and organization of the selection and must have a clear understanding of expectations for student learning. Otherwise, skillful questioning is likely to be mere happenstance. Obviously, not all of the six points of inquiry may pertain to a given reading assignment. In such cases the teacher may elect to delimit the number of categories used during the predicting phase.

In addition, the DIA, like the DRTA, does not explicitly include provisions for preteaching vocabulary. Consequently, one of the most critical contingencies for an effective learning experience is proper placement of students in content reading material. Vocabulary can be introduced "indirectly" during the hypothesizing phase, but often this is simply too incidental to assure consistent success.

However, the skillful instructor can meet the challenge of the "teachable moment" by introducing technical or specialized terms as the need emerges during student conjecture and elaboration. For example, if students describe the attributes of a given key concept without making reference to the appropriate label, the teacher may simply ask whether anyone knows the word commonly used as a referent term for those collective attributes. Given the usual range of abilities and background experiences in a heterogeneous content class, the chances are favorable that an accurate response can be elicited from some member of the group. If not, the teacher may choose either to supply the term or to request that students try to identify the label during their reading. Regardless of the course chosen by the teacher, vocabulary is a crucial factor and must be accounted for in some fashion.

In retrospect, Stauffer (1969b, p. 14) suggests that there are four fundamental aspects of the reading-to-learn process: (1) declaring purposes, (2) reasoning, (3) judging, and (4) refining and extending ideas. The DIA was conceptualized as an instructional procedure which would bring all four of these aspects into focus before, during, and after the reading of content selections. Its effectiveness in light of these goals needs further substantiation, however, and classroom teachers are encouraged to pursue this task.

References

Barrett, Thomas C. "Taxonomy of Cognitive and Affective Dimensions of Reading Comprehension," cited in "Current Conceptions of Reading," by Theodore Clymer, *Innovation and Change in Reading Instruction,* Helen Robinson, editor. The sixty-seventh Yearbook of the National Society for the Study of Education. Chicago: University of Chicago Press, 1968, pp. 19–23.

Hansell, T. Stevenson. "Increasing Understanding in Content Reading." *Journal of Reading,* Vol. 19. No. 4 (January, 1976), pp. 307–310.

Herber, Harold L. *Teaching Reading in Content Areas.* Englewood Cliffs, New Jersey: Prentice-Hall, Inc., 1970.

Manzo, Anthony V. "The ReQuest Procedure." *Journal of Reading,* Vol. 13, No. 2 (November, 1969), pp. 123–126.

———. "Guided Reading Procedure." *Journal of Reading,* Vol. 18, No. 4 (January, 1975). pp. 287–291.

Sanders, Norris M. *Classroom Questions.* New York: Harper and Row, 1966.

Smith, Nila Banton. "Levels of Discussion in Reading." *Readings on Reading Instruction.* Albert J. Harris, editor. New York: David McKay Co., 1963, pp. 285–289.

Stauffer, Russell G. *Directing Reading Maturity As A Cognitive Process.* New York: Harper and Row, 1969a.

———. *Teaching Reading as a Thinking Process.* New York: Harper and Row, 1969b.

———. *The Language-Experience Approach to the Teaching of Reading.* New York: Harper and Row, 1970.

———. *Directing the Reading-Thinking Process.* New York: Harper and Row, 1975.

Thomas, Keith J. "Perceived Needs of Content Teachers and Students." Unpublished Research Study. Tempe, Arizona: Arizona State University, 1975.

Valmont, William J. *Practical Applications of the Directed-Reading-Thinking-Activity.* Unpublished Manuscript. Tucson, Arizona: University of Arizona, 1972.

How to Question Before, During, and After Reading*

James W. Cunningham
University of North Carolina—Chapel Hill

In one way, at least, reading is like swimming. One can swim for enjoyment without being interested in its value as exercise and without being interested in becoming a better swimmer in either an absolute or a competitive sense. One can also swim to develop certain muscles or to improve one's overall physical conditioning. Finally, one can swim in order to be able later to demonstrate to others (or to him- or herself) that he or she is in fact a good swimmer. All three kinds of swimming share enough in common that all can be called "swimming," but certainly there is a difference between swimming to swim, swimming to improve physical conditioning, and swimming to prepare for swimming demonstrations or competitions. A swimming coach helps students swim for fun, swim for conditioning, prepare for swimming competitions, or all three. Likewise, one can read for its own sake, to pass the time or for the sheer pleasure of it, the way one might read a novel without caring if he or she even remembers what happened once the book is finished. Or one can read to learn, to increase knowledge or skills or change attitudes. Finally, one can read in order to demonstrate that one can read or has read well. When one reads for its own sake, we generally call that

*Written especially for inclusion in this text.

"reading." When one reads to learn, we generally call that "reading to learn." When one reads to demonstrate that one can or has read well, we generally call that "studying." A reading teacher helps students read for fun, read to learn, or study, or all three. A content teacher, however, is not really like a swimming coach. Rather, a content teacher is in the position of wanting students to learn particular content the way a physical education director might want students to improve their physical conditioning. For this physical education director, swimming is only one means to achieve the end. For the content teacher, reading is only one means to achieve the end of having students learn particular knowledge or skills associated with the content. In the case where the physical education director concludes that swimming is the best exercise for a group attempting to improve their conditioning, that director is responsible for helping the students do the kind of swimming they need to do to achieve the conditioning desired, but beyond that the director is not responsible for becoming a swimming instructor. In the case where the content teacher concludes that reading is the best means for a group of students to gain particular knowledge, then that teacher is responsible for helping the students do the kind of reading they need to learn that knowledge, but beyond that the content teacher is not responsible for becoming a reading teacher. This paper is addressed to content area teachers (and would-be teachers) and is, therefore, not an article about how to teach reading. Rather, it is an article about how to ask questions before, during, and after the reading that content area teachers conclude to be the best means for a group of students to gain particular knowledge. Teacher questioning is focused on because, whereas it is debatable whether asking students questions improves their reading ability (Durkin, 1978–1979), there is little doubt that some kinds of questions can increase learning from text materials while reading to learn (Anderson and Biddle, 1975; Rickards, 1976).

Questioning

There are several reasons why content teachers ask students questions before, during, or after they read. Sometimes teachers want to determine whether or not a student has read an assigned passage. Sometimes teachers will give students questions to answer while they read in order to guide them toward particular learnings. Sometimes teachers ask students questions in order to grade them. Sometimes teachers ask questions to diagnose what students already know. Sometimes teachers ask students questions to guide their thinking beyond the information given in the lesson or passage. (It might be expected that the questions that teachers ought to ask will vary, given the purpose for asking them.) It appears then that teacher questions can be of three general types:

1. Evaluative questions—questions that diagnose what students already know or have learned, questions that determine whether students have attended to assigned tasks, or questions that enable the teacher to assign a grade.
2. Cognitively stimulating questions—questions that guide students toward particular learnings while they read or questions that guide students' thinking beyond the information given in the lesson or passage.
3. Questions that both evaluate and stimulate.

In this paper, there will be no discussion of how to ask questions in order to grade students. Everyone knows or should know that teachers must give a range of grades and that students with few exceptions must get the kind of grades (at least relative to other students) they have been getting. The task of teachers when grading students is to figure out how to ask the kinds of questions that the students who have been doing well in school tend to answer correctly. Any teacher who has survived the politics of a public school has already figured out how to ask these kinds of questions. Nor will there be a discussion of how to ask questions in order to determine if students have read a passage. Obviously, in this case a teacher will want to ask questions that anyone who has read the passage will be able to answer. Nor will there be a discussion of questions that both evaluate and stimulate students. Such questions will occur, but no attempt should be made to develop them. Rather the teacher should endeavor to ask evaluative questions when he or she wants to evaluate and cognitively stimulating questions when he or she wants to stimulate. This paper will concentrate on how to ask questions that diagnose what students already know or have learned, questions that guide students' reading, questions that stimulate thinking beyond the information given, and questions that stimulate students to gain particular learnings.

There are two kinds of questions that one can ask students about what they know, will read, or have read: questions with a specified set of one or more right answers and questions with an undetermined set of many right answers. When we ask students questions that have specified right answers, we are concerned with knowledge; when we ask questions that have unspecified right answers, we are concerned with beliefs, hunches, and awareness of implications. These former, knowledge questions are called *convergent,* and the latter, belief questions are called *divergent* (Guilford, 1967; Cunningham, 1971).

Questions to diagnose what students already know

Until recently, a commonly held notion has been that reading requires motivation and reading skills and that anyone with sufficient motivation and reading skills can read and comprehend any well-written piece of text. In the past several years or so, this notion has been challenged by a group of theorists/researchers (Anderson, 1978) who have investigated the contribution of prior knowledge and belief to the comprehension process. In this developing view, comprehending is a process of matching language structures to existing knowledge. An example might help:

> Sums of squared deviations from means have a matrix counterpart in the multivariate case.

Presumably, you have sophisticated reading skills that enable you to pronounce every word in the example as well as divide the statement into syntactic phrases. And although the statement probably does not motivate you, for most of you motivation would not matter in this case. What is lacking—and consequently what is limiting your comprehension—is adequate knowledge structures. The author in this example, like most authors, assumed that the reader would have certain knowledge that he or she probably does not have. What if an author had written the following:

> Because it was important that they take appropriate clothes to wear while they traveled the Amazon River Valley, military regulations were relaxed.

Reading skills and motivation would only enable a reader to process the text if the reader also had some notion that most military forces have regulations concerning what is appropriate dress, what those regulations usually require, and the type of dress generally appropriate for the Amazon River Valley. The ease of comprehension of the second example, as contrasted with the first, is not attributable to either reading skills or motivation differences but to knowledge differences. Since what students already know about a topic determines how much new information they can learn from reading, content teachers often attempt to diagnose students' existing knowledge.

Unless a teacher is interested in an encyclopedic listing of all a student's knowledge and misunderstandings, diagnosing prior knowledge will always be a matter of determining if a student has the prior knowledge to learn some particular new knowledge. With respect to a text that the student is to read to learn, a content analysis of the text should be performed (Herber, 1978). Such a content analysis can be extensive but should include the principal vocabulary used and the specific background of information that the author seems to assume a reader will have. In addition, such a content analysis would require a listing of any special text features, such as footnotes or graphic aids, that students need to be able to use the text. Prior to reading the students should be required to give evidence that they can associate appropriate meanings with this crucial vocabulary, that they have the necessary background of information, and that they can use the necessary text features.

Because it is important that students be able to show what they know to avoid having teachers teach what is already known, questions to diagnose prior knowledge need to be as simple and straightforward as possible. For example, if a teacher is interested in determining whether students know how photosynthesis takes place before having them read a section of the text that describes how principles of photosynthesis can be applied to the development of new food products, two procedures are possible. In the first, students would be asked to explain photosynthesis or would be asked questions of a technical nature about photosynthesis. In the second, students would be asked to explain why leaves are green in the summer and how plants eat and would be tested separately on the technical vocabulary. The second course seems the wisest because it would differentiate between the students' conceptual knowledge and their vocabulary knowledge. In the first case students who did not know the technical vocabulary would not be able to show that they knew the conceptual knowledge. A wise procedure, then, would be to develop prior knowledge questions using everyday language and vocabulary questions using technical language.

If such a procedure seems as if it would be time-consuming—it is. Sitting down with reading material to be read by students as part of a content unit and developing jargon-free prior knowledge questions and vocabulary questions using technical language will be challenging and will take time. However, two benefits will outweigh these costs: (1) you will understand the conceptual and vocabulary demands of your text better than you ever thought possible, making you a better teacher of that content; and (2) you will become the benefactor of a "law of increasing returns"—the more practice you have in developing these questions, the less time and effort it will take to develop them. Teaching, like basketball, is a game of fundamentals. Are you willing to spend the time necessary to become a questioner?

Questions to diagnose what students have learned

Before one can determine what students have learned from reading, one must decide what is important for them to have learned. One can take several approaches to this concept of importance. Some people have defined what is important to learn from a text as the superordinate concepts in the passage (Meyer, 1977). In this case, the passage would be outlined, and those concepts numbered with upper-case Roman numerals would be the most important concepts in the passage.

Others have defined what is important as those concepts that good readers would most often include in free recalls of the passage (Kintsch, 1974). Whenever good readers are asked to read a passage and then later to recall it, they always abstract it, i.e., they only recall a fraction of the total words and total concepts. Those elements most often recalled by good readers would be defined as most important.

These two methods have serious limitations in that they define importance in terms of the text and ideal readers reading without purpose. Defining importance in these ways ignores the way in which most of us read. Whether we are reading to determine what research says about a topic or what expert opinion says about a topic or for pleasure, we often ignore the writer's purposes for writing and the integrity of the text. For example, when reading a novel for pleasure, I often skip dull parts. When in the library I often skim many articles for specific concepts, whether they are the focus of the article I am skimming or not. Also my beliefs tend to be at the forefront when I read, and I often argue in my mind with the text and make judgments about the author's real intentions without direct textual evidence. This top-down reading (Anderson, 1978) is an important and unavoidable component of reading. To require readers to read a text as a blank slate is unrealistic and antiintellectual. What is important in a text is always a function of what the student or reader brings to the text in terms of knowledge, beliefs, and purposes for reading except in the rare instances where students are reading to determine the author's stated intentions.

A new procedure for determining what is important for students to learn from reading is that of the *expected gist*:

1. In general terms, decide why you are having the students read a particular passage. What do you want them to learn?
2. Again in general terms, make a realistic, subjective assessment of your students' (as a whole) reading abilities and prior knowledge about the subject matter discussed in the passage.
3. Read the passage, keeping in mind your general purpose for having the students read and the general characteristics of your readers. Decide what different individual responses you are likely to get if the students know why they are reading and if they put forth a reasonable effort. Briefly summarize in writing the different kinds of responses you expect.
4. Write a main idea, or gist, statement for each summary you've written. These statements are statements of *expected gist*.
5. These expected gist statements provide guidelines for determining which questions to ask to students. Questions that seem unrelated or trivial when examined against these expected gist statements should not be asked.

Let us follow the procedure through a particular passage, as I keep in mind a group of sixth, seventh, and eighth graders I work with occasionally.

> The common housefly is found all over the world and is a pest everywhere. This is especially so, of course, when food is involved—particularly sweet food. Consider the problems that flies can create for a baker! In the latter half of the nineteenth century, one baker, a German named Friederich Kaiser, decided to do something about it.
>
> Kaiser was a good baker. His cakes, rolls, breads, and buns were delicious. However, they didn't look so *tempting* in his window when they were covered with flies! The baker had an idea. He coated a sheet of paper with sweet molasses and hung it in the window. The flies at once deserted his sweets for the molasses—and were stuck! Hordes of customers soon descended on Kaiser's shop—not for baked goods, but to buy his "flypaper!" (Boning, 1978)

1. Purpose for reading: "Read to find out how flypaper was invented."
2. Assessment of students: Reading ability varies tremendously; many students will have never been to or heard of a bake shop.
3. Expected kinds of responses:
   a. Some students will focus on how the baker got the idea for his invention. They will infer that the baker asked himself why flies liked some of what he baked better than others and concluded that flies liked the sweetest items best of all. From that inference, they will further infer that he decided to distract them with the sweetest substance he had—something sweeter than any of his baked items. Here one or two students will feel that he also realized that the flies would stick in the molasses.
   b. Other students will feel that he only discovered the fly-killing properties of his invention when he actually tried it out.
   c. Some students will focus on the invention itself and why it works. They will wonder why the flies are attracted to the molasses and why they continue to be attracted when all the other flies are already so obviously stuck.
   d. Other students will focus on their own sqeamishness at the thought of flies or at the thought of eating anything that had been eaten on by flies.
   e. Some students will try to think of how one could invent something now to solve a major problem and also make a lot of money.
4. Statements of *expected gist:*
   a. The baker figured out that flies liked things better the sweeter they were. He decided that molasses was very sweet and that it was also very sticky, so he used molasses and paper to make a trap that would attract flies away from his baked items and trap them for good.
   b. The baker figured out that flies liked things better the sweeter they were, and he used molasses—the sweetest thing he had—to attract them away from the baked items on display in the window. He was surprised to find that the flies got stuck in the molasses.
   c. A baker invented flypaper by putting molasses on paper and hanging it near where flies were. The flies sensed the sweetness with their antennae and flew onto the molasses paper. Molasses is very thick, and it stuck to their tiny legs. Their wings were not strong enough for them to get away.

    d.   A baker invented flypaper because his customers couldn't stand to buy what he had baked when they saw flies all over it. I sure wouldn't buy something with flies eating on it.

    e.   Today we have some problems. If we can figure out why they are problems, we can solve them.

5.   Questions to ask students after reading the passage:

What would likely be the reaction of a customer who went into a bake shop to buy something and saw the baked goods with flies all over them?

What do you think made the baker try molasses to attract the flies away?

Did the cook know that the molasses would trap the flies before he used it?

Why did the molasses work?

Can modern inventors learn anything from this story of Kaiser's invention of flypaper?

Clearly, these questions are more likely to tell you what students have learned from their reading than questions about who invented flypaper, what he did for a living, or what the seventh word in the eighth sentence means.

Fortunately, once the *expected gist* procedure has been followed a few times, with a few pieces of content writing, steps can begin to be discarded. After a while, the procedure becomes one of thinking why you want students to read a selection, thinking of how particular individual students could respond correctly given that purpose, and then thinking of questions to elicit those different responses.

Questions to stimulate students' thinking beyond the information given

Although several writers have attempted to define inference and inferential comprehension in other ways, this paper follows the logic of Cunningham (in press) that any response containing only textual information is literal. For a response to be inferential, it must contain new information *beyond* the information given. In keeping, a reader's response to a text is inferential (beyond the text) if that response is reasonable but cannot be proven using the text, a thesaurus, and a grammar book (Cunningham, in press.) (In other words, a response using synonyms and different syntax but having no new meaning is a literal response.) If it is reasonable and *can* be proven using these three instruments, it is a literal response. Consider this brief text (Rystrom, 1977) and several possible reader responses to it:

The Indian rode into the sunset.

Response 1: Into the sunset the Indian traveled.

Response 2: The Indian rode into the west.

Response 3: The Indian rode a horse into the sunset.

Response 4: The Indian had finished what he was trying to do there, and he was going somewhere else to do something.

Response 1 is literal because, for anyone who knows the English language or has a thesaurus and grammar book, it means the same thing as the text. Responses 2–4 are all inferences because more than a knowledge of language is required to relate them to the text; world knowledge must be used. (My four-year-old son knows what a sunset is, and he knows that west is a direction, but he has no idea that the sun always sets in the west.)

To distinguish among responses 2–4, we must return to our previous distinction between convergent and divergent questions. The question "In what direction was the Indian riding?" (response 2) requires the reader to make an inference, but the question is clearly convergent. The question "What was the Indian riding on or in?" (response 3) also requires the reader to make an inference, but now the question is divergent with "horse" or "car" being frequent answers and "train" or "ship" occurring occasionally. The question "Why was the Indian riding into the sunset?" (response 4) is divergent, too, but requires not only an inference but a *creative* response (an inference that cannot be evaluated by either its probability or by assessing how many average readers might produce it) as well.

Developing questions to elicit inferential or creative response is not easy. Unfortunately, there are no simple rules like "All questions beginning with 'why' are inference questions." (Many "why" questions, for example, test the literal comprehension of "because" statements in the text.) The following steps should help, however:

1. Read the text you plan to use with students.
2. With the book closed, write down statements that you *know* to be true if the text is accurate and that you feel your students ought to learn.
3. Open the book and decide which of your statements a computer with complete knowledge of synonyms and grammar but no world knowledge could prove to be equivalent to the text and cross them out; they are literal. (The remaining statements are convergent inferences.)
4. Then with the book still open, write down statements that you *believe* to be true but that you cannot prove using the text and that you want your students to consider. (These statements are divergent inferences or creative responses.)
5. Develop a question for each statement with which you will try to elicit that statement from the students. (You now have a set of convergent and divergent inference questions based on the text.)
6. Ask the students the questions *after* they have read the text and allow them to keep their books open to answer them. Remember most divergent questions have right answers you haven't thought of!

Again, this procedure can be expected to become automatic with use, though time consuming at first.

Questions to guide students toward particular learnings

Research on the effect of questions on learning from text suggests that when students are given questions before they read or questions to answer while they read, those questions are likely to improve their learning under three conditions. These conditions are: (1) prequestions will only be effective on the performance on a later test on the areas questioned (prequestions often do not increase the learning of material not questioned) Rothkopf, 1972; Frase, 1975; Sagaria and DiVesta, 1978); (2) prequestions and adjunct questions tend to be effective only when they are based on information that the author made clear as important (Rickards, 1976); and (3) higher levels of questions that ask students to infer or to apply what they have learned cause much more learning than questions that require students to restate the text (Watts and Anderson, 1971; Yost, Avila, and Vexler, 1977). In the case, then, where a teacher wishes to use prequestions or study guide questions to foster learning from text, those questions should be developed following the procedures of *expected gist* and of constructing inferential questions, both discussed above.

A Call to Action

It is clear that teacher questions before, during, and after student reading will continue to be a major tool in the repertoire of teaching behaviors of the content teacher, and there is evidence that such questions can foster learning. Unfortunately, it is not easy to develop good questions to evaluate or to stimulate students' reading or thinking. The time has come for teachers who use questions as a teaching tool to take the time to develop good questions and to develop themselves as good questioners. It is hoped that this paper has provided direction and assistance for teachers who are willing to work on this important teaching "fundamental."

References

Anderson, R. C. Schema-directed processes in language comprehension. In A. M. Lesgold, J. W. Pellegrino, S. D. Fakkema, and R. Glaser (eds.), *Cognitive psychology and instruction.* New York: Plenum Press, 1978.

Anderson, R. C., and Biddle, W. B. On asking people questions about what they are reading. In G. H. Bower (Ed.), *The psychology of learning and motivation* (vol. 9). New York: Academic Press, 1975.

Boning, R. A. *Multiple skills series,* Level G2. Baldwin, N.Y.: Lowell & Lynwood, 1978.

Cunningham, J. W. Toward a pedagogy of inferential comprehension and creative response. In R. J. Tierney, J. N. Mitchell, and P. L. Anders (Eds.), *Understanding readers' understanding.* Hillsdale, N.J.: Erlbaum, in press.

Cunningham, R. T. Developing question-asking skills. In J. E. Weigand (Ed.), *Developing teacher competencies.* Englewood Cliffs, N.J.: Prentice Hall, 1971.

Durkin, D. What classroom observations reveal about reading comprehension instruction. *Reading Research Quarterly,* 1978–1979, *14,* 481–533.

Frase, L. T. Prose processing. In G. H. Bower (Ed.), *The psychology of learning and motivation* (vol. 9). New York: Academic Press, 1975.

Guilford, J. P. *The nature of human intelligence.* New York: McGraw-Hill, 1967.

Herber, H. L. *Teaching reading in content areas* (2nd ed.). Englewood Cliffs, N.J.: Prentice-Hall, 1978.

Kintsch, W. *The representation of meaning in memory.* Hillsdale, N.J.: Erlbaum, 1974.

Meyer, B. J. F. The structure of prose: Effects on learning and memory and implications for educational practice. In R. C. Anderson, R. Spiro, and W. E. Montague (Eds.), *Schooling and the acquisition of knowledge.* Hillsdale, N.J.: Erlbaum, 1977.

Rickards, J. P. Type of verbatim question interspersed in text: A new look at the position effect. *Journal of Reading Behavior,* 1976, *8,* 37–45.

Rothkopf, E. Z. Structural text features and the control of processes in learning from written materials. In R. O. Freedle and J. B. Carroll (Eds.), *Language comprehension and the acquisition of knowledge.* Washington, D.C.: V. H. Winston & Sons, 1972.

Rystrom, R. Reflections of meaning. *Journal of Reading Behavior,* 1977, *9,* 193–200.

Sagaria, S. D., and DiVesta, F. J. Learner expectations induced by adjunct questions and the retrieval of intentional and incidental information. *Journal of Educational Psychology,* 1978, *70,* 280–288.

Watts, G. H., and Anderson, R. C. Effects of three types of inserted questions on learning from prose. *Journal of Educational Psychology,* 1971, *62,* 387–394.

Yost, M., Avila, L., and Vexler, E. B. Effect on learning of postinstructional responses to questions of differing degrees of complexity. *Journal of Educational Psychology,* 1977, *69,* 399–408.

Reference Note
I would like to thank David W. Moore for his comments on an earlier draft of this paper.

Writing in the Content Areas*

Sharon V. Arthur
Eastern Connecticut State College

Every teacher a teacher of writing? That paraphrased question will undoubtedly elicit the same antagonism and denial that its predecessor (every teacher a teacher of reading) did several years ago. And the answer, of course, is still "No!" Teachers in the content areas need not assume the responsibility for writing instruction. By the same token, they should not abrogate the responsibility they do have to provide writing experiences for students. The reasons are several, but perhaps the most crucial are that students should have ample opportunity to extend their writing skills through writing about a variety of organizational modes, that more and more research studies are providing evidence for the assumption that reading skills may well be improved through writing activities, and that students increase their understanding of information in content areas by writing about those areas.

These three reasons are closely related. The reason that students' reading comprehension can be improved through writing activities may well be that the writing in other organizational modes makes it easier for students to read in those modes. The observation is not new that the majority of the elementary students' reading and writing is performed with narrative material. Nor is it a heuristic leap to the assumption that perhaps one factor contributing to the difficulty that middle and secondary students have with expository reading material is that they need first-hand experiences with reading and writing exposition. Simply handing out the science and social studies texts does not constitute instruction in the characteristics of the mode the text uses. Through writing activities, the classroom teacher can insure that students are familiar with the structures used in the various forms of expository texts. If, for example, students are going to be reading a text that uses comparison/contrast as the dominate organizational pattern, then the classroom teacher should help students

*Written especially for inclusion in this text.

discover the characteristics of comparison/contrast writing and allow them to write several short papers to demonstrate that they have learned those characteristics. With that determined, it is much more likely that students are going to find reading their texts an easier task. Multitudinous research efforts in the realm of text analysis have demonstrated that being aware of the author's staging of information is a factor contributing to students' understanding of a passage. It is contended here that such awareness can be taught through writing.

Some may protest that that type of information should have been taught previously, or, if not, then that such instruction would become part of the secondary English teacher's curriculum. Or should it? English is, of itself, a subject area with literature as its main content. The point need not be belabored that the predominating mode in literature is narrative, though students will encounter examples of exposition, persuasion, and description. And of these, description is the one that is more frequent. The English teacher would find it a full-time job to teach students the characteristics of narration and description in their various forms, in conjunction with the other curricular concerns of vocabulary development, usage, etc.

Therefore, whose task is it to allow students to explore and develop competence in the other modes? The science classroom need not be turned into a writing laboratory, nor is it necessary to spend an inordinate amount of time with the development of these modes of persuasion and exposition. But if each content teacher would assume the responsibility for insuring that students have the skills for reading their textbooks and help to insure that, in part, through writing activities, then no one teacher would be over-burdened. Nor would those teachers have to complain about the lack of writing skills among their students, and, more importantly, students would begin to see writing as an activity that crosses discipline boundaries and is not restricted to English classes only. The rest of this paper will contain suggestions for writing activities in various curricular areas. Attempting these ideas will most certainly lead to a variety of additional writing activities.

The ideas presented here are only a start for the teacher. Nor should the teacher hesitate to take an idea from one curricular area and adapt it to another. Rarely is a strategy so restrictive that there are no other applications than the given one. Also, if a strategy does not work for the teacher as it is described, then the teacher's alteration of the activity may well accomplish the same objective through a more workable means.

A Writing Strategy for All Classrooms—Translation Writing

Very simply, translation writing is the process of converting information from text into a "translated", rewritten version. This technique is most appropriate for students at the middle and secondary school levels. Only short sections of text should be assigned at first until students become familiar with this activity.

There are several steps for doing translation writing in one's classroom:

First, the teacher presents the essential vocabulary of a passage to students and discusses the concepts that they represent. This readiness step is no different than if a traditional lesson using the text were to follow.

Second, the teacher gives each student a copy of the essential vocabulary list in outline form with an appropriate definition beside each word. This is done so that students will have a handy reference for their new terms.

Third, the teacher presents the text to the students in one of several ways. Able and less-able readers may be matched so that students with reading difficulties may listen to the good reader. The teacher may prefer to read the passage aloud to the group. A tape recording of the passage may be made so that students can listen as often as they need. Upper grade students may come into the classroom to read the passage to a student or group of students. Those who can read the text on their own should be encouraged to do so.

Fourth, during the reading and immediately afterwards, students take notes on the information they receive. Students should keep their vocabulary outlines before them at this time as an aid for spelling and to help structure their thinking. Of course, students can be directly taught some note-taking skills through modelling and other strategies. An important point is that whoever reads the text must make frequent, rather lengthy pauses so that students can write accompanying notes.

Fifth, the students next convert their notes to text by expanding the information into their own sentences and paragraphs. Their first efforts generally will consist of sparse, connected phrases derived from the vocabulary outline. This is to be expected. Displaying some sample books written by a few of the more capable students or by the teacher will illustrate the format and amount of detail that should be used. In addition, presenting the outline that students are to elaborate provides needed structure.

Sixth, a list of questions that deal with the information the students have been processing is made available. These questions act as criteria for the students' writing. If the students encounter questions that cannot be answered by referring to their translated text, then the information should be located and included.

Finally, students assemble their completed passages by compiling the essential-vocabulary outline, their translated text pages, and the teacher-prepared questions. These should be placed into a notebook, folder, or classroom-developed book cover for evaluation and future reference.

Writing in the English Classroom

The English classroom is the traditional area for student writing. Though students have accepted the "necessity" for such activity there, it does help to explain their resistance to writing in other curricular areas. They often do not see the implications and applications of such writing to the rest of their life, much less to social studies or science.

The English teacher can help by not only providing students with examples of persuasive and expository writing in the classroom, but also by discussing the characteristics of other modes of writing and allowing students the opportunity to explore those modes in their own writings. Never should the writing activities take place in isolation from the literature content of the subject. Many times teachers assume that students will transfer the skills they are taught to their curricular areas, but such an assumption is unwarranted. Using the reading materials that have been selected for the course content will make teaching both the content and the characteristics of the writing modes easier and more understandable.

Establishing the writing habit is also a function of most English classrooms. That is why so many authorities support the notion of journal writing in the English class. For many students, writing is not just a chore; it is a bore. They find it extemely difficult to let ideas flow from head to paper via the pencil. Writing that is done regularly, as a part of the daily regimen, will go some way toward breaking down the resistance of the students. This is not to say that the students will, magically, after thirty-nine days of journal writing discover that writing is a pleasure and an easy task. Rather, we might expect that they will view it as a less onerous task than they did initially and that, indeed, they do find it somewhat easier to put words onto paper.

Another more structured activity aids students in paragraph development and organization of ideas. The teacher should select a short story that runs no more than two typewritten pages. The first half of the story can be duplicated and given to students, along with another sheet which the teacher has prepared for the second half of the story. This sheet is a listing of ideas, randomly ordered, that are taken from the second half of the story. These ideas are in sentence form and contain the main ideas and supporting details (not necessarily the exact sentences) of the concluding paragraphs of the story. Students are directed to organize the randomly ordered kernel sentences into the number of paragraphs that are in the second half of the story. After the ideas are organized into main ideas and supporting details for the rest of the story, the students are to use those ideas as the outline from which to complete the story as the author might have. It is important to emphasize that the ideas provided for them are only an outline. They need to add additional sentences that are consistent as well as developing the story line. This activity helps to very clearly demonstrate paragraph structure to students. In addition, with the first half of the story to act as the background information, students need not rely heavily on their own powers of creation.

Writing in the Math Classroom

If writing is expected in the English classroom, then the math class is the last place students may expect writing activities. And yet, there are reading demands in the math text; therefore, it is likely that writing can be used to facilitate the reading. The greatest reading problems with mathematics are the same ones that occur in other reading tasks: vocabulary and comprehension. But, the math vocabulary is often a series of symbols in addition to specialized meanings for words that the students know in other contexts, such as *angle*. Those difficulties can be dealt with in the same way that vocabulary difficulties are generally handled: repetition, morphemic analysis, contextual analysis, word banks, and many other strategies. The comprehension aspect is somewhat more difficult because math reading is so different from literature or social studies reading. Mathematics texts contain very dense prose. There are few "glue" words that allow the reader to absorb the content without being overloaded with information. Also, math reading is intense and compact. A word problem in mathematics does not continue on for several paragraphs. Each math problem is a microcosm, a world unto itself. This lack of continuity from problem to problem forces a continual shift of attention, requiring many and varied reading demands on a single page.

This problem, then, suggests that a potential solution to the situation is to have students cover fewer pages in their text at the beginning of each new unit, but to deal with them in a variety of ways. For example, why not spend the first day of the new unit on instruction and activities. On the second day, have students turn the word problems into a computation format. That is, they would not be expected to solve the problems. Their assignment would be to set up the problem for solving. The teacher could even parcel different problems out to different class members for them to set up and then have others in the class do the computations.

As a final step, let the class create word problems for the computation problems that are in the text. This is a more difficult task, for they have to be able to express in writing what the different symbols mean in relation to one another. Again, rather than having each student turn the forty-five computation problems into word problems, divide them among the class members and then duplicate their problems by mimeograph and make the solution of those problems the night's homework. Students may well experience, as a group, difficulties with some of the same problems. If that occurs, discuss with them why it was difficult to figure out the computational requirements from the problem as written. Such analysis, coupled with opportunities to create word problems, will make it much easier for students to independently solve word problems in the future.

Writing in the Social Studies Class

When most of us think of writing in social studies classes, we think of reports and research papers. While these activities are not to be discouraged, they do not necessarily help the student to cope more effectively with the textbook. Social studies, in particular, lends itself to using a newspaper format, because so much of what is studied is "newsworthy" or the information would not have been included in the text. The first step is to analyze the parts of a newspaper. There are global, national, state, and local news articles; editorials, Dear Abby, comics, and other features.

Students assigned to one of these parts in heterogeneous groups can turn a chapter in their text into a newspaper report of events, people, and places. It is particularly important to emphasize that the newspaper includes more than straightforward news reporting. A chapter on the War between the States is certainly broader than a discussion of just the people and places. Allowing students to interpret the chapter through editorials and letters to the editor makes those people and places more believable and interesting.

Obviously, not every chapter should be dealt with in this manner or depth. Even novel activities can become routine. Nevertheless, if the teacher were to have students turn a couple of chapters in their texts into newspapers early in the school year, then students would have a framework for analyzing other chapters in the text as the year progresses. Future assignments during the school year could include creating specific parts of the newspaper. Thus, students reading about World War I and its aftermath might be asked to write an editorial or a political cartoon or a series of letters to Dear Abby. Such activities deepen understanding by forcing students to consider more than the literal aspects of what they have to read. Other students, who are less able to deal with the text as written, would find such additional reading material invaluable in helping build an understanding of the underlying principles and the reasons for events that occurred. An added motivation for this type of project would be to take students to a large library or newspaper and look at newspapers of the period that their text is covering. They will be intrigued when they discover that perspective and time distance affect the way that news is reported, whether that reporting occurs in a newspaper or in a textbook.

Writing in the Science Classroom

It is a logical assumption that most of the classroom lectures in the high school are directly related to the information in the texts that students are assigned to read. Operating from this assumption, it makes sense that such a lecture ought to precede the reading of the text, since the lecture would clarify vocabulary, give additional examples of the information, and provide a mind set for taking in the information in the text.

One strategy that would capitalize on the lecture format to facilitate reading of the text is described here. The teacher would have to prepare two things: a list of pertinent vocabulary for that chapter and a listening guide for the class lecture. Preteaching vocabulary must occur prior to the lecture, with a review of vocabulary for each day that the teacher lectures on the chapter material.

Once the lecture begins, students follow along on the listening guide, which includes the main ideas and supporting information in an outline format, and add other pertinent information that the teacher presents. At the conclusion of the day's lecture, students are given the assignment of converting those outline notes into a series of organized, coherent paragraphs. If the listening guide is organized so that each section can be converted into a paragraph, they will not find this task that difficult. The outline and the summations are to be kept together in a notebook, which the teacher can periodically collect and check over to insure that students are doing the required activity as well as to check for accuracy of information they are including.

Such a strategy, however, keeps the student dependent on the teacher for structure and recognition of main ideas and details unless the teacher uses "fading" to put more of this responsibility on the student. With the use of fading, the teacher gradually begins to leave out more and more of the supporting details on the listening guide. Rather, numbered spaces on the guide are provided for the students to fill in. After several experiences with that activity, the teacher can leave out one or more main ideas for the students to identify and write onto the guide. Gradually, over a period of months, the teacher-created listening guide becomes a mere skeleton of the lecture so that students have assumed most of the responsibility for filling in the guide. Additionally, if they are always required to turn those notes into a passage, there is assurance that their outlines will become fuller representations of the class lecture.

This activity helps the student to read the text in at least two ways. The most obvious is the one given earlier; students who have been listening to and converting information on a topic into their own words have a much better preparation for reading the assigned chapter than if they had not had those experiences. By the same token, when they do read the text, they will be analyzing the information presented there in the same manner that the teacher has been using with them for the lectures. Reading and identifying main ideas and supporting details will come very naturally as their experiences with listening guides accumulate. Automatic transfer of the skill will not necessarily occur, but the teacher pointing out the advantage of using the technique while they read, prior to each reading, will not be lost upon the students. Most students want to understand what they have been assigned to read, but few have a structure for doing so.

Though the content teacher is not a teacher of reading or writing, the teacher needs to keep in mind that there is a major responsibility to help students comprehend whatever reading assignments are given. Using writing approaches to accomplish this task makes both the reading and the writing of a curricular area easier and more enjoyable for students.

8

Reading/Study Strategies in Content Areas

The preceding chapters have dealt specifically with strategies that facilitate the acquisition of new information. The focus of this chapter will be on the type of strategies that enhance the retention and retrieval of acquired information. Clearly, the ability to retain and recall information is as important as the ability to acquire it in the first place. Study strategies are also intended to develop in students those habits that encourage independent learning. Therefore, teaching students study strategies should be emphasized by all content teachers.

In this chapter, Smith and Alvermann report research which points to a noticeable absence of study strategies among students. Since numerous studies have advocated study strategies to enhance learning and retention, they present three specific techniques to aid students.

Memory and Moore describe three study strategies that enable students to form connections between the information they already possess and new information they are to acquire. Specifically, they discuss reading for (1) principles, (2) organization, and (3) simple associations.

Orlando focuses his discussion on a modification of SQ3R, a widely advocated study strategy. Though originally used with college students, the authors feel the modified version of SQ3R presented by Orlando can be used with students at the middle and secondary grade level.

Developing Study-skilled Readers

Susan J. Smith
South Carolina Department of Education

Donna E. Alvermann
University of Northern Iowa

A common lament among students—"I don't know how to study"—provides a continuing challenge for content area teachers. Study skills are the application or reading-to-learn skills that most students do not automatically acquire. As Herber (1978) has pointed out, it is erroneous to assume that reading and thinking skills taught in the elementary grades will transfer to the junior and senior high. How, then, *do* secondary students who lack the requisite reading and thinking skills for effective study prepare to read content material?

To get some partial answers to that question, Alvermann (1980) asked 114 tenth graders to read an expository passage for the purpose of remembering as much information as possible on a subsequent free recall test. Students in one-half of the group were taught a specific study strategy, that of using key words in a graphic organizer; students in the other half were free to select their own "most effective" study strategy. As might be expected, the former group significantly outperformed the latter. This result is not surprising when the response category percentages for the latter group are examined.

Self-selected Study Strategy (Retrospectively Reported)	Percent of Group (N=57)
Read material over a couple of times	41%
Just concentrated on the material	16%
Studied important things	11%
Remembered key words	7%
No response (blank)	7%
Really don't have a study strategy	5%
Summarized what was read	3%
Tried to visualize	2%
Picked out main idea of each paragraph	2%
Told myself to like the article	2%
Read material fast because it's harder to read slow	2%
Tried to remember the interesting parts	2%

Although no conclusion can or should be drawn based on a single investigation, it is interesting to note, nonetheless, the noticeable absence of such familiar study strategies as

Written especially for inclusion in this text.

SQ3R, underlining, and note-taking. Perhaps, as Anderson (1978) has noted, the perceived effectiveness of these strategies is not borne out despite a long history of research and teaching.

Presently, a large body of research in reading continues to focus on identifying and developing study strategies that will assist students in selecting, organizing, and evaluating incoming information. Attempts are being made to measure differences between skilled and unskilled readers' perceptions of their reading/study strategies. Mikulecky and Olshavsky (1979), for instance, found that skilled readers see themselves reading for an overview, systematically studying text aids, and using dictionaries far more often than unskilled readers.

Since a major requirement in teaching students how to study is systematic identification and teaching of subject matter simultaneously with the appropriate reading processes (Herber, 1978), content area teachers need to be more than just aware of their responsibilities in developing study-skilled readers; they need practical implementation strategies as well. Equally important to identifying and teaching the appropriate strategies, of course, is convincing students that suggested techniques *do* work. According to Anderson (1978), "the process of studying is a criteria-related, self-directed form of reading text. . . ." (p. 27). Without active student involvement, content area teachers should expect even their best instructional intentions to go unheeded.

As might be expected, numerous studies (André and Anderson, 1978–79; Armbruster and Anderson, 1980; Barron and Stone, 1974) have demonstrated the superiority of study strategies that require students to interact with text in a meaningful fashion. Quite obviously, if the goal is to develop study-skilled readers who are flexible and versatile in getting meaning from print, it is imperative to lead students through simulation activities and to provide continual encouragement in using the techniques. Instruction should offer models and concrete examples of the desired processes. Entire textbooks, in fact, have been written (viz., Herber's *Teaching Reading in Content Areas,* 1978) that provide a theoretical framework for various text-processing strategies. A brief article cannot correlate practice and theory and give a potential reader the benefit of a full understanding of the reading process that these models provide.

Included, however, in this article are three fairly concise activities designed to acquaint content area teachers with the benefits that can accrue when study-poor readers are turned into study-skilled readers. The first strategy, originally developed as a technique in foreign language acquisition, can be used to help students retain vocabulary terms that they have selected as being important to remember. Called the keyword method (Jones and Hall, 1978), it involves learning to pair technical terms with their definitions. For example, *SA-LINE* can be recoded as *SAIL-LINE*. Students are then told to visualize and rehearse an event (or object) denoted by the code word and the technical term. In this case they might picture a sailboat with a line cast into the SALTY sea. It is a self-initiated study strategy—one that may enhance students' visual imagery as an added bonus effect.

A second strategy, known as the Chunking Study Outline (Furukawa, Sumpter, and Cohen, 1978), encourages students to organize information in a logical and easily retrievable format. To experience this method, read the following excerpts from several sections of a high school biology text (*Biological Science: An Ecological Approach,* 1978, pp. 75–92).

Communities and Ecosystems

Communities

No population lives alone. Every population interacts with other populations in a complex web of relationships. The set of interacting populations . . .

Types of Community Relationships

In the Florida river community you easily recognize some kinds of relationships that were . . .

Predation. Snapping turtles eat young river turtles. Musk turtles eat snails. Snakes swallow . . .

Parasitism. Leeches cling to a turtle's skin and suck blood. Microorganisms within the turtle absorb . . .

Commensalism. Bluebirds use a woodpecker hole after it has been abandoned. Thus the presence of woodpeckers is beneficial to . . .

Mutualism. Growing on rocks or the bark of trees, you may find small plants that have no roots, stems or leaves. These organisms are called . . .

Evaluating Relationships

The terms we have been discussing are based on the idea that some ecological relationships are beneficial, some harmful, and some neutral. Now . . .

Ecosystem Structure

To study an ecosystem, it is important to collect data on populations of . . .

Continuity of Ecosystems

What are the limits of an ecosystem? In our Florida example we would have . . .

Structure in Depth

The Florida river ecosystem obviously has structure in three dimensions—length . . .

Energy Structure

First, every ecosystem must have a source of energy. Second, this energy . . .

Now organize your response as directed in steps 1–3:

Step 1. Review the chapter title, main topics, subtopics, and details.

Step 2. Write the keywords from each of the parts reviewed in Step 1.

Step 3. Keep reviewing, progressively chunking discrete units into meaningful wholes.

Communities—Ecosystems

I. Communities
   A. Types
      1. Predation
      2. Parasitism
      3. Commensalism
      4. Mutualism
   B. Evaluating
II. Ecosystem Structure
   A. Continuity
   B. Depth
   C. Energy

For this method to be fully appreciated, several chapters must be chunked. Only then, and after repeated review, will students begin to see the benefit of using higher-order key words to tie together the lower-order words. (Notice that the chunking strategy is more concise than traditional outlining.) The organization, once perceived, will assist students in their class discussions, in responding to essay-type questions, and in sensing the author's structure. This latter factor is particularly important in determining what is comprehended and retained. Results from numerous studies (Bartlett, 1978; Meyer, Brandt and Bluth, 1978) indicate that the reader's ability to recognize and use the author's organizational pattern is a powerful predictor of what and how much will be recalled.

Finally, after students have selected and organized the material that they deem important from their texts, it is essential that they evaluate their understanding of the information gained. Carney (1978) developed a strategy that activates critical thinking about what has been read at specific points within the material. He uses the term "embedded organizers" to describe the technique for encouraging students to react critically to what they have read. The following is a modified version (to include an embedded organizer) of a passage in *Land and People: A World Geography* (1979, p. 242).

> The idea of land is very strong in most Mexicans' minds. The Mexican Revolution of 1910–1916 had as its slogan "Land and Liberty." One of the results of the revolution was that the government redistributed some of the land, enabling many poorer farmers to own their own plots. Prior to the revolution, land was mostly held by wealthy farmers and ranchers in great estates, or haciendas. (Teacher-generated embedded organizer: Finally! Justice reared its head in this, the land of contrasts.)

(Student embedded organizer: _____)

Initially, students are taught to respond by writing their own evaluation of the information in the blank following the model embedded organizer. Over time, Carney suggests that both the written response and the embedded organizers may be phased out. It is assumed that students will eventually internalize the process.

One assumption that cannot be made, however, is that the preceding study skill strategies are known to all of the students in your content area. These strategies represent a meager start, perhaps; but by continually providing students with planned instruction in reading processes that are immersed in content, the subject area teacher can help nourish the growth of study-skilled readers.

References

Alvermann, D. E. Effects of graphic organizers, textual organization, and reading comprehension level on recall of expository prose. Unpublished doctoral dissertation, Syracuse University, 1980.

Anderson, T. H. *Study skills and learning strategies* (Tech. Rep. 104). Urbana-Champaign: University of Illinois, 1978.

André, M. E., and Anderson, T. H. The development and evaluation of a self-questioning study technique. *Reading Research Quarterly,* 1978–79, *14,* 605–623.

Armbruster, B. B., and Anderson, T. H. *The effect of mapping on the free recall of expository text* (Tech. Rep. 160). Urbana-Champaign: University of Illinois, 1980.

Barron, R. F., and Stone, V. F. The effect of student-constructed graphic post organizers upon learning vocabulary relationships. In P. L. Nacke (Ed.), *Interaction: Research and practice for college and adult reading.* 23rd Yearbook of the National Reading Conference, Clemson, South Carolina, 1974.

Bartlett, B. J. Top-level structure as an organizational strategy for recall of classroom text. Research Report No. 1, Prose Learning Series, Arizona State University, Tempe, 1978.

Biological science: An ecological approach. BSCS Green Version, 4th ed. Chicago: Rand McNally, 1978.

Carney, J. Organizing behaviors that facilitate comprehension in content materials. Paper presented at the Annual Meeting of the Eastern Regional Conference of the IRA, Hartford, Conn., March 2–4, 1978.

Furukawa, J. M., Sumpter, K., and Cohen, N. Chunking method of teaching and studying: III. Paper presented at the Annual Meeting of the American Psychological Association, Toronto, Canada, 1978.

Herber, H. L. *Teaching reading in content areas* (2nd ed.). Englewood Cliffs, N.J.: Prentice-Hall, 1978.

Jones, B. F., and Hall, J. W. School applications of the mnemonic keyword method as a study strategy by eighth graders. Paper presented at the Annual Meeting of the American Psychological Association, Toronto, Canada, August, 1978.

Land and people: A world geography. Glenview, Ill.: Scott, Foresman, 1979.

Meyer, B. J. F., Brandt, D. M., and Bluth, J. G. Author's textual schema: Key for ninth graders' comprehension. Paper presented at the Annual Meeting of the American Educational Research Association, Toronto, March, 1978.

Mikulecky, L., and Olshavsky, J. E. Differences in textbook strategies good and poor university level readers perceive themselves employing. Paper presented at the Annual Meeting of the National Reading Conference, San Antonio, Texas, Nov. 29–Dec. 1, 1979.

Three Time-honored Approaches to Study: Relating the New to the Known*

David M. Memory
Indiana State University

David W. Moore
University of Connecticut

With the current emphasis on minimal competency testing and survival reading, it is easy for intermediate and secondary reading specialists and content area teachers to forget that there are many students who *can* read their textbooks and supplementary printed materials. Not all intermediate and secondary students are still trying to master the basic reading skills. Nevertheless, many competent students are quick to point out that, despite their abilities, they do have trouble remembering what they read. Helping students improve

*Written especially for inclusion in this text.

their ability to learn written information and recall it for tests and other situations is certainly one of the responsibilities of reading and content area teachers.

Based upon studies conducted since the first part of this century, researchers have described general approaches to study that enhance readers' abilities to remember written information. The more effective approaches to study resulting from this research are ones in which meaningful connections are formed between known and new information. Such connections generally move readers from the stage of initially comprehending material to the goal of storing it in accessible form. This paper describes three approaches to study that enable readers to consciously form connections between known and new information. In a sense, these approaches are planned procedures for bringing thought into the reading act. Additionally, this paper includes suggestions for teaching students how to apply these approaches to their reading and studying tasks. Several specific teaching strategies are included; however, creating a classroom atmosphere conducive to student use of these approaches should be a teacher's primary, overall strategy.

Reading for Principles

One of the most important approaches to study can be called reading for principles. Simply stated, a principle is a perceived relationship between things, states, or ideas that is maintained over time. In the natural and social sciences, most principles take the form of cause-effect relationships. That principles can be important in learning has been a view of prominent educational psychologists and other learning theorists for at least seventy years (Judd, 1908; Tyler, 1933; Bruner, 1960; and Ausubel, Novak, and Hanesian, 1978.) The attention now being given to this skill in the field of reading is best illustrated by the rather lengthy discussion of the comprehension of causal relations found in Pearson and Johnson's book, *Teaching Reading Comprehension* (1978).

The following examples illustrate some common principles that upper-level students might encounter in their content area reading assignments:

> In biology and chemistry there is the principle of *diffusion*. It states that molecules spread out in a given space from a region of greater concentration to one of lesser concentration. The principle of diffusion helps explain, for example, the absorption of water by roots, the killing of plants by the overuse of fertilizer, and the salt curing of meat.

> Most of the principles in the social sciences are not so tidy and widely accepted as the ones in the natural sciences. Nevertheless, being aware of such principles as the *law of supply and demand* and the *balance of power* can make economic and social phenomena more easily understood and remembered.

> In literature, principles of human behavior can frequently be observed in the actions of characters. Human needs for such things as dominance, novelty, and love can help explain much of the action of a story. For example, being aware of teenagers' especially strong need for affiliation with a group can help readers understand and recall much of Hinton's *The Outsiders*.

Teaching reading for principles

Identifying the causes of social and physical events is a valuable study approach, because it connects information in a meaningful fashion. However, students often need a graphic demonstration of the effectiveness of this approach in order to be convinced of its value. In an excellent article, "Organization Perceived," Niles (1965) discussed such a demonstration. All of the students in a class should be given a slip of paper with the following ordered list of words: September, December, February, November, January, October, August, April, March, July, June, and May. Students should be instructed to study the list for one minute and be prepared to write down the words in order. However, in addition to those directions, half of the class should be directed on paper to look for a pattern among the words in the number of letters and in their alphabetical order. During the minute of study time, the students who received the directions likely will see that the list comprises the months of the year ordered according to their number of letters from longest to shortest and then ordered alphabetically when two or more months are the same letter length. Students who discover this principle generally are able to reproduce the list without error after only a minute of study. By giving one point for each word remembered in the proper position, the teacher can compute an average score for each group of students. If the students who recognized the principle have a higher average than the others, then the benefit of identifying principles that underlie numerous details is clearly demonstrated.

Once students are convinced that reading for principles can be worthwhile, the question becomes how best to guide students in developing this ability. As a complex approach to reading and study, utilizing principles is not mastered through a few simple lessons. The teacher's job is ongoing. In reading and content area classrooms, the teacher regularly should discuss the reasons and causes of outcomes in both narrative and expository passages.

There are specific questioning techniques, too, that reading and content area teachers can use to help students improve their ability to read for principles. A classroom-based study conducted by one of us (Memory, 1979) suggests that with low average readers it is helpful to set purposes prior to reading that require the students to look for specific reasons, causes, and other principles. On the other hand, the same research indicates that with above average readers it may be best to wait until after the students have read a passage and then ask questions related to reasons and causes. In other words, less able readers may need to have pointed out to them what they should be looking for, but better readers may be more successful, and possibly better motivated, when they are allowed to use their own strategies while reading.

Reading for Organization

There is another approach to study that, like reading for principles, involves the formation of connections between known and new information. This approach can be called reading for organization. For purposes of this discussion, organization in information is distinguished somewhat arbitrarily from principles. Although principles are certainly at the foundation of much organization, not all organizational patterns involve definable, accepted principles. For example, information can often be arranged in hierarchical, chronological, or spatial order, even though there is no causal explanation of the arrangement. Nevertheless, such arrangements can provide a known or easily learned structure that can aid in the learning of new information.

The importance of the organization of information as a factor in learning has been known for some time (Katona, 1940; Yates, 1966), and it has been emphasized recently by research in cognitive science (Bower, 1970; McKoon, 1977). Meyer in particular (Meyer,

1975; Meyer, Brandt, and Bluth, 1978) has provided strong evidence that good readers are aware of the organizational structure of passages they read and are benefited by perceiving that structure.

The information in content textbooks is generally presented according to specific organizational patterns. For example, in life science and biology texts, discussions of types of animal life are frequently organized according to life systems—respiratory, circulatory, digestive, nervous, muscular, skeletal, reproductive, endocrine, and so on. By being presented in an orderly fashion, the facts about different types of animals are more easily fitted into students' existing concepts. Even if life science and biology textbooks do not explicitly pattern their discussions this way, students can impose such an organization on the information to help it conform to their preexisting understanding of animals.

Similarly, history and geography texts often present information about ancient and foreign cultures according to a regular pattern. Whether or not explicit headings are provided, the information can usually be divided into such categories as (1) the economic system—the ways in which basic needs were or are provided for; (2) the material culture—the things made and used; (3) the social institutions—the ways in which the people in the culture acted or act together; (4) the religion—the beliefs of the people about deities and their rules; (5) the art—the ways in which people express themselves aesthetically; and (6) the language—the ways in which the people communicated or communicate.

Once the organizational structure of a body of information such as life systems or cultures has been learned, then that structure can serve as a system of cues to help students recall specific facts. For example, students who know the standard organization of information about cultures have a structure to help them recall facts about a specific culture. If asked to describe the ancient Egyptian culture, the students could first discuss the economic system, then the material culture, then the social institutions, and so on. In a sense, the student has a set of labeled slots to fill in, rather than a huge empty space.

Teaching reading for organization

The following group activity can be used to demonstrate to students the usefulness of recognizing patterns of organization. Half of the students in a class should be given a slip of paper showing twenty-five plant names arranged by type in five columns (see table 1):

Table 1
Twenty-five Plant Names

pear	carnation	pine	wheat	cabbage
cherry	daisy	elm	rye	turnip greens
peach	tulip	hickory	rice	lettuce
plum	daffodil	maple	oats	spinach
apple	zinnia	oak	barley	collard greens

The other half of the students should be given these twenty-five words randomly scattered throughout five columns so that several types of plants are included in each column. All of the students should be instructed to study the words for one minute and then be prepared to write them down on a sheet of paper. The students given the columns organized according to plant type generally will remember more of the plants than the students given the unordered lists. The students with the ordered list can simply learn the plant types—fruits, flowers, trees, grains, and leafy vegetables—and then later plug into those categories the specific plants that they remember seeing in the list. An average number of plants remembered by the students in each of the two groups can be computed, and these two averages are likely to show that it helps to recognize the way in which information is or can be organized.

Once students are convinced that reading for organization can be worthwhile, the task becomes one of providing instruction. In order to teach this skill, the reading teacher and the content area teacher should regularly point out the organization of information in textbooks and other instructional materials. Of course, not all of the selections and textbook passages that students read will be well organized, so it is important that teachers admit when a poorly organized passage is encountered and warn students beforehand. One way to help students independently determine when their textbooks are organized in a helpful manner is to provide instruction in surveying or previewing. When headings and subheadings or topic sentences actually reveal the organization of information in a textbook, students should be directed to skim the passage to determine its overall structure. Furthermore, it seems important to provide guiding questions or orienting statements that will help students use the organizational structure of passages to actually understand and learn the information in them better (Vacca, 1975). That is, students have to see that perceiving organization in passages is a helpful means to an important end, not as an end itself.

If certain selections are found to be particularly well organized, then the teacher should occasionally provide instruction and practice in outlining. The use of a fading technique to teach outlining is especially useful. In this technique students first receive a nearly complete outline of a passage, and their task is to complete it. With succeeding assignments the amount of information provided in the outline is gradually decreased, or faded out. Eventually, students produce original outlines of the passages they read.

Many selections that are assigned will not have an obvious organizational structure, even though the information in them may be similar in a structural sense to things the students already know. In these situations, it can be helpful for the teacher to ask purpose-setting questions or follow-up questions that require the students to compare or contrast information. The effectiveness of comparison questions was demonstrated in a study conducted by Grant and Hall (1968). Experimental group subjects were asked to compare the information in a passage on the Swiss government with what they already knew about the American government. This study is one of the very few in which a purpose-setting question has seemed to enhance learning of information throughout a passage.

Reading for Simple Associations

An approach to study that is related to reading for principles and for organization is reading for simple associations. This approach calls for students to relate new information to memorable facts or images encountered earlier. Simple associations are neither explanations nor organizational frameworks. In fact, they may be neither logical nor widely accepted, since they may be peculiar to an individual's idiosyncratic view of things. Nevertheless, if the associations are based on concrete images and specific experiences, they can help individuals remember what they have read and need to learn (Bower and Clark, 1969; Montague and Carter, 1973; Steingart and Glock, 1979).

The following examples illustrate how simple associations can be formed between facts to be learned and information already known:

> Students of chemistry must learn a technical meaning of the word *sublimation*. In that field, sublimation is the change of a solid directly into a gas without passing through the intermediate liquid stage. One good way to remember this meaning is to associate the word with an image of mist coming from a block of dry ice—that is, an image of a solid changing directly into a gas. The word and its meaning in chemistry are then associated by means of a mental image.

> A more personal and consequently more powerful association for one of the authors is one that depicts an abstract term used in government, *eminent domain*. For him this term is symbolized by a house perched perilously close to a deep cut in a hillside where an interstate highway is being built. Obviously the owner of the house did not want to give up his or her land, but the government took it anyway.

> A young boy's unintentional use of an association in understanding two rather vague, abstract terms, *determination* and *willpower*, is clearly described in Wilson Rawls' *Where the Red Fern Grows* (1961). Billy spends two backbreaking days cutting down a tree to get at the first raccoon his newly bought dogs had treed. After listening to his grandfather's congratulations, Billy reports, "I couldn't see this determination and willpower that Grandpa was talking about very clearly. All I could see was a big sycamore tree, a lot of chopping, and the hide of a ringtail coon that I was determined to have" (p. 82).

Teaching reading for simple Associations

The reading or content area teacher can conduct a simple demonstration in order to convince students of the value of forming simple associations while reading. A slip of paper listing pairs of words such as the following should be given to each member of a class: dog—slope; jump—broom; hose—climb; flip—staple; basket—stumble; house—snail; slide—pistol; cap—tape; slice—hobble; blast—pencil; and crumble—pitcher. On the paper, the students should be given the instructions to study the words and then be prepared to write down each word when its paired associate is presented. In addition to these directions, the slip of paper given to half of the students should include a statement to form a vivid mental image involving both of the words in each pair. For example, *dog* and *slope* could be associated by forming an image of a dog sliding on its rear end down a muddy slope. After all students have studied the word-pairs, one word from each should be called out, and the students should write down the related word. It is likely that the average number of words remembered by the students in the group using mental images will be larger than the average number for the other group.

As with principles and organization, reading for simple associations is not an approach to study that is quickly and easily mastered. There are, however, specific activities and techniques that teachers can use to help students improve their ability to read for simple associations. When possible, teachers should provide examples that relate abstract ideas to concrete experiences with which students are familiar. Along with the traditional textbooks used in science, social studies, and other content area classes, teachers should make available and encourage the reading of popularized accounts of abstract topics discussed in class. Magazines and paperbacks written for the laymen can provide both the teacher and the students with insights into the practical significance of facts and ideas that might otherwise remain remote and go unlearned. In addition, student projects involving posters, collages, and other media help students visualize the information they are studying and thereby form meaningful connections.

Summary

These three approaches to study—reading for principles, reading for organization, and reading for simple associations—have one major thing in common. In all of them, readers use something they already understand and know or something that can be learned easily to help retain and recall new information. The known or easily learned information is a principle, an organizational structure, or a memorable fact or image. Relating known information with new facts and ideas to be learned is one way to make reading an active thinking process and, as a result, an effective approach to study.

References

Ausubel, D. P., Novak, J., and Hanesian, H. *Educational psychology* (3rd ed.). New York: Holt, Rinehart and Winston, 1978.

Bower, G. H. Organizational factors in memory. *Cognitive Psychology,* 1970, *1,* 18–46.

Bower, G. H., and Clark, M. C. Narrative stories as mediators for serial learning. *Psychonomic Science,* 1969, *14,* 181–182.

Bruner, J. S. *The process of education.* Cambridge: Harvard University Press, 1960.

Grant, E. B., and Hall, M. The effect of a thought-directing question on reading comprehension at differing levels of difficulty. In J. A. Figurel (Ed.), *Forging ahead in reading.* Conference Proceedings, Volume 12, Part 1. Newark, Del.: International Reading Association, 1968, 498–501.

Hinton, S. E. *The outsiders.* New York: Viking Press, 1967.

Judd, C. Special training and general intelligence. *Educational Review,* 1908, *36,* 28–42.

Katona, G. *Organizing and memorizing: Studies in the psychology of learning and teaching.* New York: Columbia University Press, 1940.

McKoon, G. Organization of information in text memory. *Journal of Verbal Learning and Verbal Behavior,* 1977, *16,* 247–260.

Memory, D. M. *Prequestions, prestatements, causal expressions, and cause-effect passages: A comparative study of adjunct aids and instructional approaches with low, average, and good readers in the sixth grade.* Unpublished doctoral dissertation, University of Georgia, 1979.

Meyer, B. J. *The organization of prose and its effects on memory.* Amsterdam: North-Holland Publishing, 1975.

Meyer, B. J., Brandt, D. M., and Bluth, G. J. *Use of author's textual schema: Key for ninth graders' comprehension.* Paper presented at American Educational Research Association Convention, Toronto, Canada, March, 1978.

Montague, W., and Carter, J. Vividness and imagery in recalling connected discourse. *Journal of Educational Psychology*, 1973, *64*, 72–75.

Niles, O. Organization perceived. In H. L. Herber (Ed.), *Developing study skills in secondary schools*. Newark, Del.: International Reading Association, 1965, pp. 57–76.

Pearson, P. D., and Johnson, D. D. *Teaching reading comprehension*. New York: Holt, Rinehart and Winston, 1978.

Rawls, W. *Where the red fern grows*. Garden City, N.Y.: Doubleday, 1961.

Steingart, S. K., and Glock, M. D. Imagery and the recall of connected discourse. *Reading Research Quarterly*, 1979, *15*, 66–83.

Tyler, R. W. Permanence of learning. *Journal of Higher Education*, 1933, *4*, 203–204.

Vacca, R. T. The development of a functional reading strategy: Implications for content area instruction. *The Journal of Educational Research*, 1975, *69*, 109–112.

Yates, F. A. *The art of memory*. Chicago: University of Chicago Press, 1966.

Training Students to Use a Modified Version of SQ3R: An Instructional Strategy*

Vincent P. Orlando
Metropolitan State College

SQ3R is one of the most widely recommended techniques to facilitate textbook study. Originally developed by Robinson in 1941, and designed to be applied to chapters of students' textbooks, SQ3R consists of five steps: Survey, Question, Read, Recite, and Review. Although intuitively recognized as superior to methods commonly used by students for studying, the modicum of research which compares the effectiveness of SQ3R to other methods of studying has provided inconclusive empirical evidence to support the use of SQ3R. Some research studies reported findings favoring SQ3R-trained groups as compared to groups not trained in its use (Diggs, 1972; and Nipple, 1968) while other studies reported contradicting data (Holmes, 1972; and Willmore, 1966).

The literature in the study skills area gives some insight into these mixed findings. For instance, Pauk (1974) indicated that SQ3R might be too complex for students to use. In evaluating the effectiveness of SQ3R as a study technique, he concluded that students would be more likely to use a shortened version of SQ3R as a study technique which stressed the read, recite, and review sequence.

However, a more critical issue than the complexity of SQ3R may be the pedagogical methods used by reading and study skills instructors to train students in its use. Typically, instruction in the SQ3R technique consists merely of an introduction to the steps involved. After reviewing research in the area of study skills, Dansereau, Collins, McDonald, Holley,

*Dr. Vincent P. Orlando, TRAINING STUDENTS TO USE A MODIFIED VERSION OF SQ3R: AN INSTRUCTIONAL STRATEGY, from *Reading World*, 1980, *20*, 65–70, Copyright 1980 by the College Reading Association.

Garland, Diekroff, and Evans (1979) concluded that students need detailed training in a study system. Further, even in the absence of such research, it would seem unreasonable to expect students to translate descriptions of a technique as complex as SQ3R into reasonable study strategies and to transfer those strategies to the studying of their textbooks. In order to facilitate a fundamental change in students' study habits, as the adoption of SQ3R would seem to require, instruction which involves a review of the procedures that students should use is insufficient. If students are to successfully integrate SQ3R into their studying, detailed instruction in the steps of the technique plus a system to monitor students' application of the technique to their textbooks is needed.

In an attempt to provide detailed training and monitored practice in the use of SQ3R, an instructional strategy has been developed by the author for use in his college study skills classes. This strategy presupposes that simply introducing the steps of a study technique is not sufficient for students to integrate the technique successfully into their regular study habits. Instead the student is given training in the use of a modified version of SQ3R including practice with a content related textbook. This training includes extensive interaction between students and a study skills instructor to assure mastery of the steps of the study technique. This instructor would also monitor students while they apply the technique to a textbook.

The actual study method in which students receive training is a modification of Robinson's SQ3R technique. SQ3R has been modified to be less complex and to place emphasis on a read-recite-review sequence as suggested by Pauk (1974). Although this modification is considered important, of primary significance is the instructional strategy employed to train students in the use of this study strategy. This paper outlines the modified SQ3R study technique called PSC (Preview, Study, Check), and the Instructional Strategy to train students in its use.

PSC Study Technique

As stated previously, the study technique in which students receive training is a modification of SQ3R. In the PSC system, SQ3R has been modified to eliminate the question step and to place emphasis on recitation, review of the material read by the use of written notes. Students using this technique would *Preview* the chapter to obtain an overview of its contents; begin to *Study* by: (a) reading a short segment of the chapter; (b) reciting by writing a summary of the material read without reference to the book; and (c) reviewing the written summary by comparing it to the chapter to be sure that all important ideas are included. The Study sequence, read-recite-review, is continued until the chapter is completed. *Check,* the last step in this technique, is used once the chapter is completed to review the full set of summary notes.

The Question step, used in Robinson's technique, has been eliminated because it is the author's experience that students often have difficulty determining what questions to ask. When students are instructed in the use of Robinson's technique, they are often asked to use headings or subheadings to form questions. However, many textbooks are not written so that all the important information in the chapter could be included in an answer from a question constructed from these headings (some textbooks may not even have such headings). In the PSC study technique, primary emphasis is placed on the Study sequence with closed-book-recitation considered the most crucial step of the study technique. The use of some type of recitation or review has long been recognized as an important element in the retention of material. Pauk (1976) emphasized the importance of recitation, especially in the form of written notes. He felt that the effect of the physical activity itself could help in the retention of material. Besides providing the learner with additional rehearsal time which will help him reinforce information, the notes also provide a written summary of the chapter's contents which can be used for later study.

Further, the use of written notes plays an important role in the Instructional Strategy. These notes provide the study skills instructor with a means of determining whether students are placing proper emphasis on the important information contained in the chapters they are studying. In the Instructional Strategy, the instructor reviews the notes with the student. This activity allows the instructor to compare the notes to the textbook from which they are taken and to provide feedback to the student not only on the mastery of the steps of the study technique but also on the quality of the notes taken.

While the instructor is working with the student, s/he might need to emphasize the importance of being selective while taking notes. Often, students overreact while taking notes and attempt to write out every detail. On the other hand, some students are too cursory and overlook many important details. In either case, the instructor can individually assist the student in choosing the important information from the chapter.

Instructional Strategy

No matter how good a study system is, it has little value unless students use it. A study technique is helpful only to the extent that it can be transferred by students to their studying. It is one thing for a student to listen and follow the explanation of effective study habits, and another for these habits to be used outside the classroom. The Instructional Strategy has been structured to assure that each step of the study technique is mastered plus providing sufficient time for students to apply the study technique to a textbook they are using in a college course.

The Instructional Strategy is divided into two phases: (a) Training, and (b) Application. During Training, instruction in the individual steps of the PSC technique occurs, while in Application students apply the PSC technique to a content area textbook under the guidance and supervision of an instructor. As presently used by the author, the Instructional Strategy is designed to be used over a semester. The initial sessions of the semester (approximately six to eight) are used for Training, while the remaining sessions are devoted to Application. Once training is completed, the students use the application time to study for a college course using the PSC technique.

Optimally, students should be concurrently enrolled in a college course which requires assignments from a textbook with relatively standard readings (Biology or Sociology vs. English Composition or Mathematics). The use of the content area textbook is important because it provides relevant practice plus motivation since the book is currently being used in another course which students are taking for credit.

During the Training sessions, students receive instruction in the individual steps of the PSC technique. Initially each step is explained and the procedure for using the step reviewed. Students are then given an opportunity to practice the step of the PSC technique by using not only textbook chapters from their current courses but also supplemental content chapters which the instructor can take from a variety of content areas. After the discussion the student is asked to practice the step using these supplemental chapters. For example, after the Preview step has been described and discussed, the supplemental chapters can be distributed. Students preview each chapter and then write a three to four sentence statement which encapsulates the central theme of the chapter. The student should then be given an illustrative summary statement written by the instructor for comparison. The supplemental chapters with accompanying illustrative summaries are a significant part of the Training session. The chapters provide the student with practice on content material, and the illustrative summaries provide feedback to the student concerning mastery of the steps in the study technique. Several of these chapters can be used, and while the students are working on them, the instructor is free to circulate among the students and work with those who are having difficulty. Once practice with the supplementary chapter is completed, the students should then practice the step using a chapter or chapters from their own content area textbook. The instructor should once again circulate among the students to see if the step is being used correctly.

A three-step process, therefore, is used in the Training sessions: (a) Oral discussion, (b) Practice with supplemental chapters, and (c) Practice with the student's own textbook. This process can be used on the Preview and Study steps; it is not needed for the Check step.

Once instruction in the Preview, Study, and Check steps is completed, the entire procedure is briefly reviewed in a final Training session. In this session the entire procedure is practiced and open discussion in a group setting conducted to answer students' questions. This will end the Training phase.

During the Application phase, students will spend the remaining sessions of the semester studying the content area textbook using the PSC technique during class time. During this phase the students meet together but work individually with the study skills instructor who checks with each student to ensure s/he is using the proper procedures. The students should keep all of the notes taken using the PSC study technique in logical order in a notebook. During class time the instructor can meet with students to check over their work and give assistance when needed.

The model presented here calls for the Training and Application phase to spread over the entire semester. Students can be guided during this time to apply the study procedure to more than one textbook. Also, the students can be given outside assignments which could include studying several chapters a week which the instructor can check during class time. If necessary, this strategy can be integrated into a traditional reading and study skills program with part of the time used for Training and Application and the remaining time devoted to other skill areas.

In summary, the instructional strategy suggested here calls for detailed instruction and practice in the use of a modified version of SQ3R. The strategy is significant because it provides for mastery of the individual steps of the study technique taught and in this process uses materials relevant to students' immediate needs. Future research is called for to determine if this strategy can successfully train students to study more effectively.

References

Dansereau, D. F., Collins, K. W., McDonald, B. A., Holley, C. D., Garland, J., Diekroff, G., and Evans, S. H. "Development and Evaluation of A Learning Strategy Training Program." *Journal of Educational Psychology,* 1979, *71,* 64–73.

Diggs, V. "The Relative Effectiveness of the SQ3R Method, A Mechanized Approach and A Combination Method for Training Remedial Reading to College Freshmen." Unpublished doctoral dissertation, West Virginia University, 1972.

Holmes, J. "A Comparison of Two Reading Study Methods for College Students." An unpublished doctoral dissertation, University of Northern Colorado, 1972.

Nipple, M. L. "The Relationship of Different Study Methods to Immediate and Delayed Comprehension." Unpublished doctoral dissertation, The Ohio State University, 1968.

Pauk, W. "Textbook Systems: Carrying a Good Thing Too Far." *Reading World,* 1974, *14,* 22–24.

Pauk, W. "The Study Skills Corner, Setting the Stage for Textbook Mastery." *Reading World,* 1976, *16,* 140–142.

Robinson, F. *Effective Reading* (4th ed.) New York: Harper and Row, 1974.

Spargo, E. *The Now Student.* Providence, R.I.: Jamestown Publishers, Inc., 1977.

Willmore, D. "A Comparison of Four Methods of Studying a College Textbook." Unpublished doctoral dissertation, University of Minnesota, 1966.

Accommodating Individual Differences in Content Classrooms

Individual differences are a pervasive fact of life, let alone a fact of teaching. Teaching requires making adjustments to meet student needs in various learning situations by considering changes in the methodology and materials we use to match student abilities to the demands of new learning situations. Yet, if we examine the kinds of instruction currently taking place in content classrooms, the predominant format appears to be whole group instruction, with the lecture method as the primary means of teaching. The intent of this chapter is to offer for consideration various alternatives that teachers might use in their classrooms to accommodate the individual differences of students.

Earle and Sanders provide an overview of individualizing in content classrooms. Specifically, they discuss: (1) levels of sophistication; (2) differential structuring; (3) grouping; (4) selecting appropriate material; and (5) varying assignment length.

Readence and Dishner explore the possibilities of using alternatives to the traditional, single textbook approach to teaching. Additionally, they advocate use of small group techniques as a means of aiding teachers in individualizing.

Baldwin defends the use of tradebooks to help generate among students an enthusiasm for learning which reaches beyond textbooks. Various types of trade books are described so that teachers might consider their use in content classrooms.

Gambrell emphasizes guidelines for the use of functional reading materials as teachers attempt to accommodate individual differences. Guidelines for implementing functional reading activities in content areas are provided, and examples of such techniques given.

Finally, Blanchard and Mason discuss the possible future of reading instruction in this decade. Specifically, they discuss computerized reading and its possible impact on instruction.

Individualizing Reading Assignments

Richard A. Earle
McGill University

Peter L. Sanders
Wayne State University

Any teacher who has spent more than a day or two in the public school classroom knows that students—whether they are grouped homogeneously or not—represent considerable variation in the ability to read required text material. This range of reading ability, and the variety and difficulty of subject matter text, are obstacles which can prevent effective interaction between the student and the text. Those students who are fortunate enough to have attained independence may need no special help. But what about the others? Is it "sink or swim"?

A short informal assessment of reading ability will reveal which students are less than successful in mastering their reading. Even more important are the observations of a sensitive teacher, one who feels that if an assignment is worth giving at all, differential amounts of assistance must be provided for certain individuals and groups within the class.

Individualizing subject matter assignments is an attempt to get away from regarding a class as a monolithic "they". It means providing enough help to ensure that each student will successfully master the required reading. It does not require an individual preparation for each student in the class. Nor does it mean a different text for each individual. No one means should be singled out and used exclusively. In fact, various techniques may prove useful in different situations and in several combinations.

Levels of Sophistication

Not all students will find it possible to answer sophisticated questions requiring the application of meaning from subject matter reading. Some students might well profit from questions designed to identify and generalize relationships among particular facts or ideas. By the same token, poorer readers generally find it easier to locate and verify answers to specific factual questions, rather than questions requiring interpretation or application.

This suggests the first means of individualizing subject matter reading assignments. Given an important assignment, match question difficulty to the student's reading ability. Thus, each student can experience the satisfaction of mastery at some level of comprehension, while all the essential information is gleaned from the assignment. Postreading classroom discussion can be planned to ensure that the information gained by each can be shared by all.

One note of caution: It is tempting to "pigeonhole" students using this method. We have been greeted (by teachers who *thought* they were individualizing) with such statements

Reprinted with permission of Dr. Richard Earle and the International Reading Association, *Journal of Reading,*
1973, *16,* 550–555.

as "These are my literal level kids, these are my interpretation level kids, and these are my application level kids." A permanent classification such as implied in this statement is not desirable. It may be detrimental to the child's learning, certainly to his continued reading growth in the subject matter classroom. Regarded as one means of adjusting the task to student abilities, however, teacher questioning at different levels can represent useful and constructive assistance.

Differential Structuring

One of the most useful techniques for differentiating subject matter reading assignments is to ask questions or give instructions which incorporate varying degrees of structure, according to the needs of different students or groups of students. *"Structure"* in this case means guidance built into the question itself. For example, a teacher whose "guidance" consists only of "Read Chapter 7 for tomorrow" is really saying to the students, "Some important questions about our subject matter are answered in this reading assignment, but I'm not going to tell you what questions they are. You find the answers, come in tomorrow, and in our discussion I'll let you know what the questions were. If your answers fit my questions, you will be a winner; if not, you lose."

Considerable guidance can be provided by a simple question, for example, "Read this assignment to find out such and such." While this at least provides students with some purpose for attacking the reading assignment, some students will have difficulty in locating and verifying such information, particularly in a lengthy reading assignment. For these students, a somewhat higher level of structure is in order.

Our experience suggests that reacting to alternatives is in fact easier than generating alternatives. Therefore, questions can be structured with several possible answers, the student's task being to verify one or more of the alternatives provided. Depending on the student's need for structure, alternatives can be sophisticated statements representing application, generalization, or inference, each to be supported or refuted with evidence from the reading.

On the other hand, several important details can be included in a structured question, with the student being required to verify their literal existence in the text. In some cases students who are unable to read well enough to comprehend material in paragraph and/or sentence form can be supplied with a list of single words to be verified or rejected in the light of a particular subject matter question. Combined with these techniques, even more structure can be provided by giving locational aid in the form of page and/or column number.

Some students who are overwhelmed by several pages of reading can succeed when the teacher indicates the paragraph (or even line number) where the information can be found. This approach—like most other elements of individualizing—depends on the difficulty the students are likely to have with a given assignment. It is interesting to note that some students who are labeled "nonreaders" have successfully read this subject matter assignments when questions included a little more structure. Structuring a question differentially means providing, within the question itself, enough guidance so that the student is more certain of locating, identifying, and verifying essential information contained in a reading assignment.

Collaboration by Grouping

There is an old saying that "Two heads are better than one." This particular approach to individualizing rests on the tenet that, with some reading assignments, three, four or five heads are better than one. The essential element of collaboration is teamwork—the sharing of information and skills in order to get the job done. Several forms of grouping allow the sort of team sharing that is the essence of group collaboration.

One is what we could call a *"tutor"* group, where one person who has a superior skill in reading can be teamed with one or more students who are not as effective. The tutor, with some direction from the teacher, might read portions of the assignment to the others, clarify directions, react to their answers, and generally provide needed assistance. In some cases, two readers of equal ability might help each other, combining information to arrive at a larger understanding than either could achieve alone. Another form of grouping is *"ability"* grouping, where the class is divided into two or more groups representing different levels of reading performance.

This sort of grouping, while not recommended as permanent, is particularly useful when combined with the technique of questioning at different levels of comprehension. Still another form of grouping is *"interest"* grouping, where students are teamed to complete various tasks representing common interests.

Incidentally, most students, given the choice, will not select a task that appears too easy; rather, they will elect to do that which is both interesting and challenging.

Perhaps the most common form of useful collaboration in the subject matter classroom can be achieved by *"random"* grouping. In this form of grouping two or more students are teamed on the basis of any random means, such as their seating arrangement in the classroom. As with other forms of collaboration, the object here is to share skills and information. However, the most important element of random grouping is that it encourages an interaction among the students. In contrast to the teacher-led classroom discussion, random grouping provides each student time and opportunity to verbalize his findings, support his generalization, and question other students.

Students are sometimes uneasy or even amused by the prospect of collaborative effort. Certainly they have little opportunity for such sharing in many classrooms throughout their public school career! And the teacher may feel uneasy, perhaps equating group collaboration with cheating or improper teaching. However, two facts should be made clear regarding grouping: 1) Students *do* learn from each other by assisting or challenging their colleagues in active ways; 2) Teachers, when freed from the total absorption demanded by the lecture, are able to help, stimulate, and evaluate students in individual ways. If you regard group effort as an integral part of individualized learning, your students will catch on very quickly. Collaboration on subject matter assignments is one effective way of improving learning, especially for the less effective reader.

Selecting Appropriate Material

In the ideal classroom each student operates with material that is suited to his instructional level. We know however that this ideal is rarely the case. Some subject matter simply cannot be presented at low levels of difficulty. In other cases, money is not available to buy published materials. Or a given textbook may be required by those who design the curriculum. The net result is that most content classrooms boast a single textbook, often too difficult for the student. This situation necessitates other methods of individualizing, such as mentioned in this article. Nonetheless, when curriculum-specific materials of easier readability are available, they become another excellent means of providing each student in your class with the opportunity to master his reading assignment successfully.

Vary Assignment Length

In classrooms where coverage of the entire course takes precedence over student understanding, there is little opportunity to expect more of some students than others. However, some teachers feel that mastery of fewer understandings is more important than superficial coverage of large amounts of subject matter material. These teachers have found that yet another way to individualize reading assignments is to vary their length, that is, the number of understandings to be gained. Some students can handle lengthy assignments satisfactorily. We know, however, that others are completely overwhelmed by the prospect of ten or twelve pages of text. Hence, they avoid the pain of frustration and failure by refusing to do the assignment at all. For these students, reducing the reading assignment to manageable proportions often gives them more opportunity for success. For example, some may be directed to read only the most important sections of the material, perhaps even a single page. Others may experience success in selecting a few of the important ideas or descriptive terms. In extreme cases poor readers could be asked to do no more than verify certain key words. This particular technique is especially useful in conjunction with the differential structuring of questions.

Many students need more time to complete required reading assignments. They might be much more successful if given a few additional minutes (or hours) to complete the task. It is unfortunate that the usual public school organization—the forty-five minute period, the eighteen week semester, and the graded year—makes this sort of basic individual assistance very difficult. Nevertheless, the subject matter teacher can devise means for adjusting the time factor in reading assignments while retaining the necessary degree of guidance and control. Many sensitive teachers endorse deadlines firmly but not rigidly; they do not regard deadlines as sacrosanct. Sometimes a straightforward question, for example, "Would it be helpful if you had till tomorrow, or next Monday?", can guide the teacher in his decision. Surely it would do wonders for the student-teacher relationship by communicating the concern and flexibility that is the hallmark of the sensitive teacher. Students who finish an assignment may move on to other tasks, including the task of helping those who need additional guidance. It is important to note that additional time must often be combined with other types of assistance, as suggested in this article.

It is difficult (even dangerous) for reading specialists to suggest publicly replacing printed text with assignments that do not require reading. However, the underlying premise of this article and the major concern of most subject teachers is that mastery of the subject matter takes precedence over a student's reading development.

In point of fact, the teacher is expected to teach subject matter ideas and skills regardless of students' reading abilities. Even when the student receives separate expert reading instruction, increased reading ability is a long time coming. Therefore, when the student is severely handicapped, many important ideas can be communicated through other media, such as pictures, tapes, records, films, filmstrips, and the like. Of course, we must face the fact that complete abandonment of required reading prevents the student from improving his reading ability. He becomes forever dependent on speech alone to gather and assess information in a given subject area. It therefore seems advisable to use other media as supplement rather than as replacement.

For example, material presented orally can often be accompanied by written questions structured to provide a maximum amount of guidance. Since the questions are in written form they will require reading; hence they represent elements integral to both subject matter mastery and continued reading growth. However, to the degree that reduction or abandonment of printed material is necessary to ensure student success, the technique can be effective in overcoming the obstacles presented by reading assignments.

Summary

This article has described several techniques for individualizing reading assignments in subject matter classes. The approaches mentioned herein do not represent a comprehensive list of suggestions. Nor are they all guaranteed to be equally practical, or equally comfortable to certain teachers. Experience suggests, however, that the use of these approaches has provided many "nonreaders" with the help they needed to become successful readers—at least to some degree. That alone may be reason enough to give them a try!

Alternatives to a Single Textbook Approach*

John E. Readence
University of Georgia

Ernest K. Dishner
University of Northern Iowa

One of the true "classics" in higher education is the college professor standing in front of a preservice education class extolling the virtues of individualization within the classroom; unfortunately, this extollment is usually delivered through lecture(s) supplemented by occasional classroom discussion. The end result is just one more example of the "Do as I say, not as I do!" instructional strategy!

Yet, the college professor has effectively modeled for the preservice teacher the common method of instruction found in many public schools—the whole group, lecture format wherein the entire class is taught as if it were only one person. It is no wonder that such an instructional format dominates public school classrooms.

*Written especially for inclusion in this text.

In whole group instruction the subject, rather than the individual student, is the focus of instruction. However, in reality, effective classroom teaching deals with individuals who differ in a myriad of ways. In addition to the very obvious differences in the areas of academic achievement and ability, students in a given classroom will differ in terms of experiential background, language skills, interests, physical development, emotional development, motivation, self-concept, rate of learning, cognitive style, and even in chronological age. Considering all these variables, some form of individualization seems essential in order to meet the learning needs of students.

On the other hand, "true" individualization, in which the individual student receives instruction that is specifically tailored to that student, appears to be an impossible task. Additionally, individualized instruction is probably not desirable either (Hunsaker and Roy, 1977). Indeed, such instruction neglects student interaction and meaningful student exchange.

Since both whole group instruction and total individualization seem to be inappropriate instructional formats, there would appear to be some sort of middle ground between these two extremes described above. It should be the goal of classroom teachers to discover for themselves the most effective, yet manageable, classroom organization.

One of the major deterrents to seeking the most appropriate classroom organization to accommodate individual differences is the single textbook approach. This approach goes hand in hand with whole group instruction, i.e., everyone is required to read the same assignment at the same time. While there can be no argument that the textbook is the primary means of instruction in the content classroom and that it provides an appropriate means of structuring student learning, strict adherence to the single text with all students is neither appropriate nor desirable.

Single Text Alternatives

To eliminate the constraints placed upon the teacher by a single textbook approach and to stimulate a classroom organization conducive to individual student needs, alternatives to the single text should be considered. Single textbook alternatives include: (1) adopting multilevel texts, (2) adapting the textbook, (3) using text supplements, and (4) using instructional supplements.

1. Adopting multilevel texts

If funding is possible, the use of multilevel texts is appropriate. Multilevel texts are textbooks covering the same subject matter but written at varying levels of difficulty. In this way the teacher can attempt to match students' reading levels with texts of appropriate difficulty. This match can be accomplished through the use of informal classroom evaluation instruments such as cloze test or the group informal reading inventory (Dishner and Readence, 1977).

2. Adapting the textbook

If such funding is not possible or if multilevel textbooks are not available, other alternatives must be considered. If the textbook is too difficult for many students, using the book as a resource or reference tool to supplement instruction is appropriate. Additionally, portions of the text that may prove particularly difficult could be rewritten. Students also may participate in the rewriting process by using the translation-writing approach (see Arthur article, "Writing in the Content Areas," in this volume). Once rewritten, whether by teacher or students, these revisions will be useful for future students who might experience difficulty with the primary text.

3. Using text supplements

Supplements to the original text can be divided into other textbook sources and non-textbook sources. Other textbook sources include trade books; magazines and journals; newspapers; instructional kits, such as those available from Science Research Associates and numerous other publishing companies; and programmed materials. Additionally, multiple texts by different publishers, but covering the same material, should be considered. Nontextbook sources include the use of outside "experts" to serve as resource people; films and filmstrips; audio and video tapes; study prints, i.e., professionally prepared photographs with suggestions for the teacher; manipulative material; and laboratory equipment. These aids may be used wherever appropriate to the topic considered by the original textbook.

4. Using instructional supplements

Various aids to augment the textbook may be considered. First of all, listening in lieu of reading should be utilized to aid students' understanding of difficult text material. Games and puzzles or activity folders could also be appropriate instructional supplements. Demonstrations and simulations or field trips may be more concrete means to deal with a course topic. Supervised study scheduled during class time can be an appropriate technique to reinforce text concepts. Finally, paraprofessionals or aides can be invaluable aids in the classroom to assist individual students who are experiencing difficulty with the text.

Group Instruction

In addition to the single textbook alternatives described above, the use of small groups utilizing peer tutoring procedures may be especially valuable strategies to aid teachers in individualizing in their classrooms. Earle and Sanders (1973) and Readence, Bean, and Baldwin (1981) have described the usefulness of small groups in content classrooms.

Most students tend to learn best when actively involved in the learning process. Small group strategies insure active participation on the part of students. Additionally, such strategies enhance students' social development. Small groups focus instruction on the learner, not on the subject. Small groups also permit everyone an opportunity to participate in the learning process; commitment to learning is enhanced because group members have a shared responsibility as they cooperatively learn the task under consideration. Suessmuth (1976) pointed out that small groups may be used for problem solving, case study, discussing or exploring a situation, answering a specific question, developing ideas for further study, and project preparation.

Small group strategies may be especially useful in helping individuals deal with reading and understanding their textbooks. What follows, then, is a description of two structured small group strategies, Intermix and Jigsaw, that can facilitate students' understanding of content material.

1. Intermix

Intermix (Capuzzi, 1973) is a small group learning strategy that stresses cooperative learning. It is based upon the following assumptions: (1) students learn best when they are responsible for their own learning and the learning of others (students as teachers) and (2) interdependence in learning is conducive to content acquisition. The role of the teacher in this strategy is to provide learning tasks for the small groups and to structure the groups to facilitate their learning of the content.

Intermix consists of the following procedural steps:

a. *Preparation.* Students are cautioned that everyone is in the class to learn. They are told to assimilate as much new information as possible about the learning task to be undertaken and to be helpful to each other in their learning. Students are further told that a signal such as turning the lights off and on will be used to indicate to students the need to pay attention to the teacher for new directions in the group learning process.

b. *Assignment.* Each student is placed in an appropriate four-member group and is assigned an individual task to learn. In a class of twenty-four students, six (6) groups would result. With twenty-five students, there would be six (6) groups consisting of four (4) students each and one group of five (5) students. The fifth student would be paired with one individual in the group. These two students would be assigned to study the same task and would work as a team in teaching that information to the other members in the group. Classes with twenty-six students would have two (2) five-member groups; classes with twenty-seven students would have three (3) five-member groups; and classes with twenty-eight students would have seven (7) four-member groups. This same assignment pattern could be followed regardless of class size.

c. *Study.* Students are assigned to study a particular piece of information for a designated period of time. During this silent study time, students may underline key ideas, make marginal notes on the material, or outline the information in a notebook. These aids may be used when the students then share their information with their peers.

d. *Sharing.* Students are directed to teach one member of their group the assigned task. Time limitations should be imposed on each sharing session depending on students' abilities and the difficulty of the material. In the next session partners switch roles of learner and teacher. In this way, two assigned tasks are taught and learned. Next, the partners rejoin their four-member group to gain additional learning. This time the student who functioned as learner acts as teacher of the newly learned material for the other group members. The original teacher acts as "back-up" for the new teacher. In this way the information will be adequately taught to all group members. This sequence is repeated four times, until each student has been taught and has learned the four pieces of the assignment.

e. *Follow-up.* The whole group is reassembled for further discussion and clarification of the total assignment. The teacher aids students in organizing the total learning experience.

It is suggested here that the task be one of four parts of a text reading assignment. Purpose-setting questions for reading are provided each student in their learning task. What they then teach each other are the major concepts selected by the teacher. Thus, each student has one of four learning/teaching tasks in the total assignment.

2. Jigsaw

Jigsaw (Slavin, 1978) is another cooperative learning strategy using small groups. It is derived from the work of Aronson et al. (1978), who attempted to use team learning as a means of promoting positive race relations in public school classrooms. Continuing research on this technique has shown positive results (Sharan, 1980; Slavin, 1980). As in Intermix, students in Jigsaw are asked to learn an assigned task and teach it to other students. Jigsaw consists of the following steps:

a. *Teacher preparation.* Prepare assignments for individual students and purpose-setting questions for each assignment. A two-question quiz is also constructed for each assignment. Quiz questions should be challenging to students, as they will have time to process new information in depth. Four sets of assignments, purpose-setting questions, and quiz questions should be prepared.

b. *Introduction.* The following is explained to students:
"You are going to work in learning teams to study reading material in your text. Each of you will have a special topic. You will read the material and discuss it with members of other teams. Then you will teach your own teammates about your topic. Finally, everyone will be quizzed on all topics. Your team's scores will be totaled and compared to other teams' scores."

c. *Assignment.* Students are grouped into teams representing all achievement levels. Assignments and purpose-setting questions are given to individuals. Students read their assignments to answer their questions. As in Intermix, students may be given the assignment to learn overnight. Additional students are assigned partners (see Intermix discussion) to cooperatively learn and teach their assignment when numerically uneven groups exist.

d. *Sharing.* The following directions are given:
"You will have a chance to discuss your topics with other students who have the same topic. In these groups you will have a chance to decide what are the most important ideas about your topic. Take notes on important ideas. You will then go back to your team to report your findings."

Students become engaged in cooperatively discussing their topics. Time allocated to this activity will depend on student abilities and difficulty of the assignment.

e. *Team reports and quiz.* Students go back to their teams to report what they have learned. A class discussion may follow team reports if the teacher feels this is necessary. The quiz follows the reporting and discussion. Students are given one point credit for each correct item and double credit for questions on their own topic. In this way ten points are possible on the quiz. Team members add their point totals together to get their team score.

In summary, alternatives to the single textbook are recommended as means to help teachers begin to move away from a whole group lecture method to one that focuses on individual learners in their efforts to read and learn from the textbooks. Two specific small group learning strategies, Intermix and Jigsaw, have been recommended to aid teachers in this process. Much of this discussion has been based on different means for teachers to organize and manage their classrooms. It must be emphasized that efforts to make these suggestions successful rely on an awareness that teachers need to consider such alternatives and a willingness to attempt them. Without such a "mind set," such efforts may be in vain.

References

Aronson, E., Stephan, C., Sikes, J., Blaney, N., and Snapp, M. *The jigsaw classroom.* Beverly Hills: Sage Pub., 1978.

Capuzzi, D. Information intermix. *Journal of Reading,* 1973, *16,* 453–458.

Dishner, E. K., and Readence, J. E. Getting started: Using the textbook diagnostically. *Reading World,* 1977, *17,* 36–49.

Earle, R. A., and Sanders, P. L. Individualizing reading assignments. *Journal of Reading,* 1973, *16,* 550–555.

Hunsaker, J. S., and Roy, W. The group-centered classroom: Alternative to individualized instruction? *Educational Leadership,* 1977, *34,* 366–369.

Readence, J. E., Bean, T. W., and Baldwin, R. S. *Content area reading: An integrated approach.* Dubuque, Iowa: Kendall/Hunt Publishing Company, 1981.

Sharan, S. Cooperative learning in small groups: Recent methods and effects on achievement, attitudes, and ethnic relations. *Review of Educational Research,* 1980, *50,* 241–271.

Slavin, R. E. *Using student team learning.* Baltimore: Johns Hopkins University, 1978.

Slavin, R. E. Cooperative learning. *Review of Educational Research,* 1980, *50,* 315–342.

Suessmuth, P. Training small groups: How to structure them for better results. *Training HRD,* 1976, *13,* 20–21.

When Was the Last Time You Bought a Textbook Just for Kicks?*

R. Scott Baldwin
University of Miami

"Lord, this is boring!" In the course of all your years in school, how many times have you paraphrased this thought while reading textbooks? Thousands? Hundreds of thousands? Regardless of your personal response, the fact is that being bored by textbooks is one of those little life experiences we all share.

If textbooks are not always boring, reading them is at least hard work. They tend to be impersonal, nonemotional presentations of facts; and, almost by definition, textbooks are

*Written especially for inclusion in this text.

difficult. Tremendous amounts of information and associated terminology are compressed into relatively few pages. Moreover, textbooks tend to be written to please supervisors, department heads, teachers, and intellectually gifted students. This, in turn, is often reflected in writing styles that are much too difficult for average and below average students. Add the fact that most secondary students choose neither the textbooks nor the courses in which they are used, and it is not hard to see why so many students consider so many textbooks to be so much drudgery.

This is by no means impugning the value of textbooks, for they are essential to the goals of public education. Rather, what is being suggested here is that there are rational explanations for why students reject them. It is not necessarily true that such rejection implies a poorly written textbook or an inept student. If there is a mismatch between the student's interests and the content of the text, the book may appear boring to the student even if it brilliantly written!

All of this is to say that textbooks are not inherently boring, and students who don't like them are not inherently apathetic. Whether or not a given text is boring is a matter of the student's perception, but as teachers, we must deal with the student's perception. The finest textbook on the market will be a failure if students perceive it to be boring, irrelevant, or overly difficult.

The consequences of student attitudes toward textbooks are far reaching. Students who are uninterested and inattentive will comprehend and retain less information than they should. All other things being equal, the student who perceives the textbook to be interesting will spend more time reading and learning and will retain more information. Perhaps even more important is the impact of attitude on future learning.

Mathewson (1976) has suggested that achievement motivation is the primary reason why students read, i.e., "Read this or fail!" For most students this is sufficient to produce temporary reading and learning behaviors. The problem with achievement motivation is that when students leave school and the achievement motivation is withdrawn, they have no reason to read, and they stop. Somewhere along the line students must develop an intrinsic desire to read and learn.

Assuming the validity of the assertions: (1) that students very often find textbooks boring and (2) that such lack of interest has a negative effect on present and future learning, what alternatives are available to content area teachers? The obvious alternative might appear to be to seek out textbooks that are interesting. Unfortunately, it is probably impossible to write all-purpose survey textbooks that will automatically correspond to the interest of "most" students. Also, holding textbooks to sizes that permit them to be published in single volumes, and at prices that schools can afford, necessitates limiting illustrations, supporting details in the form of curious facts and anecdotes, and the diffusion of complex ideas and new terminology.

Textbooks are a superior device for systematically surveying a general body of information. They are well organized and lend themselves to systematic teaching and easy reference. They also make it possible for the school to maintain reasonable standards and predictable learning sequences through the creation of curriculum objectives that will apply to most students and that can be met by well organized textbooks. However, textbooks are not the best means of promoting independent learning, lifetime reading habits, and positive attitudes toward subject areas. For these purposes, trade books in school libraries have far more to offer.

Advantages of Trade Books

Trade books offer teachers and students a variety and depth of information that simply cannot be duplicated in standard classroom textbooks. For example, an eleventh grade American history text may spend twenty-five to fifty pages covering all of World War II. In contrast, David C. Cooke's *The Planes the Allies Flew in World War II* and *The Planes the Axis Flew in World War II* describe in detail, and with hundreds of photographs, World War II aircraft from Spitfires to B-17 Bombers, their armaments, special design characteristics, top speeds, and other features. Such detailed topical and visual appeals are not possible in textbooks, because there is no room for them. Yet it is precisely this sort of sidelight that can turn individual students on to history in general.

Clifford Alderman's *Witchcraft in America* and Shirley Glubok and Alfred Tamarin's *The Mummy of Ramose: The Life and Death of an Ancient Egyptian Nobleman* both deal with subjects that certain students will find as compelling as anything they have ever read. In addition, these books reveal the realities of life in past ages with a sensitivity and unity that survey textbooks cannot match. This is important because young people need to know more than the simple facts of history. They need to develop a "sense" of history, a personal perspective, and a wisdom that allows them to examine the present and project the future in light of historical processes. These talents can develop if students are systematically exposed to literature that brings history to life.

Historical fiction is also a mechanism for molding flesh onto the bare bones of historical fact, for developing an awareness of that common bond of humanity forming the unshakable bridge between the living and the dead. James Forman's profound drama *My Enemy, My Brother* tells the story of a teenager who survives the horrors of the Holocaust. It is real. Elizabeth George Speare's *The Witch of Blackbird Pond* combines elements of adventure and romance with a historically accurate portrayal of life and persecution in Puritan America. Such books can create an interest in history for students who might otherwise reject it as irrelevant.

Good trade books are by no means limited to social studies. For instance, *The Ocean World of Jacques Cousteau: Oasis in Space* by Jacques-Yves Cousteau presents a panoramic view of life in the ocean. Magnificent color photographs give the book a general appeal, which makes it irresistable even to students who aren't interested in most biology textbooks. And then there is the science parallel to historical fiction—science fiction. Books such as Arthur C. Clarke's *2001: A Space Odyssey* provide exciting excursions into the world of the future as well as thoughtful considerations of the moral obligations and consequences of our exploding technologies.

Some examples of fine trade books in other content areas are:

(Mathematics) *The I Hate Mathematics! Book* by Marilyn Burns

(Health Science) *Sex, with Love: A Guide for Young People* by Eleanor Hamilton

(Athletics) *Track and Field for Young Champions* by Robert J. Antonacci and Jene Barr

(English) *I Never Promised You a Rose Garden* by Hannah Green

(Counseling) *First Step* by Anne Snyder, the story of a teenage girl who has to learn to cope with her alcoholic mother.

Trade books are available in impressive numbers for all content areas. They should be exploited.

Making Use of Trade Books in Content Area Classes

If you are not already familiar with trade books in your subject area that are written for young people, you may be in for a pleasant surprise. Adults are often surprised to discover just how good children's and adolescent literature really is, not just for children but for adults as well. Successful use of trade books in the content classroom requires becoming familiar with as many pertinent books and reading materials as possible. The following sources offer annotated lists of books that are organized by subject area:

Cianciolo, P. *Adventuring with Books: A booklist for pre-k–grade 8.* Urbana, Ill.: National Council of Teachers of English, 1977.

Donelson, K. L. *Books for you: A booklist for senior high students,* sixth edition. Urbana, Ill.: National Council of Teachers of English, 1976.

Dreyer, S. S. *The bookfinder: A guide to children's literature about the needs and problems of youth.* Circle Pines, Minn.: American Guidance Service, 1977.

Walker, J. L. *Your reading: A booklist for junior high students,* fifth edition. Urbana, Ill.: National Council of Teachers of English, 1975.

White, M. *High interest easy reading,* third edition. Urbana, Ill.: National Council of Teachers of English, 1979.

Wilson, H. W., Publishers. *Junior high school library catalog,* third edition. New York, 1975.

Make arrangements to meet with your school librarian to discuss books that are available in your subject area. Being familiar with the school's collection, the librarian will be able to help identify books and periodicals suited to particular instructional objectives. This may prove to be especially useful to you if you wish to consider using fiction titles. As you explore the library, you may want to begin your own personal card file for quick reference.

At some point you will probably want students to search for particular books in the school library; and a library orientation may be in order, especially for low ability students or reluctant readers. It is not unusual to find secondary students who have never used the card catalog and do not know that fiction titles are shelved according to the author's last name! Librarians are usually willing to arrange orientations during regular class periods.

There is no single best way to use trade books in content classrooms. They can be assigned or merely suggested to students at times when the topics of the books correspond to current class emphases. In any event, your own enthusiasm and willingness to read "their" literature is essential. Moreover, the required or suggested readings will be more positively received by students if they are given some choice in what they read and if they are not required to submit formal book reports, which they perceive to be "busy work." Book reports are often justified on the grounds that they provide a means for assigning a grade. However, book reports are notoriously easy to fake, unless you have read all of the books you assign and are willing to grill students beyond what they have written. Under such conditions the book report is likely to defeat the real purpose of having students read the books in the first place, generating genuine interest in and a deeper appreciation of your academic discipline. The following procedure may be a useful means of introducing your students to trade books:

1. Bring the books to class one or two at a time and attempt to "sell" them to the class. Tell students just enough about the books so that they will be able to make intelligent decisions about what they will read.
2. Require each student to read one book per given period of time, e.g., one marking period or one semester.
3. Allow students to make their own choices.
4. Tell students that if they select a book and it turns out to be "a loser," they can tell you about it and you will give them another choice.
5. Give students a finite period of time to actually complete the book, e.g., one or two weeks.
6. Tell students that you will assume their honesty when they say they have completed the book. Most students will respect this approach; a few will take advantage of you. Try not to worry about them.
7. Require students to critique books, not so that you can evaluate them but so that they can share their own perceptions with the class. Give students the option of critiquing books orally in class or in writing. Written critiques or reviews can be placed on 5 × 8 notecards alphabetized by author's last name and stored in some special place so that students can see what others have said about particular books. The following format for the 5 × 8 review is merely one possibility.

```
┌─────────────────────────────────────────────────────┬──────────────────┐
│                                                      │                  │
│  Author _____ , _____     _ _ _┼─Last name first  │
│                                                      │                  │
│  Title _____      │                  │
│                                                      │                  │
│  Best Adjective _____  _ _ ┼─Interesting,     │
│                                                      │   silly, etc.    │
│  Summary _____      │                  │
│                                                      │                  │
│          _____      │                  │
│                                                      │                  │
│          _____  _ _ ┼─ Circle one to   │
│                                                      │   indicate the   │
│  Overall Grade    A    B    C    D    F  _ _ _ _ ─    │   value          │
│                                                      │   of the book    │
│  Reviewer's Signature _____      │                  │
└──────────────────────────────────────────────────────┴─────────────────┘
```

Summary

Trade books are not a substitute for textbooks. However, certain limitations inherent in survey textbooks can be overcome through the systematic use of trade books, which are readily available in most secondary school libraries.

If one of the goals of public education is to engender in students a true appreciation for literature and a desire to continue learning when their formal education is completed, then educators must begin spending their resources on introducing students to the kinds of literature that will be available to them as adults. Ex-students are not going to purchase textbooks for fun. On the other hand, when teachers take the time to expose students to the marvelous realm of trade books, they are helping to generate an enthusiasm for learning that reaches beyond textbooks and lasts a lifetime.

References

Mathewson, G. C. The function of attitude in the reading process. In H. Singer and R. B. Ruddell (Eds.), *Theoretical models and processes of reading,* second edition. Newark, Del.: International Reading Association, 1976, 655–676.

Functional Reading in the Content Areas*

Linda A. Gambrell
University of Maryland

> *Whom, then do I call educated? First, those who manage well the circumstances they encounter day by day. . . .*
>
> Socrates, Panathenaicus

In today's fast-paced, highly complex world students need to develop specific skills that will enable them to be effective members of society. One of the most basic of these skills is the ability to read and understand the many printed materials common to everyday experiences (Wilson and Barnes, 1975).

Functional reading programs emphasize the types of materials that students need to read in order to function in everyday life. These materials include such items as medicine labels, danger signs, road signs, newspapers, menus, and phone books. If students are unable to read such materials, their ability to function in our society is seriously limited.

The Emergence of Functional Reading as a Curriculum Emphasis

Several factors have contributed to the increasing emphasis on functional reading during the past decade. Functional reading deficiencies of the adolescent and adult population in the U.S. received a great deal of publicity during the 1970s. Newspaper headlines reported

*Written especially for inclusion in this text.

"S.A.T. SCORES DECLINE." A study conducted by the National Assessment of Educational Progress (1975) found that approximately eleven percent of the seventeen-year-olds enrolled in high school could be labeled functionally illiterate. Whereas the validity of these reports has been questioned by some, the impact has nevertheless been strongly felt (Cassidy, 1978). Currently, over half of the states in the U.S. are involved in competency testing (Educational Testing Service, 1977). In many states a passing score on a functional reading test is a prerequisite for graduation. There is no evidence, however, that competency tests will help students learn to read better (Readence and Moore, 1979). Competency testing does not automatically result in improved functional reading ability. Educators, in an effort to help students develop real-life reading skills, are turning their attention to developing and implementing functional reading programs that are educationally sound and defensible in light of the functional reading needs of today's students.

Functional Reading—A Plus in the Content Areas

Many educators believe that learning can be greatly facilitated through the use of functional reading materials in the content classroom (Cassidy, 1977; Vacca, 1975). Functional reading materials and activities can enhance the learning environment for the following reasons:

1. High motivational value

Functional reading materials have high motivational value because they are relevant and nonthreatening to the student. Job application forms, weather maps, TV schedules and recipes are a part of the real world and have no "grade-level" stigma for the below average reader.

2. Opportunities for transfer of learning

Transfer of learning occurs when something that is learned is applied in a new situation. One way to maximize transfer of learning is to plan for similarity between a student's experiences in and out of school. Using functional reading materials that are relevant to the students' lives will assure opportunities for transfer of learning and provide for the practice and reinforcement so important for all learners.

Guidelines for Implementing Functional Reading in the Content Areas

Success in the difficult but exciting task of helping students to master functional reading skills will depend, to a large degree, upon the teacher's resourcefulness in identifying and using content-related functional reading materials that arouse and sustain the interest of the student. The following guidelines are suggested for teachers interested in incorporating functional reading into the content areas.

1. Identify appropriate links between the content area and functional reading materials

There are many obvious links between content areas and functional reading materials. It is easy to see the link between home economics, for example, and reading recipes. In science, functional reading materials such as weather maps and caution labels are easily incorporated into the curriculum. Many opportunities for emphasizing functional reading in the content are not as obvious as the ones mentioned. Teachers may find the following list of functional reading materials (Cunningham, 1978) helpful in identifying potential functional reading materials that would be appropriate in particular content areas.

Functional Reading Materials

A. Forms and Applications
   1. Checks
   2. Bank forms
   3. Income tax forms
   4. Employment applications
   5. Charge account forms
   6. Social security card application
   7. Apartment rental
   8. Change of addresses
   9. Unemployment insurance
   10. Voter registration
   11. Library card
B. Advertisements
   1. Classified ads—employment and other advertisements
   2. Specific products
C. Pictorial Materials (any information presented graphically)
   1. Maps—highway
        street
        area code
        weather
   2. Charts—bus, plane and train schedules
        calorie chart
        employee information and pay-grade chart
        tabulated results
   3. TV guide schedule
   4. Bills—bank statements, cash register receipts
   5. Road signs
D. Consumer Information and Directions
   1. Nutritional information—products
   2. Washing instructions
   3. Medicine directions
   4. Cautions—dangerous products or conditions
   5. Instructions—care of household appliances
   6. Recipes
   7. Warranties and guarantees
   8. Loan agreements
E. Information and Information Sources
   1. Short newspaper articles
   2. Newspaper editorials
   3. Requirements—registration—voter, school, etc.

4. Penalties
5. Laws
6. Constitution
7. Policies
8. Notices and announcements
9. Information for driver's license, tax deductions, etc.
10. Yellow pages
11. Index
12. Table of contents
13. College catalog
14. Dictionary

2. Survey students to determine what types of functional reading materials they encounter and can identify in the specified content area

Taylor and Wagnant (1978) have indicated that teachers would do well *not* to assume that they alone can identify the functional reading needs of students. They suggest, instead, that real-world relevance be determined by having students report on the reading demands that they actually encounter in their daily lives. Content area teachers can encourage students to identify and bring in examples of content-related functional reading materials that they encounter.

3. Locate appropriate functional reading materials

Materials for functional reading activities are usually free or inexpensive, and they are readily available. Encourage students to locate materials from home, the grocery store, in magazines and newspapers, and other everyday sources. Using local materials such as newspapers, bulletins, phone books, and maps will facilitate transfer of learning, since these are the materials that students will have to use and be skilled in reading.

4. Develop functional reading activities based upon materials identified as appropriate for both the content area and the student

Activities based upon functional reading materials are limited only by the imagination. Two priorities in developing these materials have been identified. First, vocabulary development—especially technical vocabulary and content vocabulary—is critical to success with functional reading materials (Berman and Shevitz, 1978; Taylor and Wagnant, 1977). A second priority is, of course, helping students in developing the ability to comprehend the given material (Cassidy, 1977).

The following examples illustrate a variety of techniques for developing functional reading activities:

A. *Word Puzzles.* Easy-to-construct word puzzles, matching activities, and games can be developed to reinforce commonly occurring vocabulary words found in functional reading materials. In the following example, words found on several neighborhood maps are reinforced in a word puzzle.

Reading a Map

Directions: There are many words that usually appear on neighborhood maps. Read the clues given below. Fill in the blanks in the word puzzle to make words that will usually be found on any neighborhood map you have to read. Each word contains at least one "e".

PUZZLE—WORDS FOUND ON NEIGHBORHOOD MAPS

1.   _ _ _ E _ _
2.   _ _ _ E _ _ _
3.   _ _ E _ _ _
4.   _ _ _ _ E
5.   _ _ _ E _
6.   _ _ _ _ _ E

Clues

1. St.
2. A highway with many lanes.
3. Ave.
4. A road or course to be traveled.
5. A measure of length equal to 5,280 feet.
6. Something built over a river, railroad, etc. to serve as a road or path across.

Answers

1. Street
2. Freeway
3. Avenue
4. Route
5. Miles
6. Bridge

A variety of functional reading materials can be used for this purpose; for example, reading medicine labels could be a theme, and commonly occurring vocabulary words such as *dose, physician, consult,* and *administer* could be incorporated into a word puzzle. Other possible themes include reading recipes, reading contracts, reading classified ads, and reading the TV guide.

B. *Questions.* Answering questions that accompany functional reading materials can help students to develop vocabulary knowledge and literal, inferential, and problem-solving comprehension skills. The following activity was developed by posing questions about an item from a restaurant menu.

Reading a Menu

Directions: Read this item from a restaurant menu and answer the questions below.

Country Special

What a platter! Three plump pieces of country-fried chicken. Served up hot with whipped potatoes and a fresh baked roll . . . and all you care to eat from our salad bar! Just $1.99 every Wednesday night!

(vocabulary)

1. On this menu, *platter* means:
   a. a phonograph record
   b. a large plate
   c. a member of a singing group
   d. fried chicken

(literal)

2. What is the only night for the $1.99 special?
   _____

(inferential)

3. What item would *not* be included in the $1.99 price?
   a. bread
   b. chicken
   c. beverage
   d. vegetable

(problem-solving)

4. Would you order the special? Why or why not? _____
   _____

Answers:

1. b (a large plate)   3. c (beverage)
2. Wednesday   4. _____

C. *Cloze Activities.* Cloze activities using functional reading materials emphasize both vocabulary and reading for meaning. The following example highlights some common vocabulary terms necessary for reading recipes.

Reading Directions
for Making Fudge

Directions: Read this recipe for making milk chocolate fudge. Fill in the blanks with words that make sense. Some suggested answers are provided on the answer key, but other answers may also be appropriate.

Milk Chocolate Fudge

2 tablespoons butter or _____
¼ cup milk
1 package of fudge mix
½ cup chopped nuts, if _____

- - - - - - - - - - - - - - -

    Line bottom of loaf _____ , 9 × 5 × 3 inches, with foil, leaving 1 inch of foil at each end. Heat butter in milk in 2-quart saucepan over low heat until _____ is melted and mixture just begins to simmer. Remove from _____ ; stir in fudge mix (dry). Heat over low heat, _____ constantly with rubber spatula, until smooth and glossy, 1 to 2 _____ .
Do not overcook. Remove from heat; stir in nuts. Pour into _____ .
Refrigerate until _____ , about 1 hour. Cut into 1-inch _____ .

POSSIBLE ANSWERS (*not* in order):

pan	margarine	minutes
squares	meat	pan
butter	aluminum	stirring
desired	firm	

    Cloze activities can be developed with a wide variety of functional materials, such as contracts, medicine labels, magazine subscription forms, and travel brochures. Answers to the cloze activity may be provided, as in the example, especially for slower students. With more able students, the teacher may stress filling in the blank with an appropriate word that makes sense in the given context. Word choices could then be discussed in terms of appropriateness, with no right or wrong answers being indicated. This alternative focuses the student's attention on comprehending the given material.

5. Package functional reading activities in an appealing and efficient manner

In packaging functional reading materials, use the actual label, item, or package container whenever possible. Simple file folders or pocket folders make a convenient container for most functional reading activities. The functional reading material can be stapled to or placed in the folder, along with multiple copies of the activity. Answers, when appropriate, can be stapled to the back of the folder or may be placed inside an envelope attached to the folder. Other alternatives for student self-checking include posting answers on a bulletin board or maintaining an answer key file at the teacher's desk.

6. Introduce functional reading activities in a teacher-directed lesson

Students will benefit from being helped to understand why functional reading activities are being made available to them and how they are to be used. Wilson and Barnes (1974) suggested that students be encouraged to work in pairs to complete functional reading activities. The idea, of course, is to allow students to experience success with these materials and to become comfortable with them. After materials have been introduced they can be used successfully by individuals, small groups, or the entire classroom.

7. Survey all available published materials on functional reading that may have suggestions that are applicable to your content area

During the last decade a variety of resource materials have been published in the area of functional reading. Although the most relevant materials will be generated by the students and the content teacher from local sources, additional ideas and suggestions on how to develop and extend functional reading activities can be helpful. The following resources are suggested for teacher reference:

Berman, Michelle, and Shevitz, Linda. *I can make it on my own.* Santa Monica: Goodyear Publishing Co., Inc., 1978.

A book of high-interest functional reading activities appropriate for the middle grades. It is designed to serve as a stimulus for the development of practical, functional reading programs. Activities are grouped around six high-interest units—Homebound, Shopping Spree, That's Entertainment, Errand-Go-Round, Take a Trip, and Vacationing. These materials could also be adopted for use in remedial programs in the high school.

Cassidy, Jack. "Survival Reading," *Teacher,* September 1977, pp. 62–64.

This article provides examples of materials developed by Project C.A.R.E. (Content Area Reading Enrichment). Learning centers are presented in the areas of work, home, health and safety, transportation, recreation, and citizenship.

Maryland State Department of Education. *Functional reading resource manual for teachers* (Vols. I and II). Annapolis, Md.: Maryland State Department of Education, 1975.

This resource manual (volumes I and II) contains a sampling of activities, games, and ideas to help teachers at all grade levels, and in all content areas, to provide students with learning experiences necessary for functioning and surviving in society.

Real-life reading. Paoli, Pa.: Instructo/McGraw Hill, 1980.

These high-interest, low-reading level materials for the middle grades provide practice with different types of real-life reading in the areas of: Following Directions, Obtaining Information, and Reading Forms and Labels. A variety of content-related activities are included. These materials may be used in remedial programs in the middle school grades.

Wilson, Robert M., and Barnes, Marcia M. *Survival learning materials,* York, Pa.: Strive Publishing Co., 1974.

This book contains a rationale for the implementation of survival or functional reading programs and suggestions for implementation. Activities are appropriate for intermediate grades through high school. Many content area examples are provided.

Functional Reading—A Vital Ingredient

There is little doubt that the reading development of students can be facilitated through an emphasis on functional reading. Functional reading also provides students with opportunities to develop competence in dealing with "real-world" materials and helps them gain confidence in reacting independently in real-life situations. Clearly, functional reading can and must be a vital part of the content area curriculum.

References

Berman, M., and Shevitz, L. *I can make it on my own.* Santa Monica: Goodyear Publishing Co., 1978.

Cassidy, J. High school graduation: Exit competencies? *Journal of Reading,* 1978, *21,* 398–402.

Cassidy, J. Survival reading. *Teacher,* 1977, *95,* 62–64.

Cunningham, P. M. Functional reading workshop for content teachers. Allamance County, N.C., 1978.

Educational Testing Service. *Basic skills assessment around the nation.* Princeton, N.J.: Educational Testing Service, 1977.

Maryland State Department of Education. *Functional reading resource manual for teachers* (Vols. I and II). Annapolis, Md.: Maryland State Department of Education, 1975.

National Assessment of Educational Progress. *Functional literacy—basic reading performance (an assessment of in-school 17-year-olds in 1974).* Denver, Colorado: National Assessment of Educational Progress, 1975.

Readence, J. E. and Moore, D. W. Coping with minimal reading requirements: Suggestions for the reading teacher. *Reading World,* 1979, *19,* 139–148.

Real-life reading. Paoli, Pa.: Instructo/McGraw Hill, 1980.

Taylor, N., and Wagnant, P. P. Reading logs reflect student's real world reading needs. *The Reading Teacher,* 1978, *32,* 7–9.

Vacca, R. T. The development of a functional reading strategy: Implications for content area instruction. *Journal of Educational Research,* 1975, *69,* 108–112.

Wilson, R. M., and Barnes, M. M. Comprehension diagnosis: Comprehension for survival. *Reading World,* 1975, *14,* 252–254.

Wilson, R. M., and Barnes, M. M. *Survival learning materials.* York, Pa.: Strive Publishing Co., 1974.

Computerized Reading in the Eighties

by
Jay S. Blanchard
Murray State University

George E. Mason
University of Georgia

The computer age, or at least its dawn, is upon us. For those who have worked with the computer, its potential for serving education is obvious. For those who have not, its niche is much less obvious. And regardless of one's commitment to computer technology, a point of agreement is usually reached: the computer's primary goal is to serve human needs. The need with which this paper deals is the reading and learning from text.

To understand the use of computers in reading and learning from text, one must first understand two computer terms: *hardware* and *software*.

Hardware items include the computer itself and its peripherals:

(1) the *modem,* a device that cradles a telephone receiver and transmits information to a computer from a remote (off-site) location by telephone lines.
(2) the *terminal,* a keyboard and display screen for communicating with a computer. (Minicomputers and large central processors usually serve dozens or even hundreds of off-site terminals.)
(3) the *printer,* a typewriter-type machine that prints whatever information is directed to it by the computer controlling it.
(4) other *peripheral devices,* hardware units (such as TV sets, audio recording and play-back devices, touch screens, test scorers, card readers, and light pens) that are controlled by the computer and/or feed information into it.

As critical as computer hardware is, its software is what is most important to the teacher. A computer's software is the set of programs that it can carry out to teach, test, prescribe, or manage instruction. The software described herein is for one of two purposes: *computer-managed instruction (*CMI), or *computer-assisted instruction* (CAI).

CMI can take any of three forms. First, the computer can support the clerical effort in the school or classroom, efficiently and economically storing, retrieving, and processing information, such as student scores on previous tests or class schedules. Second, the computer can be used to evaluate, diagnose, and/or prescribe reading instruction. Third, the computer can provide computer-assisted instruction (CAI) based on the data gathered in the first two stages. Thus, the computer can control, deliver, evaluate, and inform itself and others of both instructional needs and achievement.

CAI is usually programmed instruction in which printed text or TV-picture information is followed by opportunities for pupils to interact. *Drill-and-practice* is the most common

Written especially for inclusion in this text.

type of computer-assisted instruction. Lessons are short and usually limited to specific facts or skills that the learner has previously been taught. The presentation of a new information item is not dependent upon pupil correctness in responding to the previous item. Responses are rewarded before more information is presented for another pupil response.

Tutorial programs are more complex and thus more difficult to create than drill-and-practice programs. Learners master concepts through a programmed instruction technique called *"branching."* The computer, through either its CRT or its teleprinter, becomes the teacher or lecturer. The computer determines how the lesson is to be taught, presents it, and provides for review if necessary.

The third type of CAI, *dialogue* or *inquiry,* is the most uncommon and is rarely seen in the classroom. In this type of instruction, pupils respond to a variety of printed messages by typing any sort of response of their own. The computer is programmed to respond to any or all student responses, so that the student gradually solves the problem presented. Needless to say, such programming is very difficult and costly.

Computer-based Curricula in Content Area Reading

The Carnegie Commission report on higher education (1972) has referred to computer technology as "the fourth revolution," a revolution which is as fundamental in scope as the printing press. However, the revolution has not yet been manifested in most middle and secondary reading programs, even though computers are physically present in most of our public school systems. They write checks, keep time, and disguise themselves as games. Strangely enough, until Nolan Bushnell, an engineer from the University of Utah, decided to computerize games (i.e., he founded Atari, Inc.), the computer's only avenues to the schools were through business applications or very specialized instructional applications. That quickly changed, and computers now abound in the classroom in the form of small electronic computerized games. In fact, one computer game, "Speak and Spell" (introduced by Texas Instruments prior to Christmas 1978) actually converses with the child orally in a logical and coherent manner. It is both a game and an instructional tool. Teachers and parents are buying it (Gallese, 1979), and it is now part of the curriculum in hundreds of classrooms, most of them in schools where system funds were not used to purchase it. Nolan (1980) warns teachers to proceed with care in using it.

Manufacturers of large central processors, minicomputers, and microcomputers distribute CAI programs. However, the new programs becoming available for the newest and fastest-selling of the computer family—are flooding the market. The Apple Corporation, Atari, Radio Shack, Commodore, Texas Instruments, Northstar, Compucolor, IBM, Bell and Howell, and Ohio Scientific are selling microcomputers. Many of the buyers are teachers, principals, professors, and others intending to use these computers for teaching school children.

Mathematics and reading programs for microcomputers are available from Bertamax, Inc., one of a large number of companies marketing courseware for microcomputer delivery. In *The Software Exchange,* a magazine devoted to such computer programs (not computers), games and other computer programs that can be of use to the teacher are advertised. By leafing through such magazines, the content area teacher can find:

1. Games that simulate the content to be learned ("Amazing Mazes" is a CAI game that can give psychology students a "rats-eye" view of mazes. "China Trade" simulates economics of the late 1800s.)
2. Tutorial lessons for students to use to:
    (a) learn content or skills your school doesn't offer ("Typing Tutor" is designed to teach touch typing to the beginner.)
    (b) amplify learning from lectures ("Pork Barrel" is a game in which the player is a newly elected congressman who faces a multitude of problems. The player's responses result in reelection or defeat.)
3. Computerized readability formulas for use in estimating textbook difficulty.

Some of the microcomputers utilize languages for teachers to use in creating instruction for their students. Using such languages with computers available in their own schools, content area teachers can develop:

1. Computer testing and scoring programs that both give the student immediate feedback and save the marked answers for the teacher. Such programs can also average grades.
2. Vocabulary teaching programs for presenting the specialized vocabulary of their fields to their pupils. These would be completed by pupils before reading their texts. Presenting a screen full of information to be read is not a good use of a computer. In the future the computer is more apt to be used to test and/or provide interactive practice *after* pupils have first read the content in their texts.
3. Drill and practice exercises for providing the extra work that slower pupils need.
4. Cloze exercises and other devices for helping students to remember the content they have read.

This fourth type of program that teachers can create is the one that may become very common in the future. But teachers who cannot or do not wish to create computer programs for helping students to deal with their textbook content may find that a state agency can help them. In several states, schools are organized in networks for cooperative use of computers and computer programs. One such group is the Minnesota Educational Computer Consortium (MECC). MECC makes available to its members several programs for use with Apple Microcomputers (Kosel, 1980):

1. *PREFIX PACKAGE* (Tutorial and drill-and-practice lessons on five prefixes)
2. *AMAZING* (A computer-generated maze)
3. *CROSS* (Computer-generated crossword puzzles)
4. *MIXUP* (A word game involving spelling)
5. *REVIEW* (Computer-generated review questions)
6. *REVLOAD* (Computer-generated review exercises)
7. *TESTGEN* (Computer-generated test items)
8. *SPELL* (A show-and-spell game)
9. *WONDER* (Computer-generated word puzzle for any set of words)
10. *WORDGAM* (Word-guessing game, computer definitions)

Nine of these ten (all except the first) are available on a time share system using large central computers. Also available through this system are:

1. *ABC* (Students are given clues with which to guess letters)
2. *ALPHBET* (Students add a letter to an alphabetical list)
3. *CONSNTS* (Lessons and drills on consonants and clusters)
4. *LETTER* (An alphabet letter-guessing game)
5. *MNIRAP* (A readability estimating program)
6. *READING* (Drills on letter order)
7. *SNTNCES* (Drill on word usage, parts of speech, etc.)
8. *VOWELS* (Drills on vowel sounds)
9. *WORDS* (Drills on affixes and word parts)

(Using the fifth of these *[MNIRAP]*, the content area teacher can determine the reading level of the text for any course.)

Some educational software companies, such as TimeShare, Inc. or Bertamax, market programs to schools. Programs also appear in publications such as *Creative Computing* (magazine), *C-LOAD* (a magazine that arrives as a cassette tape to be entered into one's computer and displayed on its screen), *BYTE* (magazine), *Educational Technology,* or *Elementary Electronics.*

Schools Are Using Computer-based Reading Programs

With all the various organizations producing and distributing CAI and CMI reading programs, it's obvious that someone must be using them. And in fact, hundreds of school systems started using computers in their reading programs in the 1970s, and even more will initiate computer-based reading instruction in the future. Public schools in large cities such as Chicago, Los Angeles, and Memphis have been purchasing software for reading instruction for years. Others, such as Dallas and Philadelphia, have developed their own programs (Mason and Blanchard, 1979). However, few have been using content area reading programs.

Conferences devoted to issues in public school instruction have, with increasing frequency, included presentations devoted to computers and reading. In the spring of 1980 alone, four such conferences were held: one at the University of Montana; one at the NEA building in Washington, D.C. (sponsored by American Educational Data Systems); one in Nashville (sponsored by Tennessee State University); and one in St. Louis (sponsored by the International Reading Association). However, computerized content area reading has as yet received little attention.

Long-time educational materials producers have recently announced moves into computer-based instruction. Houghton-Mifflin's TimeShare Company has produced *STRIDE,* a CAI remedial reading program for grades four to six. Science Research Associates (SRA) has begun marketing Atari microcomputers and programs to public schools. The Apple Corporation has produced a special version of its microcomputer for marketing by Bell and Howell. The likelihood of content area reading programs being developed for the educational market increases with each new competitor entering the marketplace.

It appears that computers will play a larger role in content area reading instruction in the 1980s. Their decreased size and cost, along with the increase in available software for reading instruction, indicate that most content area educators will be trying computerized instruction to improve textbook reading in the next decade. Their degree of success will undoubtedly depend upon how carefully they investigate both the hardware and the available software before initiating their instruction.

References

Blanchard, J. S. Computer-based activities in public school reading: 1979. Paper presented at the Twenty-fourth Annual Convention of the International Reading Association. Atlanta, May 1979.

Carnegie Commission on Higher Education. The fourth revolution: Instructional technology in science education. New York: McGraw-Hill, 1972.

Control Data Education Company. *Basic skills learning system: Curriculum guide.* Minneapolis: Control Data Corporation, 1978.

Cummins, R. P. University of Montana computer-simulated reading fluency project. Paper presented at the Second Annual National Basic Skills Conference, Nashville, November, 1979.

Dougles, C. H., and Edward, J. S. A selected glossary of terms useful in dealing with computers. *Educational Technology,* 1979, *19,* 56–65.

Gallese, L. R. Electronic switch. *Wall Street Journal,* (25 May 1979) 1, 72.

Geoffrion, L. D., and Bergeron, R. D. Initial reading through computer animation. Paper presented at the Annual Meeting of the American Educational Research Association, New York, April 1977.

Herlin, W. R., Bance, G., and Hansen, D. M. Teaching college-level reading in a computer-assisted computer-managed setting. Paper presented at the Twenty-first Annual Convention of the International Reading Association, Anaheim, May 1976.

Kosel, M. Computers in reading. Paper presented at the AEDS Workshop on Computer Use in Basic Skills, Washington, D. C., March 1980.

Mason, G. E. Purchasing computerized reading instruction. Paper presented at the Second Annual National Basic Skills Conference, Nashville, November, 1979.

Mason, G. E., and Blanchard, J. S. *Computer applications in reading.* Newark, Del.: International Reading Association, 1979.

Newcomer, N. J. CAI development in reading. Paper presented at the Twenty-fourth Annual Convention of the International Reading Association, Atlanta, May 1979.

Nolen, P. Sound reasoning in spelling. *Reading Teacher,* 1980, *33,* 538–543.

Wisher, R. A. Using a minicomputer with voice synthesis to teach English vocabulary to nonnative speakers. Paper presented at the Montana Computers in Education Conference, Missoula, Montana, March 1980.

Putting It All Together

The Content Area Reading Program

Various types of middle and secondary reading programs currently exist. Unfortu-nately, most of these programs are remedial and/or developmental in nature; that is, they serve a few select students who exhibit abilities that differ from the average student. Yet, all students at some point experience difficulty in learning from text. Reading teachers, because of numerous constraints, rarely serve the needs of the majority of students in intermediate and secondary settings. Content teachers, on the other hand, serve all students. We are convinced that effective schoolwide reading instruction, although involving numer-ous personnel, must necessarily have content teachers as the focal point of any effective program. This chapter is an attempt to provide readers with such a perspective.

Hayes provides an overview of the various components of middle and secondary reading programs. He states that responsibility for establishing and delivering such a program rests at three levels: (1) the community/school level; (2) the supervisory level; and (3) the classroom level.

Peters describes an approach to getting more comprehensive reading programs at the upper grade levels. Specifically, he states that content teachers must be the key staff members in planning comprehensive reading programs.

Aaron deals specifically with the role of the principal in the content reading program. He describes the principal's responsibility in the content reading program and presents a scale for principals to use in evaluating programs.

Searfoss and Maddox provide the framework for putting the content reading program into perspective. Specifically, they discuss students' and teachers' rights and responsibilities in the content reading program.

Design for Middle and Secondary School Reading Programs

David A. Hayes
University of Georgia

Schools exist because it is universally believed that they can better provide opportunities for efficient, effective learning than can be offered at home. Certainly by thoughtfully arranging learners' day-to-day experiences, schools do provide more comprehensive and thoroughgoing instruction than most families could hope to offer their children. Whereas school experiences do of course vary, at the heart of nearly all school activity there is a concern for the acquisition and development of literacy. Indeed, the central concern in the primary grades is unquestionably one of literacy acquisition, the centerpiece of the primary grade curriculum being its reading program. Beyond the primary grades, concern for literacy becomes diffused and less visible, as it shifts from acquisition of reading ability to the development of reading ability. It is provision of a program to address the latter concern that provides the focus of this article. Specifically it is my purpose here to sketch the broad design of a postprimary grade reading program. Admittedly, the program design is sketched roughly and idealistically, but it should provide a backdrop against which to view specific instructional matters dealt with in the other articles of this textbook.

Beyond the primary grades the school reading program comprises all those services that the school system provides in order to promote learning through reading. Responsibility for delivering those services typically resides at three levels within the school system: at the community/school system level, at the supervisory level, and at the classroom level.

Community/School System Responsibilities

Schools can offer quality reading instruction to the extent that the public can and will provide for it. Accordingly, some understanding should be reached between school and community representatives as to what can reasonably be expected of schools, given the resources made available to them. A fundamental move toward such an understanding is the formulation of school system policy that makes explicit the community's expectations of its schools' reading programs and that pledges to make conditions possible for schools to meet those expectations. Such a policy can serve as the cornerstone of commitment upon which together the community and its school system can build a reading program. Policy takes on meaning when it is accompanied by a realistic plan for its implementation. The plan defines dimensions of the reading program, sets its goals, and indicates its budget priorities.

Written especially for inclusion in this text.

Dimensions of a reading program

Reading has no content of its own but is a process for acquiring information and extending thinking. Beyond the primary grades, reading is an important means of learning subject matter and is, therefore, intrinsic to virtually the entire curriculum. There is a reciprocal relationship between learning subject matter and improving reading ability. Success in one tends to promote success in the other. The effective reading program is fluid, its shape determined by students' reading needs in learning subject area content. The need for special reading classes can be expected to the extent that provision for special learning opportunity is lacking in mainstream classrooms.

Goals

Program goals clarify the rationale behind program process as well as spell out what is expected as a result of the program. The primary aim of the reading program is to improve the overall instructional program and thereby accrue ultimate benefit to both the student and the community.

The reading program benefits students by developing personalized reading ability. Students come to understand reading as something they do for their own reasons, not something they must be assigned to do. This means that as much as possible reading should be encouraged as a means for meeting self-determined ends within the scope of subject matter learning and recreational reading.

The reading program benefits the community by graduating literate, thinking people, who are obviously vital to the proper functioning of a democratic society. In order to protect its investment and assure desired outcomes of the educative process, the community legitimately expects schools to set reasonable goals in terms of minimum standards of reading competence for graduates. Although assessment of reading competence remains problematic, and although many educators resist outright any notion of setting minimum competency requirements, there is little doubt among the lay public that schools should be held accountable for their students' achievement. In some communities sentiment runs strong that schools unable to vouch for the functional literacy of their graduates are delinquent in their obligation to the public they serve and the illiterate persons they graduate. To ignore this sentiment is to invite external imposition of literacy standards that are unrealistic and insensitive to the reading needs of individual students and may even result in the Catch–22 of having such standards imposed, concomitant with massive withdrawal of public support for schools (Page, 1978; Rubin, 1979).

Budget considerations

A successful reading program depends importantly on community support, and that support is reflected in the quality of personnel and learning environment it can garner. A school system committed to its reading program offers the kind of compensation that can attract and retain the most qualified personnel it can get. It pays respectable salaries, and it provides for its staff's professional growth in a number of ways. It furnishes competent and supportive supervision, opportunity for paid study leave, resource personnel, opportunity to experiment, and various financial incentives for excellent results with students.

The school system committed to its reading program allocates its resources so as to provide an environment that allows many instructional options. In such an environment there is adequate clerical and instructional assistance. There is no miserly attitude toward buying textual materials, supplies, and equipment. Class size is determined by the purposes of the class. Learning spaces are comfortable and permit flexible approaches to instruction.

Positive Supervisory Processes

Appropriate supervision is critical for carrying on an effective reading program, for it is through positive, supportive supervisory processes that teachers' individual concerns are harmonized with colleagues' collective concerns and kept focused on meeting the demands of students' learning. In order to effect these processes in ways that will foster sound reading instruction, supervisors must be armed with theoretical background in reading and practical know-how to implement ideas and solve instructional problems. To a great extent they are expected to be learning specialists. As such, they provide leadership in the development of curriculum and the improvement of instruction.

Curriculum leadership

It is with schools' supervisory personnel that the leadership responsibility for carrying on an effective worthwhile program of instruction resides. Whereas teachers' concerns understandably tend to be directed toward the day-to-day aspects of classroom management and subject matter instruction, supervisors' concerns are appropriately framed by the broader goals of the curriculum which should include a philosophy of reading and which is oriented toward the development of students' aesthetic, social, and intellectual competencies. Intimately intertwined with these competencies is the ability to read critically and creatively. Accordingly, supervisors' responsibilities in the area of curriculum development properly must address the development of students' ability to deal profitably with the literature of various subject areas. In the formulation of curriculum plans, supervisors would be expected to sponsor the inclusion of components which provide for content area reading instruction. In the implementation of such plans, supervisors would be expected to provide leadership in a number of ways. They would identify resources in the school and in the community and bring them to bear in the classroom. They would work to integrate willing parents into the program. They would devise scheduling arrangements that accommodate teacher imaginations. Finally, they would see to the upgrading of teachers' instructional capabilities in connection with the use of textual materials.

Instructional leadership

By taking a supportive, facilitative role in their relationships with teachers, supervisors can motivate teachers to want to do a good job and to want to improve their classroom practices. They can open the way for teachers to see themselves as persons who can change and change others, who can take stock of themselves and grow professionally. As instructional leaders, supervisors are obliged to give continued attention to appraisal and constructive comment on teachers' instructional performance.

A promising approach to instructional appraisal has been delineated by several writers (notably Cogan, 1972; Goldhammer, 1969; Reavis, 1978), who suggest a pattern of teacher evaluation that affords teachers an opportunity to participate significantly in determining the particular aspects of their performance upon which evaluation focuses. During preobservation conferences, teachers and supervisors discuss the teacher's classroom practices in order to isolate one of those practices to be improved upon. It may be the teacher's techniques for making appropriate matches between readers and texts; it may be some aspect of the teacher's questioning strategies; or it may have to do with some other instructional method or use of materials. In any case, once that determination is made, no comment will be made about any other aspect of the teacher's performance. The supervisor then observes the teacher in action, making note of what is seen relative to the agreed upon teaching behavior. Following classroom observation, the supervisor plans a presentation of critical comments and suggestions to the teacher. In a postobservation interview only the agreed upon teaching behavior is discussed. Following the postobservation conference, the supervisor evaluates his or her own performance during the cycle of observation and comment. The pattern continues cyclically, following-up on previous cycles or going on to focus on other teaching behaviors.

By working on the improvement of isolated teaching behaviors, the positive intent of evaluation is emphasized. By giving the evaluation process a cooperative, professional tone, supervisors show teachers how observation and comment by fellow educators can actually work to improve instructional effectiveness.

Supervision cannot be a matter of perfunctorily meeting so many management-oriented objectives or keeping school along the lines of a flow chart. Rather, it has to be a matter of working with teachers to meet the demands of unique problematic situations in ways that can fit the personal style of each teacher.

Reading Instruction in Content Classrooms

The classroom is the focal point of the school reading program. It is in the classroom that community commitment and supervisory support combine with good teaching to give vitality to the reading program. It is there that decisions are made that affect the reading development of the children present. These decisions concern the material as well as the technique of instruction.

Classroom material

Classroom decisions related to the material of instruction are aimed at furnishing a setting that will best facilitate learning. Where an effective reading program is in force, the setting of each classroom encourages reading. Classrooms are library-like. Their furnishings are arranged so as to permit flexibility of student activity, which includes reading. In addition to provisions for group activities, there are cozy nooks that invite solitary reading.

In these classrooms, a variety of reading matter is not only accessible but strategically displayed so as to capture students' interest. Available are books, reference materials, and magazines for digging into the subjects under study and just for fun. Care is given to the selection of materials that will suit the range of abilities and interests of the students.

Teaching reading as a content area skill

Most of the decisions classroom teachers make are related to instructional activity. They concern the application of methods, the allocation of time, and the grouping of students. Because the use of textual materials is an important component of nearly all content area instruction in the middle and upper grades, the decisions made by classroom teachers must, to some extent, involve reading. Whenever such decisions lead to practices that enable students to use their texts productively, subject matter learning is enhanced at the same time that reading proficiencies are nurtured. In fact, it is in connection with subject matter instruction that reading instruction is best carried on in the middle and upper grades.

Classroom teachers who teach reading well introduce students to the printed material in the classroom, frequently read aloud from it, and show students again and again how to use it. Their assignment of printed matter is tempered by the knowledge that content area materials are typically written at a level too difficult for the authors' intended readership and that they are usually written by persons who know little or nothing about the dimensions of reading behavior. They continually appraise students' facility with written language and set their expectations accordingly. They are careful not to expect students to read material for which they are conceptually ill-prepared or to complete excessive amounts of reading in too short a time span. They do not draw students' attention to mechanical aspects of the reading act itself.

Central to the teaching of reading is developing students' versatility in dealing with printed language. To this end, teachers should attempt to develop in their students such broadly applicable skills as connecting facts, organizing information, appraising accuracy and completeness of presentation, and using resource materials effectively.

Versatility in reading ability is further developed by teaching students to cope with subject-specific reading demands. To develop competence in dealing with the literature of the social studies, for example, teachers might work with students on identifying and analyzing controversial issues, noting temporal sequence, reading maps, interpreting charts and graphs, and opening themselves to understand that which is not part of their contemporary experience. To develop competence with science materials, teachers might develop students' skill in following directions precisely, following step-by-step the unfolding of solutions to problems, and attending to conceptual statements that are often stated in mathematical terms. Language and literature teachers can develop versatility with literary prose, which must sometimes be read more with the emotions than the intellect, by showing students to be sensitive to multiple levels of meaning and to sort the literal from the figurative through the interpretation of symbol, character, action, and setting.

Sound reading instruction is directed at developing independence in learning. It puts students in touch with possibilities to be explored, and it extends knowledge in personally meaningful ways. It affords them opportunities for developing talents and for fitting into a context larger than the classroom.

Summary

A reading program relies on community commitment, competent supervisory support, and good classroom teaching. Its purpose is to improve students' thinking and learning capabilities through improving their facility with printed language. Since reading is inherent in most subject area learning beyond the primary grades, reading improvement can best be accomplished in the context of content area learning experiences. The middle and upper grade reading program, then, is the provision of services that will bring about the thoughtful and informed use of printed language as a vehicle for learning.

References

Cogan, M. *Clinical supervision.* Boston: Houghton-Mifflin, 1972.

Goldhammer, R. *Clinical supervision.* New York: Holt, Rinehart and Winston, 1969.

Page, W. D. What kind of reading will the law prescribe? In R.J. Harper and G. Klarr (Eds.), *Reading and the law.* Newark, Del.: International Reading Association, 1978.

Reavis, C. *Clinical supervision.* Bloomington, Ind.: Phi Delta Kappa, 1978.

Rubin, L. Educational achievement and public satisfaction. *Educational Leadership,* 1979, *36,* 537–40.

How to Get More Comprehensive Reading Programs at the Secondary Level*

Charles W. Peters
Oakland (Michigan) Public Schools

Much of the emphasis in secondary level teaching in the last several years has been upon strategies and techniques for juxtaposing reading skills with content. While no one would deny that such an approach is needed and in most cases long overdue, there seems to be proportionately less emphasis upon the synthesis of ideas, strategies, and approaches into what might be referred to as a comprehensive reading program at the secondary level.

While writers have referred to "comprehensive reading programs" in secondary schools and interest has been expressed in them at both state and local levels, very little substantive information exists as to how to develop such a program, and as Early (1973) pointed out, not much progress has been made. Most reading programs at the secondary level tend to operate in isolation without much continuity.

Traditionally, reading programs at the secondary level have developed in four ways: (1) a remedial approach, working basically with only the most severely disabled readers; (2) a developmental approach, conducting special reading/study skills classes for the disabled as well as the average and above readers; (3) a content approach, infusing reading skills into content materials; (4) a combination of the three approaches.

The extent of this diversity is revealed in the survey conducted by Freed (1973), who reported that most secondary schools with reading programs (only 55 percent at the junior high level and 22 percent at the senior high level) have a combination of remedial, devel-

*Reprinted with permission of Dr. Charles Peters and the International Reading Association, *Journal of Reading,* 1977, *20,* 513–519.

opmental, and content approaches. However, the vast majority of these programs cannot be considered as comprehensive, because their efforts are focused in the first two areas (remedial and developmental).

Unfortunately, the remedial and developmental components generally operate as isolated segments in the secondary curriculum, allowing content teachers to abdicate their responsibility for reading improvement to the reading specialist or to the English teacher assigned to teach reading. What generally happens is that students receive special assistance for one fifty minute segment of the day while the rest of their content teachers continue to treat them as if they were not a part of any special program. In other words, little is done to compensate for students' disabilities once they leave the reading teacher's class.

In high schools which are actively developing a content approach or some combination of the remedial, developmental, or content approaches, the programs tend to suffer from a number of additional weaknesses.

Weaknesses

First, where the content approach exists, only a minority of the teachers within a department use any systematic method for infusing reading skills into their content classes.

Second, few staff members reinforce the teaching of specific skills across content areas. It is one thing to say that content teachers incorporate reading skills into their materials, but yet another to have a major portion of the teachers actively involved in the teaching of such strategies. For example, if science or math teachers use a problem solving process, do social studies or English teachers reinforce that process when applicable, by drawing specific examples of how the problem solving process might apply to their own content area?

This suggests more than just a perfunctory "you might have learned about this in science." Teachers must not only make an active attempt to ascertain what common content-related reading skills exist and how they can be juxtaposed with content material, but teachers should also seek to mutually reinforce them.

Third, very few content teachers sit down on a regular basis with the remedial reading specialist or developmental reading teacher to discuss the concepts or material they will be covering so mutually reinforcing skills and techniques might be incorporated into developmental or remedial classes.

For these reasons many reading programs at the secondary level operate as nonintegrated, isolated segments.

While many high school reading teachers will state that they do indeed have a reading program, generally it tends to be very superficial or limited. One method for ascertaining how much emphasis is placed on reading at the secondary level is to answer the following questions:

1. Is there a reading consultant in your building—that is, a person whose primary function it is to help content teachers infuse the teaching of reading skills into their materials?
2. Is the reading consultant working with all teachers?
3. If your building has a reading consultant, do you also have a developmental and remedial reading teacher?

4. Is there communication on a regular basis between the remedial reading specialist, the developmental reading teacher, the classroom teachers, and the reading consultant?

5. Do classroom teachers, regardless of their departmental affiliation, share ideas and techniques for infusing reading into content classes?

6. What resources have been committed to the development of the reading program—for example, money, material, inservice time for teachers, and so on?

7. Have teachers determined what responsibilities they have for working with disabled readers?

8. Has the staff discussed and reached a consensus on what their roles should be in forwarding the school's comprehensive reading program?

9. Have the various content areas identified essential content-related reading skills needed by students to comprehend their material?

10. How many members of your staff use techniques for infusing reading into the content areas?

If most teachers would ask themselves these questions, a more precise indication of how reading is defined in their high school could be obtained. If most of the answers to these questions were "no," then teachers should seek to develop a comprehensive reading program that is designed to meet the needs of all secondary students.

The Comprehensive Approach

But what is specifically meant by a comprehensive reading program? As the figure illustrates, there are five components: (1) the content teacher, (2) the reading consultant, (3) the developmental reading teacher, (4) the remedial reading specialist, and (5) the support staff.

- For a number of reasons, the content teacher must become the focal point of the comprehensive model. First, a major portion of secondary students come in contact

Model for a Comprehensive Reading Program at the Secondary Level

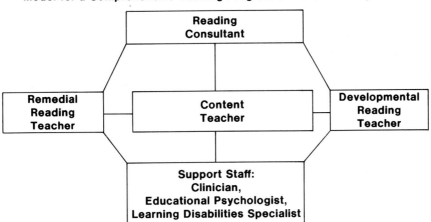

with content teachers. Carlson (1972) suggests that as much as 90 percent of students' time is spent with content teachers.

Second, content teachers disseminate a significant amount of information via the printed page. This process requires the application of specific skills if the reader is to comprehend and use such information. Content teachers must become conversant with how they can infuse these skills into their materials. In addition they must possess concern for guiding students in the use and application of content related skills.

Third, if the other components of the comprehensive reading program are to function properly, there must be systematic communication between the remedial reading specialist, developmental reading teacher, the consultant, and the classroom teacher. Therefore, if reading is to be incorporated within the secondary level, the content teacher must become a *truly functioning* component of the model.

- The second important person in the model is the reading consultant. Depending upon whose definition one uses, a reading consultant ranges from a person who functions solely as a developmental or remedial teacher to one who functions as a resource person for staff members.

In the context of this model, a reading consultant is a person whose major function is to work with teachers, administrators, and other support staff in developing techniques and strategies for infusing reading skills into content area classrooms, establish and maintain communication between other elements of the program, assess and evaluate the program, evaluate curricular materials, and work with other staff members to implement the model.

- The third person in the model is the developmental reading teacher, whose main responsibility is to teach reading/study related skills. Not only "average" students should be this person's responsibility; he/she should also deal with students who are accelerated. In other words, the developmental reading teacher would work with all readers except those who are classified as disabled.

The developmental reading teacher should not be viewed as a person who will assume the responsibilities of the content teacher for incorporating reading skills into their content area. It is imperative that the two should work closely together to reinforce mutually taught skills. The developmental reading teacher should also avoid being placed in the role of a surrogate remedial reading teacher.

In addition, the developmental reading teacher should be a qualified reading specialist, not an English teacher without the necessary qualifications to teach a developmental reading course.

- The fourth individual in the model is the remedial reading specialist. The remedial specialist works with those students who have specific skill deficiencies and therefore have difficulty reading content materials. In many instances this would mean that in order for the disabled reader to function in the content classroom, an alternative to print would be sought. Special assistance for overcoming these deficiencies would be provided by the remedial reading specialist. Therefore, it is essential that the remedial reading specialist and content teachers understand what each of their specific responsibilities are and how each can assist the other in curricular and educational goals.

The fifth component of the model is the support staff, composed of the educational psychologist, the learning disabilities specialist, clinic personnel, counselors, and administrators. They provide ancillary services that are essential to the success of any reading program, and they must therefore work closely with the reading consultant, developmental reading teacher, remedial reading specialist, content teachers, or anyone else who is involved in the reading program. In order for these elements to function properly, there must be active communication leading to mutually agreed upon roles, responsibilities, and goals.

While the concept of a comprehensive model is not completely new (Burmeister, 1974; Carlson, 1972; Otto and Smith, 1970; Robinson, 1975; Shepherd, 1973), how these various elements function in relation to one another must be reexamined, because very little attention has been focused upon the question of why so few programs at the secondary level are comprehensive in scope. In fact most secondary schools have merely attempted to incorporate an elementary model at the secondary level.

Before a comprehensive reading program at the secondary level can be implemented, teachers need to know what problems have inhibited program development and what needs to be done to improve the chances for developing an effective program.

The first problem has been the failure to obtain the necessary administrative support. Although most administrators express enthusiasm for developing a comprehensive program, their involvement has only been peripheral. Part of this can be related to the fact that many administrators still envision reading at the secondary level as an extension of the elementary model, in other words, reading being taught as a curricular subject. However, at the secondary level, reading becomes a process which should not be taught independent of content.

Lack of administrative support can take many other forms: (1) a myopic view of what constitutes a comprehensive program at the secondary level, (2) failure to allocate adequate funds for staff maintenance and development, (3) failure to provide sufficient inservice release time for the training of teachers, and (4) limited or complete absence of any reading support staff in the building.

This is not to imply that all administrators are unwilling to support a comprehensive program, but rather that in many instances reading specialists have not actively involved key administrators in the development of such a program. To prevent such problems, make sure that all key administrators are involved and that each *fully* understands the goals, roles, and responsibilities of each staff member, because there will be many important junctures in the development of the program that will require overt administrative support.

Second, problems generally result when there is no clear delineation of roles and responsibilities. It is difficult to obtain staff support if a misconception exists as to what is to be done and by whom. For example, if classroom teachers perceive the reading consultant as a remedial reading teacher and are frustrated when individual problems are not dealt with, the entire program can be jeopardized.

To prevent such misconceptions from developing, it is a good idea to ascertain how each staff member perceives her/his needs, and what person is seen as responsible for fulfilling those needs. Hesse, Smith and Nettleson (1973) have developed an instrument to assess the staff's perceptions of how a reading consultant should function. Similar instruments (Peters, 1976) should be utilized for the other components of the reading program. They can help reduce the chances for later disagreements.

A third problem has been the inability of reading program developers to establish realistic goals. For example, individuals who are responsible for inservice training have been unrealistic in terms of staff commitment, staff involvement, and the time required to develop the program.

Many of these problems can be eliminated by means of a good inservice program. Since the reading specialist assigned to develop the inservice program must rely on the support of other staff members, he/she needs to identify influential members of the staff who will assist in the initial planning. An ideal inservice program may be established, but without the support of those individuals who are needed to implement the goals of the program, chances are that it will fail.

Once key staff members have been identified, a small scale version of the program should be developed. Programs have failed in the past because they attempted to involve too many people at the outset, many of whom were either uninterested or opposed to the concept of a comprehensive inservice program. In addition to its size, a small group offers several other salient features: (1) problems are easier to resolve, (2) participants in the initial inservice group can be employed as resource personnel to train other teachers and (3) a successful program in your own building can help reduce the negative attitudes many content teachers have toward reading inservice programs.

When the program begins to function, the results should be shared with the entire faculty. At this point a committee of faculty members should be established with the idea of expanding the model to the entire school.

Once the full-scale program has been implemented, other concerns have to be dealt with. For example, how do you go about establishing a communication system between staff members? A key factor is taking advantage of available time. Common planning periods can be created for individuals who need to communicate on a regular basis. Departmental meetings can become demonstration periods where teachers share strategies. Mini inservice sessions can also be planned during common planning periods.

Developing a common file to share ideas is another good method for establishing communication among departments. Individuals should not be compelled to reinvent the wheel.

Do not assume that communication will develop by itself, because the lack of communication is a deterrent to creating a successful program.

Fifth, reading teachers must learn to anticipate potential problems. For instance, it is not uncommon to find reading programs that are merely adjuncts to an English department. Such an arrangement is not always conducive to developing a comprehensive program, because the reading program is usually subjugated to the desires of the English department.

Reading personnel must have the support of the administrator in establishing an independent department. A nonindependent arrangement tacitly conveys the administration's concept of the reading program—a curricular subject rather than a process engaged in by all staff members. If such problems can be anticipated, strategies for circumventing them can be developed.

Obviously, there may be many more problems in the development of a reading program. This article has merely attempted to stimulate thinking in regard to the most basic problem: the need for a more comprehensive approach to reading at the secondary level.

References

Burmeister, Lou E. *Reading Strategies for Secondary School Teachers.* Reading, Mass.: Addison-Wesley Publishing Co., Inc., 1974.

Carlson, Thorsten R. *Administrators and Reading.* New York, N.Y.: Harcourt Brace Jovanovich, Inc., 1972.

Early, Margaret J. "Taking Stock: Secondary Reading in the 70's." *Journal of Reading,* vol. 16, no. 5 (February 1973), pp. 364–73.

Freed, Barbara F. "Secondary Reading—State of the Art." *Journal of Reading,* vol. 17, no. 3 (December 1973), pp. 195–201.

Hesse, Karl D., Richard J. Smith and Aileen Nettleson, "Content Teachers Consider the Role of the Reading Consultant" *Journal of Reading,* vol. 17, no. 3 (December 1973), pp. 210–15.

Otto, Wayne and Richard J. Smith *Administering the School Reading Program.* New York, N.Y.: Houghton Mifflin Company, 1970.

Peters, Charles W. Alternative Models for Inservice Education. Paper presented at the International Reading Association annual convention, Anaheim, California, 1976.

Robinson, H. Alan. *Teaching Reading and Study Strategies: The Content Areas.* Boston, Mass.: Allyn & Bacon, Inc., 1975.

Shepherd, David L. *Comprehensive High School Reading Methods.* Columbus, Ohio: Charles E. Merrill Publishing Company, 1973.

The Principal and Content Area Reading Instruction*

Ira E. Aaron
University of Georgia

Reading is just *one* of many curriculum areas about which principals must be concerned. However, their responsibilities related to reading instruction take on added significance because reading achievement influences how well students perform in all curriculum areas.

The principal is *the* key person in developing and maintaining a quality program in the school. Strong support from a principal who is interested in and knowledgeable about reading is a necessary ingredient of an excellent schoolwide reading program. A few classrooms or teachers may have quality instruction without that administrative support and leadership, but such instruction will *not* be schoolwide. Though the principal does not have to be a reading specialist, he or she needs enough information about reading to discuss the school's reading program intelligently with teachers. Such knowledge also is necessary as a base for the principal to furnish leadership to program review and modification.

*Written especially for inclusion in this text.

The National Right to Read Effort recognized very early the importance of the principal in the effectiveness of a schoolwide reading program. The needs assessment and program planning materials developed for use in Right to Read schools (US Department of HEW/OE, 1974) suggested that the principal be the leader of the task force that carried out the assessment of needs and instituted program changes.

In a recent study by Samuels and Edwall (1976), characteristics associated with exemplary reading programs were isolated. Strong administrative leadership was one of five characteristics found in all exemplary reading programs. Another study (Kean, Summers, Raivetz, and Farber, 1977), conducted in Philadelphia, found that principals' experience in the area of reading and the amount of time they spent in classroom observation were two factors positively associated with pupil achievement in reading.

The Principal's Responsibilities in Content Area Reading

What are the principal's responsibilities for the content area reading program in the school? First, an understanding of content area reading skills and the content area teachers' responsibilities is essential. Second, the principal should possess enough knowledge about content area reading instruction to recognize in broad terms the effectiveness of teachers' instruction in content area reading.

Content area reading, regardless of subject field, involves two broad categories of skills and understandings. Any reading task involves use of basal skills of reading, such as recognizing words, recognizing main ideas and supporting details, recognizing relationships, and organizing material read. Most formal instruction aimed toward developing these basal skills occurs in that part of the curriculum devoted to the teaching of basal reading. These basal skills, however, must be adapted to the particular content, such as science or mathematics, that is being read. Each content area teacher—or the classroom teacher in a self-contained classroom when a specific content is being taught—must be concerned with helping students to adapt the basal skills they know to the specific content and with teaching the special reading skills that are needed for reading that particular content. Major attention here will be given to the second concern—teaching the special reading skills.

All subject matter teachers have four broad areas of responsibility for teaching the specialized reading skills in their subjects. Each of these areas of responsibility will be discussed briefly.

1. Adapting techniques to specific type of content/format

Content area teachers must help their students to read texts and other materials effectively and efficiently. How to read text materials should be discussed with students at the beginning of the school year when new materials are introduced and at appropriate later times.

Reading a mathematics text effectively is quite different from reading a literature anthology or a science text. Even within a given subject area, as in literature, students must call upon different combinations of skills as they shift from reading factual information about an author's life, to reading a short story, to reading a poem, and so on. Teachers who teach a given content have the responsibility of helping their students to read materials in that content with understanding and with efficiency.

2. Technical/special vocabularies and concepts

Each subject has its own technical or special vocabulary and concepts that must be learned by students in order for them to understand texts and other materials in that content area. The geography teacher must help students to learn such words and concepts as *island, latitude, longitude, equator, North pole,* and *desert.* Words and concepts such as *numerator, set, addition, subtraction, decimal,* and *less than* are in the domain of the mathematics teacher. Subject matter teachers should have a thorough knowledge of the key vocabulary and concepts of their subject areas, and they also should be cognizant of the vocabulary and concepts that students need for reading on specific topics in texts and related materials.

3. Special reading tasks of the subject area

Most content areas involve some reading tasks that are specific to that given content area or to several related areas. Examples include reading various types of maps and globes in geography; reading word problems, equations, tables, and graphs in mathematics; and reading thermometers, barometers, and metric scales in science. These special skills must be taught by the teacher who teaches the content in which they are used.

4. Symbols and abbreviations

Symbols and abbreviations play an important role in mathematics and in certain areas of science. To a lesser extent, they are involved in social studies and in English. Symbols, such as $+$, $-$, $\div$, and $\times$ in mathematics, involve much understanding of a process. As an example, the concept of addition is necessary for an interpretation of the plus symbol. Content area teachers must budget sufficient time for instruction aimed toward helping students to master important symbols and abbreviations that are vital parts of their subject areas.

Teachers' Instruction in Content Area Reading

Principals should know enough about content area reading instruction to learn from observations the extent to which their teachers know the skills related to their content areas, how effective their instructional time and efforts are, and how well they evaluate the effectiveness of their content area instruction. The following rating scale for principal use covers the four areas discussed above. Within each area the first point deals with teacher knowledge, the second with time devoted to instruction of that cluster of skills, and the third with evaluation of student achievement of the skills. A final cluster of four items on the rating scale deals with adjusting instruction to students' needs and interests. In addition to using the rating scale as an observation guide, it may also be utilized as a self-evaluation instrument by middle grade or secondary teachers. Staff development may be used to help teachers to improve in areas where weaknesses are noted.

Reading in Content Areas—Principal Rating Scale

Directions: The understandings/practices listed below often are recommended for effectively teaching the special reading skills in content areas. Indicate the extent to which each understanding/practice is evident among your content area teachers by drawing a line around the appropriate number to the right of each item. Use this scale:

1—Almost always	4—Seldom or never
2—Most of the time	5—Undecided
3—Sometimes	6—Not applicable

Adapting Techniques to Specific Types of Content/Format

1. Teachers know the special skills and abilities needed in reading content area texts and other materials effectively.   1 2 3 4 5 6
2. Teachers devote adequate time at the beginning of the school year (or at anytime when new materials are introduced) in familiarizing students with the content area texts and in demonstrating how they may be read efficiently and effectively.   1 2 3 4 5 6
3. Teachers evaluate the extent to which students have learned how to read content area materials effectively and then reteach and review when needed.   1 2 3 4 5 6

Technical/Special Vocabularies and Concepts

4. Teachers know the technical vocabularies and concepts to be introduced in the various units of their classes.   1 2 3 4 5 6
5. Teachers devote adequate attention to the development of technical vocabularies and concepts in each of the various units of the classes they teach.   1 2 3 4 5 6
6. Teachers determine the extent to which students have learned the technical vocabularies and concepts in each of the classes they teach, and they reteach when reteaching appears needed.   1 2 3 4 5 6

Special Reading Tasks of the Subject Area

7. Teachers know the special reading skills of their content areas (as reading word problems, formulas, graphs, and charts in mathematics; reading various types of maps in geography; and reading different types of literature in English).   1 2 3 4 5 6
8. Teachers teach the special reading skills of their content areas adequately.   1 2 3 4 5 6
9. Teachers check the extent to which the special reading skills are learned, and they reteach when needed.   1 2 3 4 5 6

Symbols and Abbreviations

10. Teachers know the symbols and abbreviations of their content areas.   1 2 3 4 5 6
11. Teachers teach the symbols and abbreviations of their content areas adequately.   1 2 3 4 5 6
12. Teachers check the extent to which the symbols and abbreviations of the areas are learned and they reteach when needed.   1 2 3 4 5 6

Adjusting Instruction to Pupils' Needs/Interests

13. Teachers use texts and other materials in their content area classes that are suited to the reading levels of their students.   1 2 3 4 5 6

14. Teachers make clear and concise assignments for reading in content area texts.   1 2 3 4 5 6

15. Adequate reference materials related to the content areas are readily available for student use.   1 2 3 4 5 6

16. Teachers take advantage of opportunities that arise to encourage students to read recreational as well as informational reading matter.   1 2 3 4 5 6

References

Kean, H., Summers, A. A., Raivetz, M. J., and Farber, I. J. *What works in reading?* Philadelphia: Office of Research and Evaluation, The School District of Philadelphia, 1979.

Samuels, S. J., and Edwall, G. School characteristics: Qualities of schools that are associated with reading achievement. In Guthrie, J. T., Samuels, S. J., Martuza, V., Seifert, M., Tyler, S. J., Edwall, G. (Eds.), *A study of the locus and nature of reading problems in the elementary school.* Final Report. Newark, Del.: International Reading Association, 1976.

U.S. Department of Health, Education, and Welfare, Office of Education. *Right to read assessment and planning handbook.* Washington: U.S. Government Printing Office, 1974.

Student Rights, Teacher Rights in Content Area Instructional Programs*

Lyndon W. Searfoss
Arizona State University

Eleanor J. Maddox
Phoenix (AZ) Elementary District No. One

Content area instructional programs should be designed to provide a broad range of learning experiences that are motivating, relevant, and which consider student rights. Students have the right to be the focal point as instructional programs are planned, organized, and evaluated. This and other student rights are not granted by schools, but are rights to which students are entitled. Consideration of student rights as an integral part of instructional programs will place additional demands on teachers. The traditional means of aiding teachers to meet new demands is through staff development. At times, however, the rights of teachers also have been ignored as staff development programs are planned, organized, and evaluated. In this article, Searfoss explores students rights, and Maddox discusses teacher rights as part of planning content area instructional programs.

*Written especially for inclusion in this text.

Student Rights

Legally, as well as morally, school systems have the responsibility of planning programs that do not violate the rights of students. Students should be able to expect that their instructional programs will lead them to successful fulfillment of any reading ability requirement for graduation. Instructional programs and any reading graduation requirement are therefore closely interwined and cannot be considered separately, if we are to be fair to our students. Fair, that is, *and* legal!

It would seem, then, as curriculum specialists plan programs for a school system, that they must keep in mind as their ultimate goal the development of programs that maximize the possibility of students meeting any reading graduation requirement imposed by that same school system. To aid in the development of instructional programs, the author would like to suggest the inclusion of two factors in the initial planning stages. One factor—*student needs*—is already an integral part of most planning phases for most programs. The second—*student rights*—must be included if we are to plan for and consider the legal consequences of a reading requirement for graduation. To aid in understanding the necessity for including both student needs and student rights in the planning of programs, definitions of these terms should prove helpful.

A *need* is defined as a condition in which something is found to be required or desirable. A *right* is defined as that which may be claimed on just, moral, legal, or customary grounds, i.e., there is an established claim to something. The obvious difference in meaning between the terms *need* and *right* comes into clearer focus when curriculum specialists begin to discuss them in relation to educational planning.

School systems are increasingly using some measure of reading ability as a graduation requirement. This attempt at accountability, although admirable, demands careful consideration and discussion before this course of action is undertaken, because it assumes that the school system imposing the requirement can guarantee both students and parents that the system's instructional program can produce a high number of fluent readers by grade twelve. Such an educational guarantee is often difficult to provide. As programs are planned in school systems, the planners are often also charged with implementing the concomitant graduation requirement and therefore will need to understand fully the legal, as well as educational, aspects of this issue. Denying a student a high school diploma on the basis of some requirement opens the door to challenges to the educational validity and the legal validity of both the reading requirement and the school system's total range of instructional programs. As Draba (1978) notes:

> But if this requirement is fairly and consistently applied, some graduating seniors will be denied diplomas. Given the "see you in court" complex that afflicts many, school systems might reasonably expect these students to make use of either the due process or equal protection clauses of the Fourteenth Amendment to challenge the procedures used to deny diplomas or the methods used to classify students according to reading ability. [p. 27.]

So, although the use of a reading requirement for graduation may seem to be attractive from an accountability viewpoint because of its simplicity, its implementation is inexorably tied to the effectiveness of all instructional programs that a school system offers its consumers—the students.

A need is discovered for students through assessment or surveying by others, usually those charged with planning educational programs. Needs are often portrayed as mysteriously hidden until discovered for students by others. This type of thinking has led us to ignore a preexisting condition to needs assessment: the unalienable rights that students possess that do not require discovering or assessing. There is no need for an instrument such as a "rights assessment." Rights exist, whether we choose to consider them or not in planning instructional programs.

Now, let us turn our attention to a specific list of student rights. As you read through them, tally to see how many of these rights are considered by the programs with which you are familiar. It may be systemwide programs, single school programs, or an individual classroom program.

Right 1: Students have the right to a comprehensive content area program that has been professionally planned, organized, and implemented

This right mandates that any content area program be comprehensively planned. If a systemwide program is being developed, then it must be planned with all grade levels incorporated, kindergarten through grade twelve. Elementary, junior high, senior high, and compensatory programs must exist as an intergrated, coordinated total with each component as part of the systemwide program. A concrete indication that any program is not comprehensive can be gleaned from comments in the faculty room such as, "If only they had taught them "down there" they wouldn't have trouble with my subject". The infamous "down there" finger-pointing by upper level teachers is frequently symptomatic of a program that is not comprehensive. However, when students enter kindergarten and go through grade twelve in our schools, they have the right to expect that their programs have been comprehensively planned, by people who knew what they were doing. That only seems fair. Twelve- or fifteen-year-olds cannot be expected to be curriculum experts. They do not know if they are students in a comprehensive program or not.

Finally, students have the right to expect that their content area teachers will know something about the reading process and how it operates in content area texts, regardless of what subject is being taught. Textbooks still carry the major burden of providing students with a single source of information in most content area classrooms. The question is not whether to make every teacher a teacher of reading; rather, the issue is that there are simply too many teachers who have had no preparation for helping students use textbooks and other printed materials to gain the information they need to succeed in school. This challenge to our teacher preparation schools is a gigantic one. They must begin doing a better job of preparing content area teachers in how to use textbooks effectively with students.

This first right stands as the most important one and the one that is prerequisite to all the other student rights mentioned in this article. However, it often receives the least amount of attention, because students have little or no control over its consideration as instructional programs are planned for them.

Right 2: Students have the right to a learning environment that meets their physical, emotional, and intellectual needs by providing acceptance, ensuring success, and developing a positive self-concept

The creation of a learning environment that accepts the prior knowledge, experiences, and learning through success-oriented, direct teaching will lead to the development of positive self-concepts by those same students. Motivation, then, becomes increasingly intrinsic for many students in such a learning environment. The content area teacher can create this dynamic learning environment by making the interaction of students and ideas the primary goal of all instruction.

However, observations of current practices in some content area classrooms bring to light teaching approaches that work against the development of a rich classroom learning environment and consequently violate the right of students to such an environment. One type of teaching found in classrooms is marked by an overemphasis on student-directed, independent, paper-and-pencil exercises where students attempt to wrestle with facts and ideas in a vacuum of cognitive loneliness, without benefit of direct, prior teaching. Students sit, practicing reinforcement activities that are devoid of active discussion and guidance on how to integrate new ideas with previously acquired ideas. This approach has been dubbed the D^3P^3 approach—the *D*aily *D*ose of *D*ittos from the *P*urple *P*aper *P*ooper! The D^3P^3 approach keeps students busy, teaching themselves in an environment lacking in sensitive teacher guidance and monitoring of student progress. It is further dehumanizing and mechanistic in that it is often fragmented into discrete, seemingly unrelated facts, to be practiced and learned in isolation. This linear, fact-dominated approach precludes students learning through the active manipulation and integration of old and new ideas. It is a trap into which elementary and secondary schools fell over the past decade in an attempt to make learning more efficient. No one ever said learning was going to be efficient. Making ball bearings, yes, but not putting all kinds of students in the same classroom with a multitude of new and challenging ideas.

The disguising of passive learning through a D^3P^3 approach has been accomplished in some content classrooms by calling these endless dittos "study guides." Even a cursory reading of the vast literature on study guides reveals that these guides are designed to foster—not inhibit—student acquisition of new ideas through active participation in the learning process. To camouflage dull teaching and dull learning by calling isolated fact exercises study guides ignores and misinterprets the underlying rationale for the use of study guides.

The use of direct teaching and the active manipulation of ideas previously introduced are two prerequisites to preparing the type of learning environment in the content area classroom that says to students that challenging and exciting ideas await them in a rich learning environment. Students have the right to expect this much from our schools.

Right 3: Students have the right to an instructional program that views reading as a communication tool

Reading is not a skill, it is a tool. Neither is it a subject. By the time the demands of content materials become heavy in the intermediate and secondary school, students should be using reading as a tool to acquire content.

For some students, however, the view expressed above is not reality. Too many elementary schools prepare students who do quite well on tests of reading achievement but who are unable and unwilling to use reading as a tool in content area classrooms. The overemphasis in some elementary schools on producing students who *can* read rather than students who *do* read is the major cause of this situation. We cannot expect students to make the necessary connections between the artificial and simplified learning-to-read settings found in many elementary schools and the reality of content area classrooms where reading must be used as a tool to acquire new concepts and integrate them with previously acquired ones.

There is a simple solution to the dilemma posed by elementary school reading programs that do not view reading as a communication tool. Why not make classrooms resemble the real world of print that students find outside of the classroom? In addition to all our teaching of reading and content area materials, we should provide daily opportunities for students—in all grades and content areas—to learn how to apply and use what is being taught in the classroom. Duckworth (1979) suggested that practical situations, real situations, that involve problem solving result in optimal learning. She states, "Learning in school need not, and should not, be different from the children's natural forms of learning about the world" (p. 311).

Although Duckworth was referring to elementary school students, it would seem that this statement might also logically apply to secondary students. Any forms of print found outside of the classroom that teachers can use to broaden the scope of what students read and learn stresses reading as a communication tool. Each content teacher should examine the curriculum for the school year and introduce appropriate real-life materials related to what is under study in the classroom. Specific applications of concepts under study in school should be found outside of the classroom and brought in for students to integrate with those concepts under study in the classroom.

Perhaps, inadvertently, we have discovered a useful measure of curricular relevance to apply to our teaching. If day after day we cannot find in the world outside of the classroom specific opportunities for students to use what we are teaching in the classroom, maybe our curriculum is out of date and irrelevant. Relevancy does not necessitate that curriculum bend to each and every whim of current fashion or fad. Rather, we should attempt to help our students understand how what they are learning in the classroom can help them make better use of the world of print to be found outside of the classroom. The right to an instructional program that views reading as a communication tool, if carefully considered, will enrich our teaching and ensure that students find school to be both rewarding and relevant.

Right 4: Students have the right to participate as actively as they can in the planning, organization, and evaluation of the total content area instructional program

Teachers who plan programs *for* students must begin to plan programs *with* students. Curriculum guides or programs of study developed during the school year or summer by faculty committees ignore the right students have to participate in the development of content area programs designed for them. One very important question comes to mind when considering students' participation. What contributions can students really make? The answer to this question lies in a deliberate search by teachers for specific ways in which student participation can become an integral part of content area instruction.

For example, as content texts are chosen by committees of teachers and administrators, each text under consideration might have its appropriateness assessed through actual use with students. A cloze passage could be constructed from selections in each text and administered to students to determine whether the readability level of the text matches the reading ability of the students for whom it is intended. Students also might be part of faculty committees charged with completing a textbook evaluation form on each prospective text.[1] Students could assist in selecting print and media materials to supplement the content texts they are using. Films, filmstrips, slides, and supplementary readings selected by a committee consisting of a librarian, content area teachers, and students insures that supplementary materials purchased are the best available and suited for use by both teachers and students. With the cost of supplementary materials in today's market, careful and judicious purchasing is already the watchword in most schools.

An additional avenue for student participation in the content area program involves the right of students to be informed of how well they are matched with the content texts they will be using. How effective are students at reading for information in content texts? Are texts at the independent, instructional, or frustration level for each student? How well developed are the study strategies, library and research skills, and organizational techniques of students? These questions point to a few of the reasons why students may succeed or fail in reading content area texts. Each question also implies that content area teachers are able to assess the ability of students to effectively read content texts. The traditional source of information available to teachers often includes the results of standardized reading tests. However, these tests of general reading ability rarely provide the specific information that teachers need to aid students who might be experiencing difficulty reading content text. They simply confirm what teachers have already observed—that students are frustrated as they attempt to use reading as a tool to gain information. Content teachers need information of a specific nature. Rakes and McWilliams (1978) suggest major problems associated with using standardized test data for instructional purposes.

1. An artificial relationship exists between test items and actual material found in adopted textbooks.
2. Many students, particularly those experiencing reading and/or learning problems, have experienced frustration while taking standardized tests. Their subsequent academic performance is not necessarily representative of actual abilities.
3. Standardized test batteries are expensive when compared to informal procedures.
4. Most norm-referenced, group-standardized tests are more survey than diagnostic in nature. Even newer criterion-referenced tests either sample a broad range of skills on a superficial basis or measure a select number of skills and exclude others on a primarily arbitrary basis. Both types usually use a variety of content-related reading matter with insufficient depth to be of instructional value to most classroom teachers. Few classroom teachers will support such instruments as appropriate or particularly valuable in developing their teaching strategies.
5. Most standardized tests require longer test intervals than informal procedures. [p. 47.]

1. See Readence, J., Bean, T. and Baldwin, S. *Content area reading: An integrated approach.* Dubuque, IA.: Kendall/Hunt, 1981.

As alternatives to standardized tests, content area teachers can administer informal tests designed to gather specific information, such as the ability of each student to take notes, use graphic aids, answer a variety of comprehension questions, read for differing purpose, or prepare a study schedule. Assessment alone, however, will not overcome the inability of students to read content texts. Results of informal tests must be discussed with students and suggestions offered for ways in which they can capitalize on strengths and improve weak skills. Students must be involved in setting goals for self-improvement if they are to use reading as a tool in content area subjects.

Finally, student involvement in the planning, organization, and evaluation of content area instruction as outlined above also requires that students share in the responsibilities for its success. Rights assume responsibilities. Students have the right to know what they must do, day-to-day, in order to fulfill their responsibilities. Their participation might range from serving on a committee with faculty who are evaluating prospective texts, to working on a teacher suggestion for improving study habits, or helping with peer or cross-age tutoring. Whatever the area of involvement, if students are actively participating in their instructional program, getting them to assume their responsibilities for its success would be easier to accomplish.

Teacher Rights

Observation of teachers in inservice settings as well as comments from content area teachers have more than established the need for looking at the rights of the content area teachers. The complaints have focused on the exclusion of teacher rights in inservice of their lack of preparation to employ reading skills as teachers of content areas.

The gap between theory, training, and practice is too large to expect content area teachers to bridge the gap without special training. Teachers have expressed their lack of sufficient training to meet the needs and rights of students in their instructional programming.

Teachers have the right to be taught how to prepare, present, individualize, and employ good classroom management in their instructional programs. The inservice process should be presented by knowledgeable personnel in a meaningful setting with plenty of opportunity for implementation. Finally, administrative support is essential.

With these statements as an introduction, the author will set forth teachers rights. What, then, are the rights of teachers?

Right 1: Teachers have the right to be participants in an inservice program that is planned, sequential, and has both short- and long-term goals

Planning of inservice is usually the weakest point of the process, since the needs assessment is usually limited, and those responsible for implementing the inservice are developing the plan based on their own perspective. This specific weakness makes inservice vulnerable to a misinterpretation of the real needs of the varied content areas. Planning should be based on improved surveys and better data collection from the teachers involved in the inservice. Some participation in the planning should be done by teachers in the various fields. Involvement on the part of the teachers is imperative to the success of inservice. Once staff has been involved and proper surveying for data collection has been completed, the involved group can readily work with the administration to develop effective short- and long-term goals. These established goals can be clearly outlined for the teachers with a timeline for accomplishment and, thus, bring about greater involvement and responsibility on the part of the content teacher for the accomplishment of the goals. As knowledge is sequential in the different content areas, so too are the skills to be learned in inservice. Sequential development of skills helps the teacher implement the knowledge gained from the inservice program.

The content area teacher must be assisted to understand how the inservice being given is related to his or her content areas, since application of skills is essential for both the teacher and ultimately for the students. Follow-up by the teacher, supervisor, and person responsible for inservice determines the effectiveness of what has been learned by the teacher. Areas of strengths and weaknesses are determined, which help to adjust goals for reteaching in the long-term inservice plan.

Right 2: Teachers have the right to workshops that are both practical and capable of being implemented

Inservice training should be conducted by leaders who have expertise in both content and delivery. Teachers have the right to expect high quality inservice training that will expand their teaching skills and abilities and provide them with practical instructional techniques and strategies that can be implemented in the classroom. They need to have inservice conducted by experts who can communicate in an interesting and inspiring manner. If the leaders of the inservice are experts but have a dull delivery, teachers will not be motivated or inspired—any more than their students would be under similar circumstances.

Whenever possible, inservice should also be conducted by classroom teachers or personnel within the area who have developed innovative instructional methods or who have developed positive attitudes towards the content on the part of their students. This is another way of recognizing master teachers and utilizing the available talent within the area.

Workshops should be "down-to-earth", interesting, and organized to allow time for presentation of new concepts, ideas, and techinques. Under guidance from the instructor, participants should be given time and materials to prepare for implementation of the ideas in the classroom. All too often teachers have received new ideas that they fully intended to implement but failed to do so because they were not provided enough time to construct the materials or because they could not remember how to prepare them. This, in effect, has made the inservices conducted—interesting as they may have been—timewasters, since no change was really effected in teaching procedures.

Right 3: Teachers have the right to be respected as human beings as well as professionals, with their physical, mental, and emotional needs taken into consideration as well as their educational needs

Teachers have the right to expect to have their human needs met as much as possible in an inservice program. A teacher who is suffering the indignity of having human needs ignored will find great difficulty in trying to be an effective learner in the inservice setting. Inservice traditionally has been a "talk at", held in late afternoon or evening, humdrum, with an uncomfortable physical setting for learning. Effective inservice requires that a physical setting be developed that is conducive to a learning environment, including furniture, equipment, and materials. The physical environment should be as well developed as that which is expected of teachers in their own instructional program for students.

When the physical and instructional settings are appropriate, with competent instructors and relevant content, the setting for learning is conducive to the improvement of respect and self-concept of every teacher within the inservice program. Teachers who feel good about the inservice process can be ready learners and thus bring about change in their own instruction for students in the classroom. Inservice conducted during the school day, with the provision for substitutes and/or released time, not only produces a better physical, emotional, and mental setting but also sets forth a commitment for improvement by teacher and administrators as well.

> Right 4: Content area teachers have the right to be taught how to employ instructional reading skills for use in their content fields

Content area teachers have spent many years in developing expertise in their content and thus have been frustrated by the continued problems that plague them with reading skills that seem to be missing with the students in their classroom. The traditional ways of dealing with this problem have been caught up in statements like, "I teach my area, someone else should teach them to read," "How can I teach my area if they can't read?", "I don't know how to help these students who can't read my materials," "What is the matter with today's students?", and "It must be someone else who did a poor job at a younger age." With many statements like these, the frustrations of content area teachers have been vented, but to no avail. The simple solution is that content teachers must be taught through inservice to deal effectively with skill development in their content area.

Some of the skills with which content area teachers should be familiar include the following:

A. Teachers should be taught to select materials with an appropriate instructional readability level.

It appears that many content area books are written with a readability level as much as two to three levels in readability above the grade for which they are intended. Unfortunately, many content area teachers have not had the training necessary in order to select textbooks at a proper readability level. Therefore, when these teachers are placed on a textbook selection committee, readability is not a factor in the selection. Thus, the teacher and the students are continually frustrated with the textbook throughout its use. The mystique of the readability formulas of the past has tended to provide a barrier to the content teachers when they select materials. Clarity and simplicity of the readability formulas need to be a goal of inservice training.

B. Content area teachers should be taught to teach readiness for learning.

A major component of any instructional program is the mind set or readiness for learning created by the teacher. The content area teacher cannot assume that

students come prepared to understand what is to be learned. Thus, the teachers must be taught to prepare lessons with the following points:
1. Development of vocabulary unique to the lesson.
2. Major concepts to be gleaned from the content reading.
3. Purpose for the reading activity clearly defined and outlined.
4. Instruction should be developed to clarify the format of the material and style of the author so that the format becomes a help rather than a hindrance to learning.

Teachers can anticipate, once a readiness structure has been employed, that improved learning will take place in their content area.

C. Teachers should be taught how to teach reading for meaning.

Too many times teachers accept the smooth "barking" of words as reading. However, unless the student can attach real meaning to the passages that are assigned, no real reading takes place. To teach for meaning, the teacher must help the students develop a purpose for reading, specific questions to be answered, an understanding of the unique vocabulary of the material, and the skills of interpreting the graphics included in the passage. The format of the content and style of the author must be surveyed and understood by the teacher so that they will not become hindrances to the extraction of meaning.

D. Teachers should be taught to develop instructional activities that use reading and thinking skills.

Content area teachers must be assisted through the inservice process in their methods and procedures for preparing an instructional lesson that goes beyond simple recall. The skills necessary in the development of questions, instructional games, and general management of the classroom are critical problems to the security of content area teachers as they are encouraged to stray from a very cognitive recall format. Clarity on the part of the inservice instructor will assist the teacher in the development of confidence for the implementation of reading and thinking skills.

E. Teachers should be taught to assist the student in the transfer of reading skills to the content area.

It is not axiomatic that because students can read well in a reading textbook, they can also read well in a content area text. The reading skills needed in both are the same. However, in the content area, these skills must be reinforced and refined. For instance, in order to outline, a student must first be able to identify the main idea and then to select the supporting details. They must then be taught the proper outline format. These are only an extension and refinement of skills taught specifically in reading. Content area teachers, then, must first be taught to recognize and to teach specific reading skills and then to be able to transfer these skills to their content area.

Right 5: Teachers have the right to expect their supervisors to be interested in and to care about what they are doing in the classroom. They also need visible, concrete evidence of administrative support and participation in inservice training

Just a quick visit by the principal followed by a sincere compliment will inspire and motivate teachers. If a teacher is particularly creative or inspiring, or has succeeded in implementing a new approach or attitude towards reading on the part of the students, this also needs to be recognized. Just as students need to be motivated or inspired, so do their teachers or motivators.

The inservice needs to take place on a regular and continuing basis throughout the year. Administrators need to show constant support by their attendance. All too often teachers are asked to attend workshops at which no administrator is present. This gives the teachers the impression that "it can't really be too important."

The major role of the school administrator has been defined as instructional leadership. Thus, the effective instructional leader becomes an active participant in the inservice process with his or her staff. To lead a staff requires the commitment of the administration to the teachers. It is also going to be difficult at best for inservice effectiveness to be monitored unless there is follow-up by the administrator. The follow-up by the administrator may take the form of monitoring, redirection, reinforcement, and support services for what is learned.

Right 6: Teachers have the right to know what is expected of them and how they are to be evaluated

Teachers have the right to be informed by their principals or supervisors as to just what is expected of them in implementing their programs and how their achievements with their students are to be evaluated. If their tasks are not well-defined, they cannot establish their goals and objectives and implement a successful content program. Instead, they are put in a stressful situation, confusion mounts, and neither the student nor the school benefits from the teacher's expertise.

Clearly defined expectancies are a joint responsibility of the teachers and administration. This task should be completed at the beginning of the school year, so that well-directed goals, objectives, instructional procedures, methods, and materials can be employed to achieve effective programming. The purpose of evaluation is to determine strengths and weaknesses so that a plan of improvement can be implemented by the teacher and administration. Inservice is one method of bringing about change as a result of evaluation. The due process procedure now required in most instructional settings requires the following points:

(a) a known procedure
(b) clear timelines
(c) preliminary evaluation
(d) development of an improvement plan
(e) monitoring of the plan
(f) evaluation of improvement
(g) determination of success
(h) cycle improvement plan

Inservice as set forth in this article can aid both the teacher and the administrator in effective teacher improvement.

Summary

In summary, if teachers are to adhere to the rights of their students to be taught skills and attitudes according to their individual needs, then the rights of teachers to be trained properly and to be treated as professionals must be respected as well.

Teaching another human being in this world of ours is complex enough as it is. If we do not give teachers the proper foundation, support, continued inservice, and respect as professionals, our students' rights to a good education will not be met.

Quality education and quality content area programs are only as adequate as the people who plan and implement those programs. Teachers cannot motivate or inspire their students if they themselves are not motivated or inspired or constantly exposed to new and fresh approaches to teaching.

References

Draba, R. E. Reading ability as a graduation requirement: Some legal aspects. In Harper, R. J., and Kilarr, G. (Eds.), *Reading and the law.* Newark, Del.: International Reading Association, 1978.

Duckworth, E. Either we're too early and they can't learn it or we're too late and they know it already: The dilemma of "applying Piaget." *Harvard Educational Review, 49,* 1979, 297–312.

Rakes, T. A., and McWilliams, L. Bridging the gap: Two alternatives to standardized testing. *English Journal, 67,* 46–50.

Read Chap 4